TRAILS OF A PAINTBRUSH

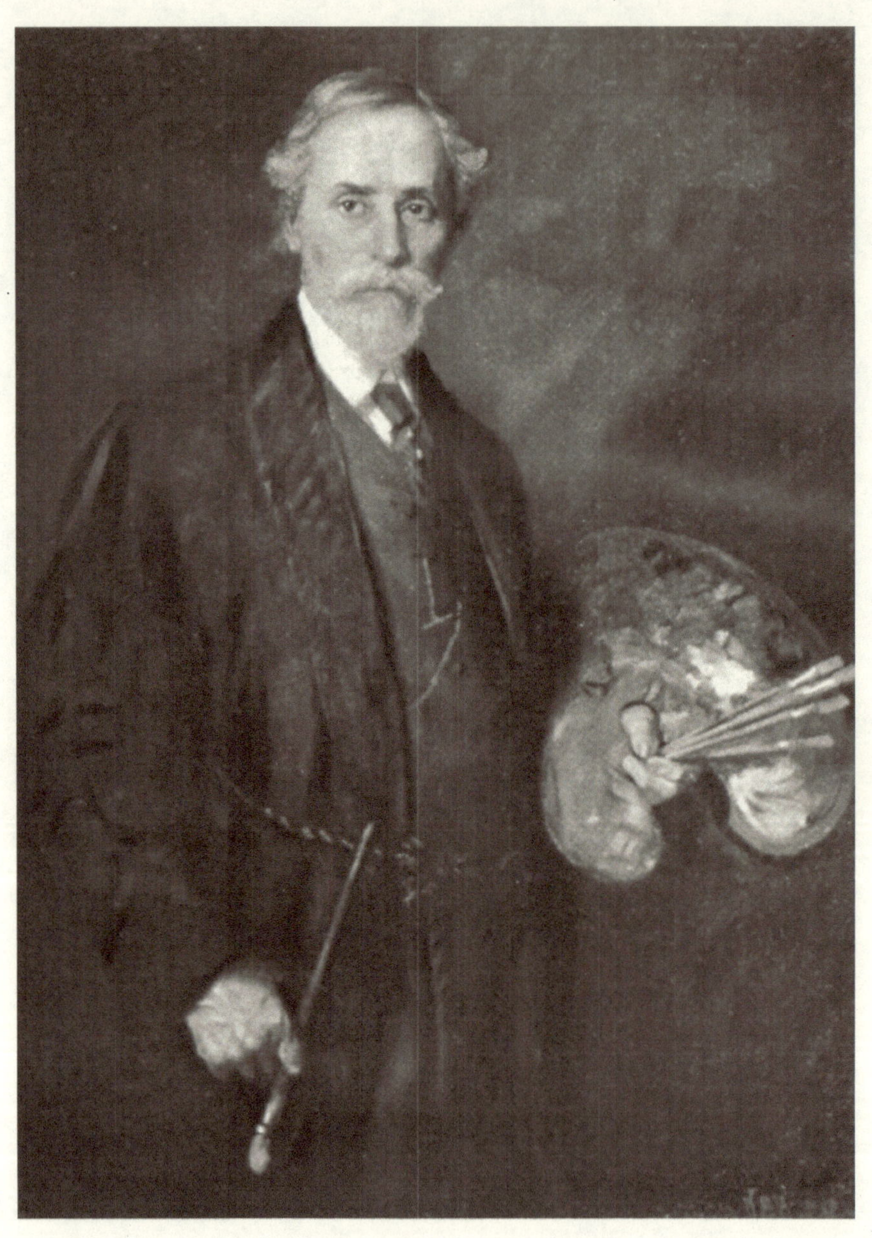

TRAILS OF A PAINTBRUSH

BY

NICHOLAS R. BREWER

New Introduction by Julie L'Enfant

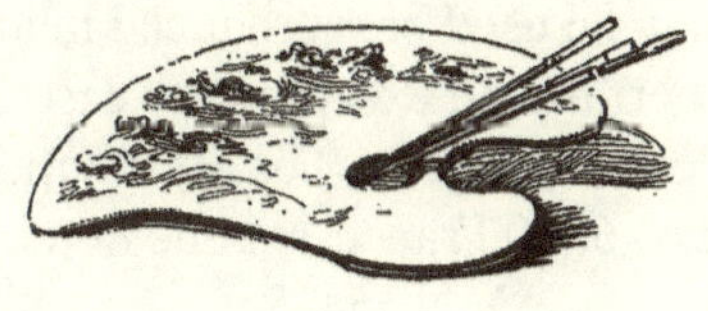

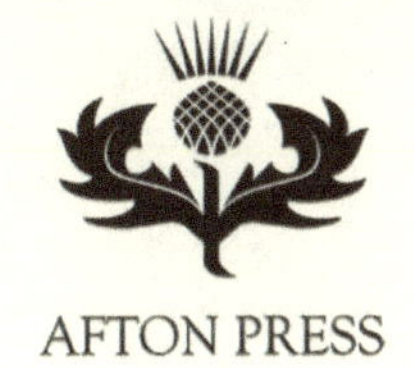

AFTON PRESS

AFTON PRESS

Minneapolis - Saint Paul
First softcover edition April 2021

Trails of a Paintbrush

Printed in the United States of America.
10 9 8 7 6 5 4 3 2 1

Copyediting and production management: Beth Williams

Cover and interior design: Gary Lindberg

ISBN: 978-1-7361021-2-1

CONTENTS

List of Illustrations

Page 257: *Ignace Paderewski*, 1921. Oil on canvas, dimensions unknown. Oshkosh Public Museum (lost). Photograph, Perry McGowan collection.

Page 263: *Most Rev. George W. Mundelin, Archbishop of Chicago*, ca. 1915–1916. Location unknown. Photograph of portrait. Mary Lou Brewer collection.

Page 298: *Hon. Ruth Bryan Owen*

Page 249: *James A. Campbell.* Courtesy of Butler Art Institute, Youngstown, Ohio.

Page 336: *Mrs. Elizabeth Jordon Gilliland*, undated. Location unknown.

Page 342: The Broken Portal of San José. Brewer called this ruin of the entrance to the church of Mission San José in San Antonio, Texas, "The Broken Portal of San José, the Most Beautiful Ruin in America."

Page 118: *Dr. Leroy Brown*, ca. 1912. Second Prize, Minnesota State Art Commission.

Page 228: *Dr. William Henry Holmes*, ca 1923. Oil on canvas, 34 1/4 x 44 1/8 in. Smithsonian American Art Museum.

Page 369: *Mr. Frederick A. Delano*

Page 365: *Mr. Justice Willis Van Devanter*, 1933.

Page 367: *Mr. Justice George Sutherland*

Page 369: *Joseph T. Robinson*, 1934. Oil on canvas, 43 5/8 in. X 31 ½ in. Arkansas Secretary of State, State Capitol.

Page 373: *Vice-President John Nance Garner*, ca. 1933–1934. Oil on canvas, 44 x 34 in. Richard Saliterman collection. Photo by Bill Kelley.

Page 377: *Franklin Delano Roosevelt*, 1934. Location unknown. Oil on canvas, over life-size.

Prologue

There is nothing so beautiful as the dawning intelligence of childhood when it begins to view the wonders of this material world. The unconscious curiosity, the ever-questioning brain seeking to probe into each new mystery—asking the reason for this thing and that, drinking with joy every bit of knowledge, and unfolding in the light of new discoveries—is like the opening of the rosebud that feasts upon the dew and sunshine of a spring morning.

One day a barefoot boy came to a log schoolhouse on the frontier and stood by the teacher's knee to learn his A B C's. To him, gaining his meager scraps of knowledge in the frontier school, the rosebud was opening. He was beginning to inhale its fragrance, though the rose was yet to reveal its full and enduring character.

A passing peddler stopped at the schoolhouse one day and showed a number of cheaply colored photogravures, the first pictures of any consequence the boy had ever seen. One of them, entitled "A New England Farm House," appealed to him as beautiful, and he offered the vendor his total wealth of ten cents, which had been saved penny by penny.

The offer being accepted, he seized the picture and scampered home to show it to his mother. Tacking it on the wall, he literally worshipped it. It was this picture that germinated within him the desire to become a great artist. He tried to copy it—first in pencil, then in cheap watercolors. The result was always dissatisfying, but the yearning to know how to paint pictures became an insatiable passion.

Another picture, an engraving that remained ever vivid in the boy's memory, and one that had much to do with shaping his veneration for aged people, hung on the wall in his mother's bedroom. It was called "Grandmother has Come." Beside a sweet-faced old lady, two children—a boy and a girl—were untying the ribbons of her bonnet. The joy expressed in their little faces as she beamed sweetly upon them held for him an alluring charm.

Someone told him of a young man named George Eberson, living about ten miles south on the prairie, who could draw wonderful pictures. The boy longed to see him and to learn how to mix the colors. One Sunday morning after the chores were done, barefooted and with a tattered straw hat, he set out to visit George. Fleet as a deer and full of expectancy, he skipped away the miles. It was hot, and the perspiration streamed down his face. Arriving at a shanty on the prairie, he knocked at the door. A slatternly woman, barefooted and with a corn-cob pipe in her mouth, opened it. He asked if George were at home. "No," she said. "May I see some of his pictures?" asked the boy. "No," she answered, "George has gone away and taken his pictures with him and won't be back until late." With this, she slammed the door in his face.

Going to the well nearby and slaking his thirst, he gazed about him. Down in the ravine, a group of boys were swimming in the stream. Thinking that perhaps George might be among them, he joined them, but George was not there. They urged him to come in and have a swim. All the while, the boy kept his eye on the shanty on the hill. As the sun lowered in the West, he began to feel a dreadful gnawing within. With ten miles ahead of him, he could swim no longer. He dressed and again went to the house, only to find that George had not returned. With harrowing disappointment, he turned his face homeward.

It was after dark when he strode in, and his mother asked him where he had spent the whole day. "Oh, down a-swimmin'," he answered. She gave him some bread and milk, which satisfied the hunger of the body, but not of the soul. Nor did his mother know the bitter disappointment that long remained vivid in his memory! I, young Nick Brewer, was that barefoot boy!

Blessings on thee, little man,
Barefoot boy with cheek of tan!
With thy turned-up pantaloons,
And thy merry whistled tunes;
With thy red lips, redder still
Kissed by strawberries on the hill;
With the sunshine on thy face,
Through thy torn brim's jaunty grace;
From my heart I give thee joy—
I was once a barefoot boy!

—Whittier

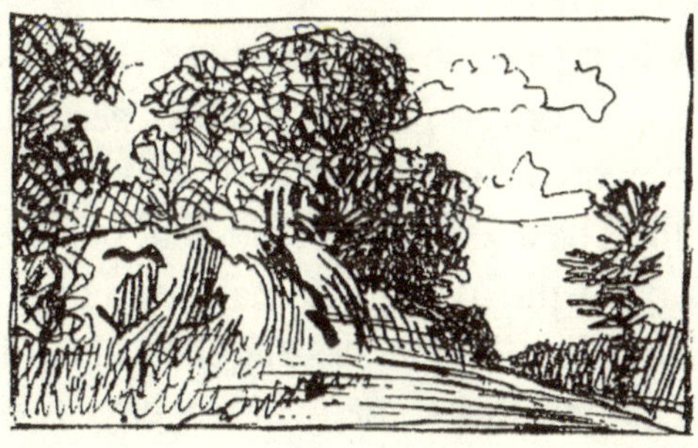

A Foreword

Stevenson said, "There is not a life in all the records of the past but, properly studied, might lend a hint and help to some contemporary." In writing the story of my life, it has been my purpose to adhere as closely as possible to the truth in the narrative of the events that have occurred along my pathway, in so far as my memory, aided by incidental notes and records, has served me. I have essayed to tell in words the things no artist can say with his brush. The art of painting and that of writing an autobiography differ widely. One school of painting, at least, requires that the artist be absolutely truthful; but to "Know thyself, O man!" and give a truthfully written record of a life's experiences is almost an impossibility.

When it was first suggested to me that I should write my experiences as an artist and portrait painter, the task seemed overwhelming; but repeated urgings on the part of numerous people caused me to feel that, after all, it might be a worthy thing to do. I believe that an intimate and truthful history of the average human life not only is of genuine interest but may be helpful to others struggling along life's rocky road. Therefore, I shall submit this comedy or tragedy, as it may be considered. With the half definite idea that I might act upon those suggestions, I began to be more careful with my notes and to jot down the accounts of incidents connected with my work and the conversations of distinguished and undistinguished personalities whom I met. These notes have aided me in my narrative.

My story begins with the hardships and hazards of pioneer life and carries on through the gropings of my youth in an untoward environment that offered no advantages for the realization of the ideals and aspirations that germinated within me as a barefoot boy. My early opportunities of acquiring an education were only those of the log schoolhouse, and I had to resort to the greater school of life in order to rise above the plowman or the wielder of the pick and shovel. The discoveries of a restless experimenter, investigator, and adventuresome traveler, always goaded on by the lash of necessity, have been my chief sources of enlightenment. My experiences and observations have been intimately associated with primitive conditions of America's great Middle West, and my love of art has caused me to note from first-hand sources its history and development in that vast region lying between Duluth and Miami, the Alleghenies and the Rockies. To become part of the educational forces at work in promoting art culture in this new land of promise was an ambition I could not smother, and the trail of my exhibitions, cooperating with Museums and Art Leagues, has extended to fifty-nine cities in twenty-four states. And so, to tell much that I have learned in that field of endeavor, I have employed the pen instead of the brush.

Whether I have always been in the right in my aims or my conclusions, whether the things for which I have striven have been worthwhile, or what measure of success has been achieved, I must leave to others to judge; and the judgment of my readers possibly will be as diverse as their tastes, temperaments, and experiences with life.

The labor necessarily incident to writing this account of my long career would not have been possible, but for the valuable assistance given me by my dear daughter-in-law, Esther D. Brewer, whose good judgment, gentle encouragement, and pertinent suggestions have been a stimulus and a help. To her, I gratefully acknowledge my gratitude. And so, I have written a book which I commend to all those who transmit by brush and paint the likeness of nature and man to canvas. To them I say in the words of Vezin:

While there is paint, there is hope.

To the Paintbrush

The humblest, yet most dignified implement of human use, is the artist's brush. Humble, because it is only a stick of wood tipped with hairs, smeared with all kinds of colored mud, thrown about, and scrubbed with soap when the mud dries through neglect.

But in spite of its humility, the paintbrush holds up its head with pride, for, after all, its footprints will be seen a thousand years hence, encased in golden frame, covered with glass, hung in fireproof buildings, guarded by men in brass buttons, gazed upon by eddying crowds, and studied by the greatest painters, poets, and thinkers.

To no other tool does immortality attach itself so affectionately, except, perhaps, the pen and the sculptor's chisel. It strokes the smooth cheek of beauty, adds dreamy lashes to sparkling eye, kisses soft lips with cherry red, and creates that marvelous, God-given thing, the human smile.

Introduction to the Original Edition

Happiest they of human race
To whom God has granted grace
To read, to fear, to hope, to pray,
To lift the latch, and force the way.

—The Monastery, Sir Walter Scott

"Man shall not live by bread alone" is so important a truism to the development and happiness of mankind that it has been thrice declared in Holy Writ. The Declaration of Independence, likewise, is of the Spirit in the classification of the pursuit of Happiness with Liberty and Life as primal, unalienable rights. The belief is the basis of our democratic institutions that it is the heritage of every one to seek a fuller and richer existence—"To lift the latch, and force the way." It is to the undying glory of both the Declaration of Independence and the Constitution of the United States that they have made possible the rise of men in America from the lowly stations of their birth, their privations, loneliness, lack of educational advantages or encouragements, and their many struggles to pinnacles of fame on the battlefields and the decks of our warships, in the councils of the Nation, on the bench, at the bar, in the pulpits, and in literature and art.

Trails of a Paintbrush is another, but different, Epic of America. It is the autobiography of a man who was born in 1857 to a home in what was then the frontier wilderness of Minnesota—twenty miles from the nearest other white family—and of a man who has lived through one of the most interesting periods in the history of the world. Through the means of his great genius and dogged perseverance, he has climbed from those early days of the rugged frontier, with its lack of educational advantages to a rich and full life, which has made it possible for him to contribute much to the happiness of present and future generations as they enjoy and treasure the masterpieces of his brush and palette. In this book is unfolded, with extreme modesty, the long journey since his earliest recollections with something of the struggles, passions, and dreams of a great and gentle man. He instantly attracted me on our first meeting, and that attraction has since ripened into a warm affection for him.

President Henry Wellington Wack of the Brooklyn Society of Artists has said of Nicholas R. Brewer that:

> The flowering of Mr. Brewer's acknowledged genius with the brush and palette has involved a poignant career of minor human adventures, of heart-breaking trials, of dire want and disappointment, of inevitable triumph, and, finally, of significant material rewards. His place among American painters has, for more than two decades, been firmly established. His signal achievements in the successful portraiture of numerous distinguished personalities have won him a gratifying renown in every part of the country, to which he has given six talented sons—three of them well-known artists—and a large group of bright, handsome, promising, and spirited grandchildren. His personal life—always clean, wholesome, and prodigiously energetic—has, with all the praise and honors bestowed upon his work, remained as modest as it is human, benevolent, and enterprising.
>
> Fame and fortune have not tinctured Mr. Brewer's spiritual concepts of art with the taint of materialism, nor stained it with the vanity that so often corrodes and hardens a versatile nature radiant under

> an exaggerated sunset of life. The Nick Brewer of the early farmyard and irresistible melon patch has not been balloon tired by the glare and the glitter, the titter and twaddle of fashion's buzzing salons, nor by the approving applause of a lay audience.
>
> Mr. Brewer has written an autobiography which I wish every art student, every occasional art critic, the profound executives of American Museums and Art Associations, and all casual art lovers could read and ponder upon. It is an intensely human document from the heights, as well as the abyss of the day's realities—so candid, so sincere, so forceful in its social example and its art message as to invest it with a precious and magnetic quality—a genuine force in the annals of American creative genius. I wonder if its author is not—after all this modernistic madness—the homely, heroic Abraham Lincoln of American Art.
>
> Read Mr. Brewer's biography *Trails of a Paintbrush* and you will see what dogged tenacity, what toughened fiber is bred in a man by this ardent ruling passion—the human soul interpreting the glory that is Nature. This Brewer self-revelation will show every aspiring boy and girl, endowed with the gift of creativeness, that however humble, they may all, by dint of vital endeavor, reach and occupy the seats of the mighty.

The love of beauty, the overwhelming desire to contribute to the happiness of mankind, and the greatest of ambitions led Brewer from that country home in Minnesota to become an artist and to commune, at least in spirit, with the masters who had gone before. He deliberately sought the more difficult road to success—and a success which has been rich—in the spiritual—if not in the material things of life.

He did not know when he left that country home that there had gone before him the painters of the early Egyptian dynasties who had recorded great events in the life of their peoples or that in Assyria, the painters had illuminated a pictorial history of great deeds. He did not know that painted tiles had been found in Babylon, historical wall paintings in India, Egypt, and in Mexico, or that Raphael and Michelangelo commenced where Cimabue and Giotto left off and had brought art to a high state of perfection. He came to know, as a devout son of the Church, that with the advent of Christianity, there was an awakening in art—the love of mother and child, the sufferings of the crucified Christ, and the sorrows of Mary and the disciples. He later learned that the art of painting advanced with the Italian Renaissance by showing its sympathy to what was then the rebirth of scholarship; that Raphael and Michelangelo were scholars and the intimate friends of scholars; that Da Vinci united the artistic and the scientific intellect; and that Rubens was both a scholar and a statesman, while Rembrandt showed a sympathy as great as his brush for all classes of people.

He has since learned that throughout the Middle Ages, the human motive of art was religious and its artistic motive was ornamental; that many of the masters of the brush and canvas in those days were encouraged by both the Church or by powerful men due to the fact that religion had an influence over the minds and hearts of the people of the fifteenth, sixteenth, and seventeenth centuries to an extent difficult for us to appreciate, and we all now know that the influence of religion is responsible for the present-day existence of many priceless and beautiful canvases which grace our art museums, churches, and homes, daily ministering to our happiness. America has been sadly lacking in patrons who could encourage the artists to the extent that was done by the Church and by wealthy men in those early days.

Perhaps it was just as well that when Brewer departed from his home as a boy of some seventeen years, determined to be a landscape and portrait painter, that he knew little or nothing of the history of art and the almost unattainable standards of achievement set by the great masters of the brush and palette in the past. Had he known, he might have become discouraged at the outset, with the result that the men and women of today and of the days to come would not have had the many landscapes and portraits which he has painted over the period of a long and busy life and which now hang in many art museums, public buildings, and homes throughout the United States.

Last but not least, we would not have this delightful autobiography which reads like fiction, truly an Epic of America, recording for all time not only some of his thoughts and dreams along the way but some of the thoughts and dreams of the subjects of his brush and palette. It is an inspiring story, this *Trails of a Paintbrush*! What would we not give today for similar stories from the pens of Stuart, Copley, West, Peale, Trumbull, or Sully, among American artists, to say nothing of the great artists of Europe? Perhaps this story marks the beginning of the end of the struggle of men in America with each other for the riches of a Midas as they settle down to a spacious manner of living similar to that in older countries with more leisure for the enjoyment and encouragement of paintings and painters, as well as music and literature.

In a word, this book consists of bits of fleece left and gathered by Nicholas Richard Brewer along life's highway as he painted, read, feared, hoped, and prayed. I know his readers will thoroughly enjoy going over that highway with him.

O. R. McGuire
Washington, D. C.
October 15, 1937

Introduction to the New Edition

Trails of a Paintbrush is an artist's autobiography, first published by the Christopher Publishing House in 1938 in a small edition of two hundred and fifty copies, with one smaller reprint in 1946. Yet it has had a vigorous underground life, an almost cult-like reputation. When I was doing research for a biography of its author, *Nicholas R. Brewer: His Art and Family,* I met or corresponded with many people who had some connection to Brewer. I would often be asked "Do you know about *Trails of a Paintbrush?*" as if it were some delightful secret. I had read it, of course (if a subject of research has written an autobiography, it is the first thing the researcher should read), but I was struck by the excitement about the book, the sense that it was special and rare. It has been posted online by the Library of Congress, which has served as a kind of guarantee that it would not be lost, but that is not the same as a physical book.

People tell about combing used bookstores and scouting online to find an available copy that is affordable. The best story about this kind of quest came from Mike Brewer Carina, one of Brewer's great-great-grandsons and an accomplished artist and designer. He tells how his good friend Nick Wormley was on a trip to San Antonio, and, knowing of Mike's long-held desire to have his own copy of *Trails*, decided to make a side trip to late author Larry McMurtry's famous used bookstore, Booked Up Inc., on the chance that he might find one for Mike. So Nick traveled some four hundred miles across Texas to Archer City and this establishment (actually four buildings). McMurtry had recently auctioned off most of his art books—indeed almost three-quarters of his stock—and the staff member doubted that they had this book. But she led Nick back through the labyrinthine shelves, finally pointing to a tall ladder where he could begin his browsing. Nick climbed up and, to his everlasting astonishment, the first book he saw was *Trails of a Paintbrush*.[1] Afton Press now puts this book in the reach of everyone.

In the early part of the twentieth century, Nicholas Brewer (1857–1949) was admired across the United States for his portraits and landscapes, the portraits for their character and grace, the landscapes for their harmonious naturalness. In *Trails*, Brewer describes his seemingly unpromising origins: a farm on the northwestern frontier of America, in the young state of Minnesota, where there were no art schools and hardly any art to see. Yet he was responsive to the beauty and plenty of his natural surroundings, and he had the drive to learn and "rise above the plowman." He was, in fact, someone born with what Wassily Kandinsky would later call the "internal necessity" to be an artist, and he had the talent and energy to realize that ambition. Like a young hero by Horatio Alger, Brewer took every opportunity and went on to create opportunities for himself.

The reader follows Brewer to St. Paul in 1875 and then, in 1885 when he was about twenty-eight, to New York for the chance to gain some academic training and experience its "art atmosphere." Happily, his still amateurish landscapes fit in with a popular mode: quiet, small-scale scenes that evoked a vanishing agrarian ideal. Brewer was born to paint such pastoral scenes—he had *lived* them. He was also fortunate that there was a particularly active market for portraits in New York. It was the Gilded Age, and portraits were an important marker of social status.[2] Having a facility for making likenesses, Brewer quickly developed into an adroit oil painter in demand by the elite and *nouveau riche* alike. He would develop no single style, although his work can be associated variously with the Barbizon school, tonalism, or impressionism. His circle included many notable artists, including J. Carroll Beckwith, Charles Noel Flagg, Alexis Jean Fournier, George Inness, Homer Dodge Martin, and Dwight Tryon. In time he became a member of the prestigious Salmagundi Club.

Had Brewer settled permanently in New York, as he so passionately wished to do, he might well be considered a major figure today. But his career was shaped by marriage and family. *Trails* describes

Brewer's crucial choice to marry his sweetheart, Rose Koempel, his years of shuttling between St. Paul and New York, and his incessant work, not only at the easel but as a farm laborer or door-to-door salesman to support his brood, which came to include six sons. Often he had to paint for money. In his portrait painting, he could be as much a "business artist" as Andy Warhol, so often did he have to paint sitters uncongenial to him—in ways too flattering to them.

Brewer's story involves dramatic ups and downs in fortune, but he reached a peak of success in 1912 with the construction, in part by himself, of a mansion on the Mississippi River. The family called it Casa del Rio ("house by the river"), which evokes thoughts of Albert Bierstadt's Malkasten or Frederick Church's Olana, although Brewer's two-story Arts and Crafts-style house was far simpler than those rambling Victorian estates on the Hudson. Unable to get enough work in Minnesota to pay his debts, however, Brewer began a peripatetic life that centered on the Midwest, where he painted numerous official portraits in North and South Dakota (aided by his sons, a collective known jokingly as "the Brewer-y"). After World War I and an attempt to establish himself in Chicago, he began traveling throughout the United States, taking the unusual step of mounting traveling exhibitions of paintings—his own and selected contemporaries—and giving lectures to the public on "fundamental art principles." Brewer might well be unique in this campaign, which lasted almost twenty years. The facilitators of these circuit exhibitions were women of the Federation of Women's Clubs and other art leagues who worked to raise the cultural level of their communities in accord with the ideas of the City Beautiful.

Brewer painted many of the most celebrated individuals of his time, such as Joseph Jefferson, the comic actor famed for thousands of performances of *Rip Van Winkle*; Maud Powell, the internationally famous violinist who was the first to record with RCA; and Ignace Paderewski, the Polish pianist and politician. One of the pleasures of this book is the opportunity to learn more about—or sometimes to be introduced to—these notables. Brewer was an eyewitness to some fascinating history. He heard his parents argue about the merits of both sides in the Civil War. He talked with Henry Ward Beecher, the great preacher and abolitionist; spent time with James J. Hill, the Empire Builder and art collector; and traveled in California with Father St. John O'Sullivan, the Great Restorer of the Franciscan missions. He painted major figures in the first administration of Franklin D. Roosevelt, including the president himself. He learned history directly from such figures as William Sprague IV, former governor of Rhode Island, U. S. Senator, and Civil War general who raised the first volunteer regiment for the Union Army, which marched to Washington in April 1861. (Brewer recounts the notorious scandal of Sprague, his beautiful wife Kate Chase Sprague, and Senator Roscoe Conklin, giving us Sprague's point of view.) Brewer also has good stories to tell about portrait subjects who were not famous: he was a canny judge of character, with a sharp eye for vanity and presumption, and no mercy for Philistines.

But Brewer's great love was landscape, and his spare time was spent painting in this less profitable genre. A particularly detailed chapter describes his only true vacation, a five-month sojourn to California. It was a working vacation, to be sure (he produced some of his most important work there), and his descriptions of the state's varied scenes are as evocative as his paintings. He also brings to life a colorful cast of characters who took part in the great boom in that state in the 1920s: Benjamin J. Brown, Jack Smith, and other artists known as the California Impressionists; Frank Miller, builder of the fabled Mission Inn in Riverside; and John McGroarty, writer and California booster, author of the long-running *Mission Play,* among others.

Some of the most exciting passages of this book are on the creative process. Brewer is explicit about his methods for portraits and landscapes, but he also speaks more generally about his philosophy of art, which we find is inextricably tied to his religious beliefs. Desiring a "rule of life," he converted to Roman Catholicism as a young man, tutored by the eminent churchman Bishop (later Archbishop) John Ireland, another of his renowned portrait subjects. Religion served as the backbone of his belief that the beauty of nature reflects divine order and ultimate truth. Art, for Brewer, as for many artists from the beginning of civilization, served the cause of beauty. Although he recognized that each age has its own standards of beauty, he insisted on naturalistic forms rendered with harmony and proportion. His work can be characterized as romantic realism, creations from the imagination embodying the truth and beauty of nature but firmly grounded in the real world. The purpose of art, for Brewer, was to communicate with, and uplift, the viewer.

Brewer's work was out of fashion by the time of his death in 1949, and we can detect his prickliness about it in *Trails*, when, for instance, he repeats a young viewer's dismissal of one of his Washington portraits as "old stuff," or when he rails against Expressionist and Cubist works at the 1913 Armory Show as distorted and ugly. Like many American viewers and critics at the time, Brewer had special scorn for Duchamp's *Nude Descending a Staircase No. 2,* "where the canvas is strewn with cubes and triangles or what not." He does not refer to Duchamp's far more radical *Fountain,* the urinal entered into the New York Society of Independent Artists exhibition in 1917, or Duchamp's cheeky defense of his provocative act that appeared later that year, declaring that the urinal was a work of art because someone *chose* it and "placed it so that its useful significance disappeared under the new title and point of view—created a new thought for that object."[3] Duchamp's subversive broadening of the definition of visual art helped open the way for conceptual art, performance art, materials and processes art—anything and everything, often with the goal of undermining society rather than lifting it up. It can be argued that art has moved on since Brewer lived. Why should twenty-first viewers pay attention to what such a traditional artist as Brewer has to say?

If the "art world" of critics and curators has moved from traditional standards and ideals, many—perhaps most—viewers have not. Brewer and the artists with whom he was most sympathetic remain very popular today. Owners of paintings by Brewer or Inness or Martin love their paintings. Much contemporary art seeks to reflect the chaos and disorder to be found in the self and the world, like a mirror. Such art as Brewer's is, in contrast, like a lamp that radiates the beauty the artist has found in the world. Brewer can be cranky in *Trails,* but he is vigorous in his convictions and mostly clear-eyed. He presents a bracing explanation of the nourishment and inspiration to be found in traditional art (and now in artists such as Matisse and Van Gogh, whom Brewer derided but whom our age has come to see as beautiful too in the kind of evolution Brewer acknowledged).

Brewer described himself as "ardent and ambitious," and these words could be applied to his own prose. He was a storyteller by nature. *Trails* was not his first effort at narrative writing. In 1881 he had produced the manuscript for a novel about an artist, although he was unable to get it published then or in the 1940s when he tried again. He sometimes kept a diary, or at least "scribbled notes" on his impressions and experiences. A few of the chapters in *Trails* are based on diaries and are thus more detailed; others are based on memory. But Brewer's style is informal—he characterizes himself as "a breezy art hound from the West"—and the book was compiled over a period of ten years in a process of gradual accretion. The original text, which might have been more rigorously edited, had some misspellings and typographical errors. This new edition contains a number of silent corrections, which have been judged preferable to annoying readers with sprinkles of bracketed emendations. Nevertheless, it has been rendered as closely as possible to Brewer's original to preserve its lively flow.

Nor has this edition been annotated. The critical commentary and explanatory notes necessary to provide a fuller context would double the size of this volume, or require another volume, and indeed such a fuller context for *Trails of a Paintbrush* has already been written: the aforementioned *Nicholas R. Brewer: His Art and Family.* There is more to discover about Brewer's life and career, and certainly more about his artist sons Edward and Adrian and the many other artist descendants than that volume could cover. But there is considerable information there. For example, the reader will discover such details as the identity of "Leon Jerome," the artist with whom Brewer's teacher Herbert Levy studied (he was Jean-Léon Gérôme, a prominent French artist and teacher of many American students); there is background information on persons and places Brewer only mentions; gaps in his account are filled in; and the reader can discover what happened to Nicholas Brewer in the eleven years of his life after the publication of *Trails.*

The reader should know a few facts about the original publication of *Trails of a Paintbrush.* The Christopher Publishing House was founded in Boston in 1910 or 1912, depending on the source, and was a family firm run by two brothers, Arthur and Joseph Christopher. Over the course of its history, the firm published hundreds, perhaps thousands, of nonfiction books on specialized topics relating to religion, history, biography, and the like. It appears to have specialized in small runs. But Christopher House was a respected publisher, not a mere vanity press, and its books were regularly reviewed in the *Boston Globe* and *New York Times*.[4]

Trails of a Paintbrush was a handsome volume, and the publisher marketed it with a four-page pamphlet containing extravagant praise for Brewer's work. The price was five dollars, a substantial sum in 1938. It was cloth-bound with "seventy-five halftone illustrations and four beautifully colored reproductions" of which the publisher was obviously proud. Many of the reproductions were tipped in, that is, pasted in by hand. (The words "beautifully illustrated" appear on the title page.) The illustrations do not meet today's digital standards, but they remain essential, particularly since many of them depict paintings that have not been located and may be lost. The layout, typography, and binding of the book were elegant but old-fashioned for 1938. (They closely resemble the format of the autobiography by Brewer's close friend Joseph Jefferson, published by the Century Publishing Company in 1889.)

The introduction by O.R. McGuire, a Washington lawyer whom Brewer probably met during his stays in the capital city, praises *Trails of a Paintbrush* as an "Epic of America." McGuire quotes at some length from Brewer's friend Henry Wellington Wack, who, among his various endeavors as lawyer, naturalist, and artist, was an accomplished booster who wrote an encomium of Brewer for an earlier exhibition catalog that dubbed him the "Abraham Lincoln of American art." The phrase stuck and was subsequently used in publicity and reviews. Although the comparison between Lincoln and Brewer cannot be taken too far, it does help evoke Brewer's character and his place in American art. Lincoln was a great hero to Brewer, and there were similarities between the two. Both came out of the frontier, had little formal education, and no connections to smooth their way. Brewer appears to have had a dignity and commanding presence that is comparable to Lincoln's. Brewer was not a pioneer in American art, nor yet a founding father, but, like Lincoln, was an eminent representative and purveyor of fundamental American principles. He was an idealist, yet realistic and pragmatic;

he was an individualist, energetic and assertive, yet modest; he was unquestionably patriotic. As the *Washington Evening Star* review of *Trails of a Paintbrush* stated, "[Brewer's] book is an important American document. It covers more than half a century of artistic development in our country, and, in the intensely American style which its author uses, reflects the spirit of our land better than a hundred treatises."[5]

Afton Press has had a connection to Nicholas Brewer and his family for many years. Patricia McDonald, who founded the press with W. Duncan MacMillan in 1993, met Edward V. Brewer, the artist's second son and himself a distinguished artist and illustrator, in 1967. She subsequently wrote an excellent article about him and his work for *Minnesota History*.[6] She wanted to write a book about his father—little had been written about him since his death, except for entries in Rena Neumann Coen's fine book *Painting and Sculpture in Minnesota, 1820–1914* (1976) and William Gerdts's groundbreaking survey *Art Across America: Two Centuries of Regional Painting, 1710–1920* (1990). Yet, due to the demands of a successful press, she never had the time. She asked Rena Coen to write it (Coen also included Brewer in her 1996 book for Afton Press, *Minnesota Impressionists*). Coen made a start, but after her death in 2001, the charge was passed to me.

Patricia McDonald died shortly before *Nicholas R. Brewer: His Art and Family* was published in 2018, and it is dedicated to her. Ian Graham Leask is now publisher of Afton Press and carries its traditions forward. It is Ian who conceived the idea of publishing *Trails of a Paintbrush* as a companion volume to my Brewer biography. *Trails* was an important source for that book, but the artist's words deserve to be read in full. It is our hope that these volumes will help preserve the legacy of Nicholas Brewer for the twenty-first century and beyond.

Julie L'Enfant
April 1, 2021

1. Nick Wormley told this story in engaging detail in his blog Eccentric Aspects, posted in 2012 as "A Bibliophile Christmas" under the pseudonym "cynick." http://eccentricaspects.com/category/bibliophilia

2. Barbara Dayer Gallati, ed., *Beauty's Legacy: Gilded Age Portraits in America* (New York: New York Historical Society and London: D Giles Ltd., 2013).

3. Calvin Tomkins, *Duchamp: A Biography* (New York: Henry Holt, 1996), 185.

4. I am indebted to research librarian Carly Stevens at the Boston Athenaeum for pointing me to information about the Christopher Publishing House from the Boston Directories of 1922 and 1925. I am also grateful to research librarian Marnie Goodbody at the Boston Public Library, who provided additional information on Christopher House publications and reviews from obituaries of Arthur J. Christopher ("Arthur Christopher; had publishing house," *Boston Globe*, July 11, 1976; "Deaths: A.T. [sic] Christopher; Hub book publisher," *Boston Herald,* July 10, 1976). Christopher Publishing House was sold in 1983.

5. Mary-Carter Roberts, *Evening Star* (Washington, D.C.), July 2, 1939, *Chronicling America:* Library of Congress https://chroniclingamerica.loc.gov/lccn/sn83045462/1939-07-02/ed-1/seq-54/

6. Patricia Condon Johnston [McDonald], "Edward Brewer: Illustrator and Painter," *Minnesota History* 47, no. 1 (Spring 1980): 2–15.

Chapter I
The Pioneers

From the Old to the New World—Westward—The Forty-niners—My Parents Meet—Chicago, to the Northwest—The Log Cabin—An Indian Massacre

Peter Brewer, my father, was born in Cologne, Germany. Being of a venturesome nature and wishing to rise to better conditions, he decided to seek his fortune in the New World. Boarding a huge five-masted sailing vessel at Bremen in 1840, he landed at Castle Garden after a tempestuous voyage.

He used to tell us of his experiences on that adventure. On one calm Sunday afternoon, he said the sun was hot. Every sail was spread to catch the breeze. The sea was like glass, disturbed only by schools of sporting dolphins. About four o'clock in the afternoon, ominous clouds arose in the west, and soon the wind began to whistle through the rigging. The first mate, alarmed, went to the captain's cabin to warn him and found him obliviously drunk. Repeatedly he beat on the door of the cabin but received only the captain's curses in response. Soon the storm broke with terrific force. The sails were unfurled. The ship rolled and tossed until the rudder gave way, and the vessel wallowed helplessly, battered by the tremendous waves. One mast after another broke and came crashing down, adding to the chaos. When the storm abated, Father said he went on deck, where he saw the seamen cutting the ropes in an effort to release the wreckage.

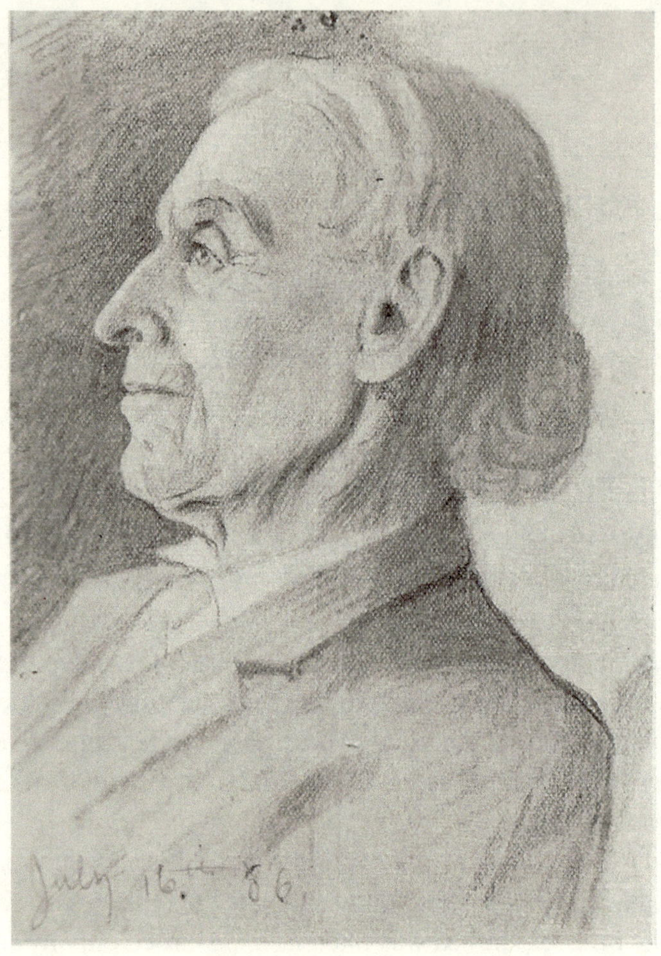

Peter Brewer, my father.

For two months, they drifted before they were sighted and rescued. Four months from the time Father sailed, he set foot upon terra firma in the New World. With gratitude for his miraculous escape and rescue, he knelt on the ground and thanked God for his deliverance.

In America, Peter Brewer became a part of the tremendous westward expansion movement, which characterized the midcentury. We were often told how he went from New York to Philadelphia and Harrisburg by canal boat, settling in Johnstown, Pennsylvania, where he worked for some years at cabinetmaking, stair building, and various kinds of construction work. In 1849 when gold was discovered in California, his wanderlust reasserted itself, and he resolved to join one of the expeditions that were crossing the plains. From Pittsburgh, he went by boat down the Ohio River and up the Missouri River to St. Joseph, Missouri, where caravans were assembled and equipped for the long trek to the El Dorado of the Pacific.

In St. Joe, he met my mother, Mary Ann Gordon Russell Rolph, who had been recently widowed. My mother and her first husband had also been on their way to the goldfields in California. At St. Joe, she was left with her two sons, Henry and Enon, almost destitute and with no one to help her. My father paid court to the young widow, and they were married. Thus, it was that, with the unaccustomed burden of a ready-made family upon his shoulders, he changed his plan and decided not to take the hazardous and exhausting trip to California. They went to Chicago instead. Chicago was one of the rising young trade centers of the nation, but a very different city from the commercial giant we know today.

Peter Brewer saw the waves of Lake Michigan break where the Art Institute now stands, not far from the spot where Fort Dearborn was once located. To the south, a few wooden buildings were scattered. He described the streets of Chicago as they appeared then by saying that at the corner of State and Washington Streets, a warning sign read, "Beware—No Bottom."

The next years were unsettled ones. The Brewers lived for a time at Waukegan, then a rival of Chicago, where my eldest brother, Albert, was born. In Rockford, my father worked at stone-cutting, stair building, and whatever else he could get to do. Iowa City, where my second brother, Hubert, was born, afforded even less incentive for permanent location, so they resolved to go to Fort Snelling and St. Paul, Minnesota, which were then on the border of civilization. After weeks of tedious journeying in an ox-drawn covered wagon across the plains of northern Iowa and southern Minnesota, they came to the stream now known as the Root River, which was then overrunning its banks from recent rains. When the subsiding waters permitted them to cross, they landed on a high promontory fringed with cedars and giant oaks—one of the most beautiful spots in southern Minnesota. There they pitched their camp and decided to build their cabin.

The land was fertile. The streams were filled with fish. Wild game of every kind abounded—geese, ducks, prairie grouse, and partridges. There were deer to supply venison, and fur-bearing animals—the otter, mink, and beaver—to provide winter raiment. After my birth, this useful wildlife still flourished close by. Often during my childhood, I watched the beavers gnawing trees to start a dam; many a mink fell victim to my steel trap. There were beasts of prey, too. On winter nights, howls of the timber wolves often struck cold terror to my childish heart.

My mother loved nature and preferred the solitude of the forest, the songs of the birds, or the rippling brook to the bustle of the city. Her life was full of hardships, but in that wilderness home, there was peace and contentment. If either my father or my mother felt, at times, a longing for old scenes or the friends they had left behind, it was never expressed.

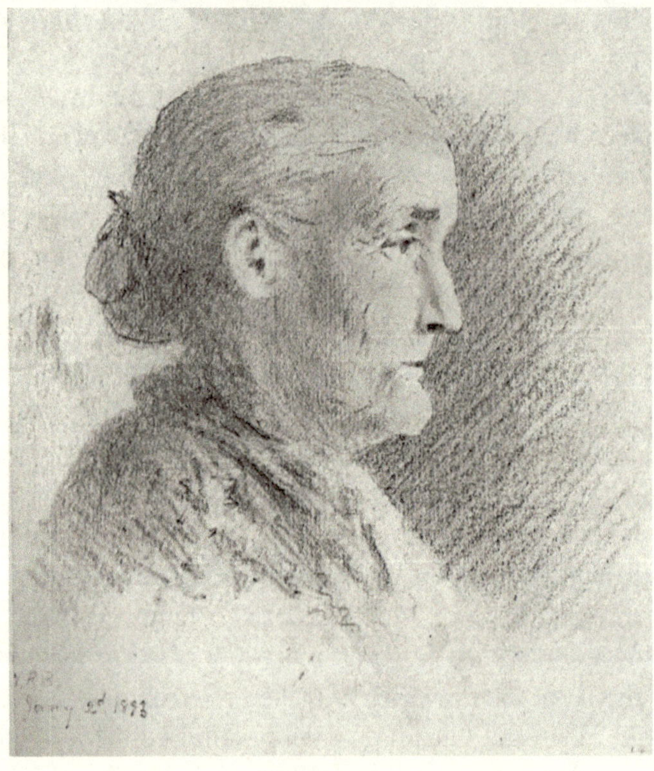

Mary Ann Russell Brewer, my mother.

It was a time of heroic adventure for them, too. My mother often told us, in the glow of the open fire on winter evenings, of an incident, which occurred before the cabin was built. While eating supper from a spread on the ground, she called my father's attention to two horsemen who appeared out of the forest about half a mile to the north. The unusual sight aroused their curiosity, and they soon discovered, with trepidation, that the riders were Indians. Father hastily adjusted caps on the guns and laid under the spread an old double-barreled brass pistol, which he kept loaded for emergency. The strangers were seated on scrawny looking ponies, wore buckskin trousers, and had blankets tightly drawn about their shoulders. They were seemingly peaceable, but the pioneers presently observed that each carried a tomahawk, a knife, and a bow and quiver of flinthead arrows. Dismounting, the foremost Indian advanced toward my parents. As he approached, he gave a grunt and nodded his head. "Injun much friend. Great Sioux Chiefs have camp on Watonwan. Much squaw and papoose," he announced. "Me Chief Cut Nose! Go to Winona. Buy toback, fire-water. Sell skins. Injun heap tired. Pony no go. Walk all day."

Mother, in her kindness, took the milk pail and filling a cup handed it to the Indian, who watched her movements with interest. Seeing this, the other Indian came forward. Each gave a grunt of thanks. Then, looking at the remnants of the meal on the ground, they motioned for permission to take the remaining half loaf of bread. Mother cut two pieces and spreading them with butter, handed one to each of the men. Instantly they drew their knives from their belts and scraped off the butter.

Having finished eating, the older savage drew his tomahawk from his belt and handing it to Father with a nod and grimace toward an axe lying close by exclaimed, "Swap!" Running his thumb over the blade, Father said, "No, my axe is better."

On the back of one of the ponies was a saddle of venison, on which one of the Indians had been riding. They made known that they wanted to exchange some of the venison for what the Indian called "Ko Koosh," the meaning of which my father did not know. The Indian lifted the lids of several barrels before finding some salt pork. He raised a piece and offered to give Mother venison in exchange, which she declined to do. The Indian then seized the axe and went to one of the tall cedar trees from which he split out a slab about four feet in length to use for arrows, leaving an unseemly gash. Father was incensed over the defacement of the tree and took the axe from him. Thereupon the Indians mounted their horses and rode away.

It was there on the banks of the Root River that I, seventh son of my mother, first blinked at the light in 1857, and where my uncertain baby steps brought me many a bump and fall, as I kicked about in that interesting period of childish exploiting when the boy is little more than legs and stomach. I had my share of narrow escapes. Like all boys, I loved to ramble. Once I tumbled down the cliff into the river, which fortunately proved too shallow for a respectable bath at that particular place. I was rescued by my oldest brother and brought back dripping wet to receive a well-merited spanking. Down through the years, I have brought a first impression which, while of no significance itself, is a poignant reminder of those happy, carefree days. One day when I was very small, my father set me on the back of our old gray mare for a first horseback ride. He held me on with one hand. I, joyfully alive to the importance of the occasion, clung tenaciously to her mane. For seventy-odd years I have treasured that memory.

Where the prosperous city of Winona, Minnesota, now stands, there was but a trading post to which small boats navigating the Mississippi River brought provisions. The world-famous city of Rochester was only a wooded valley along the Zumbro River. Winona was some sixty miles from our home, and about twice a year Father would make the journey. On one occasion, owing to the loss of a horse, he was obliged to drive the oxen. For a week we watched for his return, and when at last I spied the team on the hill, we scampered to meet him. Taking us up, he placed us in the wagon and we began rummaging about for toys or sweetmeats. From a grain sack I pulled an apple—the first I had ever seen. I smelled it and bit into it and I can taste it yet! At the table that night he related the mishaps of his trip and described the great hill at Rolling Stone down which he had to drive. At the foot of the hill, in crossing a bridge, the team made a break for the water and upset the wagon, dumping his load down the bank.

Father was wearing a new sweater or blouse, and when Mother asked him where he got it, he jokingly replied that he had stolen it. I had been taught that people who stole things would surely go to Hell. Father's words sunk deep into my childish imagination and caused me to worry greatly. Several days later, I sat down on the doorstep and began to cry hysterically. Mother asked me why I was crying. I replied that I thought that Father was going to Hell for stealing the jacket. Mother's soothing words soon dissipated my misery, and I thought no more about it.

Upon a previous occasion, the Brewer wagon went to market, but under widely different circumstances. Because of her temperament inherited from Scotch forefathers, my mother was the ruling spirit of the Brewer menage. Her courage was indomitable, and once she had decided upon a course, there was no changing her mind. Before I can remember, Father was taken ill with inflammatory rheumatism and confined to his bed for several months. Provisions ran out, and Mother was obliged to drive to Decorah, Iowa, then the nearest trading post. Her destination was over a hundred miles away, without roads or shelter of any kind, through an unsettled country which was infested with bands of marauding Indians. Taking me, a baby, and my older brother, four years of age, she drove the team, and we camped by the wayside on the dangerous two weeks' trip.

In time, after the Brewers settled on the banks of the Root River, other immigrants came in. Some built cabins quite close to our place. In less than ten years, much of that beautiful country had been settled. Only recently I motored through the same valley among the great hills. I fancied I could trace the ruts of the old-time road my father had traveled with such patience and fortitude. I thought of the vast changes that had taken place since those days of the amazing rapidity of modern transportation. Then awakening from my reverie, I realized that I had covered in less than two hours the distance Father took a week to drive.

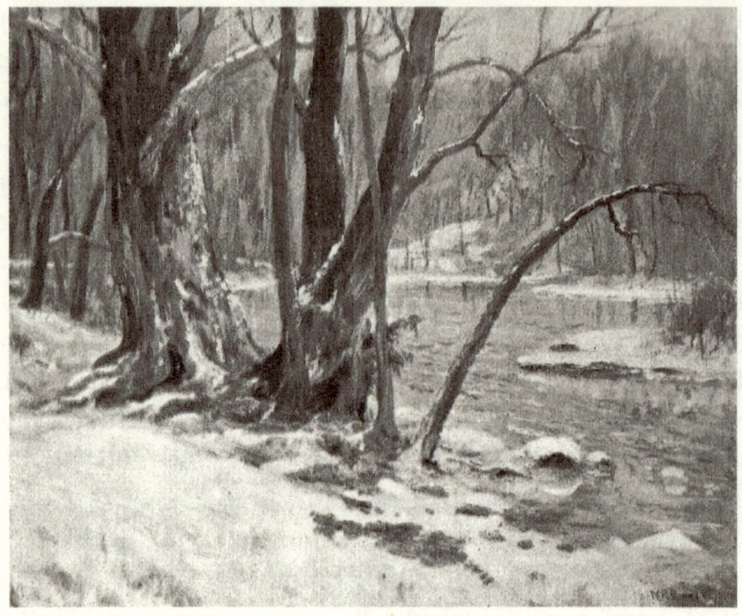

The Root River

After Minnesota Territory was organized, the Sioux Indians were induced to sign treaties ceding to the United States all their lands in Iowa, Minnesota, and Dakota, excepting a tract ten miles wide on each side of the Minnesota River, extending from Fort Ridgely to Travers Lake, a distance of one hundred fifty miles. This stretch of territory was intended as a future home for the tribes, but in 1860 the government purchased that portion on the north side of the river. As a result of systematic fraud by the government agents and the delays in the payments due, the Indians, the Red men, grew restive and, in August 1862, raised the war cry against the settlers. Little Crow, the most influential of the Sioux chieftains, resented as much as any of them the filching away of their lands and the debauchery of their homes by the unscrupulous white man, but foreseeing the hopelessness of the Indian cause and certain disaster to his people in the event of an outbreak, he sought to restrain the enraged warriors. Despite his admonitions, excitement increased. When Little Crow found himself powerless to stem the tide, he espoused his people's cause and led the combined hordes of M'dewakantons, Wapekutes, Wahpetons, and Sissetons, of the great Sioux or Dakotah Nation, in the most fiendish and horrible massacre of all Indian history. Upward of six thousand warriors descended upon the Indian Agency. After killing several people and seizing the stores, they broke up into bands and swept over the country. Fierce battles raged at Fort Ridgely and New Ulm. Couriers were dispatched over the country to warn the settlers, some of whom escaped, but by far the greater number fell victims to the rage of their savage foe.

Skies illuminated by the glare of burning homes, distant reports of guns, yells of savages, and cries of helpless people told of once peaceful scenes made hideous beyond description. Hundreds of defenseless women and children were subjected to the most frightful cruelties. The poisoned arrow, the blazing fagot, or the tomahawk were the instruments of execution. The only souls spared were those women and young girls who could be forced to march to a distant camp to meet a fate worse than death. The massacre spread in every direction until, before the frightful record was complete, over a thousand settlers perished.

I remember that fateful August of 1862. Although many of our neighbors packed their belongings and hastily fled, the Brewers remained, placing confidence in the soldiers who had been dispatched from Fort Snelling to meet the wild horde. I remember seeing Mother place the pitchfork by her bed at night and hearing her say that the Indians were not going to injure her children except over her dead body. Fortunately for us, the Indians were defeated where they were engaged by the Third Minnesota Regiment, of which my half-brother, Henry, was a member. Had they continued their march, no doubt my five-year-old scalp would have been taken, with those of the entire family. One boy, only twelve years old, Martin Eastlick, whose family had been massacred, carried his little two-year-old brother fifty-two miles to safety, traveling by night and hiding by day. I remember hearing him lecture years afterward when he showed a series of historical paintings to describe the incidents of those awful days.

When danger from the Indians was over, life on the frontier resumed its normal course. The Brewers once again felt free to roam their own woods without fear and undertake the work of clearing and breaking up more land. Father built a boat which my brothers and I used, and at night, under the blazing light of our jack, we would spear pickerel, pike, and bass. The fish were plentiful. At a shallow place we built two dams about ten feet apart of cobblestones and pebbles, leaving a gap in the upper dam. From the cliff we watched the schools of fish float downstream from the deep water to the shallow place to spawn. Once they had swarmed through the gap of the dam, we would rush in and close the opening with a piece of timber. The water in the pen was so shallow that their fins and tails would show above and it was our joy, as the frightened fish leaped about, to spring in and throw them out to the bank with our hands. We caught barrels of them and fed them to the pigs, which is not the proverbial fish story but the literal truth.

Amid these surroundings life was easy to support. Clothes, a little coffee, flour, and seasoning, and a roof overhead were all that was needed to raise a family of husky boys. Wild plums, crabapples, and berries grew everywhere. The snow-covered forest was lined with rabbit paths. As I grew older, it was often my delight to bag a dozen cottontails with my gun in a ramble through the woods.

Near the two-roomed log cabin where I was born, my father built a shop in which he had a forge and turning-lathe. The forge was an ordinary one. The turning-lathe consisted of a large wheel, a belt, and a pulley. He operated it with his foot. Upon it he turned the old-fashioned bedposts and spindles to match, which we prize so highly today. As a child I stood by and watched the whirling shaft and flying chips with wonder. Not one movement did I miss in the entire construction of a new, two-horse lumber wagon, as Father shaped the spokes and felloes and forged the iron for the tires and trim.

One day, wondering at Father's skill with tools and where he had acquired it, I asked him how long it took to learn to handle tools so easily and well. I do not now recall his answer but remember following it with the question, "How long is a lifetime?" When I was told it was about seventy years, my heart fell within me, for somehow, I had fancied a lifetime was hundreds of years, and seventy years seemed so short! I pondered over the answer for days with much disappointment, for life was so beautiful to me, and I was so full of the zest of being.

I presume I asked more questions than Mother was able to answer, for I remember her chasing me out of the house with a broom one day for talking too much. At times I would wander into the woods close by to sit and listen to the warbling of the birds. One day I fell asleep and did not appear at mealtime, which put the family into a commotion that lasted long after dark. Then it was Watch who found me and by his barking led the searchers to my forest bed.

As the land was taken up by settlers, the village of High Forest, Minnesota, came into existence. Mr. Tattersall, an enterprising miller, built a mill where the farmers brought their wheat to be ground for flour. There was also a well-patronized blacksmith shop, a couple of stores, a tavern, and two churches, Methodist and Baptist. The forest of great trees came down to the stream, which curved and plunged over great boulders just below the ford where the road emerged from the forest.

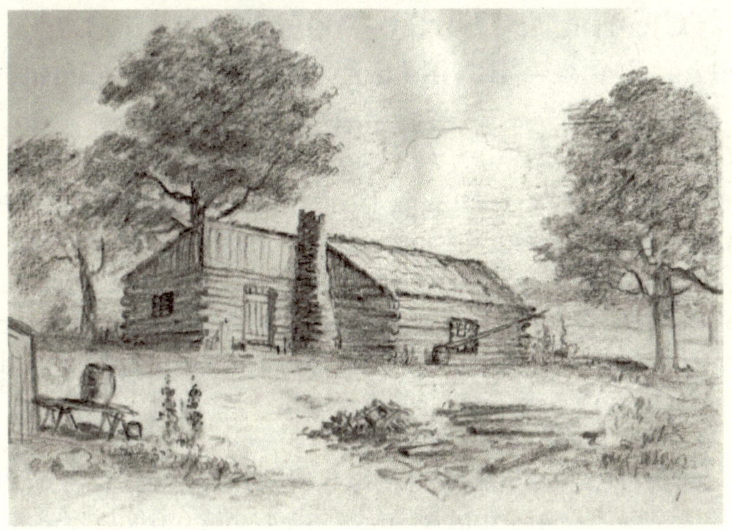

Where I was born—1857. From a pencil sketch made in my youth.

Chapter II
Early Experiences

Clearing the Forest—Wild Life—The Log Schoolhouse—Boyhood Escapades—Elementary Training

Before I was eight years of age, I had quite a collection of sketches, things I had drawn about the farm, many of which I tinted with watercolors. My mother was very proud of those early, feeble efforts and often boasted that since I was a descendant of a famous historical painter named Gordan, her seventh son would yet hang a picture in the Pope's gallery—which he has thus far failed to do.

Several miles to the north there was quite a settlement of Swedish people. One Fourth of July we heard they were going to celebrate with a picnic and a dance. I told Mother I was going to take my drawing and watercolor pictures there, sell chances, and raffle them off. After a five-mile trudge, I arrived at the picnic grounds. There was a dancing pavilion and a booth where homemade wieners, coffee, buns, and other food were served. Farther along was a stand with several kegs of beer, to which everybody was free to help himself.

Many poured whiskey into the beer to give it a stronger kic and, consequently, quite a number were staggering about in good-natured stupidity. They became my prey as I bartered chances for dimes. Some would not buy unless I would drink with them. I had never tasted beer and whiskey cocktails and knew nothing of the effects. After selling thirty chances, I, too, became oblivious of everything and staggered out into the brush, where I lay unconscious far into the night. I awoke about three o'clock in the morning, half-frozen, terribly sick with frequent stomach explosions. My only satisfaction during the three days recovery from my initial jag was in counting the ten and twenty-five cent script pieces, which totaled over three dollars. After all, it is a fact of considerable pride to me that my first earnings were made with my brush.

No one can imagine what a passion I had from that time on to draw and paint. I drew the calves, pigs, chickens, and other animals, and even attempted to draw my mother's picture. My efforts were failures. I had to milk the cows and work in the fields from early till late; consequently, I had little time for drawing, except on Sundays and in the evenings but there was no amusement, no pleasure comparable to that derived from my pencil and brush.

My muscles itched for exercise, and wherever I went, it was with a hop, skip, and jump. From the shop to the house was but so many bounds. Ape-like to climb to the topmost boughs of the tallest oaks was my pleasure. As we grew up, we boys had hard work to do, but we managed to get plenty of fun and adventure out of it.

I recall one occasion when I was riding the fleetest and most skittish horse in the neighborhood. After I had dismounted to kill a rattlesnake, the horse started off without me toward home. If I had a running chance with a barebacked horse just getting underway and could clutch his mane, he was mine, for then no horse could prevent my landing on his back. This time I cut behind a bush in the direction he was going and just grabbed the rear lock on his neck. My spring was so vigorous that I leaped just a little too far and with an unfortunate jolt, landed on the other side, striking on my head and shoulders. I was so badly stunned that I had to give up the chase.

It was my daily chore to fetch the cows from the bottom-lands where they grazed at large. Watch, our mongrel dog, was my constant companion. One night I could not find the cows. I was really alarmed when I did not hear the tinkling of the bell on old Spot's neck, so I listened and hunted far and wide. Soon I found myself in a dense thicket bordering the forest. Suddenly the dog left me, darted forward with a growl, and disappeared in the bushes. I heard a snarl and a yelp, and he rushed back with a young timber wolf at his heels. My impulse was to run, but Watch stopped near me and encouraged by my presence again charged, only to yelp with greater pain as the wolf's fangs sank into his neck.

My woodland experience had taught me the efficacy of carrying a stick of some kind with which to beat the brush or kill snakes. At this time, I had an old broom handle. Watch and the wolf came so close that I summoned all my nerve and brought my club down upon the neck of the wolf. It was a lucky stroke I made—just back of the base of the brain. With a little yelp, the wolf settled to the ground and released his hold on the dog. I followed up the fatal blow with two or three more to make sure of my victim. I have often thought of that lucky hit, for it probably saved us both some lifelong scars. Forgetting the cows, I dragged the carcass home, and the following day I related the incident to a neighbor named Pierson. He asked me to show him where I had killed the wolf, saying he was sure the wolf family lived nearby. He shouldered his gun, and taking the dog we pursued the trail somewhat deeper into the glade. Suddenly I saw him raise his gun to his shoulder and fire. The she-wolf was his victim. Later we took the scalps to the county seat and claimed the state bounty for wolves.

I tease my sportsmen sons, who annually find their greatest pleasure on the duck pass, when I tell them of a greater achievement in the slaughtering of ducks than they can ever hope to equal. I feign to forget their disdain for the old-fashioned pot shot and eloquently describe the first time I ever fired a gun.

Across the river from our home, in sight of the house, was a small lake where thousands of ducks lingered in the spring and fall on their migrating journeys. One day as the water was literally covered with birds, Mother asked me if I couldn't take the old Springfield musket, which my half-brother Henry had carried home from Civil War service and get some ducks for supper. One of my brothers had loaded the gun with buckshot for geese. The fence enclosing the field ran down close to the water. I crept out of sight of the ducks, along the fence, until within a hundred yards of them. Resting the gun on the lower rail at arm's length, I blazed away at the mass of squawking birds. The kick of the heavily loaded gun brought the stock back against me with such force that it turned me over into the ditch. In spite of an aching shoulder, I peeped up at the cloud of wings, and when it disappeared, I discovered four mallards lying on the water close to the shore. To me, it mattered not whether it was a pot shot or on the wing. I was after a good supper, and with pride, I lugged them home. While my sons' appetites have always been equal to my own youthful hunger, they have never carried home so cheap a dinner.

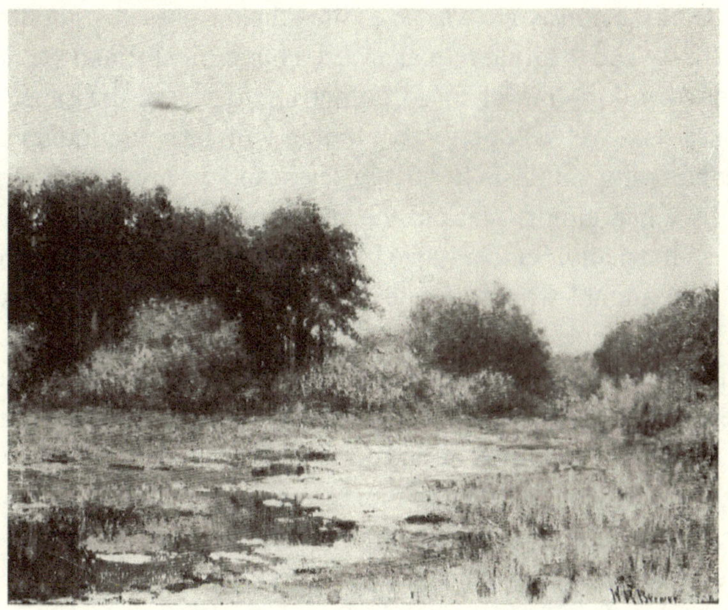

The Duck Pond

Nowadays, we hear much of wildcat oil wells, wildcat speculations, and wildcat get-rich-quick schemes. These followed in the wake of our material development during the days of pioneering when men were well satisfied to get enough to eat and maintain a respectable roof over their heads. The Brewer boys had a different scheme—a real, live wildcat with which to speculate.

One winter's morning, my eldest brother Albert, who was an enterprising lad of sixteen, sauntered forth to collect the catch of the fur-bearing animals in his several traps. Hubert, the next older, and I, knew his purpose, although he tried to keep us in the dark regarding his traps. He feared that our mischievous curiosity might lead us to frequent the places where he expected to beguile a mink, an otter, or a beaver. These animals were wary, and the trapper must disguise his tracks—a thing that roustabout boys think little about—hence Albert's secrecy.

We decided we would follow him, keeping discreetly out of his sight as he wandered along the stream and up over the bank deep into the forest. After following him for some distance, dodging behind trees and stumps in hide-and-seek fashion, we saw him quicken his pace behind a dense thicket, only to reappear, running at full speed back in the direction of the house. He was so excited that he passed without seeing us. His hasty and exciting retreat aroused our curiosity, and we debated whether to follow him or to go farther and discover the cause of his sudden retreat. We were perfectly familiar with bear and Indian stories, but our curiosity got the better of our fears, and we proceeded cautiously until we had almost reached the spot where Albert had turned and retired so hurriedly. Suddenly we heard a growl. Looking up a tree, we saw a gray animal which, in our boyish imagination, seemed a monstrous beast capable of devouring a dozen such kids as us.

In our fright, we also retreated. Our young legs carried us over fallen trees, briers, and knolls at a speed never before tried. Arriving at the house all out of breath, we found Albert jumping about telling Mother what a wonderful animal he had caught and that it had dragged the heavy timber, to which he had attached the chain of the trap, up a tree.

After much discussion of plans, Albert evolved a scheme to capture the beast alive. The idea developed into a vision of great wealth! For such an animal, we figured, would be quickly bought for at least a thousand dollars by the first circus manager who came into the country. It proved to be a huge lynx or bobcat. Anyone acquainted with the wildcat family knows the hazard of trying to capture one alive, and we only half guessed the difficulties involved. But, "Nothing ventured, nothing gained," urged Mother. "Only be careful." So, we started out with an axe to cut down the tree, a coil of strong twine to bind the animal, a blanket to blindfold him, and a large grain bag in which to bring him home. Arriving at the place, we cut a sapling with branching limbs and made a two-tined prong with a ten-foot handle, with which Hubert was to ward off the beast, should he attempt to spring at Albert while cutting the tree. Timidly the axe-man approached the tree beneath the snarling cat, which was held fast by one hind foot in the trap, with the chain tangled around a limb of the tree. Each blow of the axe brought from the maddened animal growls, snarls, and vain struggles to free itself. As the chips flew, lessening the girth of the tree, it began to sway and finally fell in the direction where Hubert and I stood. We dodged and thus avoided coming in contact not only with the tree but also with the claws of the ferocious beast. I still see his great leap toward us with outstretched claws, and within four feet of us, when the chain that held him captive reached its limit. Now that the battle was to be on terra firma, we decided to pin him down with the prong about his neck so that we might bind his feet, but the attempt only enraged the creature more, causing him to show greater ferocity. We piled heavy branches on him and beat him on the head, hoping to knock him senseless until we could bind those lightning-like feet and snapping teeth. When we thought we had him fast, he would wriggle himself loose and spring at us with terrific force.

After about four hours of constant effort, we wore him out and finally bound his feet together. We cut a block of wood and put it in his mouth as a gag and tied his jaws firmly to it. Then we got him into the bag and lugged him home.

Father had just returned from High Forest. On discovering what we had in the bag, he immediately began preparing a cage. He had a large empty box about three feet square, and by adjusting bars of straight poles across the opening, we soon had a temporary home for our victim. We placed the box in father's shop, where Mr. Bobcat could be fed and guarded until the first circus should come to Rochester and we could cash in for our morning's work.

A dispute arose between us as to how we would divide the spoils. Of course, Albert maintained that the lynx was his since he had trapped it, but Hubert and I argued he never could have caged it without our help. Mother, however, settled the wrangle by saying, "Let us see, first, how much you can sell it for; then we will divide the money to each one's satisfaction."

Father's shop was fifty yards from the house. Adjoining it was the chicken house. Feed was kept in the shop, and it was my chore to go early each morning into the place to get feed for the chickens. Each morning as I entered I was greeted by a vicious roar and growl, warning me not to come too near the bars, for those swift-flying claws meant to extract satisfaction for the part I had taken in making prisoner the subject of our future wealth. I must confess I lifted the latch timidly in the dim light of dawn, and although I did not realize it at the time, I might have met with serious trouble. One morning the usual growl was not heard. All was quiet in the room. This aroused my curiosity and I stepped closer to the cage, peering in. The brute was not there! I realized my predicament should he be hiding under the workbench or behind some timbers in the corner. Quickly I left the room, opening the door only wide enough to peep in. The silence continued. Picking up some rocks, I opened the door quickly and hurled them under the bench and behind every object until I was sure Mr. Cat had made his exit. I discovered that the upper right pane in the window above the bench, some seven feet from the floor, had been completely broken out. He had evidently sprung the two-inch wooden bars of the cage and gained his freedom. But why he should have chosen that lofty pane of glass as an opening to liberty remains a mystery. At all events, he was a wise cat. Before starting on his journey, he bethought himself of his breakfast. The crumbs of his feast were evident in the scattered feathers and feet of one of Mother's finest white Brahmas.

And thus, our wildcat scheme for quick money proved only a disappointing fiasco.

I was filled with wonderment over this creation and all its marvelous beauties. It was only natural, in my speculations, that I should wish to know something of the Creator. We were not church-going people; in fact, I was half-grown before any church in that part of the country was thought of. Pioneers often reverse the Biblical command, "Seek ye first the Kingdom of God, and all things else shall be added unto you." Mother's Protestant Bible lay on a shelf, covered with dust. I had never even looked into it, but one Sunday, something prompted me to ask her, "Who is this man, Jesus Christ, these rough harvest hands curse by?" Her reply was, "If you will take that old Bible down and read the New Testament, it will tell you all about Him." I climbed up on a chair, rooted the volume out from under a pile of papers, and she showed me the New Testament. I took the Holy Book out under the trees, began reading it, and soon became deeply absorbed in the story of the Man of Galilee. Sunday after Sunday, I perused the sacred pages.

The effect of this reading on my boyish imagination was singular and salutary, yet it left me in a state of perplexity and discomfort. I was overwhelmed with the newly found knowledge gleaned from my reading, that I had an immortal soul to save, and I felt the need of guidance, which this sacred book scarcely furnished. At least, my limited comprehension of its message left me with an uncertainty and fear which I was unable to overcome. I could not grasp the meaning of the words, "Watch and pray, lest ye enter into temptation." "What is temptation?" I asked. "How must I pray?" I could not find an answer to the latter question save in the Lord's Prayer, which I could not understand. However, I formulated certain requests which I asked daily of the Infinite Arbiter of our eternal destiny. I asked Him to bless my father and mother, my brothers, but most ardently my teacher, who was but two years older than I was and for whom I had acquired a deep and sincere affection.

To make these requests more earnestly, I frequently knelt beside my bed. Mother had placed my bed upstairs in father's shop, where the harvest hands slept. On one occasion, while I was kneeling there, two of the men came in. One of them pulled off his boot and slung it at me with the words, "Stop that, you damn little fool." After that, I said my prayers in bed, not the least disturbed by these men or their attitude toward the sacred things of which I had been reading.

With the inconsistency that is life, my experiences led me into widely divergent paths. Spiritual groupings occupied quieter moments, but I was thoroughly alive to the world about me, keenly appreciative of adventure and mischievous fun, and as liable as any boy to be led into scrapes from which I emerged the wiser for a little philosophical reflection.

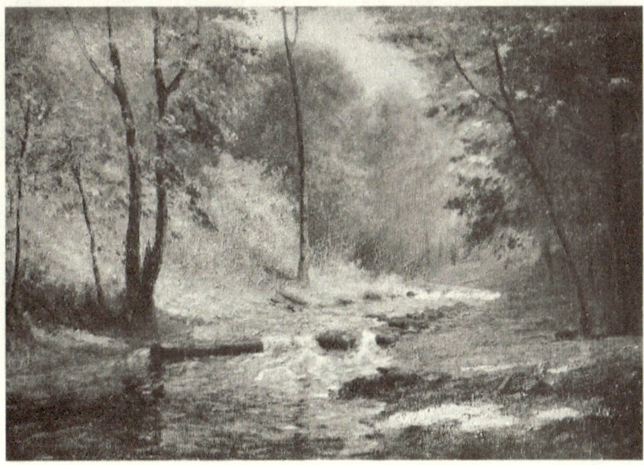

Where we built the fish pen.

Mike Foley was twelve years old, had red hair, and a freckled pug nose. He never washed his face, nor did he like to go to school. He used bad language and spoke abusively of the teacher whenever he could do so without being heard by her, played truant, and led the other boys into all manner of mischief, getting himself and them into trouble.

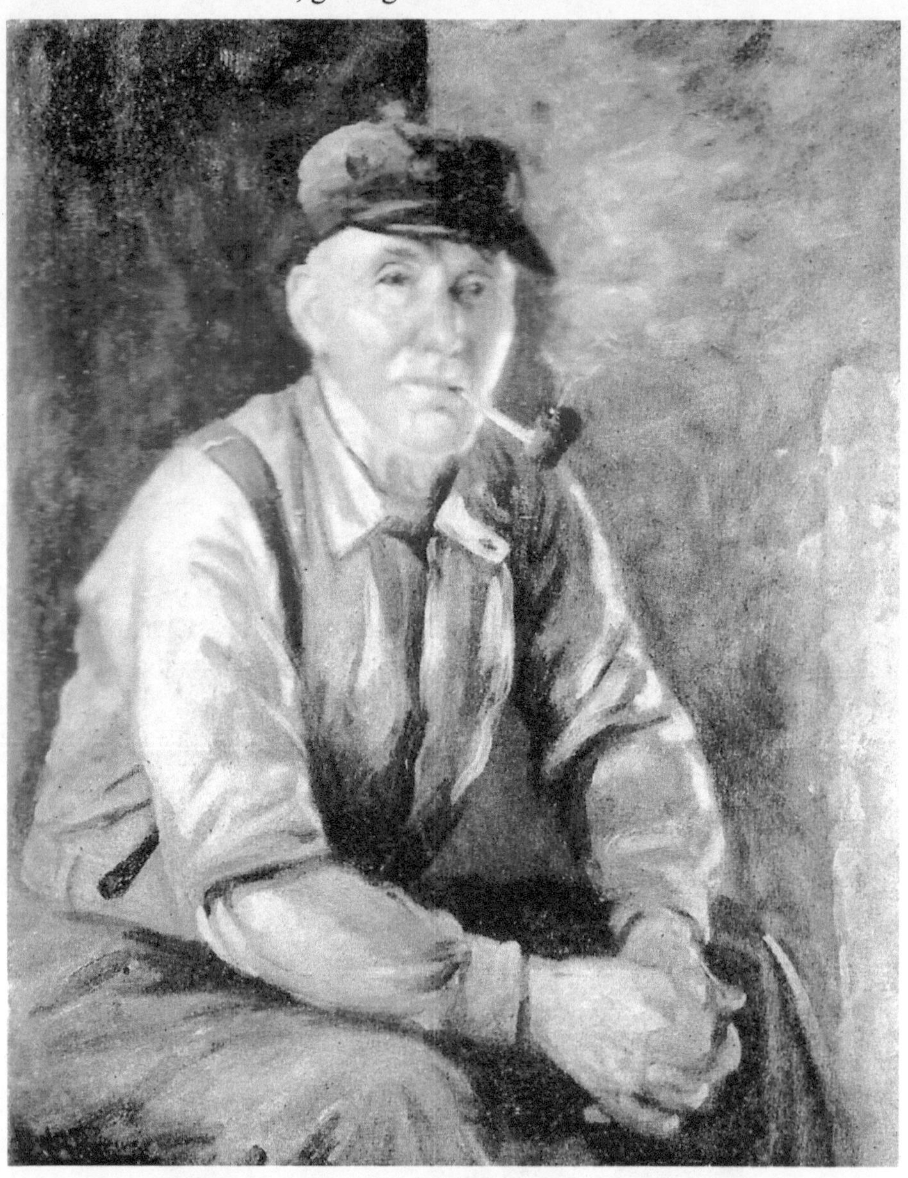

Mike

Miss Blodgett was a pious soul. She always opened school with the reading of verses from the Testament and with long prayers, which Mike did not like. One day he composed a rhyme to express his contempt:

The little black mouse ran up the stairs
To hear Miss Blodgett say her prayers.

The teacher, overhearing him recite it to the other children, summoned him. "Repeat that to me," she demanded. Mike looked down, scratched his knee, but said nothing. "Did you hear what I said?" she asked.

"Ye-s," hesitatingly, from Mike.

"Well!" said Miss Blodgett.

"T'ain't—t'ain't nothin' anyway," faltered Mike.

"Did you hear me?" threatened Miss Blodgett as she held up her ruler.

Mike thought it best to obey, so he stammered, "The little black mouse ran-ran up the stairs-to-to-hear Miss Miss-" Here the class began to giggle.

"Go on," said the teacher.

"To hear Miss Blodgett say her prayers."

The teacher's eyes flashed with indignation. "Now, I'll give you just five minutes to compose another rhyme as smart as that, and if you don't, I'll punish you severely."

Mike was nonplussed. He looked at his dirty bare feet and tried to think. The pupils tittered. The teacher threatened him and them. Her clock on the desk ticked away the minutes—one—two—three—four—five. The teacher said, "Time's up; have you got it?"

"Yes'm," answered Mike.

"Well, out with it, then," commanded the teacher.

Here I stand, before Miss Blodgett,
She's goin' to hit, 'n I'm goin' to dodge it.

As the last words fell from Mike's lips, the class broke into a roar of laughter. Mike had won the day, and Miss Blodgett, flushed and excited, had to bite her lips to suppress a smile.

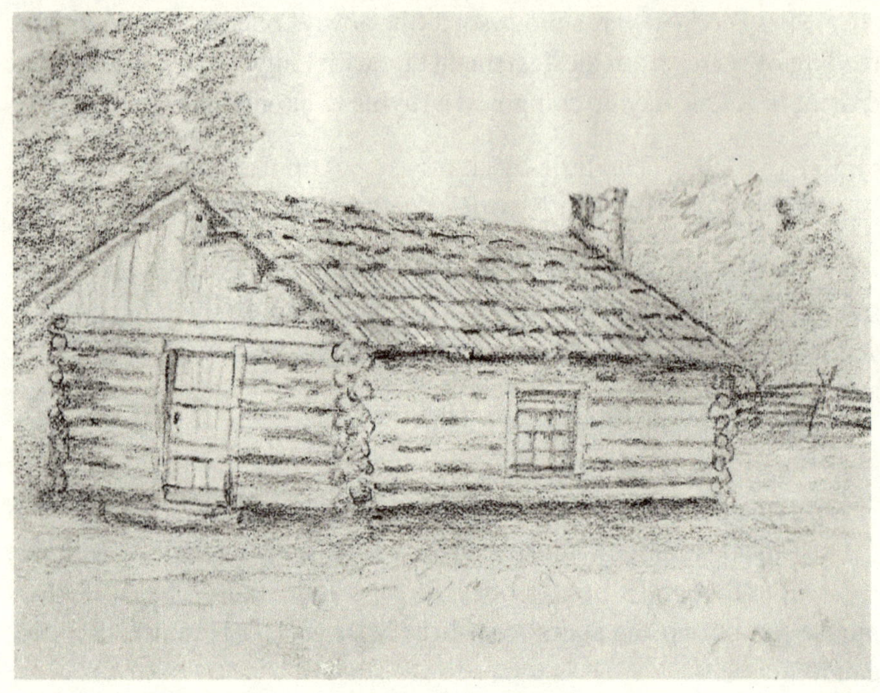

The log schoolhouse

Mike was the boisterous fun-maker of the crowd, the inventor of ingenious schemes for mischievous pleasure, into which he usually managed to embroil the rest of us. Once it was to tear out and carry away Fred Pierson's fish trap. Another time it was to raid old McFadden's melon patch.

Old man McFadden had built his home about two miles to the south of us. He had an inordinate craving for melons and had to have them no matter what else was lacking. He knew how to grow them as big as one's head and kept a savage dog that attacked anyone who came near the house. The garden was just in front of his door. The difficulties surrounding the proposed looting of the patch made the adventure all the more tempting to Mike and his clan.

One Sunday morning we had just come from a swim in the pond and were lounging in the shade of the house when Mike introduced the subject. The question, "How about the old man's shotgun?" was asked. Mike sat on the ash-barrel, kicked his heels against it, and spat on the ground. Presently he suggested that one of us take a cowbell and sneak around in the cornfield at night, commence to tinkle the clapper so that the old man would think cows were in the corn and when he rushed out with his dog in pursuit of the forging herd, we boys would skip in, fill bags with melons and sneak them down to a safe place by the creek, where we would have a jolly feast. We drew lots to see which one must assume the venture in the cornfield. The job fell to me, so that night I sneaked into the cow yard, loosed the bell strap from old Spot's neck, and we started out.

It seemed a simple bit of mischief until I heard the old man calling his dog and cussing the supposed cattle when it suddenly dawned upon me that the dog could run faster than I could. It had rained the day before and the field was quite muddy. My courage began to fail. I turned and flew toward the old snake fence and safety, falling headlong into a muddy pool. I scrambled to my feet in a desperate effort to put the fence between myself and the snapping, growling cur. I had barely reached the fence when, with a fierce growl, the dog overtook me. I felt his first tug at the seat of my pants. Using a hickory club as best I could, I made him let go, which gave me a chance to mount the fence, but while I was throwing one foot over the top rail, the brute seized me again from behind, this time sinking his teeth into my flesh. I was determined to get away, even at the risk of losing my trousers, if I could only keep him from playing havoc with my rear, so I fought free and bounded away over thorns and briers while the dog, seemingly satisfied with the remnant of my clothes, returned to his master, who went on searching for cows. This ruse had, meanwhile, enabled the boys to lug away half a dozen or more luscious melons to the appointed place, where I found them a short time later.

The boys were loud in praise of my excellent work, but that didn't heal my smarting wounds. Mike offered to go home with me to help me face my mother. She had already retired when Mike lifted the latch, and we stole into the room, but she called out to know if it were I. "Yes, Ma'am," Mike replied. "We are here, but this is me, Mike Foley. I came to tell you that Nick tore his pants. He tore the seat right out of them, and he wanted me to ask you if he could have another pair. He's kind of ashamed to show himself."

"How did he do that?" she inquired.

"Just climbing a tree," said Mike.

"Did he get hurt?" she asked anxiously.

"Oh, not much. He got scratched a bit, but he's all right. Only he's afraid you'll lick him. You won't do that, will you, Mrs. Brewer? He ain't to blame," lied Mike.

Evidently, something in the tone of Mike's voice as he pleaded for me aroused her sympathy, for she assured us that she would bring me a pair of trousers in the morning. Mike spent the night with me and next morning doctored my wounds with axle grease!

Once in a while, we boys would attend the new meetinghouse in High Forest, a newly built village which consisted of a gristmill, a blacksmith shop, and a general store and tavern. On one occasion we went to a revival meeting with some of the neighbor boys. We took seats in the rear of the church and listened attentively for a time to the minister, but Mike Foley, the incorrigible mischief-maker, had brought with him a pepper shaker. As I was next to the hot stove, he handed me the pepper and motioned that I should sprinkle it liberally thereupon, which I did. Then he led the way to the street, lest we might be the first to sneeze. Scampering away to a safe distance, we watched for results and were delighted when the congregation came filing out in a chorus of sneezes. In spite of the humorous side of the situation, I felt that I had been guilty of a serious breach of reverence and respect for the earnest preacher, who was trying to answer, perhaps, some of the very questions I had been longing to ask. But Mike's leadership was a thing we all felt and instinctively obeyed.

On another occasion, Mike's command was possibly the turning point for me between childhood and manhood. At school, the boys formed two armies for a snowball battle. Of course, Mike was the commander of one of the forces and I, the loyal henchman, was on his side. The snow was soft and in splendid condition for snowballs. The contest raged about the schoolhouse, the woodpile, and through the bushes with intense excitement. Then John Lamp, the enemy's leader, sent an icy ball right into my face and struck me directly between the eyes. The effect was terrific. My impulse was that of every child when injured—to scream. Mike, nearby, shouted, "Don't mind that, Nick; peg him one, darn him. We are all men, and we'll lick 'em!" Instantly

I felt the force of his words and choked down the impulse to cry. Ever after that his words have inspired me to control my feeling. Mike was a good example of Irish grit and fearless pugnacity.

The building of the Winona and St. Peter Railway made Rochester, Minnesota, our best trading place. Situated in the fertile Zumbro Valley, where settlement had been rapid, the village was not long in taking on the character of the small town. The long anticipated coming of the first circus was the talk of the whole country and on circus day people came from all directions in conveyances drawn by horses, ox-teams, and on foot. My three brothers and I teased Mother for two weeks to let us get tickets. They were only twenty-five cents each for children under fifteen years of age, but the outlay of even a dollar in cash meant a hardship. Mother managed to sell some chickens and gave Albert the money.

When we got to the circus grounds, I saw several large pictures of wild animals. These I observed were hand-painted. They fascinated me so much that I, forgetting everything else, was separated in the crowd from my brothers. They had the tickets and boy-like, forgot me and went into the circus without me. When I realized my situation, I searched everywhere but could not find them. I went to the door-keeper of the big tent and tried to tell him my trouble, but he brushed me aside. At one side, workmen were staking guy ropes. I lay down close to the tent and peeped in. One of the men, with an oath, grabbed me by the collar, yanked me around, and kicked me outside the ropes.

I was desperate and determined not to miss that circus. I would have climbed one of the guy ropes and with my penknife slit a hole in the roof and tumbled in. As I skipped around the tent, I noticed there was no one very close, so I raised up the canvas and rolled under. Breathless with excitement, I found myself in the midst of a dense crowd and quickly mingled with them. When sure I was not going to be captured and kicked again, I leisurely looked at all the animal cages, the clowns, and the horse riders. Nothing in that big tent escaped my eyes. The memory of it all has faded during the sixty-odd years that have elapsed, and I am sure every member of that circus has long since passed through the Valley of the Shadow. But three things remain with me—the thrill of the venture into a new world, experiences when I rolled under the canvas into the big tent, and the memory of those pictures, even as atrocious as they must have been.

John Lamp was a dear old cuss. We had much in common, but once in a while, our bristles rose toward each other over fancied wrongs. When I was about sixteen, we might have had a lively scrap if my older brother had not sprung between us. John was on a wheat stack pitching bundles of wheat onto the platform of the threshing machine, where a small boy was cutting the bands as they rolled down to me to be evenly fed into the rapidly revolving, roaring cylinder. John was a powerful chap and was piling the grain high above the boy, almost burying him and preventing his cutting the bands. I looked at John with fire in my eyes and shook my fist at him, angry to the core to think he didn't have more consideration for the little fellow. John, incensed at my threat, stopped and raised his fork handle as if to strike me. I mounted the stack to meet him. We were about to clinch, when my brother, Hubert, who was sitting on the separator, sprang between us, preventing a tussle while the empty machinery was running wild. I soon cooled off and resumed work. That evening, as soon as we had quit operations, John strutted over to me with a fork in his hands and exclaimed, "Nick Brewer, if you ever jump on a stack like that at me again, I'll run this fork right through you!" I fired up and said, "You big coward, you stick that fork in the ground, and I'll give you what you're looking for." We clinched. He was taller than I and heavier too, but slower in his motions. The best part of my physical make-up has always been in the grip of my arms and the speed of my actions, so I immediately got an advantageous hold of him with both arms around his back. After some circuitous waltzing and a sudden twist of my knee, I toppled him over on his back in the ditch, my hands gripping his throat until Hubert again came and pulled me off.

It frequently happens that people who are continually looking for trouble are great bluffers. Once you call their bluff and give them a trouncing, they meekly surrender and become your friends. This was the case with John. As long as I knew him thereafter, he never threatened me again. On the contrary, he frequently sought to do me good turns. The last I heard of him was after I had quit the farm and had assumed the title of house painter. Then he wrote me a letter and told me how much he envied me the dignity of my new profession.

The hardships of the field told heavily on me. I was obliged to plow with an ox team. The handling of the plow was made more vexatious by the meanness of the bovine brutes I had to drive. Whenever Duke, the nigh ox, spied a tuft of green grass or weeds, he would pull the other ox from the furrow to get it. Many a time I have had to let go the handles to pelt him back into line. Not being able to accomplish a fine bit of plowing and exhausting my strength on their tough old hides, I would sit down and literally weep with anger and fatigue. Beating them and shouting at them did no good. Sometimes I even felt like retaliating on Father for allowing an ox team to be yoked up and making me plow with them.

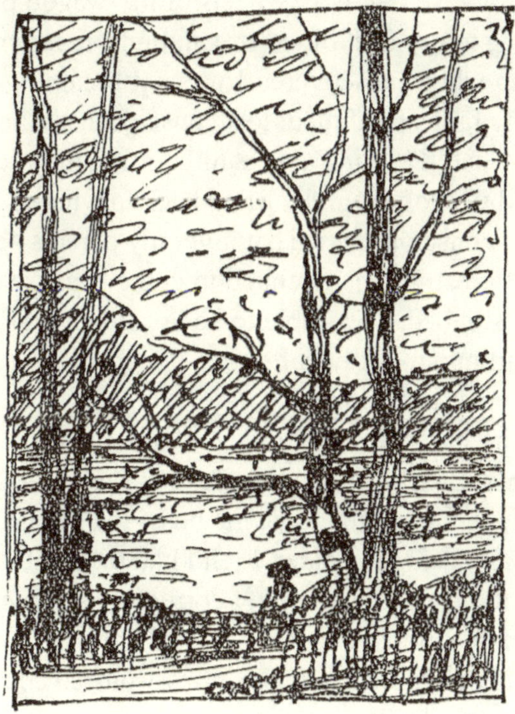

We had to bind the heavy sheaves of grain behind the reaper. My back ached, and my fingers bled from the nettles and briers. In winter, we hauled our wheat eighteen miles to market. Even though we rose at four in the morning to load our grain, we reached home long after dark.

Many a time when it was so cold that one could not remain seated on the wagon, I have walked either ahead or behind the team across the bleak prairie.

One day after I had unloaded my wheat at the elevator, I met Al Hill, a neighbor to whom Father had sold a runaway horse. We started home together, Al riding with me because he had no seat on his wagon and leading his team behind mine by a halter wound around his wrist. About five miles on our way, the runaway horse bolted out of the road on my side of the wagon. My own team took fright, and there were prospects of a bad mix up. I braced back to curb my horses while his team rushed by. He could not loose the halter from his arm quickly enough. They brushed me over the dashboard onto the whippletrees behind my own rearing horses' heels. I fell through crosswise the ruts in the road, so that both wheels of my wagon passed over my chest. Staggering to my feet, blood streaming from my mouth, I started back for my cap when I discovered I was not breathing. I struggled to draw air into my lungs but failed, lost consciousness, and fell. Al tried desperately to reach the reins, and a mile down the road he regained control, stopped the horses, and hurried back to where I lay. About that time, I regained consciousness. That night my parents sent for old Doc Grant of High Forest, but he declined to come because it was so cold. After two weeks in bed, I was able to be up and about again, thanks to Mother's careful nursing. I have felt the effects of that accident in the muscles of my back ever since that day.

With all the hardships there was a humorous side to life on the farm. My brother, Charlie, next younger than I, often tried my patience sorely. In all matters I wanted to be the boss—so did he. I thought him infernally lazy and being the older, I felt I had the right to impress upon him my authority. He never took my correction seriously. The more I pommelled him, the more he laughed. One day I was so exasperated by his conduct that I determined to make him cry out, so I beat and punched him until he screamed with pain. In resentment, he swore he would get even with me. In the barn, Father had an old organ box in which he kept the horse feed. When the food got low, it was necessary to bend way over, head down, to sweep up the grain. The next morning, after Charlie's beating, Father got a pair of my overalls by mistake, upon the seat of which Mother had put two black patches. Charlie saw Father bending over the feed box and said to himself, "This is my chance to get even with Nick," so, seizing the stave of an old barrel, he crept up behind him and with a mighty swat laid the stave upon those patches. Father was somewhat excitable, and his temper could be violent when it was aroused. His expression was quite ferocious as he jerked his head out of the box and turned about to discover the cause of the onslaught. Charlie saw his mistake and bolted for the woods and did not return till after dark. To this day we laugh at the suddenness with which Charlie's expected satisfaction was turned to dismay.

My schooling of three months each winter for a few years had only carried me half-way through the old "Practical Arithmetic" and not far beyond verbs in grammar. My education was really limited to a mere beginning of the three Rs. The school terms were short, and about every other year, the winter term was skipped. My craving to get an education was so keen that I took my books to bed with me, where my fatigue from hard work brought oblivion in sleep, and the books were forgotten.

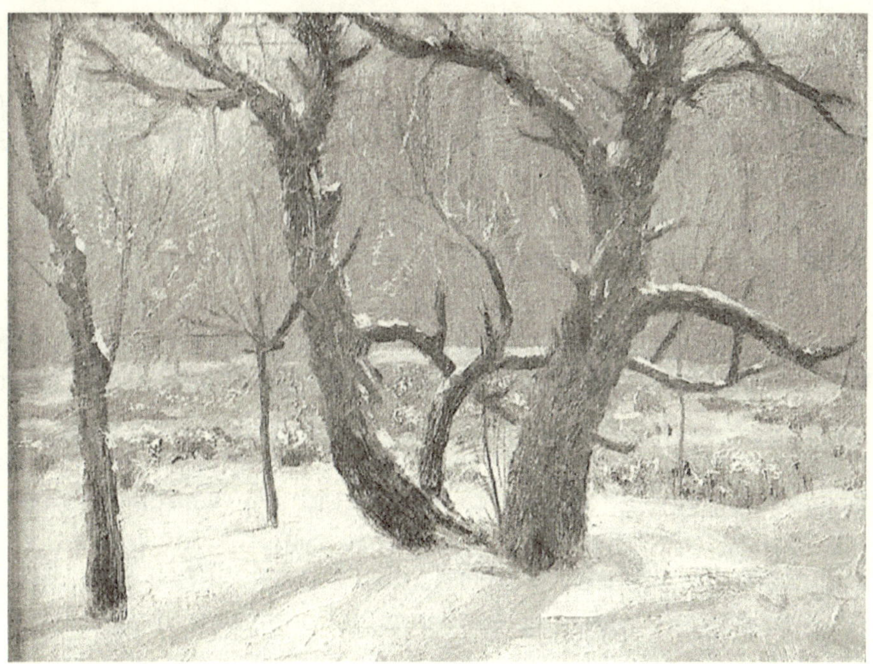

Sunlit Snow

Mother had an old-fashioned churn, which Father had made, and it was my work to do the churning. It was my habit, while sweating away at the dasher and chasing the flies that hummed about, to have my books on a chair beside me, trying to memorize some of their problems. I pondered over the possibilities of rising to something better than a farmer's life, and I said to myself, "If I only knew what all these books contain, I might become President of the United States."

It was also my duty to do the milking before breakfast. My brothers, older than I, had to feed and harness the teams and get ready for the field. To milk six or eight cows in cold or wet weather is enough to give any lusty boy a hearty appetite. When the boys went to the field after breakfast, I was obliged to help Mother wash the dishes and do little tasks about the house. She said I was the only girl in the family.

Once she was quite ill—confined to bed for about six weeks—and I had to do all the cooking, baking, and washing as well as play nurse. We always baked our own bread. My batches must have been fairly good as they were ravenously devoured by the rest of the family. I could cook as good a boiled dinner of cabbage, potatoes, onions, and turnips, with bits of wild rabbit and some pieces of pork as anybody. Dinner over, I would wash the dishes scrupulously clean.

Sweet little Mary Goodrich was our teacher one summer. It was not long before she had the hearts of all the children and mine in particular. Some of the turbulent boys whom the former teacher, Mary Powers, could not control, were submissive under the gentle touch of this girl, who was just two years my senior. How I burrowed into my books in order to win her praise! The school hours were no longer irksome. She was frail, and Mother was asked to take her as a boarder so that she might be nearer the school. After school hours it was my joy and pride to lead her along the cliff, or to give her a boat ride in order that she might be out of doors as much as possible. Day by day, my devotion grew into what people now call "puppy love." No one guessed the force of that attachment, nor have I ever mentioned it until I set it down upon these pages. The days were empty when the three-months' summer term ended, and it was with a pang that I heard she had gone East to be absent about a year.

On her return, it was announced that she had married. Mother mentioned it at the table. At once my boyish appetite vanished and I, crushed, fled instinctively to the path in the woods and to places where we had often wandered together. I even looked for a possible track of her heel where I had helped her from stone to stone across the river. To me, there was no beauty left in the sunset nor in the world about me. The labor in the fields was harder and more hopeless than ever.

A few months later, we were told that quick consumption had carried her away and that the funeral would be held in the church at High Forest. Unknown to the family, I went for a last look at the face of one whose gentle nature had awakened in me a genuine desire to live right. When the lid of the casket was removed, the congregation filed past the bier. Through timidity, I hesitated until I was the last one in line. And she was carried to the little cemetery in the forest near the village.

In my seventieth year, I visited the scenes of my boyhood and drove by her resting place, which aroused sleeping memories, sweet to recall.

My brother Albert, who was the author of the wildcat scheme, was a great enthusiast about music. One summer, my father apportioned to him and my older brother Hubert a piece of land which they could sow to wheat and keep the crop for themselves as a reward for their industry. That fall, each one had forty bushels of grain. Hubert bought a colt with the money he realized, while Albert purchased a fiddle and a nice suit of clothes. Albert went to the Pierson home and asked Fred to teach him to play his new fiddle, agreeing to cut down one oak tree and split it into firewood for every tune Fred would teach him to finger out on the fiddle, the tree to be cut before the lesson would be given.

The first tune was "Yankee Doodle," the second, "Old Dan Tucker," then "The Girl I Left Behind Me," and so on. After learning where to place his fingers on the fingerboard for each respective note, he would come home and scratch on that fiddle long after midnight to the annoyance of the rest of the family. He continued to practice until he had memorized the tune and was able to play it as well, if not better, than Pierson did. Then when ready for another lesson, he would cut another tree. He had about twenty tunes in his repertoire when spring came.

I also had an ambition to be a musician. This I shared with my brother Charlie, who really had ability but no patience for practicing. I got my father to buy me an accordion and under Albert's tutelage, Albert, Charlie, and I became an orchestra. Albert played first violin, Charlie second, and I droned in wherever I could make a noise to harmonize. Before long, we were asked to play for dances and soon found ourselves famous. Mr. John Althouse, who sang with Eliza Russell in the Methodist Church, helped me learn a few sacred tunes. After the lessons, which were always in the evening, I would go out and sit by the roadside and practice until I had memorized the tune. Sometimes it was after midnight when I got home. Finally, I traded my accordion for a fiddle. After a little practice, I found I could strum time on the chords, and it sounded better than the accordion. Fred Pierson had been earning money by playing for country dances, but before the year passed, Albert's music was preferred by all the young people of the neighborhood, and Fred found that he had made a great mistake in teaching him.

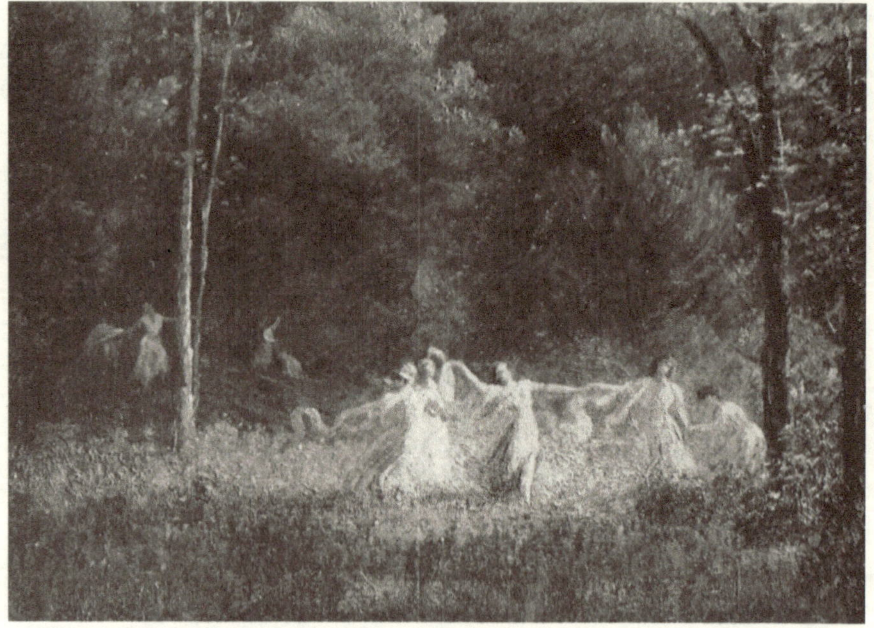

The Sylvan Dance

A couple of years later, a violinist who had better technical training came to Rochester. Albert at once became his pupil and discovered that all he had thought was music was only the acquisition of bad habits. He applied himself diligently, however, along the right road and became the leader of an orchestra before he died at twenty-seven years of age.

Whenever brother Hubert had anything to say, it was to the point—often humorous. He seemed to be lacking in artistic fancy, but had force and courage ever ready to tackle any problem.

I had only two grudges against Hubert. One was that he would not let me lick John Lamp when John needed it, and the other was the result of a disagreement we had when we were children. While roasting some ears of corn at the grate of the old-fashioned stove in the kitchen, where only one ear could be roasted at a time, Hubert took the first one off when it was ready to eat and put on another for himself in its place. While that was roasting, he ate the first one, then the second one, and so on until my patience was exhausted. I was as hungry as he and began to scrap by brushing his ear of corn off on the floor, for which he slapped me soundly. This made me scream and dance, which brought Father from the other room with wild eyes to find out the reason for the noise.

Hubert said I was making the fuss and had thrown his corn on the floor. Father was quick-tempered at times and unreasonable and gave me a good spanking, which I thought was deep injustice to a boy who was hungry and not at all to blame. Hubert had so many good qualities, however, one could not help liking him.

After Hubert bought the colt, he became a regular David Harum. He could handle any balky or runaway horse. When a horse did not suit him, he traded it off, always getting the best of the deal. He had a gelding named Dick that was very affectionate. Dick, who knew his master, would whinny as soon as he saw him in the pasture and would come trotting to him and nibble around for the customary lump of sugar. Hubert had a two-wheeled cart in which he used to make quick trips when no load was to be carried. Dick was the fleetest sprinter in the country. He could go lickety-split, except when he took a notion to balk.

His balking spells seemed always to come down with the rain, for then he would stop abruptly, hoist his head in the air, stick his ears back, and glance to both sides as if to say, "Well, what are you going to do about it?" and nothing short of a cyclone could budge him. Sometimes the lump of sugar was too great a temptation, and he would become normal again. When that failed, Hubert would put on his topcoat and walk away in the direction of home. He would not go very far before Dick would begin to whinny for him. When his horseship found that Hubert would not come to him, he decided to go to Hubert, and soon there was a reconciliation. Several times after Hubert's horse trades, he could have said, "I told you he'd stand without hitchin'."

Hubert finally sold Dick, receiving part payment in cash and a sixty-day note for the balance. When the buyer discovered the horse's balking disposition, he refused to pay the note. Hubert agreed with Frank D. Kellogg, who had recently been admitted to the bar in Rochester, to bring suit on the note on a fifty-fifty arrangement of the amount they hoped to recover, as Kellogg's fee. They were awarded something like ten dollars in the suit, so Hubert said. Very different, no doubt, from the fees received later by the author of the Kellogg Peace Pact.

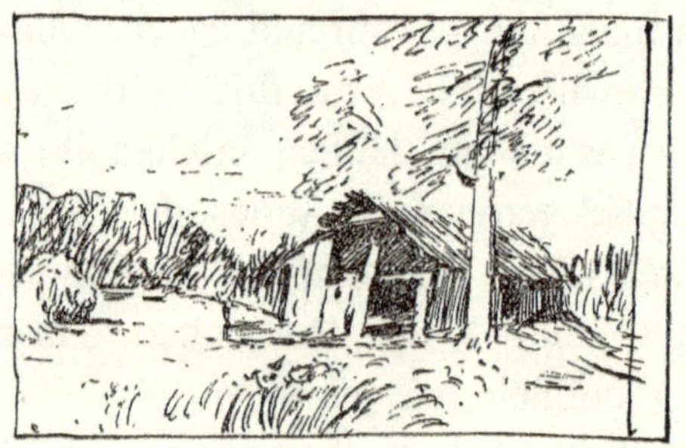

Chapter III

Breaking Home Ties

St. Paul—An Embarrassing Incident—House Painting—Spiritual Gropings—Unfamiliar Scenes

At eighteen years of age, I urged my father to let me leave home and seek an education. He could not afford to pay my expenses at an art school. The best he could do was to give me the price of a load of wheat. On the morning of December 9, 1875, Hubert and I rose at four o'clock to load the wheat we were to haul to Rochester to sell. We had hitched a fractious young half-broken colt with one of the older horses to the wagon. Forty bushels of wheat was, of course, a heavy load. The colt, no doubt, also considered it heavy and refused to pull. In starting, we had a scrap with him, and he slipped, falling flat on his side. My brother jumped on his head and held him down while I gave him a sound trouncing by way of discipline. This took the spunk out of him, and he decided to do his horsely duty.

I received thirty-four dollars from the sale of the wheat and boarded a train for St. Paul, my brother Albert accompanying me. This was the first time that I had ridden in a railway train. We stopped overnight in Owatonna to make train connections at three o'clock in the morning. Albert and I parted the next day, and I found lodging in St. Paul at Mrs. Stone's boarding house. Albert went farther north.

The boy who had spent the first eighteen years of his life on a pioneer farm breaking broncos, milking cows, and ploughing with an ox team found many surprises when he stepped off the railway coach for the first time in a city of twenty thousand inhabitants.

When I first saw St. Paul, on December 10, 1875, there was only one four-story skyscraper and about half a dozen three-story buildings in the town. There was not a paved street. One streetcar line ran from Mississippi Street down Jackson and up Fourth Street to Seven Corners. These cars were very short—not longer than a lumber wagon. They bobbed along with a jolt at every splice in the rails, on a thirty-minute schedule of service. Each passenger deposited his nickel in the slot inside, when the driver would "chop" it down, carefully watching to see that no one forgot to pay. The car was drawn by one horse, except on the steep grade for a couple of blocks on Fourth Street. At the foot of the grade an intelligent old horse was hooked on at the side of the other to help boost the load up the hill. At the top, the reinforcement nag was taken off, turned around, and told to go down to the foot of the hill, dragging his single-tree and chain behind him. There he stood, ready to be hooked on to the next car that came along.

On my second day in the big city, while sauntering around taking in the sights, I spied this animal in harness, driver-less, his trappings jingling behind him. At once I thought he was a runaway and should be arrested before he strayed so far, he could not be found.

Thinking I was doing the owner a good turn, I caught the horse and tied him to a telegraph pole. I remember that he looked at me in a way that said, "Mister, why don't you mind your own business?" After hitching him securely, I was about to go on my way, when the horse car came around the corner and stopped. The driver sat down and began to call, "Here, Prince. Here, Prince." Prince looked up and whinnied but didn't budge. Then the man got off the car and walked up to him. Not knowing his purpose, I remonstrated, telling him I had tied the stray animal so his owner would find him. With this, the roughneck car driver gave me the first real tongue-lashing of my life. Some girls in the car, who heard it all, began to giggle at my well-meant blunder, which made me feel very much ashamed of myself. I never go down that street to this day that I do not recall what a hayseed I was.

The city seemed wonderful as I strolled about. I had never seen a four-story building before. I had never had any money of my own nor any necessity of providing for myself. There I was with thirty-four dollars, less my railroad fare, in my pocket. It had never occurred to me how long I might subsist on that amount.

My big ambition was to find someone who could give me lessons in painting. My hopes were dissipated when I discovered that the town possessed neither art nor artists. There was one photograph gallery, and on its walls were several Prang chromos—reproductions of Dutch paintings. I frequently went to see these, but something told me that they were not real art. I was told of a German named Henry J. Koempel, who painted copies of pictures and decorated churches and who might give me some instruction. I called on him and asked about lessons. He said he could teach me for fifty cents a lesson, which I agreed was a fair price. We began work immediately. Just one week after my arrival in town I met, in his workshop, one of his daughters, who three years later became my wife.

After two or three weeks, my funds were completely exhausted. When I left home, I had taken my fiddle with me. I was timid about practicing at the boarding house, where there were so many strangers. When the money ran out, I came to the realization that I must either earn something or sell something. Since I had no work and was absorbed in my painting, my fiddle became the sacrifice. Old man Thomas, who kept a picture framing shop on Third Street, wanted to buy it. He would not pay cash but offered to trade me a couple of chromo landscapes, unmounted, saying I might try to sell them. If I could not, he would return the fiddle.

With the roll under my arm, I walked all one day from house to house, but nobody wanted to buy the pictures. Mrs. John S. Prince, wife of the banker, scanned me from head to foot and offered me a fifty-cent piece, saying I looked as though I were in great need. My pride came to my rescue, and I instantly thought, "If I accept it, I will not be able to say I have never been the recipient of charity." I said, "No, thank you, lady," and backed out of the door.

Dear Mrs. Prince! Three years later, when I became known as a crayon artist, I was employed to give instructions in drawing in her house, to a private class of her own and her sister's children. She never recognized the peddler of chromos, who had enlisted her sympathy but would not accept her charity.

My fiddle deal having failed, I was compelled to find something to do. The old Clarendon Hotel was being remodeled at the time, so I went there to secure a job at house painting. Being asked by the agent of the building if I were a painter, I replied, "Yes," remembering that I had once painted a wagon on the farm. The wages were a dollar and half a day for ten hours' work. I had to furnish my own brush. Not having money enough to buy one, I borrowed an old one from Mr. Koempel. It was so short and stubby the paint would not flow but dripped from it to the floor. When the foreman came to examine my work, he shoved both hands into his pockets and stared at the floor with a look that filled me with apprehension as to the permanency of my employment. This man was none other than Mr. Partridge, of the firm of Bazille and Partridge of more recent years, who developed more respect for my ability later.

He said, "It seems you have not done much painting," and taking my brush, he looked at it, then threw it across the room in disgust and brought me a better one. I was now able to put the greater portion of paint on the woodwork instead of the floor. By Saturday, I had so progressed in facility that he reported me a good "brush hand," and I drew the same pay as other workmen. At the end of a month the job was finished, and I was again without work.

This month's experience enabled me to master the art of house painting, graining, and paper hanging. Graining in those days was considered by the craftsmen to be a great art. By studying the grains of oak in furniture I was able to imitate it so closely that the firm of Beck and Rank sent for me to do a job they said they wanted specially well done. They had been paying ten cents per yard, but as this job must be extra fine, they promised to give me twelve cents. I started work the next morning, and by six o'clock, I had finished one hundred twenty-two yards, netting me fourteen dollars and sixty-four cents. Suddenly I was famous! Afterward, I was employed to grain front doors at five dollars each, which took me one hour and twenty minutes. There was such a demand for my work that I began contracting in the spring and soon found I had to employ help.

At the boarding house there was an Irish laborer who was out of work. He had never painted. I told him that if he could handle a paintbrush, I would give him something to do. I put him to work painting an iron fence with black paint for Mrs. Monfort, on Dayton Avenue, and went to another job. Returning an hour later, I found he had upset the pot of black paint on her cement sidewalk. From her window, Mrs. Monfort had seen the accident and rushed out in a huff. There he stood with hands, feet, and overalls spattered with black paint. After giving him a good scolding, she said she would prepare a bowl of hot soapsuds with which to clean the sidewalk. While she was in the house, he covered the paint with dust from the street and brushed it off several times until the dust had absorbed the stain and concealed the spot completely. When Mrs. Monfort came back with the soapsuds, she was surprised and asked to know how paint could be so easily removed, whereupon he straightened up, and with the dignity of a house painter, replied, "We painters don't be givin' away the tricks of the trade, Ma'am."

My experience as a house painter taught me things that I have used to this day. I learned the effect of oil when employed as a medium and its tendency to cause white to grow yellow in the course of time, for when painting indoor woodwork to remain pure white, I found that no oil can be used; that pure lead and zinc with turpentine only can be relied upon. Ever since then, I have avoided as far as possible the use of oil in my paintings. I also learned that lead cannot be used over zinc without danger of cracking and that paint should not be varnished until perfectly dry and hard.

I had a roommate, Joe Young, a fine fellow from Chicago, about my own age. He and I spent hours scheming and planning how we could get into a paying business. Once we thought of opening a butcher shop, having had a chance to rent a place on St. Anthony Hill in the residential section, and we were so sure a fortune could be made that nothing under Heaven but our empty pocketbooks prevented our opening up as meat carvers.

Another time it was a poultry farm. We got books and papers on the business, studied poultry diseases—the pip, the roup, the cholera, and so on. Here, too, our dreams failed for lack of cash. Joe was just as ardent and ambitious in his way as I was in mine. He had a temporary job in a shoe store, while I plied the brush on any house, barn, or fence I could persuade the owner to think needed a coat of paint.

Joe soon became tired of St. Paul and returned to Chicago. To my regret, I have never seen him since. I had formed a great attachment for him and many times while in Chicago I would scan the crowd, hoping to see his face.

When work came slowly and I could not keep one or two men busy, I did the work alone. I always had the habit of rising early and going to roost with the chickens. Poor Bridget Maloney, the maid at the boarding house, was kind enough to prepare my breakfast at five o'clock so that I could get out on the job. She grumbled a bit at times but could be easily won over when I told her I had to walk two miles out of town to some of my work. My dinner pail was always ready and full. Then, smeared with paint after my day's work, I would saunter in after the other boarders had finished their meal, and she would smile in a tired way and scrape up a supper for me as best she could.

After Joe Young left St. Paul, I had another roommate, Joe Mathews, a Frenchman, who had a temperamental and excitable nature. He was an adventurer from Montreal. A bookkeeper by profession, he was employed by Priedman, the grocer. Joe imbibed strong drink at times, never getting very drunk but occasionally disagreeable. When he absented himself until sober again, I was glad of it.

Joe formed the acquaintance of my sweetheart's sister. On one occasion, I happened to be in a parade when I saw the two girls in the crowd on the corner. Farther down the block, I spied Joe, also. I motioned him to step toward the line of march and called to him that the girls were up on the corner. He became so excited that he swallowed his burning cigar stub and nearly choked on it, he said.

Joe lost his job, and needing money, he got me to sign a note for him for one hundred dollars so that he could buy a stock of celluloid collars to sell on the street corner. The first day he made fifteen dollars and ten by noon the next day. Then a burly policeman asked to see his license to vend on the street. Joe had never thought about a license. The policeman pulled him in, and they not only made him pay a fine but took away his stock of collars. This so discouraged him that he left town. I never heard from him afterward. Of course, I had to pay the note I had endorsed for him. This was the first and last time I ever endorsed a note, but I have often loaned money, which was never returned. Somehow, I must have been an easy mark—too trustful.

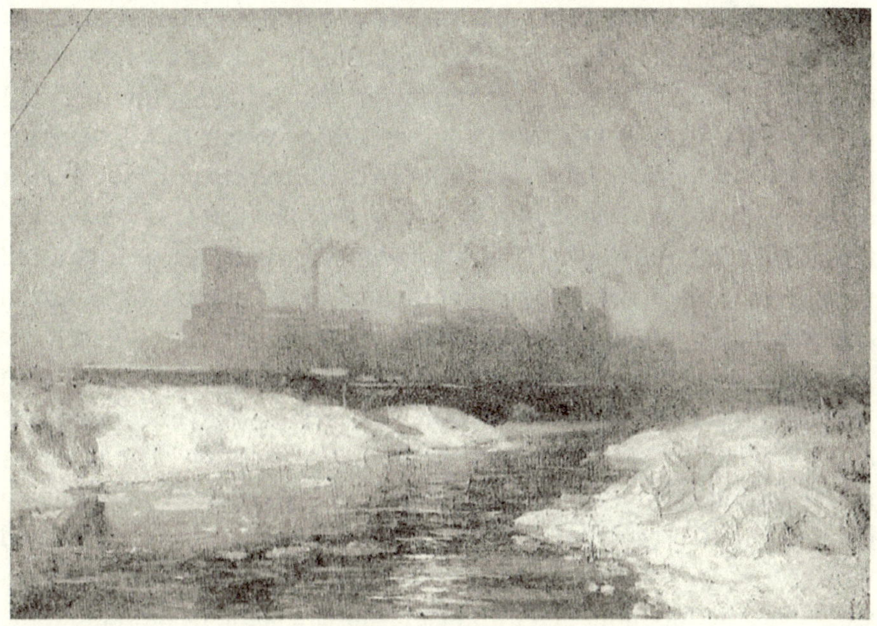

Mills of Minneapolis

A new boarder came to the house shortly after I had bought a nice Prince Albert suit for Sunday wear. This fellow learned that I often went to church, and one Sunday morning, he told me that he would like to go to church also, only he had no decent clothes to wear. This particular day he wanted to meet a girl at the church and asked if I would be so kind as to let him wear my suit for just two hours. I cheerfully loaned him the suit, meanwhile putting on my old clothes and waiting in my room. If I had waited until the man and the suit came back, I would still be waiting there.

In the fall of 1877 work was scarce and it occurred to me that I might make a deal with my landlady to paint her house in exchange for board. She accepted my proposition and offered me five months' board to do the work on the outside, but as it was already too cold, it had to be put off until spring. Thus, she paid in advance for the job, but in the spring she bought the material and the work was done to her entire satisfaction. This place seemed almost like home to me.

There were several young people boarding there and our evenings were often taken up with arguments over things we knew nothing about. I did not enjoy these discussions as much as I did reading, for reading was my chief means of learning. But the subjects we discussed and things I heard from some of the older men led me to investigate. I got some books from the library, but as I read slowly, I often kept the books overtime and had to pay the penalty. I preferred to buy a book occasionally, when I could afford it, that I might read it slowly. I preferred Dickens, Hawthorne, Balzac, and history, and I soon discovered the difference between good literature and poor. I thoroughly enjoyed and read many religious controversies.

The realization that came when I read in the New Testament in Mother's old Bible that I had a soul to save had remained with me, and I worried a great deal over the matter of religion. The sense of moral responsibility, not only in regard to my relations with human beings, but also to my Creator, weighed heavily upon me. Coupled with the joy of living and working out ideals, ambitions, and desires were ever the thoughts that all must terminate some day, and that the Arbiter of my Eternal Destiny would judge my every thought and deed. I felt that I must find a rule of life, a system of belief, an authority to guide and enable me to know right and live accordingly. I had formulated certain prayers in my early youth and continued to say them daily, but that did not suffice. I hungered to know more of the different religious creeds.

On the windowsill in the dining room one day, I saw a child's catechism of Christian Doctrine of the Roman Catholic Church. Glancing through it, I concluded I wanted to read it and slipped it into my pocket. I found that it outlined one's duty and answered certain questions that had been troubling me. I remembered arguments that Mother had had many years before with a Methodist neighbor. My mother had backslided from the Methodist Church after meeting my father and joined the Catholic Church but failed to live up to its precepts. All this led me to a thorough investigation of the claims of the Catholic Church. In certain Protestant churches where I had gone, I heard emphatic denunciation of the Catholic belief, the doctrines of Purgatory, Papal infallibility and priestly power of pardoning sin, as well as of hideous crimes of the middle ages said to have been committed in the name of religion, and I had been stirred with a desire to know the arguments on the other side.

About that time, Bishop John Ireland and several Protestant ministers were engaging in religious controversy, and the full text of their sermons was being published in the papers. I made a scrapbook of these, read and pondered over them, and finally, I had a talk with Father Shanley, a young priest who later became Bishop of the Fargo Diocese. He gave me two books, Milner's "End of Controversy" and "The Faith of our Fathers" by Cardinal Gibbons. Bishop Milner, I believe, was a disciple of Newman and seceded from the Church of England at the time of the Oxford Movement, when several of the most distinguished lights of the Anglican Faith joined the Church of Rome. His treaties on the different rules of faith, and his views on the Bible question impressed me profoundly.

William Cobbett, a Protestant, in his history of the Reformation seemed to give a convincing refutation of things I had heard and read by Protestants. Little by little I began to feel an inner assurance in the doctrine that something more than the Bible is necessary to a restful confidence in the teachings of Christianity.

The thought that the early Christian Church had spread throughout the Roman Empire until it had undermined the very foundations of that gigantic tyranny and caused it to crumble before the New Testament was even declared the inspired Word of God, or had come into general use at all, seemed to minimize the belief that the Bible is the sole and only rule of Faith for the guidance of man.

Many things about the teachings of the Catholic Church I did not fully understand, and I might have been disposed to question them had it not been that there were so many satisfying and consoling things about it that I felt like crying out with St. Peter, "To whom shall we go? Thou hast the word of eternal life." Amidst the hazy interpretations and contradicting beliefs of many outside the Mother Church who professed Christianity, I found no unity or cohesion and often a woeful lack of the real spirit of Christian charity.

Those conversations with Bishop John Ireland, Father Shanley, and others had the effect of causing me to make a decision favoring the Roman belief, nor have I ever regretted the step and as the years and experience of life have ripened my understanding, I have come more and more to see the wisdom of Catholic philosophy and its potent aid as a stepping-stone to a higher spiritual life.

I have always felt that every man's religion should be to him a sacred thing, and I respect every man who feels a responsibility and an inclination to worship the Infinite Creator, for no man ever knelt in sincere prayer without rising from his knees a more worthy creature. It is not my intention, therefore, to say a word that would lead others away from their own beliefs or put forth any arguments for or against any particular religion, but I simply record here the gropings of a lone soul—that of Nick Brewer sixty years ago.

I made my first confession to Bishop Ireland. That was to me a tremendous revelation as to the right and wrong of human conduct. The voice of a profound and conscientious churchman and philosopher to a young man whose religious experiences had been but mere spiritual searchings in the darkness left an impression that still lives with me. I went out of that confessional into my room at the boarding house a new man. That night were born to me new ideals which raised a lifelong conflict within me—a conflict for the mastery of the spirit over the flesh—that will continue to the end of my life, for as St. Paul says, "The flesh warreth against the spirit and the spirit against the flesh."

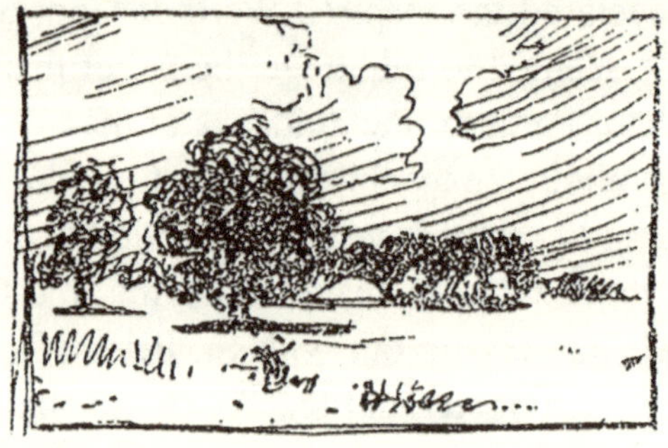

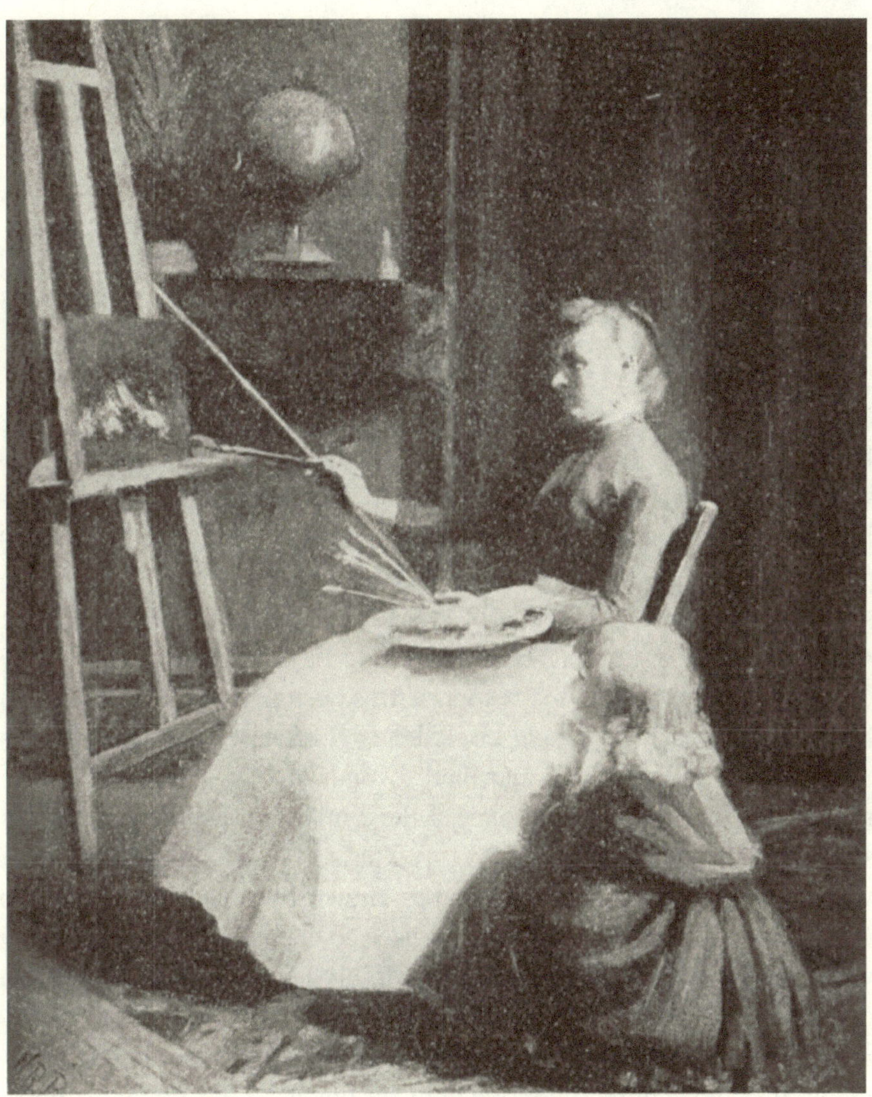

The artist and the critic

Chapter IV
Beginning Life's Work Together

Love Postpones Art—Building a Home—Violin Practice

In the summer of 1878, I had little to do. Henry Koempel, who afterward became my father-in-law, got a job decorating a church in Hastings and wanted me to help him. I worked there for a while. As he was paid poorly for his work, he could not pay me good wages, so when the grain harvest opened, I hired out to a farmer whose place was twenty miles out in the grain belt. He promised to pay me three dollars a day to bind the grain behind the reaper. It was customary to have five men bind the sheaves as the reaper circled the field. There were four stations for the five binders. Each man had to bind out his station while the reaper went around the field once. If he could not reach the end of his station, the reaper would overtake and pass him, which meant that he was not keeping up. Thus, the reaper, drawn by four horses, was the whip to goad the men on. I was not used to such heavy, backbreaking work. At seventeen, when constantly doing heavy farm work, I could do as much as the average man, but town life must have softened my muscles. The weather was warm. The hours were from six in the morning until seven at night, with one hour for lunch. At the end of six days, I was completely lagged and had to quit. The farmer hated to see me leave and kindly told me not to worry about keeping up my stations, but to do the best I could, and it would be all right. But my pride, as well as my aching muscles, were put to the test. I told him I would have to go, and he reluctantly brought me to town and paid me off.

During the following winter, times were hard and I was in despair. I had fallen very deeply in love and wished to marry but had no money. I had been bitterly disappointed in my longing to paint pictures and I had no prospects, not even house painting, to brighten my future outlook. While in this hopeless mood I saw an advertisement in the paper telling of a man who claimed he could teach anyone to make a perfect crayon portrait in one lesson.

Partly out of curiosity and to satisfy my great longing to paint, I went to see him. In his room, he had many crayon pictures on the wall. He explained he could really teach me to make a portrait in a single lesson. His charge was ten dollars. With only eight dollars in my pocket, I felt that I would have to pass it up and told him so, whereupon he was willing to take my eight dollars. Back of a curtain he had a pantograph attached to a table, with which he deftly enlarged the outline of a girl's picture. Then, tacking the paper on a board, he quickly brushed in with his chamois skin and paper stumps the dark hair and masses of the face and shoulders and clouded the background. Of course, he got no real likeness of the person represented by the photograph, but only a crude resemblance to it. "That is all there is to it," he said and showed me out. I was not only out of doors but out of money as well. I felt that he was a trickster, but since he had my money, I had to make the best of it.

In my room I had a photograph of my friend Father Valentine that I thought I would practice on. I got paper and proceeded to work according to the instruction I had received and after wrestling with the thing for a day, I made a copy of the photograph, which proved to be a very good likeness. When I showed it to Father Valentine, he was surprised to know I did that kind of work and asked what I charged for it. "Oh, eight dollars," I said. He straightway brought me the money and another photograph, which he said he liked better than the one I had used and told me that if I would make a larger picture, he would give me fifteen dollars for it. The following day when I returned with the larger copy, the Bishop happened to be there. He, too, was interested and asked what I charged for such pictures.

I said, "Oh, fifteen dollars." "Well, I want to have three made; one for the house, one for the school, and one for a friend," he said, and gave me a photograph. On the second day following, I had completed the three pictures, delivered them, and received my forty-five dollars. A gentleman who happened to be there ordered a couple more portraits at that price.

Then I realized that the faker who had so ruthlessly emptied my pocket, compelling me to face my landlady with an unpaid board bill, had in truth conferred a blessing in disguise, for he had shown me a way to earn a livelihood. From that time on, I had no trouble in getting orders for crayon portraits. Of course, I knew this was not art, but at least it was more agreeable than house painting. While occupied as a house painter, I had abandoned all hope of becoming an artist, and I recall that those two years were years of extreme regret and sadness. Moreover, I now realize that this mere incident was the turning point in my artistic career.

My acquaintance with Father Valentine dated from the time I went to him to solicit the job of painting the fence about the parochial schoolhouse. I agreed to paint his fence for twelve dollars, provided he would buy the material. It proved a bigger job than I had expected and took over a week to complete. This was much less per hour than he afterwards paid me for doing his portrait. Once he wanted the vestibule of the church varnished. Not being familiar with the action of varnish, I mixed some oil with it, with the result that it never dried and remained so sticky that if one leaned up against it a year later he would stick to it.

About that time the sexton of St. Mary's Church, on East Ninth Street, died, and the pastor, good Father Cailett, was put to the necessity of finding someone to take his place. Father Valentine suggested my performing that duty temporarily, and it resulted in my going to live at the parsonage, where I was to get my board and room in exchange for the light chores of ringing the Angelus bell three times a day and lighting the fires in the school rooms. This left me most of the time for work and study. Father Cailett, a kindly man, took a deep interest in my work, helped me with my reading, and secured quite a number of crayon portrait orders for me.

Our conversations were always a source of pleasure and profit to me, and I still remember many bits of the information he gave. Outstanding in my recollection is one that became more interesting as I read of events that culminated in the assassination of President Lincoln.

Mrs. Surratt, at whose boarding house in Washington several of the suspected conspirators resided, was accused of complicity in the plot and, with others, was hanged. The priest who attended her and heard her last confession, for she was a Catholic, happened to be a friend and classmate of Father Cailett. This priest afterward told Cailett that from his intimate knowledge of the case, he was sure Mrs. Surratt was wholly innocent of any connection with the plotters and was but the hapless victim of circumstances.

Father Cailett urged me strongly to go to New York to enter an art school and went to the trouble of writing to ascertain the cost of such items as tuition and board. While I seriously thought of going, Father Valentine, knowing that I was very much in love urged me, on the contrary, to get married and settle down. When it came to a contest between reason and sentiment, the latter prevailed, and poor Father Cailett was little less than disgusted with my lack of practical common sense. He argued that I should put marriage off until I had secured an art education and established myself professionally and insisted that New York was the place for me.

I now see the wisdom of his advice, though I was blind to it then, for, as I shall explain later, I have always felt the need of more thorough academic training in my younger days. At all events, the arguments of Father Valentine seemed to my sentimental longings the more agreeable. Rose, my sweetheart, and I decided to marry. My roll of cash after buying my wedding outfit had simmered down to one hundred fifty dollars. The 20th of May was set for the wedding, and it was not until the morning of that day, before stepping into the carriage to go to the Assumption Church, that I bade adieu to my respected and beloved pastor, Father Cailett.

The ceremony was performed at seven o'clock in the morning by Father Valentine. After breakfast together, we went to a gallery to have our pictures taken, then left on the train for Mendota, where we were the guests of friends.

We joined our hands and bravely, blindly started
Along life's winding, stormy way;
With eyes aloof and hopes aglow
And hearts that daily beat to ne'er be parted
Through clouds and storms, we knelt to pray.

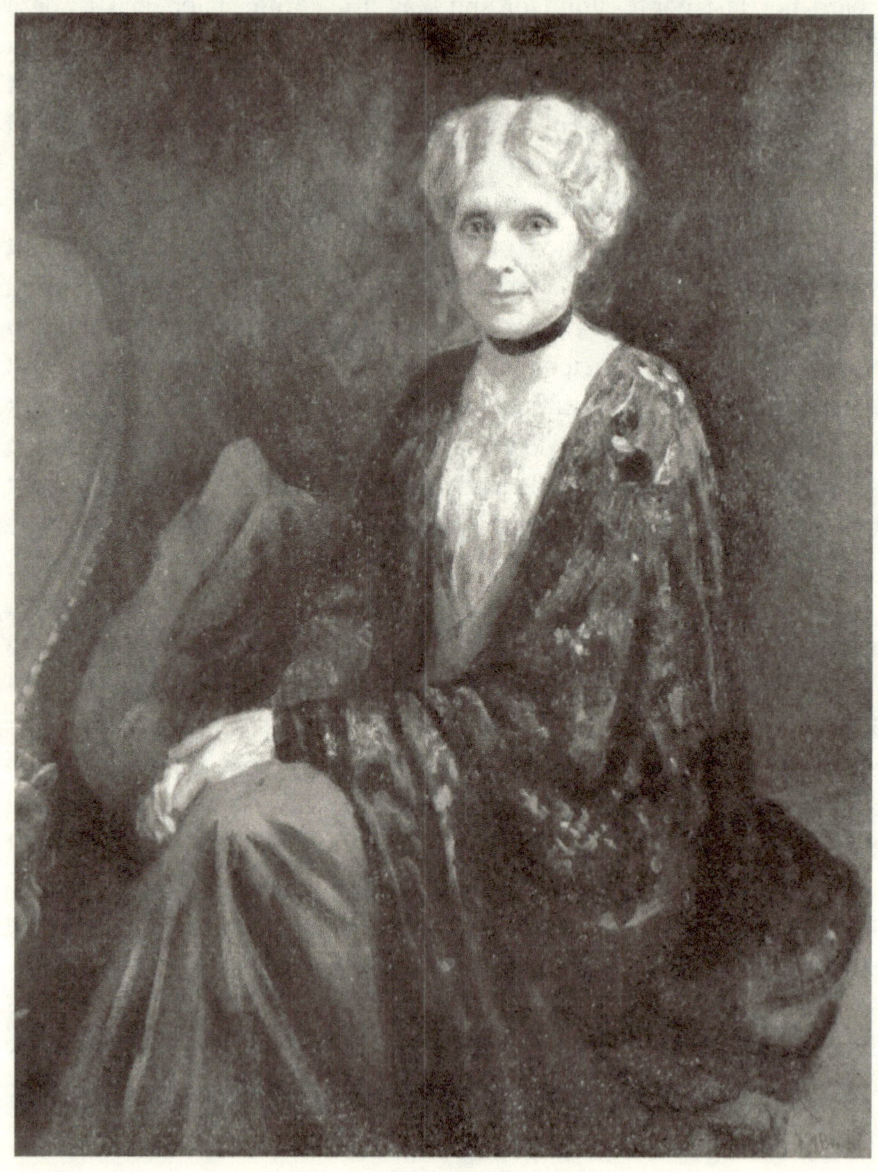

Mrs. N. R. Brewer

Under the high cliff at the confluence of the Minnesota and Mississippi Rivers lies beautiful Pike Island, containing about eighty acres of level ground fringed on all sides with trees of various kinds—cottonwood, maple, ash, elm, and willow. The island had been used for pasture purposes for many years. Fort Snelling surmounts the cliff and looks downstream to the distant hills around and beyond the city of St. Paul. To the south, across the Minnesota, up the sloping bluffs, lies the historic village of Mendota. The old stone church of early days crowns a high projection and is reached by a long stairway from the road below. Lower down is the old mansion built by General Sibley when commandant of the Fort. It was in this romantic hamlet we spent our wedding night before boarding the train to my old High Forest, and as the evening sun was gilding the distant hills, we talked up to the church and for a time sat on a step of the long stairs to view the beautiful scenery while the peal of the Angelus bell re-echoed from hill to hill. This lovely scene that evening and ever since has been tinctured with romance for us. Nor had these quiet dales been strangers to romance, for a short way up the Mississippi is the beautiful glen leading to the Falls of Minnehaha, made famous by Longfellow's Hiawatha. In the shadows of that primeval haunt, the Indian brave wooed his dusky mate. There, Laughing Water still croons the same melody for the ears of white lovers, and romance lives on.

* * *

From the wigwam he departed
Leading with him Laughing Water;
Hand in hand they went together,
Through the woodland and the meadow.

* * *

All the birds sang loud and sweetly
Songs of happiness and heart's-ease;
Sang the bluebird, the Owaissa,
"Happy are you, Hiawatha,

Having such a wife to love you!"
Sang the robin the Opechee,
"Happy are you, Laughing Water,
Having such a noble husband!"
From the sky the sun benignant
Looked upon them through the branches,
Saying to them, "O my children,
Love is sunshine, hate is shadow,
Life is checkered shade and sunshine,
Rule by love, O Hiawatha!"

Within two stones' throws of where we sat that memorable evening, the first river craft that ever rode the waters above Prairie Du Chien was moored just sixty years before. In 1819 a troop of soldiers was sent by the government, in rowboats, to build a fort where Snelling now stands. They arrived in the fall, and as the weather was getting cold, they constructed temporary winter quarters in which to await the spring before commencing work on the fort. Shortly before this expedition was begun, a little girl was born to the commanding officer and his wife. The voyage lasted nearly the entire summer, because their craft had to be rowed up stream by the men. The child, Charlotte, was nourished by porridge made from the flour in barrels among their supplies. The dampness of the river had caused the flour to mould, yet the little one thrived on it and grew into maidenhood at the fort. Afterward she married a Mr. Van Clive and but a few years ago, at an advanced age, passed away in Minneapolis. Her autobiography is a most fascinating narrative of army frontier and Indian life at the fort. I must not omit to mention that she was the first white child born in a vast territory then called Ouisconsin, which included Wisconsin, all of Minnesota, and much more of the Northwest, before present state lines were established.

Today Fort Snelling borders the corporate limits of both the Twin Cities with their vast population of eight hundred thousand. Nowhere in the United States will one find more beautiful and progressive cities with their scenic highways and lovely mansions fringing lake and river. Their great universities, cathedrals, and skyscrapers rival the best in the country. The old blockhouse, with its portholes for protection against Indian warfare and other buildings erected in 1820, still stand at Fort Snelling, mute reminders of a rapidly changing world. The hum and bustle of modern city life is everywhere. But a hundred years has seen this wondrous transformation in a land where once the smoke from the quiet Indian teepee ascended on the breezes and where the war cry of the Sioux, the Chippewa, and the Blackfeet will never be heard again. It was near Mendota that my friend Alexis Fournier, the artist, was born and there he painted the thistles about which I will tell you later. On Pike Island he got his foreground for an important picture of the old fort, crowning the brow of the cliff.

Previous to our wedding, I had rented three upstairs rooms which had none of the modern conveniences. On returning a month later from our wedding trip, I went to see Mr. Frank Bass, an artist who had abandoned the profession and gone into the furniture business, and he let me have two hundred dollars-worth of necessary household articles on time, at the rate of five dollars down and five dollars monthly. With this meager equipment and a few other utensils, which had been given to us, we began housekeeping.

Bass afterward failed in business because of a poor head for business and too much heart, but the little household he had made possible throve. I had made a deal with King, the liveryman, to make him a crayon portrait in exchange for the use of a horse and buggy that we might enjoy an occasional ride into the country. So, on our first wedding anniversary, we drove to Fort Snelling and Mendota where we had spent our wedding night. Our course lay along the country road, which today is the beautiful Summit Avenue, lined with magnificent homes of millionaires. The rolling common to the left, where cattle grazed, was very beautiful. Large oak trees and clumps of hazel brush dotted the slopes, and to the west was a grove of heavy timber, through which the road wound.

On that drive, we noticed a sign, “Lots For Sale, Ed Simonton, No.—Wabasha St.” The thought of buying a lot where we could build a home of our own out in the suburbs of town was uppermost in our minds, and this beautiful spot seemed the fitting one. On the next day, I went to see Mr. Simonton. During the first year of our married life my earnings had not been as great as I had expected. My monthly income averaged not more than sixty to seventy dollars. Having our furniture bill to pay and many things to buy, I had accumulated in cash but seventy-five dollars. Simonton had seven lots he wanted to sell in a group.

The price was six hundred dollars for the group, terms one-fourth cash, the balance to be paid in three annual installments. To raise the one hundred fifty dollars, I had to borrow seventy-five from good old Mrs. Rittle, whose thrift had enabled her to become something of a banker to her friends in the neighborhood. She did not even ask a note in security, only that I should pay six percent interest. I paid the debt in odd sums as money came in and the interest was figured accordingly. And so I bought the lots.

It is strange how insignificant incidents sometimes leave an ineradicable impression on the mind, while more important ones are forgotten. My little wife has never asked for the things that contribute to a woman's pleasure or comfort if she felt it involved the least hardship for me. This first year was the beginning of our struggles, and her old threadbare coat had been discarded when warm weather came, and I was not able to buy her a new one as winter approached. She was compelled to wear a light dolman or cape fit only for summer use. I had taken a room on the fourth floor of the McQuillan Building, which I called a studio, although it had only a table, an easel, and two plain chairs as its equipment. Rose frequently brought my lunch to the studio in the middle of the day.

Once when it was bitterly cold, she blew in wringing her hands, weeping, in a half-frozen condition. That she should suffer so, without complaining, when I could not provide her with comfortable clothing made me very unhappy, but the worst came a few days later. She incidentally told her sister Christine how cold she had gotten and the latter gave me a sound scolding for not buying my wife a new coat.

It was hard to get orders. One day I heard that a man, Tom Brennan by name, who was superintendent of the St. Paul & Duluth Railroad, wanted a portrait of his dead brother. Brennan lived some two miles out of town in the Arlington Hills district. There was no streetcar in that direction, and this was before the days of the telephone, so I had to walk.

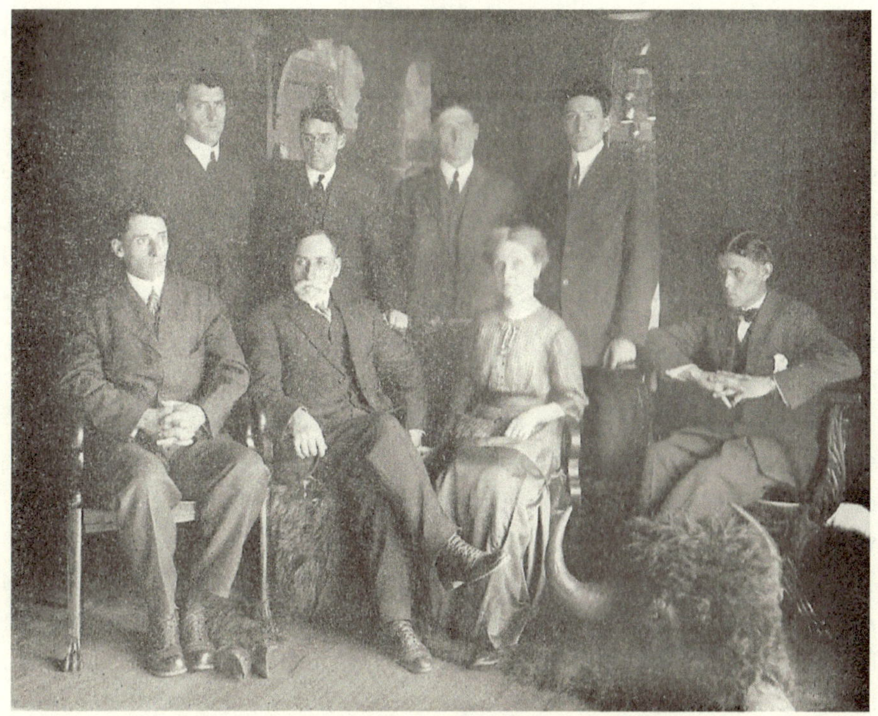

My family thirty-five years later.

They say that thirteen is an unlucky number, but on my thirteenth trip on foot to his place, I found him at home and got the order for a ten-dollar crayon portrait. When it was finished, I took it to him. He asked me what I would charge to do nine more, one for each of his brothers and sisters. I told him I would make the whole bunch for one hundred dollars.

When I returned with the rest of them, he was pleased with them and gave me a check on the Second National Bank for the amount agreed upon. I presented the check at the teller's window and received a bag of silver dollars, which I lugged home. My wife greeted me at the door, and as she led the way into the room, I slipped my hand under my overcoat and pulled out a handful of silver coins and sowed them about the room. Indeed, they rang cheerily as she sprang to gather them up. Soon I let her have another handful and another and another, and believe me, a hundred silver dollars thus scattered about can create a musical impression of wealth far beyond their intrinsic value.

We joyously scraped them up and counted them over. With them, I was enabled to pay off quite a grocery bill, which I owed to one of the finest grocerymen with whom I have ever dealt, for he had credited me long and patiently. When I paid the bill, I made excuses for the delay. "Well," he said, "I never worried about your not paying it, Nick, and you could have added greatly to it, just the same." I also bought the much-needed coat for Rose. It was in this groceryman's store that fall that I first talked over the telephone. I urged good old Dr. McDonald to be hasty; it was the day on which our eldest son, Angelo, now celebrates his birthday.

My income grew less and I was obliged to look about for other things to do. I solicited collections for doctors and tramped about, many times far out in the outskirts of town, and many a day returned without having earned even streetcar fare.

In November of that year our first son was born. We named him Angelo, hoping that he might prove a second Michelangelo in art, but the name hoo-doo'd him, for of all our boys he has the least artistic instinct.

The following spring, when I had reduced the mortgage on our lots, we started to build a house. As I was not able to employ carpenters, I did practically all the work myself, and it took almost three years to complete the six-room home. I rented five acres of adjoining land and did market gardening. Every Sunday, before we bought a horse, we walked two miles to church, wheeling the baby carriage. On pleasant Sunday afternoons, I sketched in the woods. Making an occasional portrait, painting signs or houses, collecting doctors' bills, and market gardening, I was able to earn enough to meet my payments and add other improvements to the home.

After we had had three children, I again yielded to the old instinct to play the fiddle. The start came with an opportunity to trade a picture for a fine French violin—Audino was the maker's name. This time I was determined to begin right, so I arranged to take lessons from a well-known violinist named Kleist. This, too, was a trade deal. He must have had the patience of Job to endure me, for twenty-six-year-old fingers are not easy to direct. He was so anxious, though, to get a portrait of his child that I think he would willingly have carried me across the

Jordan on his back. After he had labored with me for nearly a year, and in lieu of the difference still due me on the pictures, he induced me to take a better bow, which he said I needed. Furthermore, he seemed glad to recommend me to a Professor Guilbert, who was thought to be an excellent teacher.

Guilbert, too, was inveigled into a trade. In exchange for my work I received lessons and a lot of manuscript music, including selections from the operas and other high-class music.

I was getting so I could read music fairly well, although my execution was still amateurish. Guilbert was likewise patient, as long as he still owed me something on the pictures, but as soon as they were paid for, he passed me on to a Professor Amato who had just come from Chicago, where he had been playing in Thomas's Orchestra. But Amato was no trade victim; his terms were cash only. He was a real musician, living constantly in the high heaven of musical dreams. To him, teaching was a bore, even with the cleverest pupils, but with a dunce like me, I could plainly see it was exasperating. At times, his temper would get the better of him, and he would thump my fingers with his bow. Of course, I would take it good-naturedly, because I knew that I deserved it and that he was putting me through worthwhile exercises. His Latin temperament was interesting. When completely out of patience with me, he would wheel his back to me and sail off into an improvisation of exquisite melody. Then, no doubt, thinking of which side his bread was buttered on, he would come back to me as I stood in enraptured chagrin and start over again, enduring me until the hour was up, when down went the fiddle and I was dismissed.

I had little time to practice. I rose at five o'clock to put in two hours before going to work. Always an early riser, I was compelled through exhaustion to retire early. My wife reversed that plan and loved her morning sleep. Consequently, my scratching on the fiddle at that outlandish hour greatly annoyed her. In summer I would go into the barn to practice. We had chickens and when I began to play the rooster began to crow. Somehow my fiddle awakened a sympathetic chord in Mr. Rooster, but since he made no effort to crow in tune, he only disturbed me and I would have to rid the barn of his presence. We once had a dog who, when the church bell rang, would set up a most unholy howl until the bell ceased ringing. I presume my music was as unpleasant to the poor rooster's ears as the bell ringing was to the dog's.

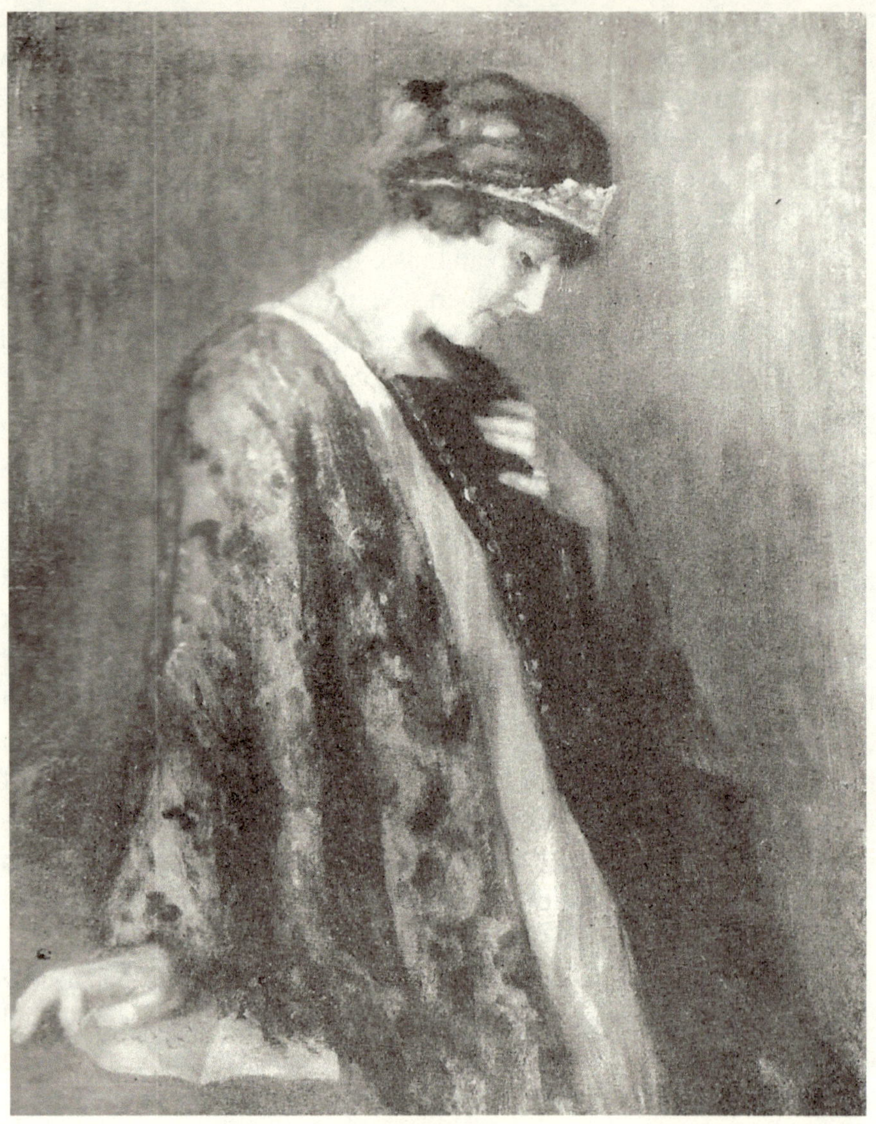

The Letter

When the panic came, we had to move to the farm, and I had no time to practice; my fingers and muscles became stiff from physical work and I said to myself, "What is the use? One art is all I can handle," and with reluctance I sold the fiddle. Ever since, I have contented myself with listening to the music of others. Now our grandson, Francis, only seventeen, promises to become a worthwhile violinist, and I love to listen to his splendid work.

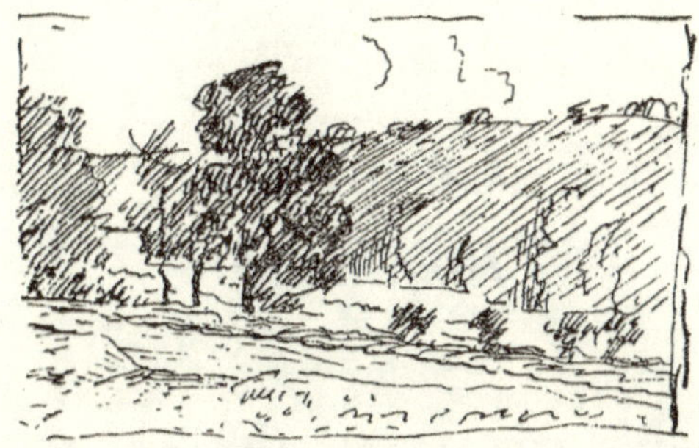

Chapter V
Inspiration

Homer Martin—Charles Noel Flagg—New York City

The truly great rarely mount gilded pedestals; they more often kick them over.

On April first of the second year of my married life, I opened the studio door to a vigorous knock. There stood a man of medium build, in a slouch hat and shabby brown coat. "My name is Martin," he said. "I'm looking for a place where I can do some painting." It was Homer Martin, who afterward became one of America's foremost landscape painters. He was the first real artist I had ever met. I had never heard of him before. He said he thought I might let him use my studio for painting. I welcomed him, delighted at the thought of his being an artist and curious to know more about him.

We soon became devoted friends. He brought in a few small canvasses and an unfinished head of Doctor Charles Smith, which he was making for the family. He came almost every day to do a little work on his pictures.

His way of working was just the opposite to that of George Inness, whom I have often seen at work. Inness was actuated by an intense concentration and an all-absorbing enthusiasm—a kind of frenzy, which did not permit any interruption or pause for conversation. Martin worked leisurely, talked half the time, often laying down his brush when becoming interested in a foreign theme. Some days after an hour's work he would become so involved in conversation that the rest of the day would pass without accomplishment. He was a great reader and I fancy he got as much pleasure from his books as from his brush. Great readers are usually great thinkers and only thinkers become great painters. All of Martin's pictures show well-thought-out schemes, with little left undone.

Although I had painted a great many landscapes, I frankly confessed to him that I was not an artist, that I had never taken a lesson from a real artist nor from anyone competent to teach the rudiments of drawing and painting. But when I saw Martin's pictures, watched him paint, and heard him talk, I knew that he was a real painter. I drank with avidity every word about drawing, painting, color, nature, and life, and I can still see his large blurred eyes, hear his voice, see his gestures, and remember many of his arguments.

I had acquired a great many books by trading my pictures for them at a book dealer's. I mentioned the fact to Martin, and he came to the house to see them. After that he often borrowed my books and took them home to read. One book especially interested him. It was Ranke's *Lives of the Popes*. He read it with great interest and talked over his impressions with me. Another was *W. M. Hunt's Talks about Art*. Fortunately, Hunt's conversations with his students had been jotted down by one of them, a Miss Helen M. Knowlton, on backs of canvasses, scraps of paper, or anything she could find in the classroom. Otherwise, those valuable impromptu sayings by one of America's great painters and educators would have been lost. The direct, terse lines expressing a profound philosophy intrigued Martin, and he read and re-read the book. Another favorite was the *Autobiography of Marie Bashkirtsev*, in which she wrote of Bastien-Lepage, Tony Robert Fleury, Carolus Duran, and the great Frenchmen of her day. Martin's comments on these works were most illuminating and enabled me to comprehend them better.

I had just completed a couple of portraits in oil of Judge John Oliver and his wife, which I showed to Martin. These pictures, of course, had been made from photographs. I had made a careful note of the flesh coloring of my subjects, and Martin commented on the fact that he did not know I was so "well up in color." He had no other praise for my work, since work, such as I was doing at that time, did not admit of artistic criticism. My portraits were just commercial pot-boilers, and no one knew it better than I.

Up to this time my only source of enlightenment on the technical principles of art had been from reading, but I was unable to find any textbooks of rudimentary instruction on which I could depend. Occasionally Martin would drop such words as "values," "masses," "tone," "composition," and "balance." When asked the meaning and application of these terms, his explanations were dear and easy for me to grasp. "Values," he said, "means the relation of tones to each other. There are two kinds of values, light and color values. Upon the accuracy of these relations, other things being right, depends truthfulness of impression, a necessary quality in every picture." When alone I would scribble down his sayings and reflect upon them. Despite my limited comprehension of these principles, I tried to apply them to my outdoor landscape work, which occupied all my spare time.

Martin worked on several landscapes, though none of them was finished when he left. He was extremely reticent about his private life. On one occasion only, he mentioned having a family. Before leaving, he turned one of his pictures to the wall behind the door, where I might not observe it readily. I never saw him after that. Some days later, I noticed the picture and fancied he had left it as rental. I valued this picture greatly, but unfortunately, it disappeared. I think that when in a hurry, lacking a stretcher for a piece of canvas, I tacked a canvas temporarily over his picture. Now both canvasses have disappeared. No doubt somebody has a valuable Homer Martin under a worthless Brewer.

Years afterward, I frequently saw Homer Martin's *Harp of the Winds*—now a valuable treasure of the Metropolitan Museum—at the art shop of Stevens and Robertson on Sixth Street, without a frame. I was told the price was one hundred fifty dollars, but I was too poor then to think of buying it. I did not know that about that time Martin was living on Rice Street, St. Paul, where he died. There was not money enough in the house to buy a grave in Oakland Cemetery, where he sleeps. The good sisters of the Visitation Convent had given him employment as an instructor and helped the family in its struggle.

A few years later, this same picture that I could have bought for one hundred fifty dollars was sold at auction in New York for about fifteen thousand dollars and presented to the Metropolitan Museum, where it now hangs.

One day an article appeared in the newspaper about Charles Noel Flagg, a New York artist who had come to St. Paul to make some portraits. Flagg, at that time, was spoken of as the best educated artist, technically, in America, and had been in charge of the life class at the National Academy of Design. After returning from Paris, where he had been an instructor for a decade or more in one of the schools, he opened a studio in Hartford and lived there until his death. He was a member of the famous Flagg family of artists in New York. His father was well known as a portrait painter. One or two of his brothers were painters and one was a very famous architect.

I had just finished a sketch of a landscape and decided to show it to him and beg a criticism. When he looked at it, he said, "This is interesting; I should like to see more of your things." I told him I had several at the Stevens Art Store. "Well," he said, "I shall be there at one o'clock tomorrow." When I arrived at the gallery, they told me he had been in, looked at my pictures, and gone. This was a keen disappointment, but on the street, I met him returning. "Come back here," he commanded, "I want to talk to you," and he led me into the gallery where the pictures were. "Young man, you have a future before you," he said. In going over the pictures, he picked out one which he praised. His advice was, "You should go to New York and I know the man with whom you should study. It is Dwight Tryon. I will give you a letter to him."

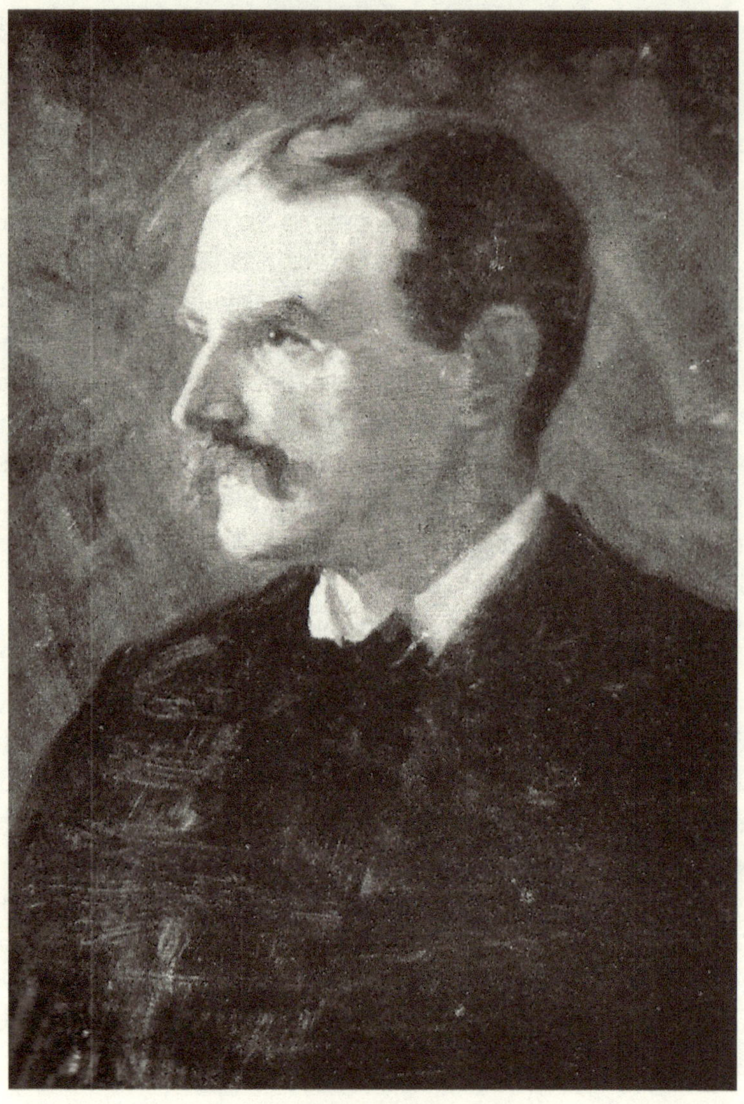

Charles Noel Flagg

It seemed impossible to go to New York. Being heavily involved in St. Paul, I had to continue to earn money to meet my obligations and support my wife and three children. But I dreamed and thought and planned, and in six months, I had worked out a scheme by which I could get away for a couple of months. Renting the place, I moved the family into a little house near my wife's mother's place and went to New York. That was the first time I had ever been in a Pullman. I had been told of the wickedness of Chicago and of all great cities and that it would be advisable for me to carry a gun for self-protection. I carried that gun for about two months without any provocation to use it and finally discarded it for good and all.

Arriving in New York, I went into McNabb's photograph gallery, where enlarged portraits of all kinds in black and white were displayed. I told the proprietor that I did free hand crayon portraits and asked if he would be interested in seeing them. He said he would not, that he had tried many free hand pictures and they had never proved good likenesses, so he used pictures made over solar enlargements instead. I had never made portraits in that way, but I insisted upon his letting me have a photograph of someone he knew so that I could make one for him to see.

When I returned with the picture, he was very much pleased and said he liked it even better than the enlargements he had been using, because it was not so black. He was having a dozen pictures made every week by other artists. When I told him that I could make him a dozen pictures a week like this one, he looked at me with consternation. I assured him that I had put only one hour on this picture. He remarked that he had never heard of such a thing. "Well, here are three photographs you can do," he said, handing me the pictures. "I'll pay twelve dollars and fifty cents each." The next day I delivered the pictures and drew thirty-seven dollars and fifty cents. I discovered that there was quite a ready market for crayon portraits and that I could get ten to fifteen dollars each, from the local photographers, for more portraits than I could do.

I took rooms at a boarding house and in a short while I was making money. I haunted the galleries in the Metropolitan and visited several artists' studios, with open eyes and an open mind. I realized for the first time that New York was the place for an artist to begin a career. There were schools under the direction of the best artists, who had recently returned from abroad. The Art Students' League was then a young institution imbued with the spirit of the French school. The Society of American Artists was a rival of the old National Academy, giving exhibitions annually. Galleries on Fiftieth Avenue constantly displayed foreign works, which I studied daily.

In my amateur excursions into the galleries and studios, I stumbled into the huge atelier of Albert Bierstadt, at that time the most famous painter in America. A foreigner by birth, Bierstadt had become the leading representative of the Hudson River School. His studio contained many large canvasses, one of which representing the Yosemite Valley, stood in the middle of the room. Before it sat Mr. Bierstadt eating an orange. A man bordering on seventy years with a fine shock of curly gray hair, a Bismarckian white mustache and goatee, a fine physique, he nodded "Good day" to my rather sudden invasion of his sanctum. The bravado of a breezy art hound from the West must have impressed him judging from the scrutinizing stare he gave me. I told him of my ardent wish to enter a school, how much I admired his great pictures and the like. When he had finished eating his orange, he became more communicative and gave me, what I then considered, wholesome advice.

Time, however, has put its stamp upon his works which is much lower than my then worshipful estimate of his overelaborate, panoramic sweeps of snow-covered mountain ranges or Indian buffalo drives, so much admired by American art lovers and buyers of 1885.

My feeling in seeing those great canvasses no doubt agreed with those of the young German street sweeper at Boston of whom, it is said, that on reading about one of Bierstadt's pictures having been sold for $30,000.00, declared that painting pictures must be a good trade to learn, and scraping all his earnings together started for Paris, where he was told such trades were taught. But after three months of experience there he returned to America by way of the steerage a saddened but wiser boy.

Five months later I returned to St. Paul with many pretty things for my wife, family, and relatives. In addition, I brought back nearly one thousand dollars, a fabulous sum, beyond my most optimistic dreams. I decided to move the family to New York in spite of the mild protests of my wife and relatives. In November I rented our Grand Avenue home, and we packed all our things, moved to New York, and set up housekeeping in a flat on East Ninety-First Street.

We had just settled in our new environment when I found that my fame as a great crayon artist had gone before me. John V. Stout, a photographer of Easton, Pennsylvania, who was a friend of McNabb, called at our flat with a dozen photographs, which he wanted reproduced in crayon. A few days later, Dick Richardson of Napanee, Ontario, also a friend of McNabb, came to see me with several photographs. He wanted to see something that I had already done, but I had nothing to show him. I said to him, "If you will come here this evening at seven o'clock, I will do one of you without a photograph." In an hour I had a beautifully shaded and nicely stippled portrait of him, which closely resembled my other photographic pictures. From then on, he sent many portraits for me to do. A photographer from Springfield, Massachusetts, also came. Before long, I had more work than I could do. I employed an assistant to do the draperies and background effects, giving me time to finish the faces. This scheme did not work, so I had to limit my output. That December, my books showed that I had delivered one hundred twenty-three crayon portraits, working from seven in the morning until nine or ten at night.

My schedule was too strenuous; my nerves went to pieces, and I became ill and had to stop work entirely. I went to Easton, Pennsylvania, to visit Stout, for whom I had formed a great liking. He was not the kind of photographer who thinks photography the greatest of all arts. We took a trip to Mauch Chunk and Allentown, Pennsylvania, sketching together. It was in Easton that I made the sketch for a landscape, which became my second exhibition picture at the National Academy.

My first exhibit in the National Academy was hung that fall. It seemed to me a reflection on the judgment of the jury. It was the study that Charles Noel Flagg had liked when he first saw my work in St. Paul and which I painted before I had ever taken any regular instruction or had ever met an artist. It was an amateur's effort, yet it was hung on the line. It showed a grove bordering a meadow. I had not thought of principles of art for the very good reason that I knew none. To think that the work of an amateur, who had never seen an original painting or an artist, should be accepted and hung on the line by the august jury of the National Academy provokes a smile—even though it were not hung wrong side up as was a prize picture recently. Flagg said the picture showed care. I remember I had difficulty in my limited experience with colors and I make this statement for the ears of artists and people who know: I rubbed in that grove with pure asphaltum and terre-verte, two colors flatly condemned by the profession as dangerous and fugitive. I still have that picture, and the colors I used are as luminous and perfect today as when I painted it. But I do not wish the student to follow my example, for I have long since learned that the use of those colors is impractical.

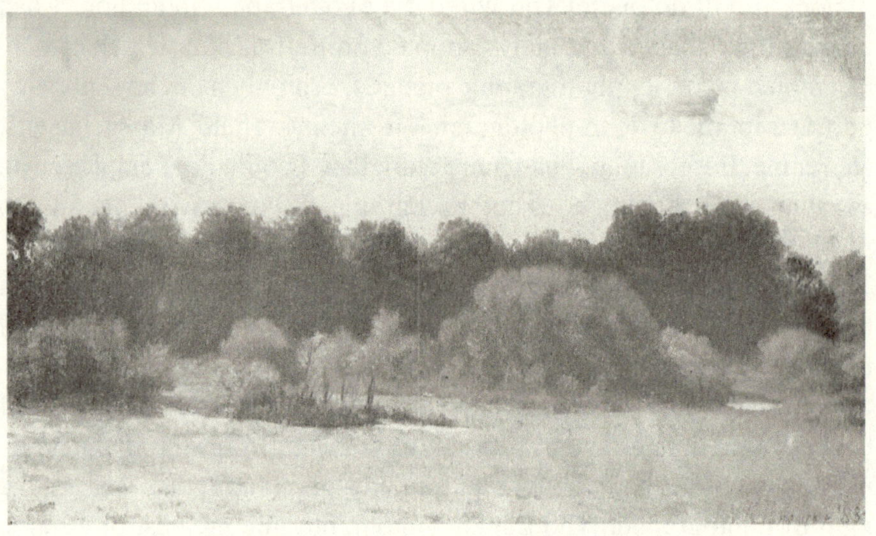

The Winding Stream in the National Academy Exhibition 1885.

Chapter VI
Hobnobbing with the Masters

Tryon, My Teacher—Inness, the Great—Gay, the Patient Wayfarer Among Fields of Waving Grain—A Miserly Model

That winter my crayon portrait work left me little time for real study. I arranged with Mr. Dwight Tryon, to whom I presented Flagg's letter, to join his class two afternoons each week. His studio was then in the Rembrandt Building on Fifty-Seventh Street. I recall the first day I attended. He set me to work in charcoal on a head of Germanicus, from the cast. I went about the task in practically the same way that I had been doing the crayon portraits from photographs—beautifully shaded, soft, pretty pictures. He seemed to pay me little or no attention until I had the work completely finished—so smooth and pretty that Germanicus would have groaned in his grave if he could have seen it! Finally Tryon came to me and said, "Well, I see now what you can do. You have been working, no doubt, a long time by yourself. You have learned too much and not enough and it will be necessary for you to start with the rudiments of drawing." With that he pulled out his handkerchief and, with a few vicious slaps, wiped away almost every vestige of my beautiful work. I must confess I felt some chagrin, for no doubt the other pupils knew what was coming when he arrived at my easel. Then he demonstrated how I should sketch out the big angles of the outline and parts of the features and told me then to wait until he saw it. On the second round, he found I had followed his instruction perfectly. "All right," he said, "now try to determine the outline and shapes of the masses of light and shade, ignoring the little details such as reflected lights, half tones, and the shapes of minor features." Again, he complimented me on grasping his ideas. Before the end of class time, I had a very differently constructed piece of work.

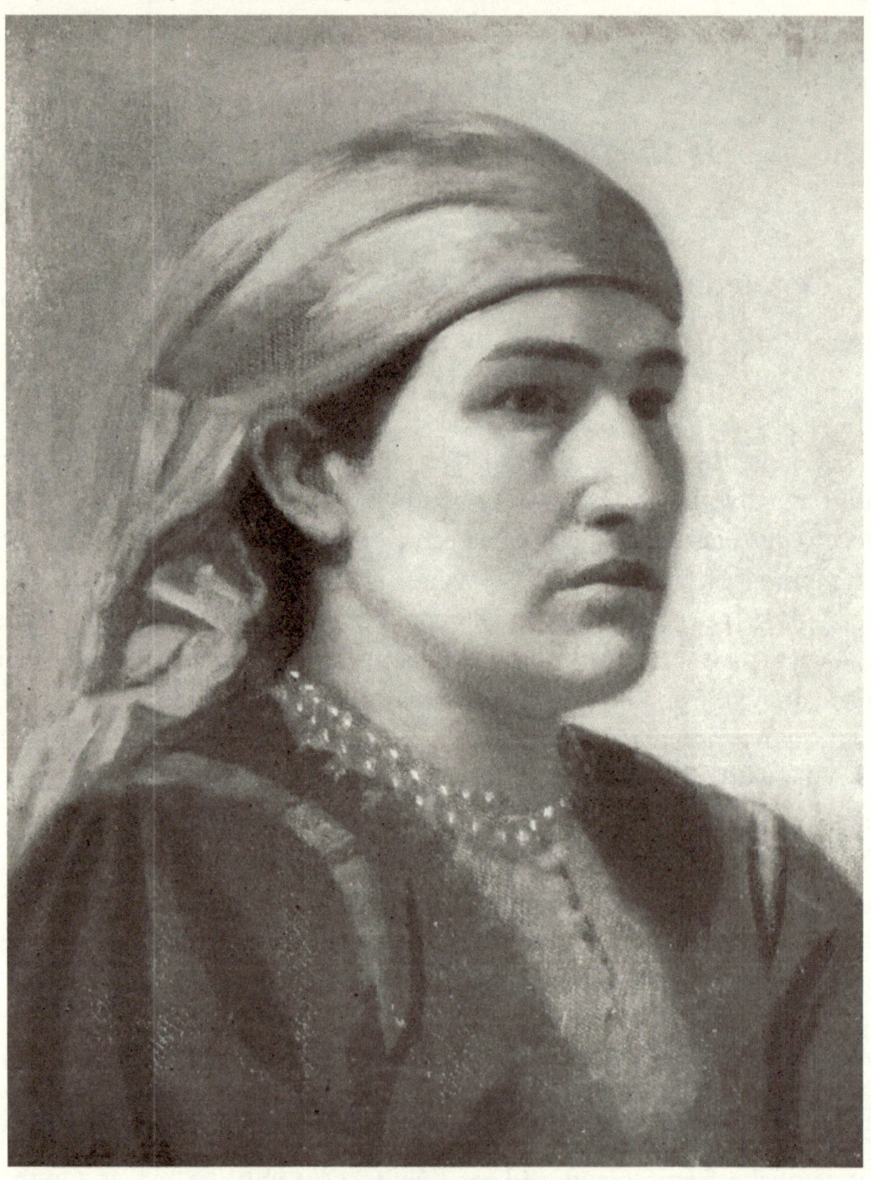

My first study under Dwight Tryon.

The second day I was told to draw the head of Vitellius. The head of St. Francis was my third model. Four or five afternoons I devoted to drawing heads from the cast. Then he told me to bring my colors and he would have me work from a life model. The model was an Italian woman with a red bandana around her head, and a blue dress. She was the wife of John Mundaro. John had been a famous model in Europe, posing for Munkacsy in his *Christ Before Pilate* and other famous painters. My familiarity with colors enabled me to proceed with facility and by night I had completed a very creditable head. Tryon gave me quite a bit of encouragement, and suggested my sending it to the Academy.

I think my success in class was due to my ability to grasp the principles and apply them readily. After all, what can be said or taught of the technique of drawing can be written on ten pages. The difficulty with most students is that they have to be reminded over and over again to keep them in the correct groove of technical work. I have always had an excellent memory, except of late years when names and faces play me tricks; but in those days when I understood a principle, I made it my own and never forgot it. To this day, I seldom go to work that I do not recall some of the advice of Tryon, Flagg, Inness, and others. After studying for some time with Tryon, I began to understand many of the things Homer Martin had said to me. I needed a concrete demonstration and once I understood the principles, they were mine.

I was, unfortunately, obliged to discontinue my studies with Tryon after about three months. The following year he had quit teaching and I joined the class of Herbert Levy. Levy was a pupil of Leon Jerome and Jerome was a draftsman. Levy, however, was extremely fussy about the way I mixed my paints, the way I placed my colors on my palette, and things that seemed to me trivial and unnecessary; so after a month I quit the school. Yet he made clear to me the necessity of accents and massing and gave me some very good ideas on composition.

This was the extent of my technical training, although I derived great benefit from the criticisms of other painters. I knew George Inness quite well and went to his studio occasionally to show him some of my paintings. The first time I went to his studio, I asked him if he would tell me of a good teacher with whom I could study, not telling him that I was already a pupil of Tryon. He said, "Well, Bruce Crane has a very excellent technical method." Then I asked what he thought of Tryon. "Well," said he, "there is greater feeling there." Those were the brief comments on the subject of perhaps the greatest painter America had produced up to that time.

Homer Martin, Inness, Wyant, and Blakelock have been classed as the four outstanding painters of this country. It was my good fortune to know all of them, except Blakelock. A few years later, as we shall see, the criticisms and intimate relations with Charles Noel Flagg helped me to develop whatever style and knowledge of technical art I have acquired. I shall ever hold an unfading memory of Wyant, who, with Inness and Martin, wielded an influence that shall always abide with me.

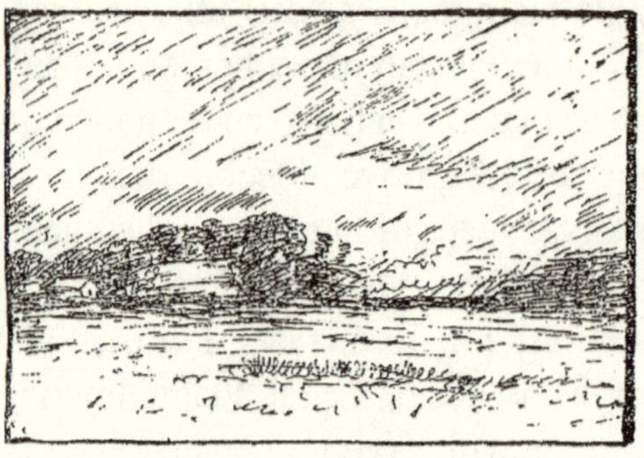

Poor Wyant, handicapped by ill health, toiled and suffered patiently under most distressing circumstances at a time when there was no market for American pictures. Once he said to me, "If I could make fifteen hundred dollars a year with my brush, I would be so happy." Today, the pictures he sold for one hundred dollars sell for one hundred times that amount.

In 1887, I happened to be an exhibitor at the National Academy of Design. This was the same year that George De Forest Brush was awarded the first prize for his fine canvas, *The King and the Sculptor.* I do not recall if there were any other prizes given, but in those days the prize was awarded by the popular vote of all exhibiting artists. On Varnishing Day, we artists gathered to see how our pictures were hung and do such touching up and varnishing as we thought necessary. In fact, it was the artists' day, and each one registered his vote for what he considered the best picture. That good old custom no longer exists. It was perfectly fair and just; politics played no part in it. Who should be more competent to pass upon a picture than a body of artists? Strange to say, the vote on Brush's canvas fell little short of being unanimous.

At the reception that followed, when the verdict was announced, Brush, who was then a very young man, was elated beyond measure over his success. It may have been his first honor. At least we inferred that from the way he proffered his right hand to each of the artists, with a hearty, grateful smile, as much as to say, "Congratulate me, Jim. Congratulate me, Bob," and so on around. Conditions have been reversed since then and now people ask for the privilege of grasping the hand that was so freely offered then.

It was on the afternoon of that Varnishing Day that a man wearing a broad-brimmed slouch hat entered the gallery. Soon the artists began to crowd about him. It was George Inness—the first time I had ever seen him. As he passed along the walls, his criticism was solicited by various artists on their work, and his comments were listened to by all with keenest interest. Inness' pictures, at that time, were not so popular with the dealers or buying public. The prices he asked for them would be considered shockingly cheap today, but the artists all knew that he was a truly great painter. All American art then was a drug on the market. I doubt if more than one of the well-known dealers handled it at all, while foreign works were bringing handsome prices. When we consider the returns artists receive today, it is easy to see that American art has surely come into its own.

Inness' studio was a veritable treasure house of beautiful creations. Racks two and three tiers above the floor held numerous unframed pictures of all sizes and subjects, standing on edge. There were perhaps a thousand canvasses in that room. He painted every season of the year—spring, summer, autumn, and winter; every mood and hour of the day—morning, noon, and night, the dawn, the sunset, and the moonlight, the clear blue sky, and the rolling storm clouds; every phase of nature—mountains, plains, woodlands, and meadows, the sea, the surf, the rocks, and the rivulets. Here and there he would throw in the corner of a house among trees to denote human habitation. He peopled his fields with a figure or two, usually without much action, a cow or perhaps an old wagon. Inness was not a one-story painter; he was more catholic in scope than any of our American artists. Nor did he trouble himself about the craftsmanship of technique. The poetry of nature meant more to him. He sang of the ever-changing moods of the scenes he loved. I have watched him while at work under his usual great enthusiasm. While engaged on his large things in the studio, he would dip his brush into the oils, mix his colors on a palette lying on a table, step forward to his canvas and nervously lay on a few strokes, then run back to a mirror placed at right angles to reflect his easel, study a few minutes, and then return to his palette and canvas. To speak to him while at work caused him annoyance. At other times he was affable and agreeable in conversation.

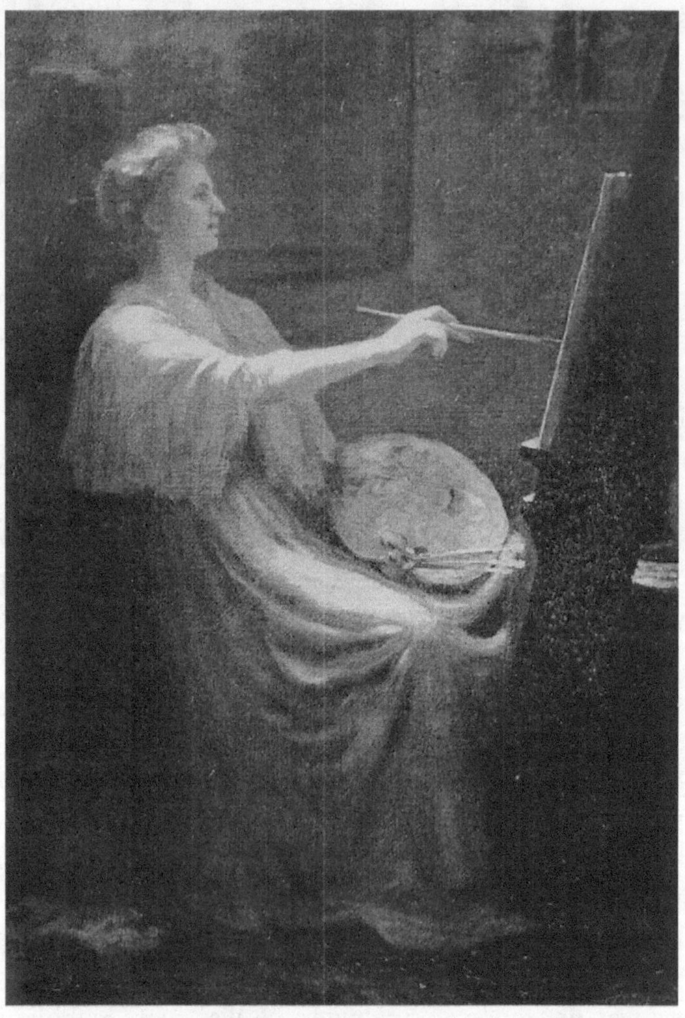

At Work

I remarked to him one day that when I had saved enough, I was going to buy one of his pictures. He turned around and abruptly asked me how much money I could raise. I said I had only one hundred fifty dollars on hand at home. "Well," he said, "for that sum you can have that one," pointing to one on the floor. I gladly accepted the offer and became the owner of a real Inness—a New England farm scene. After enjoying the picture for several years, I sold it for five thousand dollars.

A few years after the master's death, a memorial exhibition of his works was held, followed by an auction sale which netted the estate something like seven hundred fifty thousand dollars. From a subsequent sale, his smaller canvasses brought two hundred fifty thousand dollars more. Inness never guessed the vast wealth he was storing on those racks in his studio during the ripening years of his career, nor that the meager sums he received for his canvasses during his lifetime would be multiplied twenty to fifty times by eager dealers and collectors after his death.

One morning, years later, when I was painting the portrait of that delightful elderly gentleman and artist Edward Gay, he told me an interesting story. He had just come from the Knoedler Gallery, where, at Mr. Knoedler's request, he had gone to look at a picture they had found in their storeroom. The picture was unsigned, and they knew they had never bought it. It must have been left there long before by some artist who neglected to call for it. They suspected it was the work of Homer Martin and thought Mr. Gay could identify the style, since he had been an intimate friend of that artist. As soon as Gay saw the picture, he said, "Yes, that is Martin. I was with him when he made it." The painting proved to be a good example of the dead master's work and was very valuable. As they knew it did not belong to them, what disposition should they make of it? Gay suggested trying to find the artist's family, which after his death had moved away. Gay had some leads, however, and promised to try to locate them. Some days later he told me they had found the widow in California. In the meantime, Mr. Knoedler had received an offer of five thousand dollars for the picture. Gay had told Mrs. Martin of the discovery and that the picture could be sold for a couple of thousand, he thought. She replied that she hoped the story was true, as it would greatly relieve her pressing needs. They sold the picture and surprised the poor woman with a check for five thousand. Her gratitude was unbounded. Martin was not a prolific worker and those pictures he left at the time of his death had to be sacrificed for family necessities. Surely this windfall of so large a sum must have brought joy to worried hearts, and Gay's pleasure over the matter was as great as theirs.

Gay, better than most people, could appreciate the joy of that find, for he had spent years in the same struggle to support his large family. When we lived near their place in Mount Vernon, New York, we knew the biting poverty that was theirs. In those days, most American landscape artists were in the same boat. To consecrate one's time and thought to creative things with a worried mind and empty stomach is not conducive to satisfaction nor happy in results. Yet the Gays lived through it while the husband and father painted those beautiful fields of waving grain that promised a hopeful harvest for both farmer and painter.

The American Art Association awarded a two-thousand-dollar prize one year on one of his large wheat field canvasses. Of this picture Inness said, "It is the greatest picture ever painted in America to date" (or words to that effect). On Varnishing Day, Gay went to see how his pictures had been placed and was met at the door by someone who said, "Gay, you have drawn the prize." "No! Impossible!" he exclaimed as he rushed in to see if it were really true. Seeing the first prize card on his picture, he fainted and had to be revived, so the story runs, with a cold-water lotion. When they lifted him to his feet, his first utterance was, "I must take the first train home to tell my wife." Without waiting a moment, he started for the station. As he left the room, someone heard him mutter, "Two thousand dollars." There was joy in that Mount Vernon home that night, for now there would be enough to eat.

Two years afterward, I met Mr. Gay on the street, and he told me he had orders from seven museums for landscapes.

John Mundaro, the professional model and erstwhile pushcart banana man, was a real character. He was an Algerian who married an Italian woman and had become the father of twelve children. His appearance was typically Arabian, with strong features, heavy black eyebrows, dark complexion, and a certain ferocious expression such as

Schreyer would have chosen for one of his chieftains. John could not make himself clearly understood in English. One had to guess at the meaning of more than half his words. His eldest son, Tony, from what he said, must have been "some boy." "Oh, my Tony—fine feller. My Tony—him lick six beeg, beeg fellers." John's pantomime to reinforce his defective language made his narratives amusing, and he would take off Tony's fistic victories in a fashion so real, one felt it safer not to get too near him. I had him for a model in painting the three Magi, one of the figures almost prostrate before the Blessed Mother and Babe at Bethlehem. He had the real Oriental costumes, but was unable to hold the position on account of the gourmandish frontal rotundity he had acquired in late years, so I thought I would take a photograph of him to aid me in getting the outlines. But when John saw the camera, he rebelled and gave me to understand if he posed for a photo he would surely "go in fi'" (meaning in fire). I ridiculed his superstition, whereupon he stepped to the corner of the room, raised both hands and eyes to Heaven, and prayed for deliverance. As I could not persuade him, I told him to leave the costume and I would get a substitute to put it on, but that was even worse—someone else to pose in his clothes for a photo? He shook his head and went again to the corner and prayed. Coming back with a less agitated expression on his face, he said complacently, "Five doll'—me no care go fi'." I paid the five dollars, and the photo was taken. Occasionally, John would come in late in the day and say, "Mr. Brewery, me no sell banan' today. Me musta pay beega, beega bill. Please lend me car fare." Taking his story for gospel truth, I would lend him a quarter or a half dollar, which loans were never repaid. One day, he entered with a troubled look. I could see that he was really worried. He wanted me to advise him about some person he called his "part" (meaning partner). I said, "Part? What part?"

"Part in house," he answered.

"You have a house? Where?" I questioned.

"In Eighty-first Street," came the answer.

"What kind of a house?"

"Oh, four store (meaning stories) brownstone," he said.

"You have a four-story house on Eighty-first Street—a brownstone house?"

"Me and my part."

"How much did you pay for it?" I asked.

"Twenty-tree tous" (meaning thousand), he replied.

"Cash?" I asked in amazement.

"Cash," he repeated. "My part ten tous, me tirteen tous."

He staggered me. "You rascal," I said. "You ask me to lend you carfare. I thought you were a poor man."

"Me poor man?" he said—"Bluff!"

He and his family were living in the basement and the remaining rooms were rented to tenants.

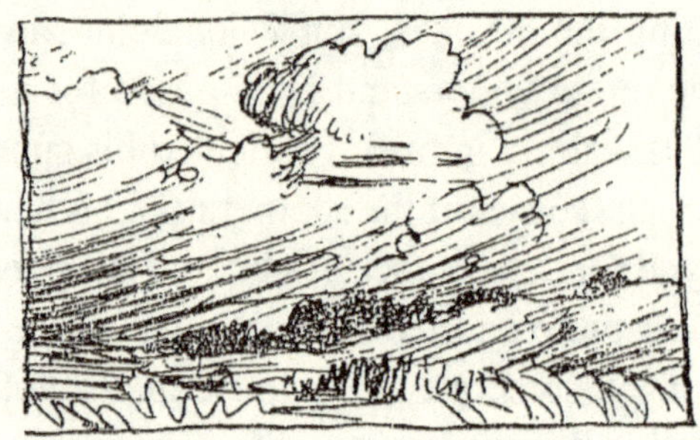

Chapter VII

Henry Ward Beecher, the Great Divine

Blessed are the Happiness Makers. Blessed are they who know how to shine on one's gloom with their cheer.

—Beecher

I was nearly twenty-two years of age before I first heard Henry Ward Beecher speak, and it was another ten years or so before I had the pleasure of meeting him and painting his portrait.

My father and mother were Democrats and southern sympathizers, and my impressions in childhood were gleaned from hearing them read and discuss political affairs during those stirring times. In spite of Mother's political predilections, she permitted her older boys to go to the front, urging them to be true to the call of the country and to lay down their lives, if necessary, in the cause of the Union. Prejudice was rife on all sides; some Democrats were anti-slavers—some Republicans supported the Confederate cause. John Althouse, our nearest neighbor, had been a staunch Republican, but when the news came that Lincoln had been shot, he rushed in excitedly and exclaimed, "They have killed old Abe, and I am damn glad of it, too!"

Father would become greatly excited over reading Beecher's condemnation of slavery and his abolitionist sermons. I think his dislike for Beecher arose from the fact that the latter was a minister, who, he said, should attend to preaching the gospel and let the government conduct the war. Beecher had made his influence felt throughout the nation and strongly reinforced Northern sentiment against the injustice of slavery. My parents talked about this frequently. Beecher did not favor Lincoln's conservative policy, and loudly denounced it. The single defeat of the Union troops at Bull Run aroused the lion in him, and he never lost an opportunity, by voice or pen, to express his censure of the administration's hesitancy and the ill-advised and partisan appointment of generals. His fiery editorials in the *New York Independent*, as well as his sermons, had a far-reaching influence; yet they called forth hostile criticisms from equally patriotic Northerners.

His sermon on the first anniversary of the attack on Fort Sumter will go down in history as an example of that spirit he helped to arouse, and that determined the breaking of the shackles of slavery that had, for so long, smirched the fair brow of Columbia. "We will give every dollar we are worth, every child that we have, and ourselves. We will bring all that we are and all that we have and offer them up freely. But this country will be one and undivided. We will have one constitution and one liberty that is universal. The Atlantic shall sound it and the Pacific shall echo it back, deep answering deep and it shall reverberate from the lakes on the north, to the unfrozen gulf on the south. One nation, one constitution, one starry banner! Hear it England. One country and indivisible. Hear it Europe! One people inseparable. One God! One hope! One baptism! One government! One nation! One country! One people! Free, cost what it may we will have it."

Criticism of the Washington government appeared in his editorials when McClellan failed to take Richmond.

"Did the government frankly say to this nation, 'We are defeated?' To this hour it has not trusted the people. It held back the news for days. Nor was the truth honestly told when outside information compelled it to say something. It is even to this hour, permitting McClellan's disaster to be represented as a piece of skillfully planned strategy.

"After the labor of two months, the horrible sickness of thousands of men poisoned in the swamps of the Chickahominy, the loss of probably more than ten thousand as noble fellows as ever lifted a hand to defend their country, McClellan, who was four miles from Richmond, finds himself twenty-five miles from the city, wagons burned, ammunition blown up, parts of artillery captured, no entrenchments, and with an army so small that it is not pretended that he can reach Richmond. The public is infatuated. The papers that regaled us two weeks ago with visions of a fourth of July in Richmond are now asking us to rejoice and acclaim—not a victory—but that we have just saved the army; McClellan is safe and Richmond too!

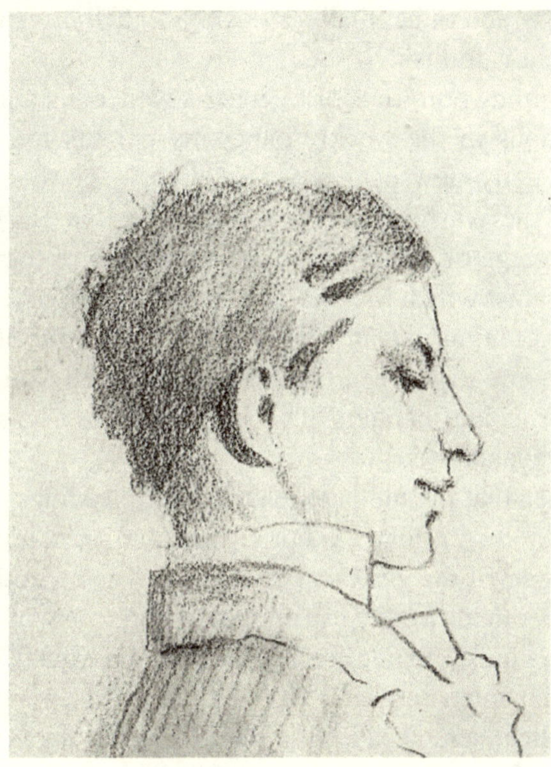

A sketch (the portrait in profile)

"It is not enough that we increase our men and means. We shall never succeed until we have the idea latent in the conflict. Slavery must be crushed. Liberty must have absolute and unquestioned dominion on this Continent. We will not have oppression under the symbol of a sceptre or of a whip—neither exported from abroad nor sprouted from our own soil. This Continent is dedicated to Liberty. It is the mission of this generation of men to establish free institutions from ocean to ocean. We sought to do it in peace. Since war has come, we will seek to take from its repulsiveness and horror by making it serve the noblest ends of human liberty. If it is for liberty upon a whole continent that we fight, then every son or brother that falls is a sacrificial victim. By his blood, we ransom generations of men. Richmond determines, Washington reasons; Richmond is inflexible, Washington vacillates; Richmond knows what it wants to do, Washington wishes that it knew. Richmond loves slavery and hates liberty; Washington is somewhat partial to liberty and rather dislikes slavery. Rebellion is wise and sinful; government is foolish."

These flaming editorials of Beecher's were constantly appearing with his sermons in the weekly paper my parents took. (The rural West had no daily newspapers at that time.) Nor was Beecher the only critic of the Washington government. For the North was trembling, on the verge of hysteria over the resistance of the Confederate stronghold against which McClellan had hurled his forces only to fall back in disheartening defeat. The President's call for 300,000 more men, struck home to the hearts of the people, and volunteers came forth from farms and hamlets. The fife and drum corps were heard throughout the land.

It was then that my mother yielded to the pleadings of her second son, my half-brother, Enon, a lad of eighteen, to be permitted to go to the front and "smell the gun powder of battle," as he said. After Enon enlisted, Mother made a daily trip on foot through the woods to the Post Office at High Forest, hoping for a letter from the front. On these trips, I always accompanied her. Once she was handed an envelope bordered with a black line, scratched with a pen, the usual sign announcing a death. I noticed her turn pale and stagger to a seat and hastily tear open the seal. Glancing quickly over the lines, she soon resumed her composure, and a calmer look came to her troubled face. She said, "Someone has made a mistake." Possibly in the mail shuffle, a clerk had marked the wrong envelope.

I remember Father hiding his horses, two lively steeds, by leading them far into the most inaccessible and densest part of the forest, fearing that they would be commandeered by government officials. I used to go with him to help carry feed to the animals in their silent retreat. Once on our approach, we were greeted by a shrieking whinny from one of them, which aroused father's apprehension lest they would make their whereabouts known to officers who might be near.

I was only five years old at the time of McClellan's defeat, but hearing my elders read and talk about it, I formed impressions I have never forgotten. There is no telling why the childish mind will take this or the other side of a controversy, for surely it is not reason that makes decision at that age. Beecher became a great man in my boyish imagination. Perhaps it was because Father and Mother did not think quite alike about him. Father frequently would sneer about his sayings, while Mother often expressed admiration. Perhaps I formed my conclusions because of the innate boyish disposition to take Mother's word for it before all others. When the boy merges into the man, he begins to think and reason as men do. It is then the mother loses some of her power to control or shape his logical deductions. Not until I was past fifteen, did I begin to side with Father on disputed questions.

In later years, I read of the poems of that wonderful Southern patriot and priest, Father Ryan, author of *The Conquered Banner* and *The Sword of Lee*—poems that will live as long as poetry shall live. Everything he ever wrote was tinctured with as deep a patriotism, as honest a purpose, as sincere a conviction as ever animated the utterances of Beecher. Chaplain Ryan of the Confederate army, after days of weary marching, barefooted and in tattered rags, late one night heard that Lee had surrendered. In his own words, he was "crushed with grief and threw himself on a cot where he wept long and bitterly." The beating of a saddened heart robbed him of sleep, and he fell to wording lines of poetry. Seizing a scrap of brown paper that had contained some fresh meat, he scribbled, hot from his fevered brain, those immortal verses of *The Conquered Banner*, and in the gray dawn he cast it down on the floor as he sank into a stupor, to awake and to rise again when his regiment received orders to move on to a place of surrender. That scrap of paper was afterward found by the woman of the house where Ryan slept. She must have discerned its merit, for months later it appeared for the first time in a Louisville newspaper, and ever since has been accorded a place among the finest American literature.

In my sojourns in the South, I have often met men and women whose allegiance was entirely with the Confederate cause. They were cultured people possessing as fine instincts of right and justice as I have ever found in the North. Yet the spirit of justice and freedom that fired the North to wipe forever the stain of slavery from our fair land will ever remain the noblest in human history. Nevertheless, it is to be questioned that had the North been the slave-owning section with millions of dollars invested in colored "property," would the spirit have been the same?

When I left home ten years after the close of the Civil War, I carried with me the vivid impressions gleaned during those fervid times. Of all the heroes of that great struggle, Henry Ward Beecher held first place in my mind. It was with no small pleasure that I heard Beecher was to lecture in the opera house in St. Paul in 1876. I went to hear him. And it was a pure delight, a real treat I shall never forget; nor will the picture of that massive head, those rugged features fringed with long hair, set on powerful shoulders, ever be effaced from my memory, nor the great voice that reverberated over that vast audience.

In those first years away from home, I had a passion for hearing public speakers, and never lost an opportunity to do so. Little did I dream that night, as I sat listening, that I should ever know Beecher personally or paint those powerful features. He held his audience breathless as he reviewed the great catastrophe of the war and the misfortunes that speedily followed the death of Lincoln on the assumption of the reins of government by Andrew Johnson. The question that agitated Congress—where to place the blame for the rebellion and how to punish the leaders and discipline the Southern states—had been heard on all sides. The victorious North was divided, however, on these issues; some fanatical radicals advocated the execution of all the leaders; some the exclusion of the Southern states for a period of years from participation in the government; others, more magnanimous, pleaded for mercy for the conquered leaders and for legislation to aid the rebuilding of the devastated and ruined Southland. Beecher said he stood firmly for the latter course, and no political layman had a wider influence. "It is a new South we must build; the passions of war must cease. The Confederate states have come to their knees, have pleaded for reinstatement in the Union. I say, bury all resentment and put forth a helping hand to the vanquished, as brother to brother in the great cause of humanity."

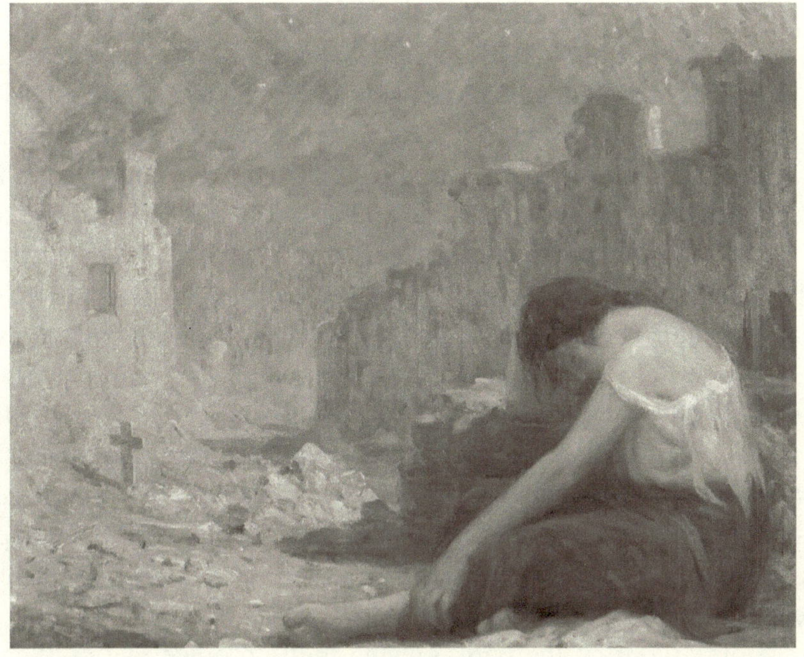

"Belgia" War's Desolation

Then he went on to tell of the immediate industrial boom following the war, the hectic exploitation of material resources, wild speculations, frenzied inflation of values, "until all the other nations looked on and saw that we were rushing on to ruin." He dwelt on the awful climax—the crash of '73, "when millionaires of today became beggars tomorrow; when millions of laboring men walked the streets and highways in search of work that they might feed their families;" then the slow coming back to normal conditions, not yet quite restored. He concluded a wonderful peroration on the potential glory of a reunited nation and drew a picture of our country fifty years hence, when a hundred million people would abide in peace and plenty, and when foreign nations would look up to us as the balance of power for peace and goodwill. I often think how truly prophetic were his words.

That lecture of Beecher's at a time when I was groping about for information and knowledge, which had been denied me while following the plow, I drank in with avidity, garnering impressions that have never become clouded and to which my thoughts have reverted a thousand times.

On the following day, he gave the prayer at the opening of the state legislature in the old Minnesota Capitol on Wabasha Street. The building was burned one night in 1881, and in the morning only blackened walls remained. One of my earliest pictures, a portrait of Governor Pillsbury, like everything else, went up in smoke. I had recently finished the canvas, and it was placed on the wall in the House Chamber.

About a year before Beecher's death, a Mr. Rockwood, a member of Beecher's church in Brooklyn, engaged me to paint a portrait of the great preacher. Then I came in personal contact with him and enjoyed his conversations. When I referred to my having heard him speak in St. Paul many years before and mentioned the subject, "Reconstruction Days," he launched into a review of those dreadful times following the war. An occasional leading question on my part was all that was needed to stir his reminiscence, and he would grow eloquent over the happy termination of that awful struggle and the permanent establishment of freedom, to which it was a delight to listen.

As my work on the portrait came to a close, we met only occasionally, and because I soon had to take the family back to St. Paul, my intercourse with Mr. Beecher terminated. The impression I formed in personal contact with him was that he was a most sincere, enthusiastic, and warm-hearted man, but somewhat lacking in tact, which sometimes no doubt gave an opening for attacks from designing and jealous people.

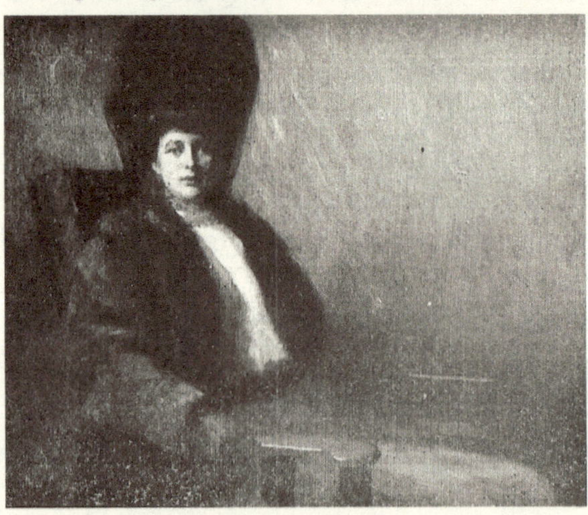

A scheme in brown

Chapter VIII
Handicaps

Art in the Northwest in the Eighties—A Chicago Art Exhibit—An Art Auction in New York

It would be hard to find a more devoted family than the one into which I married. There were three boys and five girls, devoted to each other and to their cousins, nephews, nieces, uncles, and aunts. All of them possessed the usual characteristics of the German race. They were good cooks and housekeepers on the feminine side, and industrious wage earners on the masculine, with the exception of Daddy Koempel, who was a dreamer, a painter, an inventor, a horticulturist, something of a doctor, and an all-around poor money-maker. The family was home-loving and satisfied with the lot of plain people. Consequently, when I took my wife to New York, being a total stranger there, she experienced agonies of loneliness. Her health was not good; she had three small children to care for, and she longed to be back in the old environment. At the end of eight months, her homesickness became so marked that I yielded to her request to send the family back to St. Paul. As I had hitherto been doing my work at home, I opened a studio at 21 University Place, shipping back to St. Paul our furniture, excepting the few things I should need for my bachelor's quarters in the studio. On the twentieth of May, I put my wife and children on the train in Jersey City. It was before the invention of vestibules on Pullman cars. As the long train pulled out of the station, I felt that I was parting with all that I held dear. The reluctance to let them go was so great that I sprang upon the platform of the last speeding car and went with them, intending to get off at the next stop. It was one of the through trains and I was carried far down into New Jersey. I came back to my lonely quarters late at night to cook my own meals and work from seven in the morning till six in the evening at my easel. It was my intention to earn all the money possible and then return to my family.

It was not a pleasant life, this living all alone. I am pretty good at cooking and washing dishes, but I can't say that I get any particular thrill out of it; yet I did that rather than patronize a cheap restaurant. After retiring the first night I discovered that I was not alone; there was a presence in the room that made me very uneasy. I had to scratch to keep alive. I arose and struck a light; they were creeping everywhere. The largest, a whopper, evidently the captain, was measuring the width of the rim on my bedstead. I undertook an experiment—dipping a little paint brush into turpentine I gently touched the curve of his back which made him quiver and curve still more and straighten his legs as if on stilts. After a few shivers he stood still and never moved again. I left him there for a week as a warning to his offspring. A turpentine war ensued until I had cleaned them out.

Frequently, I would seat myself at the window for fresh air in the evening, when some Italian with his dancing monkey and organ would grind out doleful airs that somehow enhanced my loneliness and made life all the more miserable. I was making money at the rate of fifteen to twenty dollars a day and anticipated paying off the mortgage on the home; but I experienced this first long separation from my family with genuine homesickness.

After my wife returned to St. Paul, leaving me to this unwelcome bachelor's existence, Mrs. Stacy, wife of General Stacy, became interested in my work and undertook to introduce me to some prospective patrons. She had me go with her to a very beautiful reception on Riverside Drive. I was presented to the hostess and a few of her guests, then I stood about shivering with stage fright. I had never seen such an array of beautiful women. How freely and gracefully they deported themselves, especially about the punch bowl! What a din and chatter of elegant language! Seeing me standing there so meek and forlorn, the hostess presented me to a couple of charming ladies, saying, "Here is an artist I want you ladies to know. Mr.-r-r—" Having forgotten my name, she paused—but I was frozen dumb. I stuttered and bowed without uttering a word, until Mrs. Stacy came to my rescue and most cleverly broke the suspense by a brilliant description of "Mr. Brewer's wonderful paintings." The twinkle in the eyes of one of the young ladies betrayed her amusement over my blushing embarrassment. I had forgotten my own name! My transfer from frontier conditions to more refined circles was a staggering experience. It took forty years for me to completely overcome that dreaded self-consciousness and diffidence.

In August, I received a letter from home saying that some old friends were to be there for dinner on Sunday. Homesickness got the best of me and I said to myself, "I shall be there, too." Consequently, I stepped into the house at St. Paul just as the family were being seated at the dinner table. Angelo, the eldest boy, saw me from the dining room and shouted, "Oh, there is Papa!" and flew to my arms weeping as though his heart were breaking with joy. I spent two weeks and then returned to New York to go on with drudgery. On the morning of December 31, I received a telegram announcing the birth of our fourth boy and requesting me to come home. I left for St. Paul on the night train! Proud to welcome the new addition to the family, I loitered for about six weeks, then took the family back to New York with me. This time they stayed a year and a half.

The pangs of homesickness again brought us back to St. Paul. The tenant who leased our house moved out and we took possession of the old quiet environment and spacious grounds we had labored so hard to build. This time I opened a studio at Seven Corners and started a class, hoping to secure pupils enough, with the small sums I could otherwise earn, to take care of the family. There was still a mortgage on the place. Times were getting hard. The boom days of the administration of Grover Cleveland had passed.

The worst financial panic that the country had ever experienced was breaking. Millionaires of the day became beggars of the morrow. Banks and business houses closed one after another. A few years previously, in St. Paul, the carpenter's hammer was heard everywhere, but now houses stood vacant and were available to tenants if they would only care for them.

Upon opening the studio at Seven Corners, which was large and well lighted and had a couple of smaller rooms, I found the place admirably suited for class work. I purchased a large number of antique casts—the Venus de Milo, Michelangelo's David, heads of Vitellius, Germanicas, Saint Francis, and others—torsos, feet, hands, etc., to provide suitable equipment for the antique class. I had a number of brass pots, kettles, jugs, a fine Russian samovar, in fact, every kind of object to tempt the students to do still-life work. There was a model throne for the figure model in the life class, also draperies and costumes. When the finishing touch had been added, my studio could be compared with any in the best private schools in New York. St. Paul had really never heard of such an institution, for this antedated the opening of the art school in Minneapolis under the able direction of Douglas Volk. Some of the academies and private schools had art classes, but the instruction usually given there was with a view of enabling the students to paint pretty pictures, copies of studies, colored prints and chromos, suitable for framing. These canvasses, after being touched up by the teacher and signed by the pupil, could be pointed to by the proud mothers with happy effect, and redounded to the reputation of their offspring.

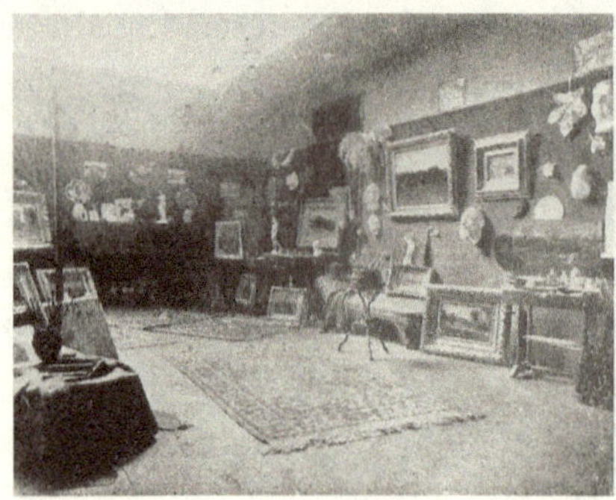

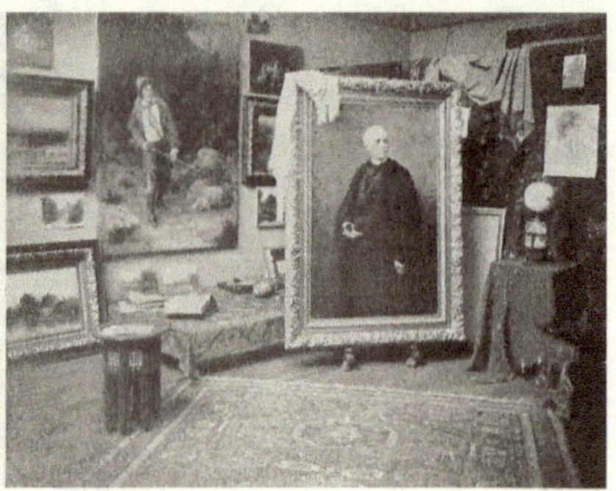

1886 My studios in New York 1902

I caused an article to be written for the newspapers describing my school equipment and classes, and pupils began to trickle in. On discovering that I taught drawing and painting only from the object or life model and that I would not allow the students to copy other pictures, many hesitated and did not return. Others would make a heroic effort for a week or more and then drop out. Only about one out of four remained.

Had I permitted my pupils to copy my own paintings or other pictures and helped them finish pretty subjects as other schools did, I could have had the rooms crowded with potential talent; but pursuing the courses of giving honest, worthwhile instruction as the schools of New York did, I failed to increase my list of students above a pitiful few. As an indication of the limited appreciation of real art in the Northwest at that time, and the way it was commercialized, the following narrative is significant:

Brown and Smith were a firm of portrait makers, Smith the artist and Brown the business manager. Smith was advertised as the greatest artist in the world. He had painted all the crowned heads of Europe, Asia, and Africa and was ready to paint the President of the United States, the Chief Justice of the Supreme Court, and every Senator and Member of Congress if they would only come to St. Paul and see his wonderful achievements.

His portraits were invariably made from photographs. Their price was one thousand dollars if the firm could get it—if not, they would accept five hundred, two hundred, one hundred, or less. Brown put out agents all over the country to take orders. The agents would collect their commission with the orders, the photos were sent in, and the finished product delivered afterward. They had a store for a gallery, with a big window filled with beautiful portraits, works of art. Once a great civic celebration commemorating some notable event in the development of the Northwest was given. In the parade were beautiful floats festooned with flowers, bearing goddesses of this and goddesses of that, drawn by prancing horses; lines of policemen, fire engines, hook-and-ladder wagons, Masonic and Odd Fellow bodies in glittering regalia, brass bands (every fellow tooting until red in the face), carriages bearing city and state officials, etc. Then came commercial and industrial wagons laden with products of factories, furniture, groceries, hardware, the product of butchers and bakers and candlestick makers. And in the line was a beautiful bandwagon with Smith and Brown's wonderful works of art, portraits of prominent people whom everybody knew, life size, in life-like pastel colors, in gorgeous frames gaily dangling on the sides of the bandwagon! The drum major directed the brass horn tooters, and the drum pounder hammered away to attract more attention than all the rest of the show. And why not? Art is the most important thing in the world, you know!

Smith and Brown had prospered beyond expectations during the great boom, from '84 to '88, but finally strife developed between them, which led to disastrous results. They could not agree. Criminations and recriminations took place until Smith, who was a wiry scrapper, decided to blacken Brown's eyes. This he did in truly pugilistic style. But Brown was the heavyweight, and when he landed a solar plexus blow it meant something. Smith punched with one oath, Brown with half a dozen. Which one scored the knockout, I never heard. Some said one; some said the other; others said both landed in jail for disturbing the peace. Particulars were aired in court afterward. The judge ordered the books of the firm brought in and an expert accountant to examine them. It was found that during that year the cash receipts of the firm had been over seventy-five thousand dollars. That is the story, which was circulated abroad. And thus, they came to the parting of the ways.

Brown was left without an artist, Smith without a business manager. Each opened a rival establishment, and both continued to make money.

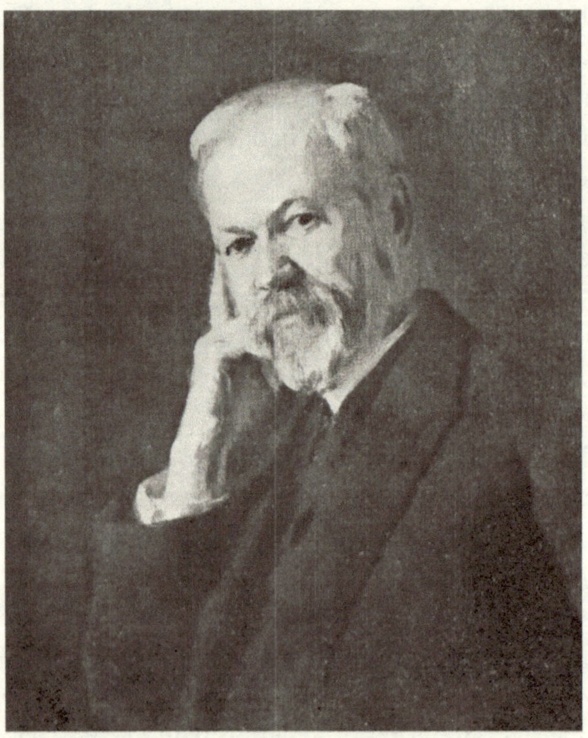

Dr. Leroy Brown, Second Prize, Minnesota State Art Commission, 1912

As the financial panic pinched tighter and tighter, the floating population left for other parts wherever employment might be had. Many who had thought themselves well fixed in professional positions moved to the country and planted potatoes and other things to be sure of having something to eat. Lawyers and doctors became small farmers or country peddlers; musicians became piano tuners, and artists sawed wood. How in all thunder Smith and Brown managed to float under such conditions was a puzzle, but they did, and I believe they are both living now.

Cultural conditions in the Northwest in the '80s were still in an embryonic state. There were no art schools, no public exhibitions, no symphony concerts, or grand opera. This condition could not remain always, for human nature is never the same, aspiring to better things. The enterprising businessmen of Minneapolis had organized an exposition association and had erected a building with eight or ten large galleries for the display of painting and sculpture. They had commissioned Mr. H. J. Smith to take charge of the Fine Arts Department. Smith was a connoisseur and critic—one of the best. Many of the heads of art institutions know nothing about technical art. Smith was a most efficient executive, and a rare critic of pictures and art generally. He was sent to Europe with *carte blanche* to bring to Minneapolis the best he could get of contemporary art. There in those spacious galleries we enjoyed the finest collection ever seen in this country up to that time, excepting perhaps that of the Centennial at Philadelphia in 1876. The World's Fair at Chicago was not yet dreamed of. Indeed, this small frontier town was a pioneer in the progress of art in the Middle West. It has been said that the example of the Mill City inspired the movement for the World's Fair at Chicago. I had painted a picture I called "Feeding Baby," using our curly-headed boy Wallace, of one year, and our maid as models. Seated by a window in the kitchen, she was feeding baby his porridge. Smith had invited me to exhibit, and I sent this picture. It was sold—my first sale out of an exhibition. One hundred and twenty-five thousand dollars-worth of painting were sold from this first exposition. These annual displays continued until the hard times preceding the great financial panic of 1893, and then had to be discontinued.

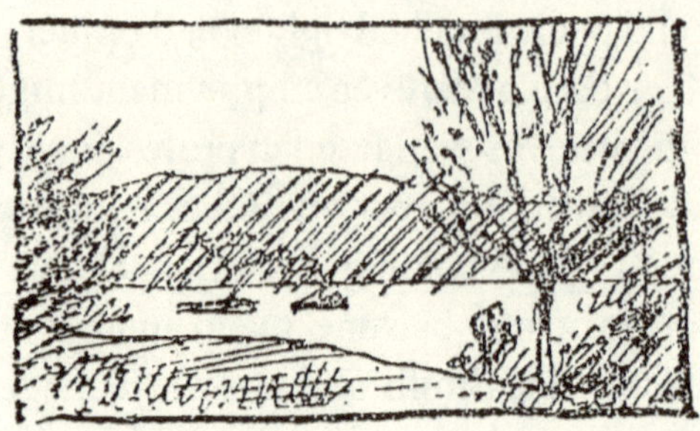

However, the business people of Minneapolis realized they could not have a progressive, cultured city without art, so after a lapse of several years, when the financial storm had blown over, they called a meeting one night and within an hour subscribed one million dollars for an art institute. Mr. Dunwoody, whose portrait I afterward painted, gave seven acres of ground practically in the heart of the city, and bequeathed one million dollars as a fund for the purchase of works of art. Mrs. Dunwoody repeated this magnificent donation.

When I first went to St. Paul, in 1875, there was scarcely art enough in the Northwest for a respectable cigar box label, nor was there much art west of the Alleghenies. I vividly contrast conditions then with now. With our millions on millions invested in both private and public galleries and art schools and endowments, when it is hard to find a city of twenty-five thousand population where there is not an art league or association promoting exhibitions, one concludes that culture and taste are growing by leaps and bounds.

One day Mr. Robert J. Wickenden, the artist, formerly of Chicago but now of New York, called and presented me with an invitation to join the Chicago Society of Artists. This society was an organization of energetic painters led by such men as Vanderpoel, Grover, Boutwood, and others, who had returned but recently from the Ateliers of Paris or Munich and represented about the first real art society west of the Atlantic Coast. How they spotted me away up in the frigid Northwest has always been a mystery, unless, perhaps, they had kept their eyes on the National Academy and noted some of the things I had sent to these exhibitions. Acting upon Wickenden's advice, I accepted the invitation. Later I received the following letter:

Chicago Society of Artists,
Chicago, Illinois,
Nov. 10th, 1891.

Mr. N. R. Brewer,
St. Paul, Minn.

Dear Sir:

I have the honor to inform you that you have been elected, unanimously, a member of the Chicago Society of Artists.

Your paintings examined critically at an unusually large meeting of the Association met their full approval and received hearty praise.

We feel assured that your excellent standing in art will add prestige to our Association.

Respectfully yours,

Win. W. Vernon, Sec'y.

To the exhibition that followed a few months later, I contributed four canvasses, two figure pieces, and a couple of landscapes. All were accepted by the jury and well placed on the walls. The display was given in the galleries of the old Atheneum Building, a wooden structure.

The present Art Institute building was not yet thought of. The World's Fair of 1893 had not become a reality. Chicago with her vast population of a million had paid little attention to the value of art as a civic asset. It needed a great International Exposition to stimulate local sentiment in that direction, and after the World's Fair of 1893, plans were perfected for building the present magnificent Art Institute on Michigan Boulevard.

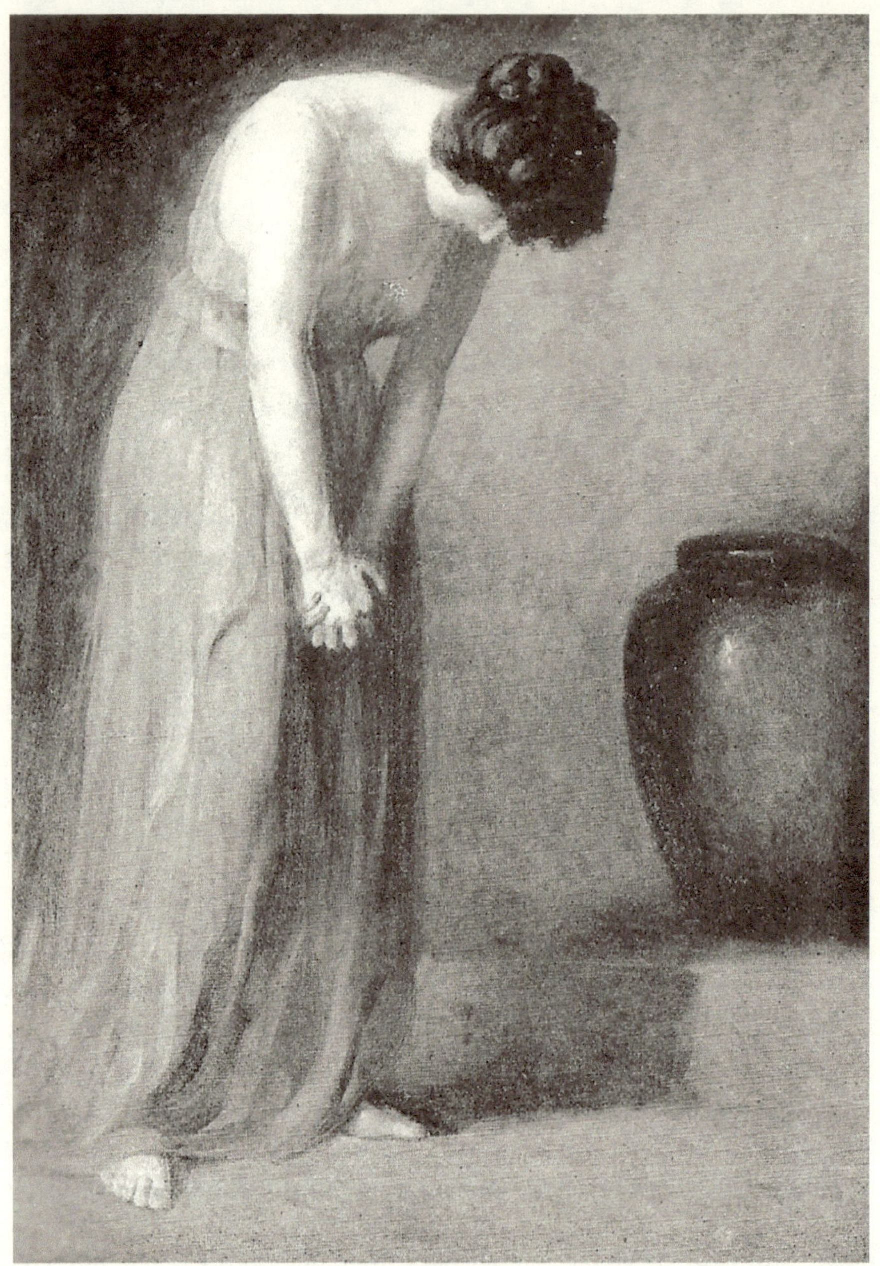

The Pot of Basil

Later, while on my way to New York to arrange a sale of my pictures, I stopped in Chicago to attend the reception at the opening of the exhibition. There I met Grover, Vanderpoel, Wickenden, and others, who were extremely cordial and enthusiastic over the display. A few days after I arrived in New York, I read in a New York paper of the burning of the Chicago Athenaeum Building and the destruction of the art collection. I immediately wrote Mr. Vincent for particulars and received the following reply:

> Chicago Society of Artists,
> Feb. 24th, 1892.
>
> Dear Mr. Brewer:
>
> Answering your query of the 21st inst. I regret to have to tell you that your pictures, with the entire collection, did 'go up in smoke.' Not a vestige of the exhibition remains. The artists, too, who had their studios in the building, lost their all.
>
> The origin of the fire is not known. It happened all so quickly no one was able to save anything. The committee had failed to take out insurance and so it is a total loss.
>
> The artists have decided however, to hold another exhibition in the near future, and we trust you will again be a contributor.
>
> Respectfully yours,
>
> Wm. W. Vernon, Sec'y.

Among my pictures destroyed in that fire was one I regretted to lose. I named it "The Artist and the Critic." It showed a young woman before an easel, painting. Beside her on a low footstool was a curly-headed boy, still in skirts, leaning toward the canvas. The model for the child was our fourth son, Wallace.

In spite of a half empty larder, I applied myself vigorously to painting landscapes, visiting the old scenes at Rochester and High Forest. I painted cattle, sheep, and still life, and in the course of a couple of years I found that I had over a hundred studies and finished pictures, which I could not sell. In New York I had seen paintings sold at auction, and I concluded that I might dispose of some of my pictures in that way. Not having the money for frames for them, I borrowed a thousand dollars on our household furniture and other assets and ordered Newcomb Macklin of Chicago to make modest frames for the pictures, which had been shipped to New York, the frames to follow. There I awaited them for several weeks and at last discovered that my frames had been smashed to kindling wood in a railroad wreck. Then I scrambled about and bought small moldings and had them knocked together, arranging with Lovett & Co. to put on a sale in their downtown gallery. The sale was advertised for March 17 (St. Patrick's Day). On the night of the 16th it began to rain and snow. I awoke in the morning to find a foot of snow and slush. Not even the elevated trains were running. I walked two miles from my boarding house to witness the slaughter of my pictures, for only three dealers were present and they had their own way in butchering me. I saw my pictures selling from five to twenty-five dollars each. The gross proceeds from the sale were something like six hundred dollars, or an average of less than six dollars each. Thus we live and learn. There must be a first and last time in all experiments. I returned home and paid off four hundred dollars of the thousand I had borrowed; the rest went for expenses.

We had spent a great many happy hours in the house I had built in St. Paul, and we had many experiences in the planning and building, the planting of trees, the garden and flowers so skillfully handled by Gust Malmquist. We used to raise great numbers of chickens and fought with the rats and other rodents that took our small chicks. I invented an incubator that was quite a novelty. With it I hatched ninety percent of the eggs. Our difficulty was in caring for the small chicks. One bright moonlight night I was awakened by a commotion among the chickens outside. Looking out, I saw a huge muskrat prowling about. Slipping on my socks, I seized a cane and went after him. When I came close to him, he showed fight and went for my stockinged feet. I struck at him wildly, but he dodged my blows. Knowing what he would do with my toes if he reached them, I tried to keep them high in the air, sometimes both feet at the same time. I was in my nightshirt, with ample freedom of action, yet the nearness of his lunges made me catch my breath and almost shriek, and he kept me dancing the liveliest jig of my life. I finally succeeded in landing a blow that finished him. But oh, my!—the excitement spoiled my sleep for the rest of the night.

One summer a herd of cows owned by a milkman annoyed me very much at night. They would break out of their enclosure and spook about our home and garden, doing much damage. Frequently, I had to get up and drive them off. There was a young bull with them. One night, dressed in the same ghostlike garb in which I attacked the muskrat—or rather when he attacked me—I was so exasperated at the damage done by the cattle that I proceeded to maul the bull with my cane, a thing which he resented, turning in defiance. By a lucky chance, I was able to grab his tail, and by beating him with the cane vigorously, I started him on a stampede. Hanging on for dear life, I was taken on a gallop down the slope, then he halted to turn at me. All I had to do was to hang on and play a crack-the-whip game until he decided that the whaling I was giving him was more than he wished, when he started ahead. Then I let go his tail and returned to my room, out of breath. This taught me that when confronting a bull the safest place is clinging to his tail.

My original purchase of ground on Grand Avenue consisted of lots on both sides of an alley, and when I built I placed the barn across the alley. Later on I sold the lots on which the barn stood and had a verbal agreement with the buyer that in a short while I would move the barn to my own lot. Time passed and I let the removal drift. One day I met the man who had bought the lot and I made excuses for the delay in moving the barn—to which he did not reply. A few days later I got a letter telling me that when he bought the ground, the barn was to go with the lots and warned me not to move it. With him in the purchase was his sister, who was a devout Seventh Day Adventist. Not trusting my memory, I went to talk with her, first asking her what she remembered regarding the agreement. After a few moments of thought, she said, "I believe you were to move the barn off the ground." I told her about her brother warning me not to move the barn and asked her what she thought I should do under the circumstances. She replied, “Well, I always leave such things to the Lord.” I concluded that here was a case where the Lord helps those who help themselves, and, having heard that possession is nine points in the law, I engaged a house-mover, Mr. Craig, a venerable old Scotchman, and arranged with him to start next morning on the job. Before noon that day, the barn was safely on my own lot. I said nothing to the man who had bought the property, but after a couple of weeks, discovering that he had lost a barn, he wrote me threatening dire consequences if I did not place the barn back on his ground, to which request I paid no attention. I never heard from him again.

All these incidents, and many more, connected with the building up of a home over a period of five years had rendered the place dear to us, and now to have to lose it caused no slight grief. However, “Let the dead past bury its dead” has always been part of my creed. So, we started out anew to establish a temporary home at Stacy, Minnesota, in a more simple way on a farm and to take up the toil with which I had been so well acquainted in my youth.

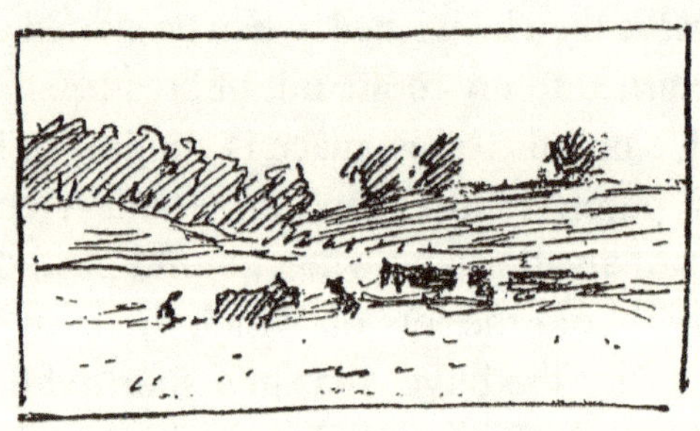

Chapter IX

Back to the Minnesota Farm

Henry W. Wack—Bill Irwin—Art and Holstein Cows—Strawberries and Potatoes—Finding My Backbone—Delightful Experiences with Charles Noel Flagg

When the sun of joy is hidden
And the sky is overcast,
Just remember light is coming
And a storm can never last.

Some years before the Panic of '93, Father had lost the greater part of his property and had moved to Stacy, Minnesota, where he bought a poor piece of land upon which was a small house. There, Father and Mother expected to spend their remaining days. When the financial storm broke, all I possessed was swept away, and as there was no market for my paintings, Father urged me to move to this piece of land. It edged the village where there was a school for our children. Here we could let them romp around barefooted in overalls, and we could raise sufficient food to satisfy their lusty appetites. A mortgage was negotiated, and the new house completed in November.

The children hugely enjoyed the change to the country. Always while in the city during the winter months, they had the usual spells of sickness—colds, sore throat, and croup. Strange to say, this winter in the country none of them showed any indisposition whatsoever, but all had wonderful appetites and went to school in the village.

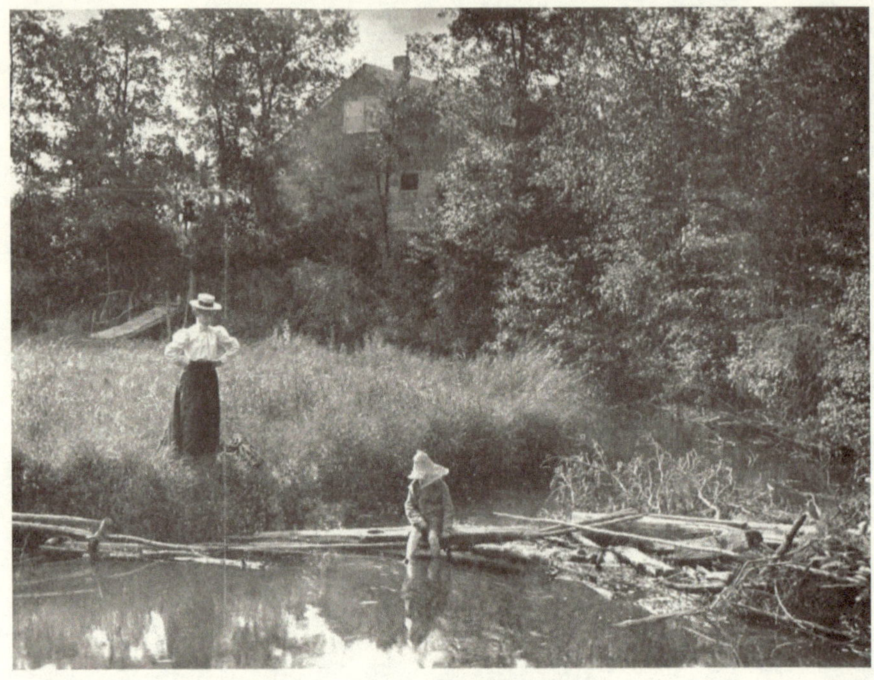

On the farm at Stacy, Minnesota

Returning home one cold day after a heavy snowstorm, I found them all coasting down the bank onto the ice in the creek. They were greatly excited over their new amusement. Reuben had completely torn half his trousers away, leaving exposed the postern part of his body and legs, which were red as a beet. The cold and the snow did not seem to faze him in his less-than-bathing-beach costume.

My wife, a wonderful mother, never failed before retiring to see that the babies were safely tucked in for the night. On one occasion, she found Reuben slumbering under piles of covering and wet with perspiration. Curious to know the reason for the extra warmth, she uncovered him and found that he had a dozen hen's eggs close beside him. He had turned incubator in the hope of hatching some little pet chicks he had longed to have.

However strenuous the effort we put forth to feed and clothe our six boys, we enjoyed the change from the congested conditions of New York. The beauty of the winding, tree-fringed stream that flowed close by the house, with the low-lying meadow on the opposite side, furnished numerous subjects for landscapes, which I could not resist painting whenever leisure permitted. Here the children romped and swam, chasing frogs and butterflies. They were given their pets to care for—chickens, little pigs, a few lambs, and so took their first lessons in animal husbandry and the practical life of the country. This life developed a love of nature that has led three of them to become landscape painters. I was constantly painting landscapes. I remember rising frequently at three o'clock in the morning and wandering through the wet grass down by the meadow to sketch the rising mists before the sun came up. One morning it was chilly, and my clothes got wet almost to my neck. I contracted a cold that kept me in bed for several days. On this farm I also painted many cattle pictures. One represented the herd crossing the bridge led by old Spot, the cow whose milk had nourished our twin boys through their babyhood.

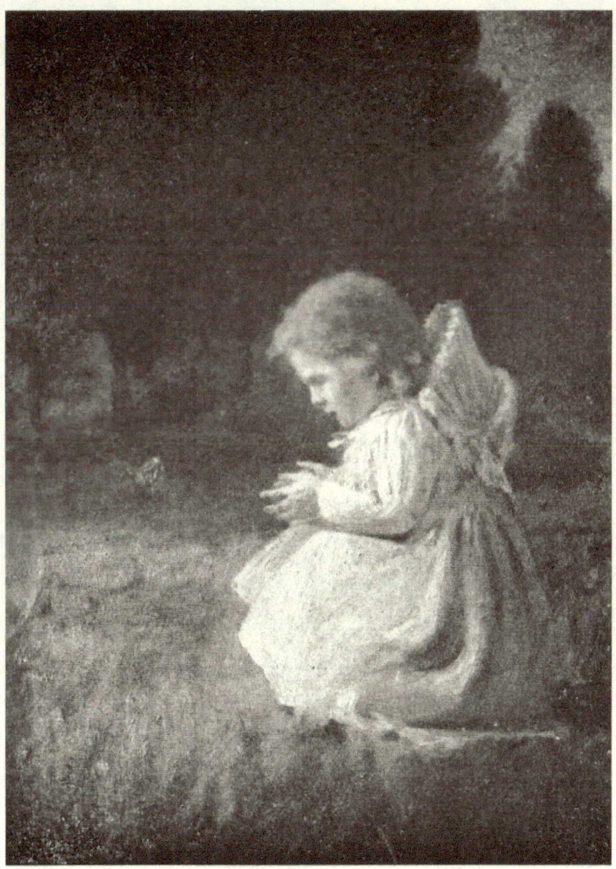

Chasing Butterfly

I kept my studio in St. Paul and returned to it each week or fortnight to pick up what I could in the way of ready money.

My friend Henry Wellington Wack, an all-around enthusiast in art and literature, a lawyer, writer, artist, lecturer, and general genius, used to spend much time at our farm, and I was indebted to him for many favors. He wrote for newspapers and magazines and persisted in writing me up whenever he thought I did a creditable picture. He had a blind confidence in my ability and has remained my friend throughout the years.

Wack was exploiting his friend Ellen Beach Yaw, as a concert singer. She was already famous for her beautiful high soprano voice and general musical attainments. Much had been said in the press of her slender, girlish beauty, her swanlike throat, and delightful stage presence. Wack was a great sportsman and would come to the farm with gun and rod, or snowshoes, and take the boys on long hikes in quest of game. They once bagged a family of wolves, and Wack actually brought in the wolf pups in his hunting coat. The first summer he was accompanied by the prima donna. She appeared to be quite as fond of nature as he was. Later it was said the twain were engaged to marry. Ellen enjoyed the country and the frugal hospitality my wife offered her, rambling along the stream and in the meadow with our boys, chasing butterflies and gathering birds' eggs, and singing charming lullabies to our twins, Adrian and Clarence, then one year old, while with an arm about each she jostled them on her knees. For a time, she lived with some relatives in north Minneapolis, and I went there to paint a picture of her clad in a pink gown with a broad-brimmed Gainsborough hat. Ellen was insistent on my working out a certain kind of expression to her features, which she fancied she wore. She would say, "You have me painted this way," assuming her normal look, "can't you catch this other expression?" thinking her look had changed, but for the life of me I could see no difference. I told her to try it over again. The result was the same—the change was only in her mind. In all of her moods, she was a very lovable woman.

On the farm, Wack would enjoy the work in the field or the hay meadow. One day he and I, with the aid of the boys, put up a huge stack, and he did all the pitching from the wagon while I shaped it.

While topping it off, with Wack under the last forkfull, one of the boys snapped the kodak at us. Another day they caught me plowing behind a horse-team. It was said that J. F. Millet could handle the scythe, as well as any of the peasants he painted. I am sure I could handle the plow as well, however badly I painted.

About this time I painted a portrait of Bill Irwin, dubbed *The Tall Pine*. Bill was a great criminal lawyer, said to be about the ablest manipulator of criminal evidence in the country. I think, although I am somewhat hazy on the matter, that he was appointed defense attorney in the famous Homestead Strike Case in Pennsylvania. It was said the Tall Pine could secure acquittal of three-fourths of his criminal clients in a jury trial. Consequently, he was much in demand. Tall and slender, with a large Ciceronian head and sensitive features, a square jaw and firm-set mouth, he was a splendid subject for a painter. Of my portrait he said, "It is the mask of Memnon." His eloquence was irresistible. He was a wit, a philosopher, and a widely read man. At times, in the presence of men only, his language was not edifying. His professions were inconsistent. Pretending to believe in spiritualism and religion, he was blasphemous in his use of the name of the Deity.

Once he told of going to a country town to defend a man accused of grand larceny. He went to the jail to get the man's story and concluded he had not a ghost of a chance of escaping a prison term and told him so. "There is only one thing under high Heaven that will save your damn carcass from doing time," he said, "and that is, you have to get down here with me on your knees and pray to the God of Abraham, the God of Isaac, and the God of Jacob with your whole damn heart, and if you don't do it, you damned idiot, you will crack rocks the rest of your damn life." Continuing the story, he said, "And we did, we prayed for an hour. Then we went into court, odds against us—a clever prosecuting attorney, overwhelming evidence in his hands, an intelligent jury. The trial over, I boarded the train for home. At the second station a telegram was handed to me. It read, 'Acquitted,' and I'll be damned if it was not the grace of God that did it."

My portrait of Irwin and one I had made for Mrs. Davis, wife of Senator Cushman K. Davis, were hung side by side in the exposition in Minneapolis. Mrs. Davis was a beautiful woman, and as the wife of the senior United States Senator, who was Chairman of the Foreign Relations Committee, she was popular in Washington. She had the fairest, most rouge-like skin I have ever seen. In those days, it was not customary for ladies to paint their cheeks as they do now. After one of the sittings, I asked her please to use less rouge the following day. Her companion, a delightful little lady, stepped up and pinched her cheek, leaving a perfectly white spot. "Do you call that rouge, Mr. Brewer?" she asked. I had been completely deceived by that wonderfully translucent skin and apologized for my blunder. These portraits were both for exhibition pictures; that is, they were not orders. A year or so later, both Irwin and Mrs. Davis came and offered me ridiculously low prices for them, which I was glad to accept for obvious reasons.

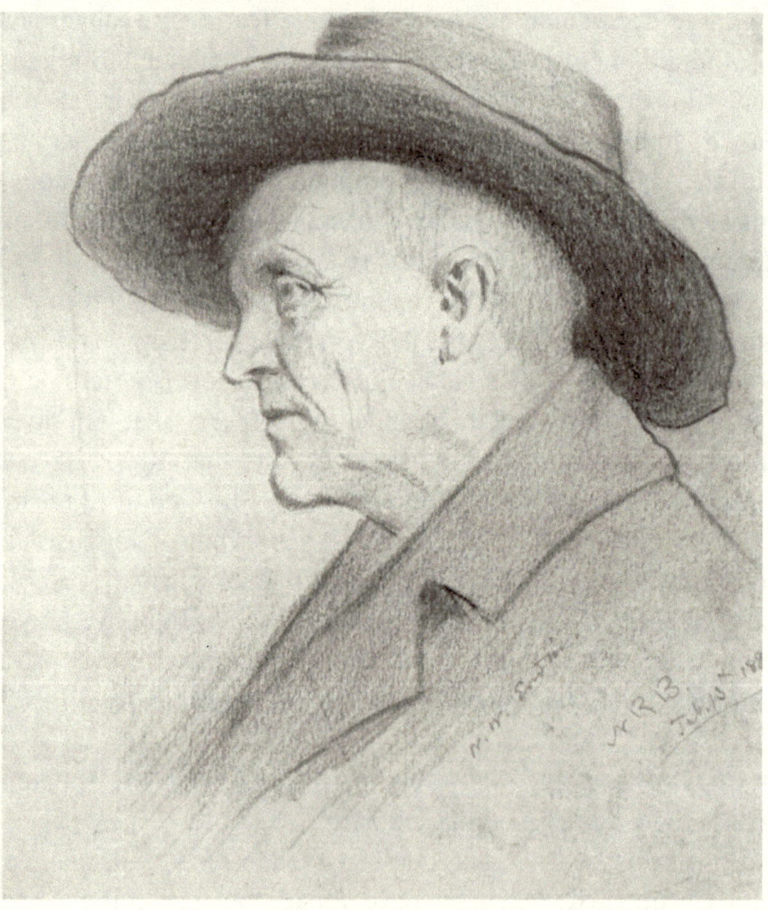

Bill Irwin "The Tall Pine"

I began stocking up the Stacy farm, and wherever I could trade a picture for a cow or horse or pig, I did so. In the spring, we planted four acres of strawberries. I rented land adjoining our field and planted corn, with a view of raising hogs and cattle. We hired men, and during my absence each week from the farm, they would sit down and rest in the shade or play high jinks in the village, but when I came home, they suddenly became industrious. They complained to others, however, that when I was home, I was too much of a slave driver. I felt I had to be to get equivalent work for their wages.

The first winter was a hard one, and I must confess that if it had not been for some of my city friends who came to my rescue, we would have seen quite a few hungry days. As it was, New Year's found our cupboard empty. Nevertheless, there was something wonderfully beautiful about the winter landscape, and I took the boys down to the meadow, where we built a fire, and I painted a 20 by 30 sketch. I had no money with which to buy colors, and as there was a keg of white lead in the house, with some black and yellow ochre and red, I used these. The effect was quite good. We ran onto a tiny stream in the meadow, which was literally filled with frogs. All we had to do was to scoop them up. Sending home for a pail, we brought back frog legs, enough to last several days.

I traded a picture to Isaac Staples of Stillwater, who was an importer of Holstein cattle and a breeder of fine racehorses. I was to have five thoroughbred Holstein cows and a bull for the picture. When we went to get the cattle, Staples called his men and told them to bring out the five poorest cows in the bunch. When I saw them, I protested. He said, "Well, if you don't want them, keep your damn picture." I acquiesced, and we drove the cattle to the farm. Later that bull made us lots of trouble. He became very ugly and hard to manage, and I felt uneasy every time I left home lest something might happen. Roxy Reber, who had a restaurant in St. Paul, said he would give me thirty dollars' worth of beef for the brute if I would bring him in. The men refused to take him that long distance—about forty miles through a sparsely settled country, with no road, save a wagon-track, through the sand. I asked my sons Angelo and Ed if they would not like to go with me to deliver the bull, and they were delighted. Angelo was fifteen and Ed younger. We hitched the bull behind a lumber wagon, and as the weather was warm, we drove during the night. After going some two or three miles, I noticed the horses were having hard work and that the bull was pulling one way while they were pulling the other. Nothing would do but for one of us to walk behind and pommel him with a club to inspire a different gait—with the result that I had to walk nearly all the way. It was a clear, beautiful night, with a full moon. At midnight we let the animals rest and spread some blankets on the ground, thinking we might sleep awhile. The boys did, but no sleep came to me. I lay gazing at the moon and wondering about the possibilities of getting rich on a farm. We resumed our journey and I realized what a grand companion the moon may be to the lonely traveler, for we saw it rise in the East and lower in the West as we labored along the dusty road. At daybreak we arrived in town and disposed of the bull.

At that time, I was working on a portrait in Minneapolis for a lady by the name of Tourtellot, for which I was to receive one hundred dollars. So letting the boys go to their aunt's home to sleep and spend the day, I boarded a streetcar for Minneapolis to work on the picture. The old lady was fussy, especially about her dress, but the lash of necessity goaded me on to labor to please her. You can imagine my physical condition after a day and night without rest. I worked on the picture until about four o'clock in the afternoon and on the way back to St. Paul, seated by the window in a crowded streetcar, I leaned against the wall, soon falling into a profound slumber and began to dream about an incident which had recently happened on the farm. We once had a large colt, which was a congenital runaway. One day Angelo and I were driving in a buggy when the brute suddenly took a notion to run. She seized the bit between her teeth and dashed forward. There was no more use in trying to restrain her than to stop an avalanche. Springing to one side of the road, the buggy struck a tree, and she crashed the shaft free from the rig and pulled us both over the dashboard. I fell heavily on my neck and shoulders; in fact, for a time I was literally stunned, and the injury somehow affected my nervous system for several weeks. So when I fell asleep in the streetcar I began to dream of this fractious colt. Only this time she seemed to be backing up instead of bolting forward and was about to upset the rig, when I rose up excitedly and shouted, "Get out of here!" A lady sitting beside me screamed, evidently thinking me drunk or perhaps something worse. My own voice awakened me, and I realized my position. I quietly sat down again, and pulling my hat over my eyes, leaned against the window pretending I was asleep.

Coming back to Mrs. Tourtellot, I subsequently finished the picture and received my pay; but a couple of years later, the fashions having changed, she insisted on my painting the dress over to bring it up to date!

After supper we hitched up and drove back home that night, arriving just at breakfast time only to discover that the railroad train had killed one of the imported Holstein cows. This cow had a prize record, but she had outlived her usefulness to a great extent and was one of less actual value than an old scrub. I was urged to put in a damage claim against the railroad. They ignored the claim, and I took the case to court, securing a compromise settlement for one hundred dollars, which was more than a good price, as the best graded cows could be had for twenty-five dollars. I had just been sued for back pay by one of the farm hands, whom I discharged for the good reason I had nothing with which to pay him. This time he won, and the hundred dollars I received for the cow enabled me to pay and satisfy the judgment, thus saving more trouble.

Occasionally, I got a picture to do in pastel from a certain picture-agent who was willing to pay ten dollars a piece for them. For four years it was one long, desperate struggle to find enough to eat and pay the men. The farm soil was unproductive because of extreme drouth for two years. Many people can remember the awful period of drouth the year of the great forest fires that wiped away the towns of Hinckley, Sandstone, Willow River, and other Minnesota villages, when over six hundred people lost their lives. The cornfields withered. The potato crop was a total failure. The frost and drouth destroyed the strawberry blossoms and no crop resulted. The third year they blossomed beautifully and promised a bountiful harvest. A caterpillar scourge passed over the country devouring the leaves on all trees and shrubs and some of the grain crops. They crawled by the millions in one direction from southwest to northeast, and as the berries were just beginning to ripen, the caterpillar army put in its appearance. I saw that our crop was doomed unless something was done to block its advance. A hasty trench must be dug. I took the team and setting the plow to a great depth made a furrow around the border of the field; then with spades we dug it deeper, with a bank on the inside having walls sloping under. The soil was of such a character that no caterpillar could crawl up it without falling off. Then we got many gallons of kerosene. The pest army swept down into the trench, but none of them was able to scale the wall. We went along and sprinkled the squirming pests two inches deep in the trench. No caterpillar could stand a kerosene bath. The first touch made him wriggle into all kinds of shapes for a moment, then lie still forever more.

My scheme was effective, and our berry crop developed beautifully. We bought ten thousand boxes for shipping the berries. We had some thirty pickers and shipped the crop to a commission house, only to find that the price was so low that it would barely pay the expense of picking, boxing, and shipping. I went to town hoping to collect quite a sum and came home crushed. The bubble of hope had burst. About half the berries, some ten thousand quarts, had been gathered. Buying sugar, we canned the rest of the crop. On the day of the Battle of Santiago de Cuba, in the Spanish-American War, my wife and I labored in a temperature of nearly one hundred, over a hot stove, canning fruit. That winter there was no sale for our product, and our storehouse of preserves lasted for several years. I shipped three carloads of potatoes, for which I realized but thirteen cents a bushel.

Wack had been induced to publicize the musical career of the late Mrs. William Sprague of Rhode Island. who thought she had a wonderful voice. He obtained a commission for me to go to Boston and paint her full-length portrait. He hoped to use it for advertising at the time of her debut with the Boston Symphony Orchestra. This was to take place in a short time. To execute the commission, I was obliged to leave the farm to the care of the hired men. There were several acres of potatoes in the field ready to be dug and marketed and acres of corn to be husked and fed to the swine. When I returned from Boston early in December, my wife, ill and disgusted with farming, had moved back to the city and taken a house, leaving the men in charge. I found the potatoes had frozen in the field, the corn was unhusked, and the animals were starving through neglect—some of them having actually died. I paid off the men, sold everything to the neighbors for whatever I could get, and closed the place. Father had died two years previously and Mother came to live with us in St. Paul.

After moving away from the farm, there were many distressing times when the cupboard was empty, while I was trying to pass for a measurably successful artist. For ten dollars per month we were living in a two-story, eight-room cottage on Fairmount Avenue. The exterior of the house looked comfortable, but inside at times there were no savory odors of frying steaks coming from the kitchen.

Christmas Eve I tried hard to collect money from my pupils to buy some presents for the children and food enough for a Christmas dinner, but in vain, and without carfare I walked the three miles home. The children gathered about me with expectant eyes. My wife came into the room, and realizing that there was no food in the house, I could bear up no longer and broke down completely. Taking her in my arms, I told her my sad story. Presently she went upstairs and returned, handing me a ten-dollar bill. "Well, dear," she said, "I have been saving this a long time, and we will have a Christmas dinner at least," and she bade me "cheer up." The anxiety born of the desire to feed, clothe, and educate my family properly wore upon me. As I opened my eyes each morning, the reality of the struggle came back with harrowing force. I took a smaller studio in the Schutte Building. Eight dollars a month was the rent and it became a task even to pay that small sum.

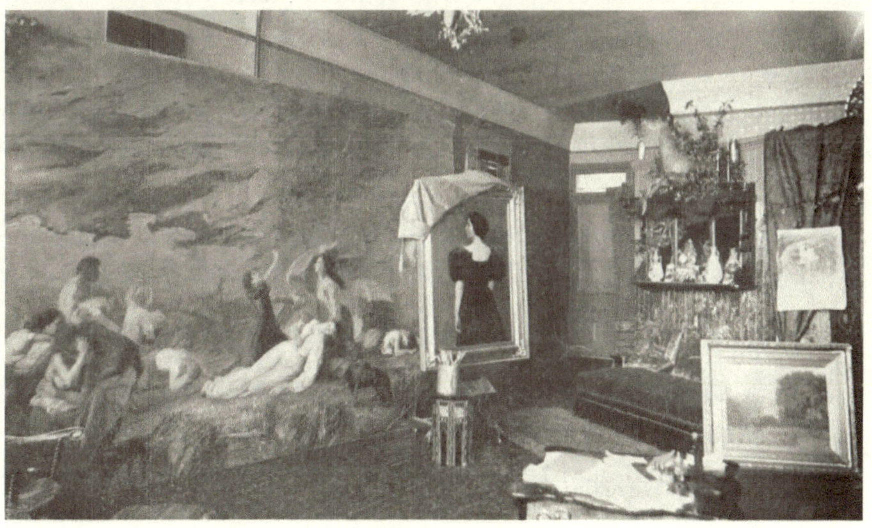

My St. Paul studio—1895

A bill for certain hardware that I had bought at a store on Rice Street had been running several months because I was unable to pay it. The man, a brusque roughneck, had come for his money several times, when I always explained my situation and assured him that just as soon as I could possibly get the money I would let him have it. One morning he came in with fire in his eyes, determined to collect the bill. I again began to explain, but he interrupted and demanded his pay by the following morning or he would sue me. His words aroused something within me, and the thought occurred to me that here was a man who would take the bread out of my children's mouths, their clothing from their backs without the slightest remorse. Did I not honestly want to pay him? Was I not doing everything in my power to care for my six little dependent ones? And yet this man would haul me into court! My temper rose; I stepped to the door and threw it wide open. I said, "You heartless cur, you would take the bread out of my children's mouths. You get out of here, and if you ever come back with that bill I'll kill you!"

On that day something was born in me. No longer did I slink around the block to avoid meeting some man whom I owed. My pictures had been accepted by the National Academy; I was honestly striving to do the right thing and to make the most of my art; so why should I blush in the presence of anyone who could not realize that art is something higher and better than mere money-getting. It is said of Whistler that he once sold a picture and sometime afterward borrowed it back for an exhibition. He failed to return it to the owner. In time, the latter demanded it, asking Whistler to return the property. "My dear sir," said Whistler, "this is not your property. You happen to be the custodian of it only. It is the property of the world—it is ART." I am by no means trying to compare my work with Whistler's, but I believe there are some men who could not appreciate that situation.

Another man to whom I owed a bill for fuel, a Mr. Dowlan by name, was a splendid, kind- hearted fellow who had two sons. One of them had charge of collections for the concern. Frequently, he came to collect what I owed, and I made the usual promises to pay as soon as possible. One morning when he quietly handed me the bill again, I was about to speak when my feelings overcame me and choked my voice. I turned away. Noticing this, he put the bill back in his pocket and in a kind voice said, "Well, Mr. Brewer, I realize your circumstances, and I shall not bother you anymore. If you are able to pay it sometime in the future, it will be acceptable; if not, it will be all right anyway." He left me feeling less bitter toward circumstances.

One winter Charles Noel Flagg again visited the city of St. Paul to execute some portrait commissions. He lived at the Minnesota Club, and as soon as he heard that I was in town, came to my studio. In fact, he spent many leisure hours there. A more pleasing personality or delightful conversationalist I have never met. At that time, I was painting a portrait of a prominent society lady whose name I dare not mention, for she is still living. She was well-known in the city as a crank and a snob. No one was ever able to please her. Her husband had requested me to paint her portrait, and when I first began to lay it out in charcoal and had but a bare outline of the head, she stepped around in front of the canvas and exclaimed, "Why, that doesn't look like me!" All through the work she never had an encouraging word to say, for this was wrong and that was wrong. Flagg used to come in and frequently would hear her denunciation of my picture. One day he said, "Brewer, do you know how I would treat a woman like that? I would kill her with kindness." "Well," I said, "she is a cat with nine lives, and you would have a job on your hands." Finally, the husband on seeing the picture called me aside and said, "Don't pay any attention to my wife's criticisms. I like the picture, and when you are ready to put your name on it, I will give you a check." I was never more prompt in writing my name. In about a week, Flagg came to me and said that she had requested him to paint her little boy's picture, but since she was a patron of mine he didn't want to do it unless it was all right with me. I cheerfully said, "Go ahead, Charlie; you can have all the fun there is in it." The picture was painted at her home. In answer to a vigorous knock at my door one morning, I opened it and Flagg brushed in past me in a great temper wearing a cape—handsome, his black eyes flashing. He began to shout maledictions upon that "awful woman." I said to him, "Well, Charlie, why don't you kill her with kindness?" His temper melted, and after a moment he said, "I would like to have you come up to the house and see the damn thing." This I did, and while waiting at the door I said, "I presume Mrs. — is home now." "Home now!" he repeated; "no, not when I come." They had so many disagreements that she absented herself every time he was expected. Looking at the picture, I advised him to consider it finished, and he went to the husband and got his check. A few days afterwards, I met the lady on the street, and she said, "Mr. Brewer, I'm sorry I didn't have you do my boy's picture, as I do not like the one I have had painted." Of course I had to be polite, and joined my regrets with hers, but at heart it was another story—no money could have tempted me to tackle another picture for her.

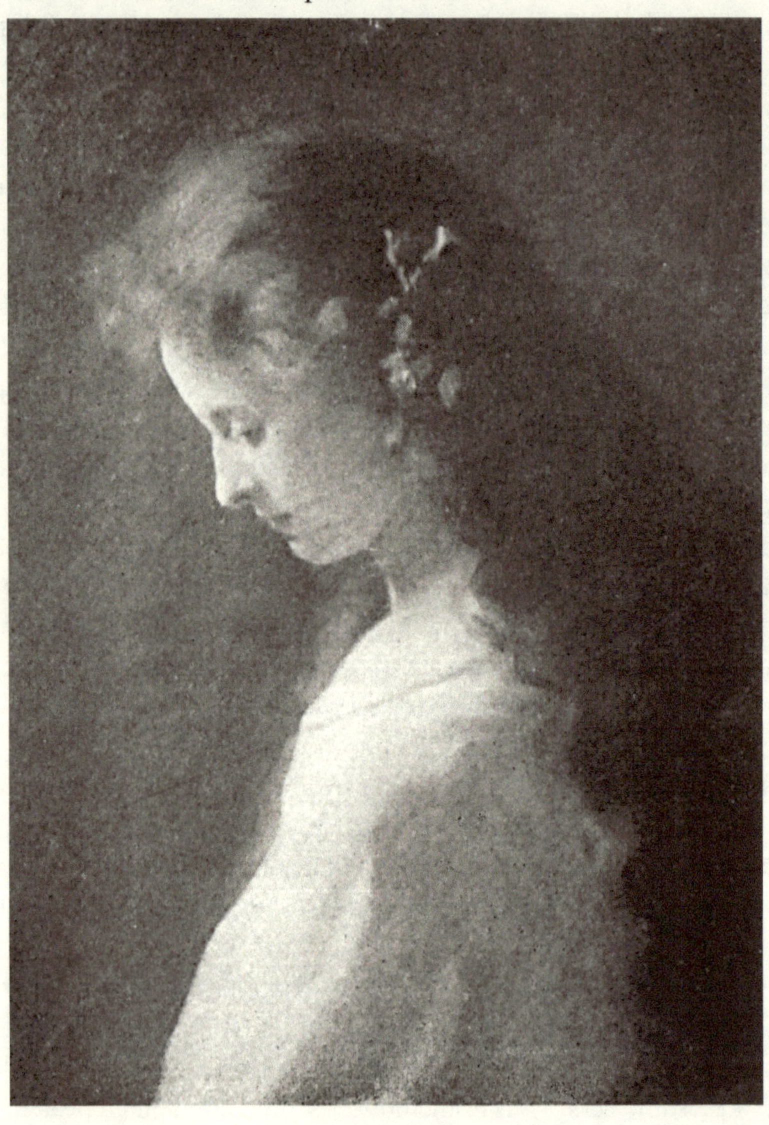

Alice

When Flagg was whiling away the time in my studio that winter, I often began a still life, usually a fruit piece, and worked while he talked most entertainingly about his experiences—of his life as a student in Paris or his engagements as a portrait painter or teacher— all of which I craved and enjoyed, since such experiences had never been a part of my own life. Flagg was very complimentary of what he termed my facility in handling color and getting quick effects. I would hit off a still life in two or three hours, and several times he exclaimed, "My God, I don't see how you do it!" His way of working was slow and deliberate, with a heavy brush and thick impasto of color. When he got the thing *premier coup*, it was masterful for its technical quality, always conservative, consistent, and well-drawn. but I could not work in that way. I brushed in the planes and masses loosely, in my heat of enthusiasm, in a manner he seemed to admire, while I would have given anything to be able to do it in his way. One day I proposed his sitting for me to paint a head of him, and no finer subject could be found. His strong features, dark piercing eyes, waving black hair, black mustache, and wonderful flesh color would tempt the brush of any artist. In two hours I had a fine head, with which he was delighted—I recall how the brush strokes on the lapel of his coat did not quite please him, and how he seized a dry brush and whipped the fresh paint crisscross in a few places but would not touch the rest of the picture. He urged me to send it to the Academy Exhibition, but I never did. It appeared, however, in one of the Salmagundi Club displays. I held it a treasure, as a memento of a valued friendship, and had it in many of my one-man shows.

One day I told Flagg I wanted to return to New York and go into a school for at least a year to freshen up. "No, you don't need to do that," he replied; "you can teach most of those fellows down there. You should go on painting what you see and feel in your own way. You will thus develop your individual style, which after all is the thing that makes any artist great." Several times Flagg urged me to come to Hartford, Connecticut, where he lived, and once he said, "I should like to see you paint my eldest daughter."

At the close of my exhibition at the Salmagundi Club in 1904, New York papers published extensive notices of my showing. There were in the exhibition several portraits of notable society people, including the Jefferson and Anglin pictures. Flagg wrote, "I see you are much talked about. When are you coming to see us?" It was my intention to visit him, but I delayed too long and meanwhile my friend passed away. A few years later, while I was going through the galleries of the Herron Art Institute in Indianapolis with the director, three people entered from another room, and as the director knew them, he left me to greet them. Presently, he returned and asked me if I would like to meet Mrs. Flagg and her daughter, whom I had never met. With them was a gentleman, a writer on one of the big papers, who years before had written an article on those very sketches Flagg had seen in the Stevens Art Shop, where our acquaintance began, which resulted in my going to New York with his letter to Tryon. It was Flagg who found me, a groping Western waif in art. My gratitude will never die for the good counsel he gave me, as a father gives a son. In my heart's fullness, I decided to part with my treasure, Flagg's portrait, and told Mrs. Flagg I was going to send it to her. Later I received this letter:

> "Tuesday 16th
>
> "My dear Mr. Brewer:
>
> "I hardly know how to thank you for that very interesting picture of my husband, which has just arrived—our meeting and also the history of the portrait. I shall have it framed at once and will always count it one of our greatest treasures. Everything connected with the picture is most interesting. I am very glad that you are coming to Hartford, and I hope you will surely come and see us. Thanking you again for your kindness, I am, with kind remembrances from my daughter and myself,
>
> "Your sincere friend,
>
> "Ellen F. Flagg
> "234 Washington St."

Chapter X
Sons of the Northwest

Most Rev. John Ireland, the Churchman—James J. Hill, the Empire Builder—Hon. Pierce Butter, the Jurist—Hon. Frank B. Kellogg, the Statesman—Governor John A. Johnson

During the exhibition of my pictures by the Little Rock Art League, a gentleman and lady stopped before the portrait of Archbishop John Ireland, and the lady was heard to remark, "What an expressive face! But I don't like him; he is both Republican and Catholic." "That is just why I do like him," retorted the man. "While I am not a Catholic, I am a Republican, and there is one of the outstanding Republicans and patriots of this country. As to his religion, that makes no difference with me. Once I heard a speech of his in Chicago, and ever since, I have had the greatest respect, not only for Archbishop Ireland but for the great Church he represents, in its attitude toward politics and government in these days of political-church meddling."

One could not fail to be attracted by Archbishop Ireland's dignified yet active, nervous, executive manner. Those large expressive eyes, the broad forehead, firm mouth and chin, benign yet serious countenance, the downward bend of the handsome nose, resembling the face of Dante, stirred admiration and made a lasting impression.

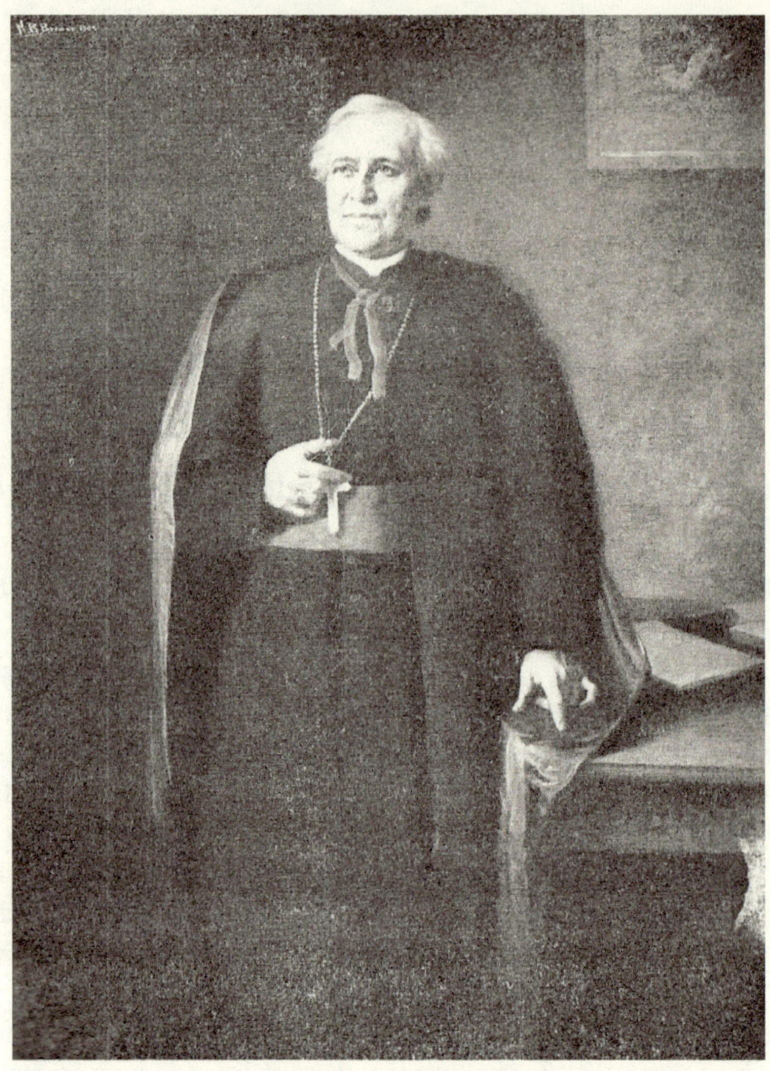

Most Reverend John Ireland

The first time I met Father Ireland was the day before his consecration as Coadjutor Bishop of the Diocese of St. Paul, in 1875. On the following day, I attended the solemn consecration services in the old Cathedral on St. Peter Street. The sermon was preached by the Rev. Thomas O'Gorman, a classmate of the new Bishop. O'Gorman, famous for his eloquence, afterward joined the Order of Paulist preachers in New York, where his Lenten sermons in St. Patrick's Cathedral attracted wide attention. Later he resigned from the Order and accepted the Chair of History in the Catholic University of America, to be followed some years subsequently by his appointment by the Pope to the Bishopric of Sioux Falls. On the occasion of the elevation of his friend Bishop Ireland to his new position in the hierarchy, O'Gorman's eloquence was masterful. I had not, up to this time, heard many sermons of any kind, none by Catholic preachers, and I must say the eloquence, as well as the substance of O'Gorman's discourse drove home with exceptional force to my open, hungering consciousness.

Sometime later, I became intimately acquainted with Bishop Ireland, who aided me in my readings and spiritual gropings. At that sensitive time of my life, coming in intimate contact with a man of Ireland's exalted intellectual and spiritual attainments, it is not surprising that I should have received impressions that are still vivid with me after more than half a century. And all through the long years, up to the time of his death, I was more or less in contact with him. Some of his achievements during his administration were his colonization scheme in bringing the poor Connemara peasants from Ireland to the fertile prairies of Minnesota; his organization of Father Mathew Temperance Societies in most churches throughout his diocese; his experiments in the matter of religious training in the schools, controversies with several prominent ministers of other churches who frequently attacked his Church's doctrines and policies; his fight against the Cahensly movement and staunch defense of the Americanization principles in the Catholic Church in this country; his intercession with President Roosevelt which resulted in Secretary Taft's being sent to Manila to settle the Friar land question after our acquisition of the Philippine Islands. Nor did the Bishop meet with easy sailing in all his efforts for the welfare of his beloved Church and Country. No man ever takes an active or aggressive part in any uplift or altruistic work of a semi-political character, that he does not become a target for the criticism of narrow-minded and jealous people even within his own camp. And Ireland had his critics. He was accused of being more politician than Bishop. His total abstinence crusade was sneered at by liquor-loving people both outside and in the Church. Especially was criticism ripe at the time of his war on Cahenslyism.

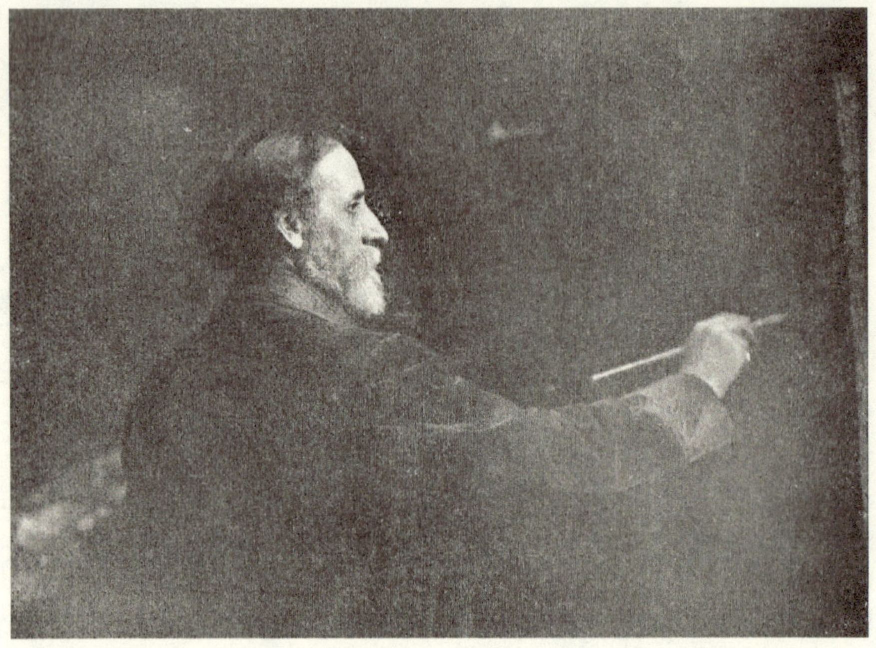

The author at fifty years.

Bishops Ireland, Spaulding, and Keane were foremost in a movement to establish a great Catholic University at Washington, and Ireland and Keane were commissioned by the American Episcopate to lay their plans before the Roman authorities. During their stay in Rome, the information reached them that a certain Father Abbelin, of the Archdiocese of Milwaukee, was there representing the German Bishops of the United States in a petition for certain legislation, which would greatly promote the power and influence of the German element in the Church in the United States. For a long time, this subtle German influence had shown itself in the churches, schools, and parishes presided over by German pastors, whose sermons were always in the German language. The catechism and principal studies in the schools also were in German. Efforts were never wanting to segregate German immigrants from English-speaking parishes wherever possible, to perpetuate German customs and prejudices in the United States. It was hinted that German state authorities were even sympathetic and aided the practice. German newspapers never failed to inspire German patriotism and love of the Fatherland. Conditions like these, especially in the Northwest, where the German immigrant population was large, rasped the soul of Ireland, as well as of other members of the Episcopate. Consequently, on learning of the movements of Father Abbelin, Ireland and Keane lost no time in presenting a counter memorial to the effect that the German demands were needless and dangerous to the Church.

The Roman authorities, on hearing both sides, approved the petition of the American Bishops and not only rejected the German appeal, but also administered a warning that no such petition should ever again be presented at Rome. The Roman Tribunal adopted, in their entirety, the views of Bishops Ireland and Keane. Thus did the first attempt to fasten foreign influence on the Church in America come to an ignominious end. But in December 1891, there was held at Lucerne a conference of presidents of Catholic immigration societies of various European countries. This conference commissioned Herr Peter Paul Cahensly, Secretary General of the St. Raphael Society for protecting German Catholic immigrants, to present to the Pope a memorial, substantially the same as that presented by Father Abbelin.

Again, Archbishop Ireland took the lead in opposing these proposals. He pointed out that what the legislation sought, if granted, would aid in the perpetuation of German customs and influence in the heart of the Church in America. That it meant the Germanizing of parishes and dioceses and had for its aim the establishing of a permanent Germany in the United States. He was opposed to stamping the Catholic Church in America as an alien institution, which would be regarded as a menace to the country. It was again due to the efforts of Ireland in a large measure that Cahenslyism and the German movement was at last defeated. Time has vindicated the wisdom he showed. He always stood for the principles of a great "melting pot"—to make all immigrants who come to our shores and their descendants, loyal citizens of his beloved America. And no man has had a wider influence in fostering and developing that sense of loyalty to our national institutions and our flag, now held by the twenty million of American Catholics, than John Ireland.

In later years with a very dear friend, Mr. Lucien Warner, a delightful gentleman and a good Presbyterian, I attended the solemn services of conferring the pallium that made Ireland Archbishop, with jurisdiction over a vast Archdiocese. This time the sermon was preached by Archbishop Ryan, who said, "The Pallium conferred here this morning in the presence of this august assemblage of ecclesiastical dignitaries of the Church, I can assure you, will rest on strong shoulders, shoulders capable of bearing the grave responsibility with honor to the recipient and to the Church."

About 1905 several of the Archbishop's friends prevailed upon him to permit me to paint his portrait. The sittings were made at the episcopal residence, and like most busy men he proved a poor sitter. His countenance and manner, however, were not of the sphinxlike character of some others I have painted. He talked a great deal, leading the conversation from subject to subject—too interesting to allow me to concentrate on my work. I had to dismiss him at intervals and work from memory. In drawing the hands, I had to use a substitute, for his hands were never still. I have often seen his Grace walking on the street, head up, talking aloud to himself, those wonderfully expressive hands gesticulating as they did in his sermons. His thoughts at such times seemed to dwell in the skies, utterly oblivious of those who passed by! St. Thomas College in St. Paul has a replica of the portrait I painted; the original I still possess.

The closing ambition of the Archbishop's life was the completion of the wonderful cathedral, which he built to crown the brow of the magnificent bluff that overlooks the romantic and saintly city. It is said, the dome of the church is the fourth largest in the world, being one hundred twenty-four feet in diameter, surmounted by a cross three hundred feet above the street. Its copper ribs have turned a beautiful greenish color, and it is seen for miles in all directions. During Archbishop Ireland's illness and before he passed away, he was asked by those near him to express his wishes regarding his burial—if it should be in the crypt of the Cathedral. He hesitated, then said, "No, bury me in the green cemetery among my people." His passing brought mourning to Catholic and non-Catholic alike, and the funeral cortège extended from the church to the cemetery two miles away.

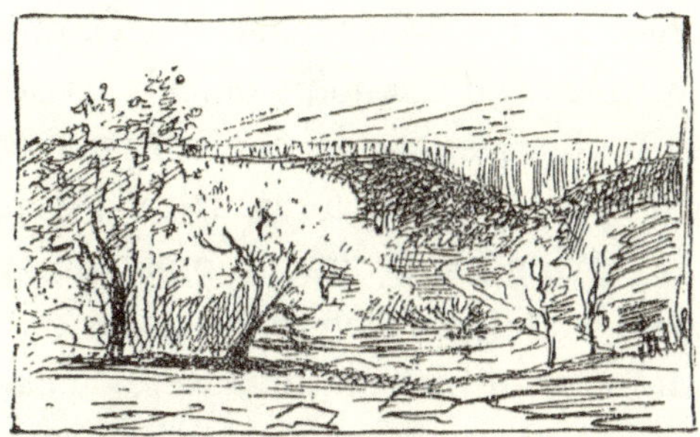

* * *

In the fall of 1888, after returning from New York to St. Paul, I was asked by Conde Hamlin, one of the editors of the Pioneer Press, to accompany him to see the art collection of Mr. James J. Hill. When we rang the bell, about nine o'clock in the morning, the door was opened by Mr. Hill himself, hat and overcoat on, ready to go to the office. When Mr. Hamlin presented me, Mr. Hill immediately showed us into the gallery. As I glanced about, I was surprised to note the great pictures hanging on the walls. Corot, Daubigny, Millet, Diaz, Dupre, Troyon, and many other masters of the Barbizon School were represented in his collection. There were pictures by Benjamin Constant and Delacroix; but, alas, no examples of American artists, nor the great living Frenchmen of the day. I mentioned a number of the artists whom I recognized without their signatures. Mr. Hill silently received my comments regarding his excellent collection. He became at once interested in the subject of art and talked very enthusiastically, pointing out many of the good qualities as he saw them, expressing the views of a layman of more than ordinary artistic comprehension.

He voluntarily mentioned prices he had paid, running as high as fifty thousand dollars for some of the canvasses, and seemed to feel proud to be regarded as an exceptional critic and collector. I remember his thorough analysis of a small picture by Fortuny and his comparison of the artist's style with that of Puvis de Chavannes, which to Conde Hamlin meant more than it did to me. The viewpoint of the literary critic is usually very much in line with that of the average laymen, since neither seems to grasp the technical views of the painter. Mr.

Hill seemed to forget any possible engagement he might have had. He talked about his pictures and the hours quickly passed until a quarter of twelve o'clock. Before leaving, he cordially invited me to come in whenever I wished to study his pictures, and if I were doing any pictures that might be giving me a difficult problem, I might bring my easel and canvas and work right there in his galleries.

I noticed that many of his paintings were cracking badly on the surface and called his attention to it. "Yes," he said, "I employed a man from the art shop to clean and varnish my pictures. One morning I saw him with a pot of thick coach varnish, which he was applying to give the pictures a wonderful gloss. I immediately gave him his check and dismissed him. I presume that is the cause of the cracking." Six months or so later, the picture, *The Spaders* by Millet, was brought into the art shop of Stevens and Robertson to be shipped East for restoration, they said. The picture was so badly cracked that paint hung like dried scales of a fish all over it—many of them had dropped off leaving patches of canvas without any paint. How anyone could believe that such a picture could be restored was beyond my understanding. Several months afterward, supposedly the same picture was returned beautifully restored. I had an opportunity to examine it very critically and formed the impression that it was not the original canvas at all, but a clever copy on new canvas.

In Sensier's *Life of J. F. Millet*, *The Spaders* is beautifully illustrated, showing the two peasants plying their spades and turning over the soil. It is a wonderful work. The rhythm of action, as these hardy sons of toil labor in the field, is well expressed, as is the case with all of Millet's peasant pictures. *The Sower*, in his stride casting the seed of the future crop as the sun sinks behind the West, is a song expressive of the poetry of peasant life. The stooping figures of *The Gleaners*, as they gather up the scattered ears of wheat, tell of the toil for daily bread, and *The Angelus*, we all know, expresses the peasant's prayer. In this *Life of Millet*, Sensier, who was Millet's friend, on being asked by the artist for his opinion of *The Angelus*, declared, "I can hear the angelus bell." Millet replied, "I knew that truth of impression would do it."

The story is told of a connoisseur, a wealthy American collector, who had heard of Millet and his picture, going to Barbizon to study the man and his art. Millet at that time had not yet been recognized by the "powers that be." It was said that the Salon and the Luxemburg had rejected his works, which is not surprising since such institutions the world over, are slowest to perceive merit in a great work of art. This connoisseur requested the privilege of taking the picture home so that he might better study it. Returning it six weeks later, he said he did not want it, though the artist had offered it for five hundred francs (about $100.00). This collector lived to see *The Angelus* sold at public auction for something like one hundred seventy thousand dollars. This digression shows the high quality and value of many canvasses in the Hill collection.

A pretty little story is told of Mr. Hill's courtship days, when he proposed to the girl he afterward married. The young lady concerned was employed at the Merchants Hotel, St. Paul, and it was there Mr. Hill did his courting. She was an Irish Catholic and he, a Scotch Presbyterian. His suit was not favored by her for religious reasons. My good friend, Father Caillet, happened to be her spiritual advisor, and she would not seriously entertain Hill's proposal without first consulting him. After learning her request Father Caillet said, "Well, Mary, I know you and I know Mr. Hill, and I believe I would advise you to accept him. He is a fine man and will, no doubt, someday amount to something." With this advice she consented to wear an engagement ring. "Now then," Mr. Hill said, "Mary, in time I am going to be a very wealthy man, and you will need a better education. I want you to go to a convent school for two or three years to perfect your studies, and I will pay your expenses." Mary emphatically declined, saying she could never accept his money in that way. "Well," said Jim, "why not consult Father Caillet and ask him about it?" He persuaded her to do so, but Mr. Hill reached Father Caillet first. When she spoke to the good priest, he said, "Well, Mary, I think you will need a better education, as Mr. Hill says." "But Father, I cannot accept his money for my education," was Mary's answer. "Well, let us see," said the good priest. "I know the Sisters at the Convent. I have done them a good many favors, and I am sure I can fix it so you can get your education and it will not cost you anything." With this she was willing to enter the school, and Mr. Hill's checks found their way to Caillet and Caillet's to the Convent.

Mrs. Hill possessed fine traits of character and discretion and made use of her opportunity in the fullest manner. During their long married life, she was able to take her place in the best society and had the respect of everybody. I recall meeting her once at the Governor's reception. I had already heard this little story, and I reflected on the position she now held, as well as the prophetic statement of the man who afterward became the "Empire Builder." Most young lovers will not plan their domestic affairs with that far-seeing vision, and thus many of them "marry in haste and repent at leisure." Evidently Mr. Hill saw in this girl the future lady who was to be his wife and the mother of his numerous children. One might readily prophesy that the man who so well planned his domestic affairs was destined to be a leader of men and an executive of the highest order. He showed the same foresight when he conceived the plan of taking over the bankrupt Manitoba Railroad and reorganizing it. The vast wealth that fell to him as a consequence of his railroad, immigration, and financial ability was but the realization of his dreams of earlier days.

A story is often told that for some years Mrs. Hill was frowned upon by a few of the ultra- snobbish society people because she had been a working girl, and Mrs. Hill's retiring disposition was construed to be due to her not having been "to the manor born." It became known that Mrs. Hill was the possessor of some beautiful jewels, and a lady holding a high social position, wishing to satisfy her curiosity, called at the Hill residence one day and asked the maid, "May I see Mrs. Hill's jewels?" In response to her request, Mrs. Hill very cordially brought down the jewels, and the visitor was most flattering in her praise of them. The mistress of the house then withdrew to her rooms above, leaving the visitor waiting for her return and the usual good-bye. As time elapsed, wondering at the delay, the caller questioned the maid, who returned with the word, "Mrs. Hill says you called to see the jewels, and she has shown them to you."

During Charles Noel Flagg's second stay in St. Paul, he was commissioned to paint a portrait of Mr. Stanford Newell. Newell was one of the active builders of the city. The portrait was intended for the Minnesota Club. In connection with the execution of this work, Flagg told an interesting story. The last sitting was taken up in finishing the face.

Flagg's way of painting was usually in a heavy impasto of color laid on without much blending or joining of the tones. When the sitting was done Newell asked permission to bring in a friend to see the picture at the noon hour. The request was gladly granted, the artist saying that he would be absent but would leave the painting on the easel and the door unlocked. On his return, he said, he was filled with consternation to discover that somebody had redrawn the face with a piece of charcoal right in the fresh paint and had ruined one of his finest pieces of work. "The sight of the picture made me literally sick at the stomach," Flagg said. "I could hardly believe my eyes. Finally, I threw the canvas into a corner, determined never to touch the damn thing again. Late that day Newell came in and not seeing his picture on the easel, asked where it was. I told him there was a thing in the corner that somebody had been trying to paint—that it was not my work and that I would never put another stroke on it. Newell felt very bad about it and wanted to know what he could do to make the matter right with me. I told him there was only one thing and that was for me to take a new canvas and start all over again—and that I would expect my pay for both pictures. This adjustment was agreed upon and I finished the second picture. The culprit who had had the audacity to mutilate my portrait was none other than Mr. James J. Hill." Whether Hill ever learned of the ire his ill-advised criticism had aroused in the soul of Flagg I do not know. It required as great a genius to be a good portrait painter as it does to manage a great railroad, only in a different way. Few men are big enough to be both.

In 1889 I painted the portrait of Mr. Bruno Beaupre, senior member of the wholesale grocery house of Beaupre, Allen & Keough, in St. Paul. During the sittings Mr. Beaupre told me many things about early life in the Capital City, but nothing more interesting than the fact that his firm had employed Mr. J. J. Hill in the early days as a truckman and shipping hand at a salary of $50.00 per month. He said, however, that Hill did not stay with the house very long but struck out for something better, and that it was but a short while before he was on the upward climb that led to his title of "Empire Builder."

In his selection of works of art, Mr. Hill bought only those things that had already established a permanent commercial value; consequently he favored the works of the Barbizon painters and such artists whose fame he was sure rested on a safe foundation. He was not apt to speculate on any living artist, however popular. Many times he passed by Homer Martin's *Harp of the Winds*, (now a valued possession of the Metropolitan Museum) when it stood unframed on the floor in a St. Paul art shop while its author lived in a cheap flat on Rice Street unable to buy enough coal to keep his family warm, or to obtain shoes for their feet. This beautiful canvas could have been bought then for the modest sum of one hundred fifty dollars, while Hill was paying twenty-five thousand for foreign works which today are worth far less than the *Harp of the Winds*.

This ultra-conservatism on the part of collectors often proves to be poor business policy when viewed from a speculative standpoint. Ten thousand dollars wisely invested in the works of George Inness, A. H. Wyant, Homer Martin, and Blakelock previous to their death would today easily represent a value of one million dollars, and should any one or two or even three of those artists have proven a disappointment as to the niche they were to occupy in the gallery of fame, the investment would still have yielded a fabulous profit.

The Hackley Gallery owns a beautiful Blakelock for which it paid a very nominal price—if my memory is correct, something like twelve hundred dollars. The directors say they have had an offer of fifty-five thousand for the canvas but declined to part with it. I told them that if they had accepted the offer and reinvested the money in the works of twenty of the best artists of today, in twenty years when those artists will have passed away their institution would be richer by several million more—even if they had to discard half the pictures in the purchase.

I knew Inness when he was selling for three to five hundred dollars the very canvasses, which today are being bought by collectors for prices above twenty-five thousand each. There is something in being able to recognize a work of great genius when one sees it.

* * *

It is needless to say that Justice Pierce Butler of the United States Supreme Court is one of the outstanding lawyers of the country. For years he practiced law in St. Paul, was a railroad attorney, and I believe was chosen by the Government to prosecute the Beef Trust in Chicago, and finally, was appointed by President Harding to the high position of Associate Justice of that august body which constitutes the balance wheel of our government. My first meeting with Justice Butler was in 1898, when he entered my studio with two other distinguished attorneys, Moses Clapp, who afterward became United States Senator, and Judge Wilson, Chief Justice of the Minnesota State Supreme Court. Clapp was a picturesque character, a striking face with a black mustache and eyebrows. Seated on my model stand in his shirt sleeves, he reminded one more of a cowboy than a distinguished lawyer. Butler was tall and dignified. They had come to see my portrait of Wilson, painted for the Supreme Court room. After several good-natured jokes about Wilson's homeliness, they decided that I had made the most of a poor subject. Both Wilson and Butler agreed that Clapp would have better stood the beauty test.

It was Saturday afternoon and these men seemed to have nothing else to do but stand about and argue over legal questions. The call resulted in Butler's giving me a commission to paint a portrait of his father. During the progress of the work, Butler came in several times and asked many questions relative to the artist's profession. He was apparently soliciting information concerning something about which he frankly admitted he knew nothing. The picture was finished to his entire satisfaction, and owing to our absence from the city, I saw nothing more of him for several years.

Having signed a real estate contract which was rather ambiguously drawn and promised to involve me in financial difficulties, I went to Butler and asked him to read over this contract and advise me what to do. The matter related to the purchasing of a block of lots situated in the Midway, between the Twin Cities, and provided that I had a limited amount of time to fulfill its conditions. Butler read the document and after a few moments, reflection said, "Well, Mr. Brewer, I would advise you to pay off and take title to the land." This seemed an impossible thing for me to do, considering the short time allowed and I told Butler I could not. After a little more reflection he said, "Well, I'll lend you the money, because I want to see you secure that property, as I think it will soon be very valuable. You can give me a mortgage payable on or before the expiration of two years." He examined the abstract, and the day before my time limit expired, he handed me the check. In the course of a year I paid one-half the amount he had loaned me but was unable to pay the balance for several months after the two years had expired. When my obligation to him was finally canceled, he said, "Well, it required a little more time than you thought, but I was glad to give you all the time you needed for I wanted to help you and I am sure your speculation will prove a fortunate one."

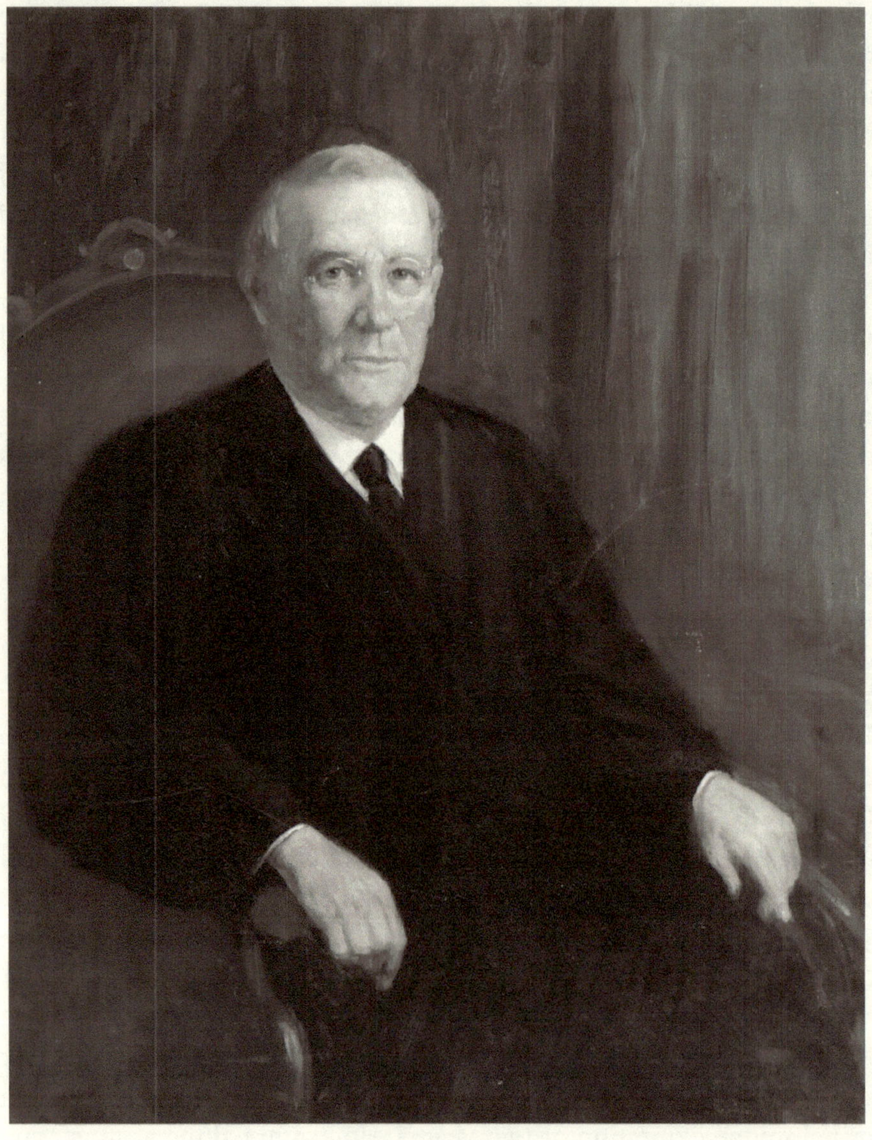

Mr. Justice Pierce Butler

These lots were situated on the plateau above the Mississippi River, but because of springs near the hill, were flooded with water most of the time and were unavailable then for building purposes. I knew that the proper drains would dry them out and make them valuable. I persuaded the City Fathers to have a system of sewers installed. Today the lots are covered with beautiful residences, paved streets, boulevards, and form one of the most beautiful residential sections of St. Paul. After our home, "Casa del Rio," in the same locality was finished, my wife gave a silver tea for the benefit of the church. She had arranged a fine musical program upon which Mrs. Hoffman (who at the time was the accompanist for Madame Schumann-Heink) with a noted local contralto and an equally famous violinist rendered several delightful selections. The guests were far more numerous than we had expected and our reception rooms were jammed to overflowing. Judge and Mrs. Butler were among them. When the music ceased, there was a rush to the dining room where the table was heaped with delicacies. I tried to assist the Butlers and Mrs. Hoffman in squeezing through the crowd to get into the room, but it was impossible. We rushed around to the garden entrance which led into the dining room, where a long line had also formed, but with enough pressure and squeezing we managed to reach it safely. The grounds were illuminated and festooned for the entertainment, and everyone said it was a very pretty affair. We afterward sold the place to Mr. Emmett Butler, brother of the Judge, who still lives there.

Six years later, while in Washington, I called on the Butlers and arranged to paint the Judge's portrait. The sittings were made at his home, usually early in the morning before he went to the Capitol on judicial duty. The Judge was an early riser and had always had his morning walk when I came to work. I must say he was a poor sitter. He fidgeted about and talked constantly. Before I began the picture, he suggested my being in the Supreme Court room when the nine judges, with Chief Justice Taft leading the procession, filed in to take their respective seats. The chairs are in a straight row; the background, between a row of marble pillars, is hung with a dark red draping. This I used for the background of my picture. It is an impressive sight, this dignified jury of great men entering to listen to the pleas and arguments of lawyers from all parts of the country, who have carried to the court of last resort complicated questions of law where final definitions and interpretations settle all disputes.

When I arrived at his home for the last sitting, I entered a large hall leading through a portiered doorway to the parlor where the picture was painted. There sat the Justice with the portieres nearly closed, peering through the small aperture at his portrait beyond. "Come here, Mr. Brewer," he said, beckoning me to him and pointing with his finger, "does not that look as though I were really sitting there against that red curtain?" Suddenly rising to his feet, he said, "I haven't had my breakfast yet; come with me and have a cup of coffee." He seemed to be in a talkative mood, evidently not thinking of my doing any more work on the picture; and as he ate his toast we fell to discussing many subjects of popular interest, which prolonged the hours until nearly time for him to go to the Capitol. The subject of Prohibition came up, on which in many ways we differed. His logical analysis was quite convincing, and I am still guessing if my own convictions are well founded. Before leaving, however, the Justice took me to his study on the floor above. The walls were lined to the ceiling with books. The desk and tables were littered with documents and briefs of a legal character, bordering on confusion. "Here," he said, "is my work room." "And it shows it," I added. He continued, "We judges haven't much time to play during sessions. Frequently I don't get to bed until past midnight. The work is hard, but I enjoy it." By this time the Judge's car was at the door, and he drove me back to my hotel on his way to the court room at the Capitol.

* * *

The coldest subjects I have ever painted are Judge Frank B. Kellogg and Governor Dan Moody. I posed both of them in very much the same way, standing beside a library table with bookshelves in the background. Moody was so tall and lanky that I had to cut his feet off just below the knees. Kellogg, I represented somewhat taller than he really is. During the long sittings neither of them would utter a word unless I asked some questions or made some comments to draw them out. Then the brevity of their replies would send the shivers through me. How can an artist paint a good portrait of one who never comes out of his shell with more than a curious or critical stare?

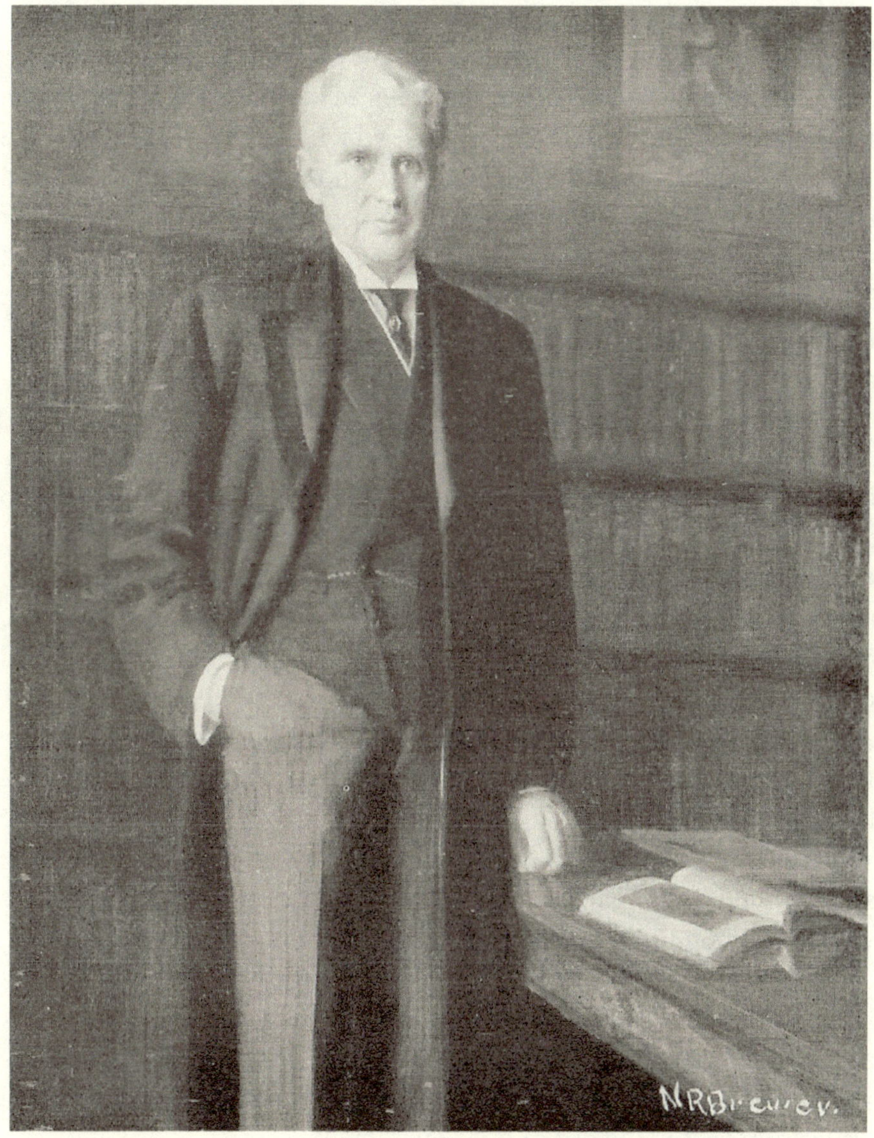

Hon. Frank B. Kellogg in 1908

In the winter of 1906, an exhibition of my paintings was given under the patronage of several prominent society ladies of St. Paul, at the gallery of Brown & Bigelow. A reception with a delightful musical program was given, with Mrs. Peet pouring tea while Mrs. Shepard, Mrs. Tighe, Mrs. Kellogg, Mrs. Wann, and Mrs. Stem were in the receiving line. The place was filled with the elite of St. Paul's society. The social festivities took place chiefly in the front gallery. In the rear room were hung several of my portraits of well-known local people, as well as several New York portraits, which had been loaned for the Western Exhibition. In the back gallery I noticed, standing alone in a corner, a small man with a full head of partially gray hair, somewhat stooped, gazing at the portraits of Mrs. Oelrichs, Natalie Schenck of Newport, and Joe Jefferson. He was pointed out to me as Mr. Frank B. Kellogg, whom I had never met before. Later Mrs. Kellogg introduced me and also remarked that Mr. Kellogg was thinking of having his portrait painted.

I was soon obliged to return to New York and forgot about the incident until a subsequent visit to St. Paul, when I was asked to do the work. The sittings were made in a large library at his home. There I came to know intimately the man who has since risen to the exalted positions of United States Senator, American Ambassador to England, Secretary of State, and now to a seat in that dignified body, the World Court. Astute to a superlative degree, apparently high strung, active, energetic, clear and forceful in reasoning, Kellogg forged his way up from the ranks, so to speak, for in his youth he was no stranger to the hardships and toil of the life of a pioneer farmer boy, his parents having settled in an early day in Olmsted County, my own native birthplace, several miles out of Rochester. I had, however, never met the Kelloggs while living on the farm at High Forest. But I knew lawyer Eckholdt, and the story goes, with truth in it, that Kellogg first read law in Eckholdt's office and trudged the weary miles daily to help his father milk the cows and do chores on the farm. It is said that he never had the advantage of a college or university education, yet he rose to the highest diplomatic post in the gift of our government.

* * *

One of the most outstanding characters it has been my pleasure to paint was the late Governor John A. Johnson of Minnesota. Johnson was born in St. Peter, Minnesota, of humble parentage. As a mere boy he became a printer's devil in the local newspaper office. Forced at a tender age to help in the support of his mother, he stuck to the routine of the printing office and rose in time to be the editor. Naturally, his mind turned to politics, and he became an ardent advocate of Democratic principles. He was elected to the State legislature, eventually being placed in the Governor's chair. Four terms he served as governor; twice he was virtually elected over his own veto. Because of his remarkable personality, his wise administration, and several notable speeches made in the East, he attracted the attention of the national leaders of the Democratic party. It has been said that he was slated for the presidential nomination and many believe that, had he lived, he, instead of Woodrow Wilson, would have been President. Governor Johnson died in office a very short time after sitting to me for his portrait for the "Gallery of Governors" in the State Capitol. His death caused profound grief among the people of the state, and as the bells tolled at the hour of his burial, in every town and village the people paused on the streets and all work ceased for five minutes in honor of one of Minnesota's greatest sons.

Sons of the Gopher State!
A heritage they gave mankind,
No broader space nor bluer skies,
From budding spring to winter late,
An empire fair they left behind.

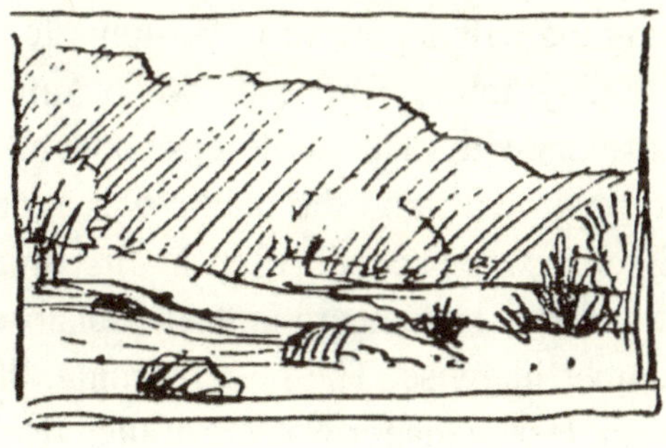

Chapter XI
The Spragues of Rhode Island

Kate Chase Sprague—Governor Wm. Sprague—Echoes of Sumter and Bull Run—Lincoln—Conkling—Chase—Grant—Portia Sprague

Mrs. Inez Sprague, who aspired to fame on the concert stage, was the second wife of William Sprague, the widely known Governor of Rhode Island of Civil War days, with whom the reading public is well acquainted. She had a sweet soprano voice, and her teacher told her that if she would work hard, she could become famous. I first met the Governor while I was painting his wife's portrait in Boston a few days before her debut with the Boston Symphony Orchestra. My picture of her was reproduced in the newspapers with many write-ups about her. In fact, she was over-advertised to begin with and the public was expecting something phenomenal. The house was packed. After the first aria from Gioconda, the fall of a pin could have been heard in the awful absence of applause, and after each number likewise. The next morning. the critics literally riddled her to pieces. Her manager was crestfallen. He had mapped out a tour for her to follow an expected successful debut; but those engagements were canceled and nothing more was heard of the wonderful soprano voice that was to delight the ears of music lovers.

In the solitude of Canonchet, Mrs. Sprague sought comfort after the death of her ambition at the hands of critical and heartless Boston. Canonchet, the palatial home of the Spragues at Narragansett Pier, had been the scene of the social triumphs and political intrigues of that most remarkable and beautiful woman, the Governor's first wife, Kate Chase Sprague; of the scandal involving Roscoe Conkling, once termed the "Adonis of the Senate;" and of the tragic climax of her exalted reign. Here, the brilliant daughter of Chief Justice Salmon P. Chase, had spent lavishly of her husband's wealth in entertaining the great political and social leaders of the time. She had planned and directed the building of the sixty-room mansion, with its wonderful mahogany carvings, its spacious halls, its playing fountains; she had furnished it with the rarest pieces to be found in Europe, here a mantel from the ruins of the Tuillеries, there a divan from the boudoir of Marie Antoinette, or a cabinet used by Empress Josephine, and numerous works of art of the great masters. The great house was situated in a tract of three hundred and sixty acres of beautifully wooded land and one could view from its towers the smoke of steamers far beyond the horizon, distant Newport, and at one's feet the hotels and other buildings of Narragansett Pier. Canonchet was named for the last great chief of the Narragansett Indians.

At the time I knew him, Governor Sprague, past seventy, had retired from active public life. He whiled away the time in the quietude of this romantic retreat. Once the apotheosis of Rhode Island's political and industrial life, when he could write his checks for fabulous sums, he was now a comparatively poor man. Before the Civil War, Sprague was the foremost manufacturer of fine linens and fabrics. His mills dotted New England wherever water power could be found, and thousands drew their weekly pay from his treasuries. He was the idol of Rhode Island's people. Quoting his words to me, "Wealth poured in upon me so fast that it became a burden and to get rid of it I built more mills to give employment." Two years before the first gun was fired at Sumter, he foresaw the conflict and organized and equipped a regiment, both artillery and infantry, at his own expense and helped drill them himself.

"Previous to the Battle of Bull Run," he told me later, "I wired President Lincoln that my men were ready to start south. His answer was, 'Wait,' and I replied, 'My regiment will go forward tonight.'" Sprague, in command, led the Rhode Island men in that first defeat of the Federal forces. His losses were tremendous. "When we went into the engagement," he said, "I noticed that my boys, white-faced, were shooting wildly in the air. Exasperated, I rode along their lines, shouting, 'Lower and shoot at something,' and I hacked their guns with my sabre. On the march to the engagement, one of the wheels of our mounted guns was broken and we left it behind. In the routing of our troops, that gun was the only one we saved, and I afterward presented it to the State. It now stands in front of the Capitol at Providence. My horse was shot from under me and fell on me in such a way that I was unable to extricate myself. They found me afterward, and thus I was prevented from being taken prisoner." He showed me his sabre with its battered blade.

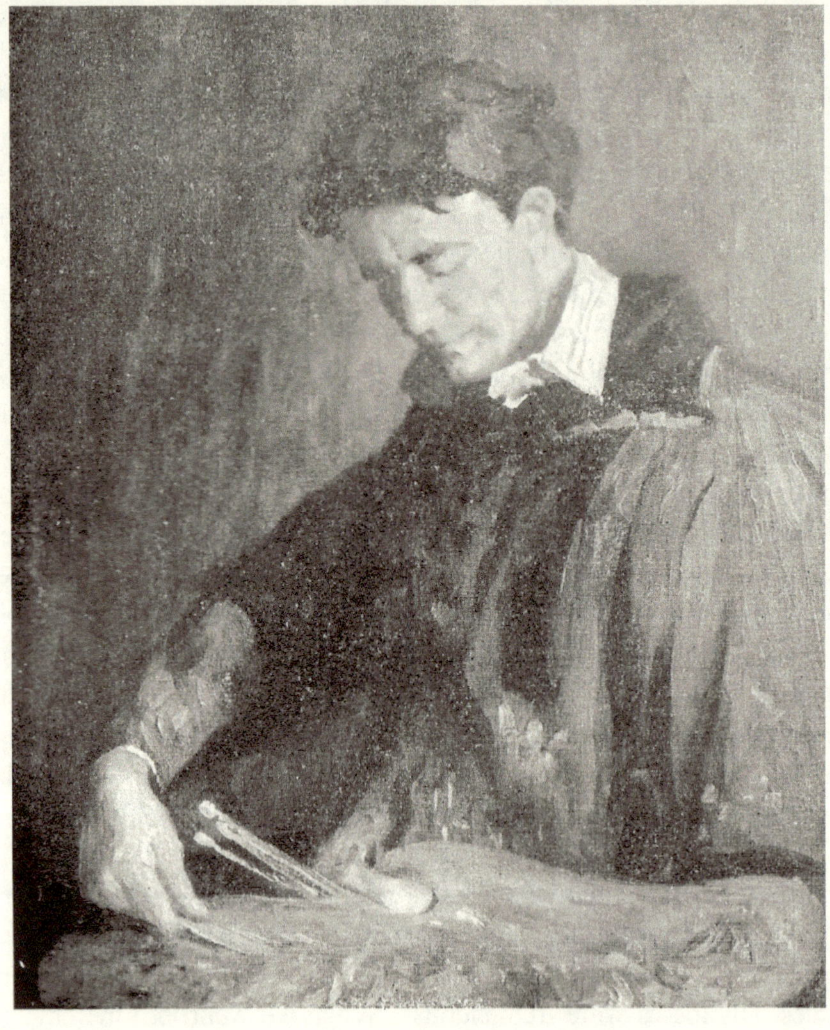

Cleaning Up

In August 1898, the last summer we spent on the farm, two years after I had painted her portrait in Boston, I received a letter from Mrs. Sprague requesting me to come to Canonchet and paint a portrait of the Governor to be hung in the State Capitol at Providence. She said the state had appropriated the money to pay for it and my personal expenses would be taken care of while I was her guest. So, considering my depleted treasury, the amount of the state's fund was a real temptation. The hard work and worry of the farm and the failure to realize anything out of our berry crop had so worked on my nervous system that I was not in a condition to paint well. When today I look at some of the things I did then, I feel utterly ashamed of them! If I could only buy them all, what a grand bonfire I would make of them! The only consolation I have is in the thought that I did them the best I could, under almost unbearable conditions.

When I arrived at Canonchet I was given the Salmon P. Chase room, which faced the south lawn and the great elm trees. The Governor, a grave, reticent man, appeared in a bicycle costume. He was cordial, but reserved, seeming to take little interest in me at first. Not until he discovered that I could ask leading questions and was a good listener did he court conversation. Gradually, at table, he began to warm up and after dinner frequently engaged me in desultory talk. At first I felt overawed in his presence, but that soon wore away and we became great friends. Mrs. Sprague told me that the Governor would have to be won over to the idea of allowing his portrait to be placed in the Capitol, as many of his former political enemies or their successors were still in power, and he harbored considerable resentment and would be averse to placing his picture there. She advised me to bide my time until she could bring him to a favorable decision to sit for the portrait. The Governor was in the habit of retiring to his room after dinner. His apartments were on the third floor in the tower section of the building, and here among his books and records and war relics he was something of a recluse. He separated himself from the family and social gatherings except at mealtime. Many evenings later on, he would invite me to a comfortable chair on the wide veranda on the west side of the house, where we could quietly talk. He would prolong these conversations late into the night. To me those hours were an unusual opportunity to learn at first hand many of the stirring events of the Civil War and the intimate sketches of the great characters of that time. Sprague had been in the midst of it all, one of the actors, and his wife Kate Chase Sprague, the foremost leader of Washington society.

Here in Canonchet she had entertained most lavishly in the hope that her father, Chief Justice Chase, would be nominated and seated in the White House. Canonchet, under her régime, became what might be termed the Summer Capital. Here President Lincoln and members of his Cabinet, and Chase, Conkling, Horace Greeley, Generals Grant, Sherman, and Sheridan, and numerous other great political leaders had gathered, either in conference or in social diversion with the beaux and belles of ultra-fashionable society. In *Memories of a Sculptor's Wife* by Mrs. Daniel Chester French, we read:

"Especially one evening do I remember the passage through the great room of Mrs. Kate Chase Sprague, who was, I suppose, more of a professional beauty than had at that time ever been seen in America, with a beauty and a regal carriage which we called 'queenly', but which no real queen ever has—unless it be our own Queen of Roumania. She would have been famous even without her beauty, for the position of her father, Chief Justice Chase of the Supreme Court, was at that time the most dignified one in the Capital. She was tall and slim—the universal art of being slim had not been discovered in those days—with an unusually long white neck and a slow and deliberate way of turning it when she glanced about her. Wherever she appeared, people dropped back in order to watch her. It was said that when she walked abroad in a small town of Switzerland or France, where she sometimes spent her summers, the people ran out of their cottages to admire her. In Washington she was always the first lady of the land.

"There is a story that, when one of the Presidents took his seat, his wife decided upon Thursday, if I remember aright, for the reception day at the White House. As soon as some of their friends heard of her choice, they hurried to her and told her that they were afraid that she had made a mistake, that that was the day that Mrs. Sprague and the Chief Justice had had as their day at home for years.

"'Why, my dear,' one of the visitors said, 'I'm afraid you don't understand. All the diplomats, all the great men of Washington go there. Sometimes even the President—Why, nobody will come.'

"And the lady of the Executive Mansion, on the eve of her social career, changed the day of the White House reception because, if her day clashed with the day of the Chief Justice and Mrs. Sprague, nobody would come.

"Later when I came to see her and to know more about her, it was at the time when Conkling was very devoted to her. He was Senator from New York, and one of the brilliant men of the country. I remember, suddenly, out of a clear sky, as it seemed to us young people, there was a scandal. The papers came out one morning in big headlines that Sprague had come home one evening, had found Conkling there, and had kicked him out."

The first six weeks or so of my stay at the Sprague's, which covered a period of eight months, I spent in a leisurely way, resting from the work of garnering and preserving strawberries. On moonlight nights the Governor and I would take long strolls along the ocean shore. At seventy-two, he could put me out of breath, so vigorous was his tread. Always on such walks he wore a bicycle suit. It was his great joy to wander about in the rain, with a rubber outfit furnishing protection. Having two such suits, he often asked me to accompany him. On these long walks he seemed to want to tell the intimate things of his past, going into the life he had led with Kate, as he always called her. He spoke of the great scandal, the tragedy that had come into their lives, and I could see that the thorns driven into his heart by the infidelity or weakness of the wife and mother and the treachery of an interloper had left aching wounds that could never be healed. He had loved Kate Chase with all the ardor of a passionate nature and had lavished upon her all that wealth could buy, everything, perhaps, except the kind of love or romance she craved.

It seems a trait of some women to be satisfied only with a certain kind of Beau Brummel gallantry, a uniform and the devil-take-'em eyes, all of which they soon tire of, then cast about for other worshippers. Sprague was democratic, wrapped up in big enterprises. There was nothing of the make-believe about him. Formal social rules he constantly violated, in spite of his wife's protests and admonitions. She was fond of sham and glitter, the glamour of social functions, ambitious to shine, aided by her father's high place in the nation's judiciary and her husband's vast wealth. Possessed of the rarest beauty and the most wonderful personal charm, she was able to captivate men and make them her devotees. A most valuable aid she would have been to her father, had he but won the nomination. Three daughters and a son were born of the Sprague-Chase union. The girl Portia was but a year old when the separation came. In telling the story, at times the aged man's voice grew husky. Sprague's love was of the die-hard kind. His second marriage, to Inez Weed, was a marriage of convenience, aiding him in saving the homestead Canonchet, and this was all he saved of his vast wealth. He always treated Inez with the greatest consideration, but I had reason to believe that Kate Chase Sprague carried away with her his broken heart as well as the three daughters, leaving the boy with the father.

One evening we had been walking some time when he led me to the top of the sand dunes where a little plot of grass had rooted close to some shrubs. He said, "I often come here in the night when I can't sleep. I love to listen to the surf—it is so cheering, you know, if you will notice the way the waves break and run along the beach and come back in crisscross fashion and then seem to die, laughing." To one who understands the sea, this is a picture, particularly under the moonlight, when everything is vague and indefinite and you hear the gentle wavelets chasing one another back and forth—they suggest the play and frolic of the nymphs of the deep. The swell of the great billows beyond is not seen until the thunderous roar of the breakers tells you of the power and treachery of the undertow.

After the separation of the Spragues, Kate Chase was aided by some of her father's friends in procuring a life's tenure of the old Chase mansion in Washington, where she lived with the daughters in seclusion for several years. But the need of maintenance finally drove her to engage in berry farming and chicken culture. In her mental stress she adopted spiritualism as a palliative and died a sad and broken woman.

Miss Portia Sprague was now past twenty-one. Unlike most young women she was not averse to telling her age, but I have forgotten it. Sometime before I arrived at Canonchet, she had written her father, whom she had not met since she was taken away when a baby, that she would like to see him some time should he come to Washington. Thinking that her request might have been inspired by her mother, he replied that he thought it best to let bygones remain as they were. This piqued her, as she told me, and she again wrote him that if he thought she wanted any of his money or help of any kind he was greatly mistaken; that her reason for writing him was that she wanted to know her father. This frank statement drove home to the heart of the parent who had not seen his baby girl for twenty years or more, and he wired for an appointment and took the next train for Washington. A reunion with the three daughters resulted. Portia then held a government appointive position secured for her by friends of her grandfather. Soon afterward she came to visit at Canonchet. From the photographs I had seen of Kate Chase, I noticed Portia was the counterpart of her mother; tall and slender in figure, she carried herself gracefully, with a certain diffidence due to her youth. This wore off after a few days. Mrs. Inez Sprague, the stepmother seemed to regard it a pleasure to welcome her to the old home where she was born, showing her through the many rooms and about the place. She had religiously preserved the furnishings, the choice things her predecessor had selected and valued so highly and never allowed them to be changed from their original positions. There was the Greeley room, the Chase room, the Conkling room, the Lincoln room, and her own magnificent boudoir with its spacious lounge and sleeping rooms and tiled baths that had been the sanctum of Portia's mother and where Portia was born.

Other suites were occupied by Mrs. Avis Weed Wheaton and Mrs. Eaton, whose first name I have forgotten, both sisters of Mrs. Sprague. They were spending the summer there. Mrs. Wheaton lived in Washington, and Mrs. Eaton was the wife of an army officer who was in the service in Puerto Rico. Mr. Oris Weed, a brother, also had a room on the same floor and Mathilde, Mrs. Sprague's French maid and secretary, one nearby. Oris was an only brother and was idolized by his sisters, who supplied him with more money than was good for his moral well-being. He never arose before one or two p.m. and never retired much before five a.m. Handsome, vain, suave in manner, he had not depth enough to interest himself with anything serious. He was exceedingly fond of women, but his smiles and manner were about his only recommendation. He had his own way with many of the fair damsels of the Pier and was the concern of many jealous husbands.

Miss Portia, coming into the family for the first time, was, of course, a stranger to the peculiarities of the different members of the family; nor was the reticence and reserve of her father in his general bearing modified by her sweet, youthful personality. For a time, he would seek her out for conversation, but he never seemed to love her in a fatherly way. Was she a reminder of happy days spent with Kate Chase? It would seem that the old wound was reopened by the presence of this sweet girl, whose every step and smile and gesture was but a duplicate of those which beguiled him in his younger days and brought him to the feet of the most captivating feminine personality of that time. Oris began to show special attention to the newcomer. In the reception room, glowing fires robbed the nights of their chill, and here Oris and Portia would spend the hours in low conversation, long after the rest of the family had retired.

Mrs. Sprague had commissioned me to redecorate the walls of her boudoir. I had canvas mounted on several panels. On these I had laid out a series of figure compositions and had begun work in oil on one of them. Coming in one day from a sketching jaunt, I found Oris on the stepladder, my palette in hand, slamming away with colors all over the canvas. He had entirely obliterated my drawing of the figures, to my dismay and disgust. No doubt he meant it only in a spirit of play, but it was not fun to me. My temper got the best of me, and I gave him a real scolding. An hour or two later, the Governor came in and glancing about said, "Has that young sprout been cutting capers to your annoyance, Mr. Brewer?" "Oh," I said, "nothing that is irreparable." "Well, if he annoys you, just kick him out."

That evening neither the Governor nor Mrs. Sprague appeared at the table. Conversation was desultory, when Miss Portia asked me what success I was making with the pictures. Then Oris in a joking way mentioned how successful his own attempt had been. He guessed the reason why the Governor and Mrs. Sprague were absent from the table was that they had had a few words about it, and also that he thought the Governor did not approve of their sitting up so late at night. Referring to the Governor's cleverness with a shotgun, he thought it might not be well for him to incur his displeasure. The expression on Miss Portia's face was one of surprise and curiosity. Till the end of the meal, a strange silence pervaded the group.

That night about twelve o'clock, I was awakened by a shout in the large hall outside my room, "O, Governor, don't shoot!" Presently I heard someone bounding down the winding stairs, three or four steps at a time and slamming the front door in a hasty retreat. Then followed the light tread of the Governor in slippers, and from the door he called, "Come back, young man, I'm not going to hurt you." I did not wish to manifest any particular interest in what seemed like a family row and dozed off to sleep. Sometime later I was again awakened, this time by Miss Portia, who called to know if I'd seen anything of Oris. She said something had happened and he had fled. She and Mathilde had been searching with a lantern for him about the premises. As both the Governor and I were early risers, we usually had our breakfast together. Next morning he related the incident of the night and said, "That young sprout came to me with some sort of an explanation or apology he wanted to make for his conduct, and in a false repentance wanted to fall on my shoulder and weep. I said, 'Stand back there, young man; I can hear you!' I am in the habit of paring my nails with my jack-knife when listening to men talk. I reached into my pocket for my knife, which gesture he mistook for an effort to draw my gun, and he immediately fled with a shout. We have not been able to discover his whereabouts yet."

A little later, Miss Portia asked me if I would accompany her to the Pier on our bicycles to see if we could find him. We searched the hotels and every place possible and concluded he might have gone to Wakefield and bought a ticket for some other abode. Neither did we find hide nor hair of him there.

On our return we sought a shorter route direct to Canonchet, along a less traveled road. Having to cross a small stream on a long narrow bridge, not more than four or five feet wide, and not being an expert cyclist, I met with quite a serious accident. A lady on foot about in the middle of the bridge, was coming toward us. Surely, I thought, I can navigate those boards without hitting her. When an amateur cyclist tries to avoid a catastrophe in a case like this, he often misses his guess. To be on the safe side I looked straight at her while my wheel followed my gaze and struck her a walloping punch right in the side, knocking her off the bridge into the water. The crash threw me off my seat and I tumbled over the side after her, letting my wheel look out for itself.

Sprawling up out of the shallow water, I helped her, dripping wet, to her feet. From the way she looked at me, I saw apologies were in vain. She indignantly said, "Have you no eyes?" I replied that she appeared so attractive I couldn't do otherwise, and to prove that I was at least a gentleman, I helped her up the steep bank where Portia awaited the rescue. My prank was too hazardous and damaging to be considered a joke, yet Portia often referred to it humorously as such. How the dripping victim considered it was doubtless otherwise.

My enforced baptism, Portia afterward said, seemed only a diversion from the mysterious family mixup of the night before, which was distressing to her since she did not understand the cause of the trouble. She asked me to enlighten her, if possible. I realized her embarrassment and perplexity and felt that I should acquaint her with something of the strained relations between the Governor and the "sprout." Perhaps the old man had been keeping his eyes open for any mischief the latter might attempt to put over. She said she was very much grieved, because she had thought she was perfectly safe in her father's home. When we returned, we found that Oris had sent a note to Mathilde, requesting her to pack his things and send them to him at—naming the house of an old servant of the family—and that the Governor had sent a note telling him that no harm had been meant and that he might return home.

A day or two later, Oris gave me his version of the scrap: "When I saw the Governor put his hand in his pocket, I was sure he intended to shoot, and I ran out and down to the beach. I could hear him after me, and I hid in some brush in the dunes. Then I realized how unsafe I'd be there and took the road around beyond the swamp. Gee! I got out of breath! I sat on the stone wall a while until I got so cold, I couldn't stand it. If I could only cross the thin ice to the barn, it would be warmer in the haymow or on Corinne's back. (Corinne was the Governor's favorite saddle horse.) So I tried to cross the ice but broke through and I got into the water almost up to my neck. When I reached the barn, I saw the Governor coming with a lantern. I was so frightened that I jumped the wall into the old cemetery. Then I thought of the ghosts of those people buried there and how cold I was. I ran down to the Pier and woke up Mrs. — and told her to take me in, as the Governor wanted to shoot me. I said, 'Pull down those parlor shades quick, so he can't see me.' But I guess I was just scared. The Governor said it was all right and for me to come home."

From Sprague's quiet, reticent way, no one would ever suspect that anything had happened. While out riding alone with me a few days later, he again referred to the incident and said he would stand no pranks from the "cuss." Knowing Mrs. Sprague's fondness for her brother and her excitable temper, I suggested tact on her account. "Tact," he said, "it will be tact, damn him." From what the Governor had told me about the Conkling affair, I knew that he meant what he said.

One day while walking with me on the beach, he referred to Portia's likeness to her mother and ran on in a detailed account of the Conkling incident. First, he spoke of Conkling's ability as an orator and his political views, in what I thought something of a laudatory vein. Sprague was big enough to be magnanimous even to his worst enemy and not until he got deeply into the story of their domestic tragedy did his voice or words betray any rancor.

This is the Governor's story:

"I had suspected for some time that things were not right at home while I was absent at the Senate in Washington and arranged with my butler to inform me if Conklin should come. One day a message came, and I took a train that landed me at Wakefield after one o'clock in the morning. I could not, at this hour, get a conveyance and had to walk the nine miles home.

"In the morning I went down to the second floor and I saw Conklin come out of my wife's apartment. He was quite close to me and I said, 'Young man, I will give you just twenty minutes to get out of this house, bag and baggage.' I went back and got the gun and walked down to the beach and returned, timing my return to the minute. It was fully my intention to kill him, but not in the house. At some distance, I saw the villain step into a cab with his luggage and drive rapidly toward the Pier. I followed as fast as I could walk. Before I reached him, three or four men whom I knew well surrounded me and took the gun away. I then went back to the house and told my wife to pack her things. I could not take the children from her and we agreed that she should keep the girls and I the boy."

The Governor finally consented to sit for his portrait, provided I would paint him astride his beloved Corinne, a handsome chestnut bay. Sprague, however, proved about the poorest model I ever had. He could no more hold the pose than a two-year-old child. In conversation Sprague was most delightful. With his vast fund of experience, he would recall event upon event and character after character of scenes and personages that today form important pages of history. Intimate accounts of his relations with Lincoln, Grant, Sherman, Sumner, and many others, if fully written would be most interesting reading matter.

He was particularly fond of describing Lincoln's peculiarities. "Once," he said, "a squad of Rhode Island boys had been condemned by court martial for desertion and were about to be shot. The parents and relatives of these boys requested me to take the matter to Lincoln and try to have them pardoned. After I had looked into the facts of the affair, I felt that there were certain extenuating circumstances and argued the case before the President. While I was talking, Lincoln paced the floor, his hands clasped behind him; and when I had finished, he wheeled about and with tears in his eyes said, "Well, Sprague, what would you do with these boys if you were in my place?" I felt that he was putting the decision up to me and I said, 'Well, Mr. President, I would shoot them.' Lincoln looked at me in surprise and said, 'Then why do you argue for the parole?' 'Because,' I said, 'I told these people I would do what I could in their behalf, but now that you ask me, I must say that I believe in maintaining the discipline of the army.' The next day the boys were paroled.

"Lincoln was aggressive, determined, methodical. When meeting resistance he was adroit, often seeming to waiver, but when it came to a show down, he was adamant. There was always tenderness in his deliberations. He was human, sympathetic, humorous—he would delay the most serious discussion in his cabinet meetings to tell a humorous story—open, direct, frank, but never unpolitic."

The following letter, which I copied from a newspaper clipping in Governor Sprague's scrapbook, is convincing evidence that in addition to Lincoln's ability as a statesman, his vision far exceeded the vision of his fellow mortals:

President Lincoln's Prophecy

President Lincoln wrote to a life-long friend just before his tragic death the following:

> "Yes, we may congratulate ourselves that this cruel war is nearing a close. It cost a vast amount of treasure and blood. The best blood of the flower of American youth has been freely offered upon our country's altar, that the nation might live. It has been, indeed, a trying hour for the republic, but I see in the near future a Crisis arising that unnerves me and causes me to tremble for the safety of my country. As a result of the war, corporations have been enthroned, and an era of corruption in high places will follow, and the money power will continue its sway by appealing to the prejudices of the people, until all wealth is aggregated in a few hands and the republic destroyed. I feel more anxious for the safety of my country than ever before, even in the midst of war. God grant that my fears may prove groundless."

It has been said that friction frequently existed between President Lincoln and the Lady of the White House. Denials of such facts have come forward. In answer to my query regarding these statements, Governor Sprague related an incident when he called to see the President on some legislative matter. "In the course of conversation, Lincoln shrugged his shoulders a few times and laughingly said that his wife had been too vigorous in his chastisement. I said to the President, 'I did not think you would stand for feminine correction quite to that extent.' 'Oh, well,' he said, 'as long as she enjoys it, and it doesn't hurt very much, why not?'"

Regarding Grant, the Governor said, "I think Grant was the greatest general of modern times, a far greater success at commanding armies than in handling executive matters as President. It took much to stir Grant to action, but once aroused he was sublime. After his victory at Vicksburg, upon meeting Rosencranz in Chattanooga, Grant said, 'Rosie, you know I'm no general, but at Washington they think I am, and I am going on!'"

Sprague told of his going with General Sherman on a buffalo-killing trip. "Buffalo killing was then thought rare sport, and I assure you it was exciting. The Western plains were infested by millions of them. We would ride into their herd to scatter them and then shoot them down on a gallop. Often the bulls would turn on us; then there was danger of having our horses gored. The thing to avoid was the stampede. Once going, a thousand buffaloes are like an avalanche, sweeping everything in their course. Returning by way of the Southern Pacific Railroad, our train was caught in a cut some twenty feet deep, by a stampeded herd. It was a tremendous herd, and the buffaloes piled up so deep in the trench and over the train that some of the cars were almost buried beneath a struggling, bawling mass of animals. In our car every window was smashed in by kicking legs. The trainmen were two days getting the tracks clear."

Early in October I received a commission to paint a portrait of the Reverend Father Byrne, who had been a member of a well-known order of preachers, the Paulists, but had resigned from the order to become a secular priest and was appointed pastor of a church at Wakefield, Rhode Island. A man of rare learning, his bearing was that of a dignified churchman, resembling in features Cardinal Manning, of England.

The Spragues were not religious people; in fact, they never attended any church, nor was a minister ever invited to the home; but Mrs. Sprague, knowing that I was painting Father Byrne's portrait, asked me if I should like her to invite him to dinner on Thanksgiving Day and to spend the night at the house. Byrne accepted the invitation. There were other guests also, and an elaborate spread with beautiful decorations awaited them. Mrs. Sprague, always fond of bright colors, appeared in the drawing room in a brilliant cardinal décolleté gown. Taking the arm of Father Byrne, she led the procession to the dining room. The Governor likewise appeared in evening dress, an unusual thing for him. As I have said before, Sprague was a reticent man, hard to draw out; but I might say of him, as he said of Grant, that, once inspired, his language was sublime and on this occasion he seemed to respond to the presence of this cultured and brilliant cleric.

The meal over, the ladies retired to the drawing room and the men to the coffee room, where Byrne and Sprague continued their conversation on serious subjects. Oris and several of his male companions soon withdrew and joined the ladies, while I remained, and as the conversation drifted from one subject to another the hours passed quickly. Never before nor since have I had the pleasure of listening to the language and the reasoning of so great a statesman on one side and so profound and learned a philosopher and theologian on the other. While not agreeing on all points, it is plainly evident that at heart nearly all great thinkers are of the same school. Not a devotee in any sense of the word, Sprague was, nevertheless, a believer in the main fundamental and dogmatic truths of religion, in the existence of an all-wise and provident Creator, and the immortality of the human soul. Modern conditions of civilization were discussed and the tendency of the times, they said, was pointing to a general evolution and improvement of human society. Both admitted, however, that the finger of criticism could be placed upon things which, if allowed to continue, would result in a decadence of the spiritual and an over-development of material resources and activities. Sprague said that society was no doubt ill, and religion was the nurse to the sick man, and with efficient nursing recovery was sure. Byrne made one remark I clearly recall, "If we can save our girls, we can save society, for the influence of woman has always been a potent factor in the regeneration of mankind." I must say that I never spent a more pleasant and profitable evening.

I also painted for Mrs. Sprague a portrait of Mrs. Wheaton in a white gown, seated at a harp. which she played. She once asked me to paint a head of Oris, but I found excuses and deferred the work so often that she ceased to speak about it. Somehow I had conceived such a dislike for him that I feared the expression would have been Satanic rather than human. I made a head, however, of Miss Portia, which pleased the family immensely. She and I were very congenial and frequently strolled down to the beach together. Occasionally she would go with me to church at Wakefield to hear Father Byrne preach.

Four years later, when I was painting some portraits in Newport, she came there and said, "I came just to see you." After a pleasant visit, she left for the Pier, saying she would soon return to Washington, and I have never seen her since. In 1925, while painting a portrait for the director of the National Gallery in Washington, I tried to locate her in the department where she had been employed, but I could find no one who knew her. Upon looking over the records, they found that she had resigned many years before, but they were unable to give me her address. In all my travels and in the many cities where I have lived in giving exhibitions and painting portraits, there are certain outstanding characters, my acquaintance with whom, however brief, I love to recall; but of them all, my recollections of Miss Portia Sprague are the most vivid and lasting, not only because of her personal charm, her great sincerity, and sympathetic understanding of the things with which I had been most concerned, but the thought that she felt most deeply the sad tragedy in the lives of her parents aroused my sympathy.

Governor Sprague's son Willie grew to manhood and married Mrs. Inez Sprague's sister Avis. Some years later I was told he committed suicide and she married a man of vast wealth by the name of Gerrit Smith Wheaton, in Washington. I never met the other daughters of Governor Sprague.

When the portrait of the Governor was finished, hearing about it, the Providence Journal sent a reporter to see it, and quite a lengthy article appeared about it in that paper. Later the Secretary of State, Bennett, came to the Pier with a memorial from Governor Dwyer and several State officials, requesting the picture for the State Capitol. After some time, Governor Sprague relented and signified his willingness that a replica of the picture should be made for the Capitol. Shortly after, a message came that Mr. Wheaton had died very suddenly and in the midst of a snowstorm the Sprague's, with the exception of Miss Portia, hastily left for Washington. As we bade the Governor goodbye, he said, "Be good." Those were his last words to me. The picture was packed and shipped to Providence. The appropriation spoken of by Mrs. Sprague for the purchase of Governors' portraits, I considered inadequate, and the Secretary of State said that he would introduce a measure assigning the sum I required. During the last hours of the Legislature, the bill passed both houses unanimously.

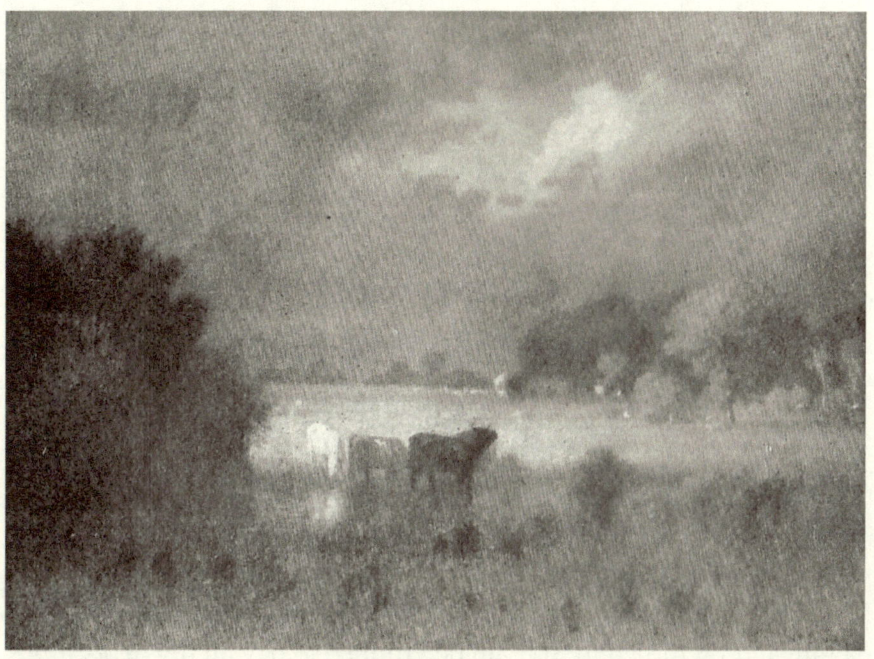

Scenting the Storm

An interesting incident in this connection arose. Young Anthony Dwyer, son of Governor Dwyer, who since then has become an artist, on seeing the painting and learning the price I asked, protested that he thought it was too high. A committee of artists composed of H. Cyrus Farnum, Eugene Smythe, and Whitaker, had been notified to inspect my picture, by Secretary Bennett, and had pronounced it a worthy piece of work. Farnum, on being informed of Dwyer's objection, said, "Well, Anthony doesn't know anything about pictures anyway, and I think the State of Rhode Island should be very glad to have such a portrait of its famous War Governor."

Not many years ago I was informed that while the Spragues were living abroad, Canonchet with all its pictures and all its art went up in flames.

Chapter XII
The Student Clan

Sketching Excursions—Alexis Fournier—Landeau—Pike Island—A Cyclone

It was a handsome sum the Rhode Island legislature approved for my picture and I returned to St. Paul determined to pay all my debts if possible. My good friend Wack suggested that if I could find a house that could be bought cheaply on easy terms, he would put up the initial payment. So, we moved into new quarters in the respectable neighborhood of Ridgewood Park.

To include all the interesting characters I have known would make a book so large that no library shelf could hold it; but Alexis J. Fournier, an old and dear friend of mine, must not be overlooked. I first noticed his work at the Minneapolis exhibition, of which I have already written, way back in the '80's. He was then living in Minneapolis, and like most Western artists at that time, was eking out a poor existence by painting landscapes, houses, signs, and everything to which he could turn his hand. Some of his landscapes were extremely ambitious and so carefully drawn and labored in detail that they were noticeable. They were well composed and true in value, but very lacking in luminosity. The promising amateur was evident in everything he did. I remember, however, a picture of thistles, with Fort Snelling in the background, which was very interesting on account of the care with which he had drawn the thistles.

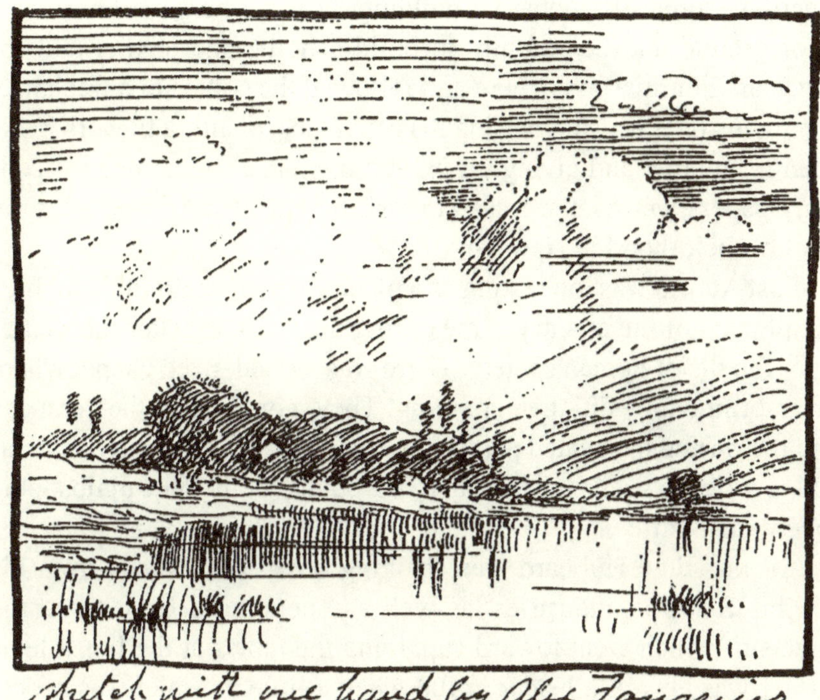

Sketch with one hand by Alx Fournier
from a hand paintin by Prof. N. R. Brewer
this 9th day of Dec. 1911.

I lost sight of him for ten years, during which time he had been sent by some philanthropic women to study in France. They provided him with funds, and he left his family in Minneapolis. He tells of the hardships of the time, when his home with all his pictures was burned and he was stranded in Europe. He studied with Laurens, Constant, Harpignies, and the Julian Academy, later with Cazin, from which master he acquired to a marvelous degree the quality of light in his work. He brought back with him many beautiful pieces, mostly sheep subjects, and told how, with a thumb box on his arm, he followed a ram all day long in the pasture, to study the anatomy of the nibbling brute, just as he drew the blossoming thistles in earlier days. One was impressed by his indefatigable capacity for work.

About this time Fournier fell in with Elbert Hubbard, who became interested in his work and wanted him to go to East Aurora, New York, to decorate some of Hubbard's buildings. I think he gave Fournier a plot of ground and helped him to build a home and studio, and for many years Fournier lived there and followed the course of a freelance, pursuing his own way, increasing his canvasses, planting flowers in his garden in summer and giving his exhibitions, or, as he termed it, "selling my papers," in winter. I used to visit him at East Aurora, after my annual bachelorhood in New York.

East Aurora was interesting as a place where pseudo-philosophers from all parts of the country came during the summer to air their cure-alls for the ills of human society. There was a good-sized chapel where every morning they did their spouting. They would sit on the verandas of the Inn during the heated part of the day or evening and exchange rational theories to such an extent that one could cut the blue philosophic smoke with a knife.

All this time Hubbard was chalking down the shekels from his hotel, his Roycroft industries, as well as operating a large farm, the products of which went toward supplying the tables at the Inn. Alexis Fournier was always a leader in fun when a little mischief was necessary. A genial and mutual friend of ours was Mr. Turner, a publisher and editor from Cleveland. He had recently gone through a serious operation for appendicitis; in fact, his case was so alarming that his life had hung by a delicate thread for some weeks. With a drainpipe still in his side, he went about Aurora as though in perfect health. He had all the wit and humor characteristic of his Celtic blood and craved something more in the way of diversion than the somber arguments of the learned theorists about the place.

Richard Le Gallienne had a shack down the river some six miles, in the dense woods, where he did his writing. A well-known actress and her daughter from New York, two or three other artists whose names I do not now recall, La Gallienne, his young daughter Eva (who has since distinguished herself in the theatrical world), with Mr. Fournier and myself formed a hostile group in the Hubbard camp. We had come there for congenial recreation and pastime and to break the monotony of the place, we formed what we termed the "Tommyrotters' Club." Our antics, for grownups, to say the least, were not always dignified. On one occasion, when we became a little too hilarious, Hubbard shook his finger at us lest we might disturb the deliberations of the reformers. This was before the days of prohibition, in spite of which fact we, at least, were always sober. In the evening we would retreat some distance from the Inn and sing comic ballads. This called down upon us a severe reprimand from His Majesty, Fra Elbertus. Then we decided to carry our fun-making to the woods at Le Gallienne's place. Chartering a boat, the party would sail down the river on moonlight nights.

One night, Fournier and our New York actress friends staged a comedy which I shall never forget. It was entirely impromptu. Fournier was the star—an Italian minstrel. A picturesque costume, with scarf about his shoulders, a little hat with a feather, a banjo in his hand, combined with his ability to sing an Italian ditty, made him appear the real thing. He was so enamored of his senorita, Eva Le Gallienne, who at her window threw blossoms at him in the moonlight, that he decided to kidnap her and make her his own. Stealing out of the dense woods, he sang to attract her, and when she appeared at the window, he scaled the balcony and sang sweeter than ever. Suddenly he seized her, carried her to the ground, and dashed away with her into the wilderness. The alarm was given, the villagers were aroused, and pursuit was taken up. Another act showed the capture and a farcical trial of the culprit, and a heavy fine of thirty cents was imposed. Le Gallienne and I sat leaning back against the walls of the shanty as the moon broke through and dimmed the faint lantern light, laughing and enjoying the fun.

Fournier seldom sent anything to the art exhibitions. Why, I do not know; nor did he court the acquaintance of prominent artists, men who could place him in the front ranks—a thing which I urged him to do. One winter I insisted upon his bringing his paintings to New York and offered him the use of my studio as I had ample room where he could retouch his things and invite artists in to see them. It would be a grand relief from the monotony of bachelor life, I thought, and it would also help him. The three months he spent with me there were, indeed, pleasant ones.

Fournier was always a comedian, and an absent-minded one at that, making appointments and forgetting them, carried away by some momentary enthusiasm to do the opposite thing from his original intention. I remember his making an appointment with a Madam Holliday and her daughter for us to dine at her home on a Thursday evening. The next day he made the same appointment with another family in Harlem. Thursday morning our friend Graff came in and invited us to dine that evening at his place. Thursday evening came and we got ready and went to dine at the Graff house, forgetting altogether the other two engagements. We had a fellow artist named Tousey, who was doing some lettering in the room, and we left him in charge. Some time after seven o'clock a telephone call came to the Graff house for Mr. Fournier from Mrs. Holliday, reminding him of the broken engagement. Suddenly he sprang to his feet and said, "My God, we were to go to Mrs. Holliday's for dinner. What'll I tell her?" Turning to me he said, "You go to the phone— tell her I have been sick all day—tell her anything!" I took up the receiver and she said, "Why, Mr. Brewer, the dinner is getting cold." I began to apologize, saying Fournier was ill, when she said that Mr. Tousey had informed her that we had gone to Mr. Graff's for dinner and she asked, "How is that possible?" I was terribly embarrassed. I forget exactly what I did tell her, but I know I got rid of her by saying that I would have Fournier call her in the morning. She and her daughter called a few days later at the studio and the well-deserved scolding we received was a scorcher. The lady with whom he had made the other appointment wrote him a letter, which made him regret his rudeness. She was a prospect to whom he expected to sell a landscape. Whether he ever did or not, I do not recall.

One summer my friend Wack and I spent our vacation in the Berkshire Hills. Wack, an enthusiastic artist, wanted to do outdoor sketching with me and we whiled away some happy weeks together. As I had to go West, I proposed a trip by motor to Buffalo and East Aurora. He had met Fournier many years before and relished the idea of painting around East Aurora. Landeau, Fournier's friend, whom I had never met, was then having an exhibition in Aurora. Landeau had studied abroad, had painted some good things in Paris, having occupied a studio with Henry O. Tanner, and was withal a well-educated and capable artist. He was short and stout, with a tremendous frontal rotundity due to his gourmand-like habits. He could eat more than Fournier, Wack, and myself put together. A man of high ideals, he had some eccentricities, which had led to separation from his wife.

We made sketching excursions to the hills south of Aurora, where the country was romantic and beautiful. Each time Landeau persisted in doing the cooking and would build the fire in the woods and cook a great kettle of goulash, throwing in all kinds of meat and vegetables, which he served with good French wine. In fact, he spent nearly all his time preparing the meals, while the rest of us worked.

One day it rained, and we had to work in Alex's studio. I began to paint a large canvas from my study of the previous day. We all worked away very industriously, except Landeau. I had laid out a scheme about which I was very enthusiastic, and which, when it was finished, I called *The Grove on the Hilltop*. But the poor canvas was almost wrecked before being finished. As Landeau sat contemplating the next meal he was to prepare for us in the woods, he watched me paint. When I sat down to rest, in a spirit of mischief he seized a large brush, dipped it in a lot of color and banged away at the trees on the hill, obliterating completely the forms I had so carefully limned. While his trick was intended as a joke, he soon aroused my indignation. Alex and Wack stopped work and with eyes and mouths wide open looked on. I said something to prevent Landeau's going further, but he did not heed, and as the first few strokes of the big brush, I thought, had spoiled my picture, I said, "All right, you can finish it now; it is your picture." Then he began to realize that I was in earnest. I grabbed the thing off the easel, turned its face to the corner and said, "That is the last of that." He began profuse apology, which we did not think very consistent, and left the room. He felt extremely bad about his mistaken humor and the following day wanted me to go on and finish the picture, but I declined. We went to the woods, however, and he was extremely nice and agreeable, ending the feud with a peace offering of a finer meal than he had ever prepared for us before. I relented and a few days later recalled the work I had done on the painting. Perhaps it was a better work of art due to the joke, because in repainting it, I departed from the photographic exactness in that bunch of trees. Freyermouth, the dealer, shortly afterward wanted some of my pictures to take to Texas, and sold the large picture to the Art Club, Waxahachie, Texas. Later, when the Dallas Art Association gave an exhibition of my pictures, the ladies of Waxahachie wanted their picture included in the exhibit, and two of them carried the large canvas on the train to Dallas, where it was hung.

Landeau's very large figure, representing a group of fisher people in prayer for those at sea, was a most ambitious and meritorious work. The French Government had offered to buy the picture for the Luxemburg Gallery, but he declined, thinking that he could get more for it in America. Because of its great size, it was a white elephant on his hands. What disposition was made of it after his death, I do not know.

Sometime after that, Mrs. Fournier passed away, and as their two children had married and left home, Alex was left alone. Meeting him in Toleda sometime later, I noticed that my poor friend seemed all broken up and so low in spirit that his work showed the effects of his grief. The next year while in Miami, I got a letter from him from South Bend where I was soon to give an exhibition, saying that he had met the widow of Clarence Ball, the artist. She seemed so sympathetic and appreciative of his art and work that he contemplated proposing marriage.

Three years ago, I saw Fournier and his wife where they were living in his wife's home. He had rented his East Aurora house and was happily painting better than ever.

And there is our son Ed, whose character has a peculiar combination of traits. In some ways, he is a genius. In his youth he was simply an abstract dreamer, no good for any practical purposes. It was useless to send him on an errand; he was sure to forget it and wander off chasing butterflies, poking after frogs, or robbing birds' nests. He would always show up at dinner, sometimes having forgotten the errand entirely. It was a custom of ours, when we wanted an errand quickly performed, to send Reuben, who was fleet of foot, always returning promptly.

When a child, Ed showed a predilection for drawing and sketching. He loved to explore the woods in search and study of birds and other things in nature. He frequently attended my class in 1897. He had a manner of scrawling his name at the top of his paper, saying, "Well, I have to make my name first!"

I placed him in the Art Students' League, New York, but it was difficult to get him up in the mornings to go to work. However, he did some notable drawing in the class.

He was successful in making covers for the sport magazines. His knowledge of bird and animal life proved of great value in this work. To this day he can tell you the characteristic markings of every bird that flies and every animal from a skunk to a giraffe. He soon became known as an illustrator. Finally he became better known as the creator of the Cream of Wheat smiling-faced darkey who featured their ads for several years. This darkey became internationally known and was dubbed "Rastus," usually being pictured as presenting a steaming bowl of breakfast food to a hungry boy or girl.

His first picture of Rastus, entitled *Dat's mah Boy*, spurred a new school in commercial art. Reproductions of his Rastus ads were bought by the thousands. Ed used his own children and their numerous cousins as models to depict compelling little heart interest stories that were as fine as they were popular. The press commented extensively on the influence of his work. In his better things, he ranges from oil portraits to miniatures, murals, and landscapes. And these are of no mean order.

Outstanding in his many large works are five mural panels for a bank in LaCrosse, Wisconsin, representing the beginning and growth of the city. On the panels the game of lacrosse is shown as being played by the tribe ere the white man came. Pioneer industry is shown in the snow-laden pineries, with men felling trees and skidding them to the river to be floated on their way to the sawmill. Another scene depicts the smoking stacks of the mills busy in the lumber industry, and still another a panorama of the city and the river bluffs from "Old Granddad," a sentinel mountain that stands guard over the curving cliff-banked "Father of Waters." A mural in the Spokane and Eastern Bank of Spokane, Washington, which he titles *Builders of the Inland Empire*, portrays the conquest of the covered wagon of early days.

He is represented by a group of portraits of the District Court Judges of St. Paul, a commission awarded him by the State Bar Association; also, in the State Capitol, by a portrait of Abraham Lincoln, which hangs in the House of Representatives, and by numerous other portraits throughout the country.

Among the six Brewer boys, their talents and occupations run as follows:

Francis Angelo, our first born, is a plain, blunt, businessman. For several years he assisted me in handling and managing some large exhibitions and did it very effectively.

Edward Vincent, an artist—portrait, murals, and illustrations form his line of work.

Ruben Joseph, a landscape painter, did not take up painting until after forty. His pictures have some fine qualities, especially in color.

William Wallace is an inventor and manufacturer of some of his inventions.

Adrian L., portrait and landscape painter. He won a $2,500.00 prize with his "Bluebonnet Year", a Texas wildflower picture.

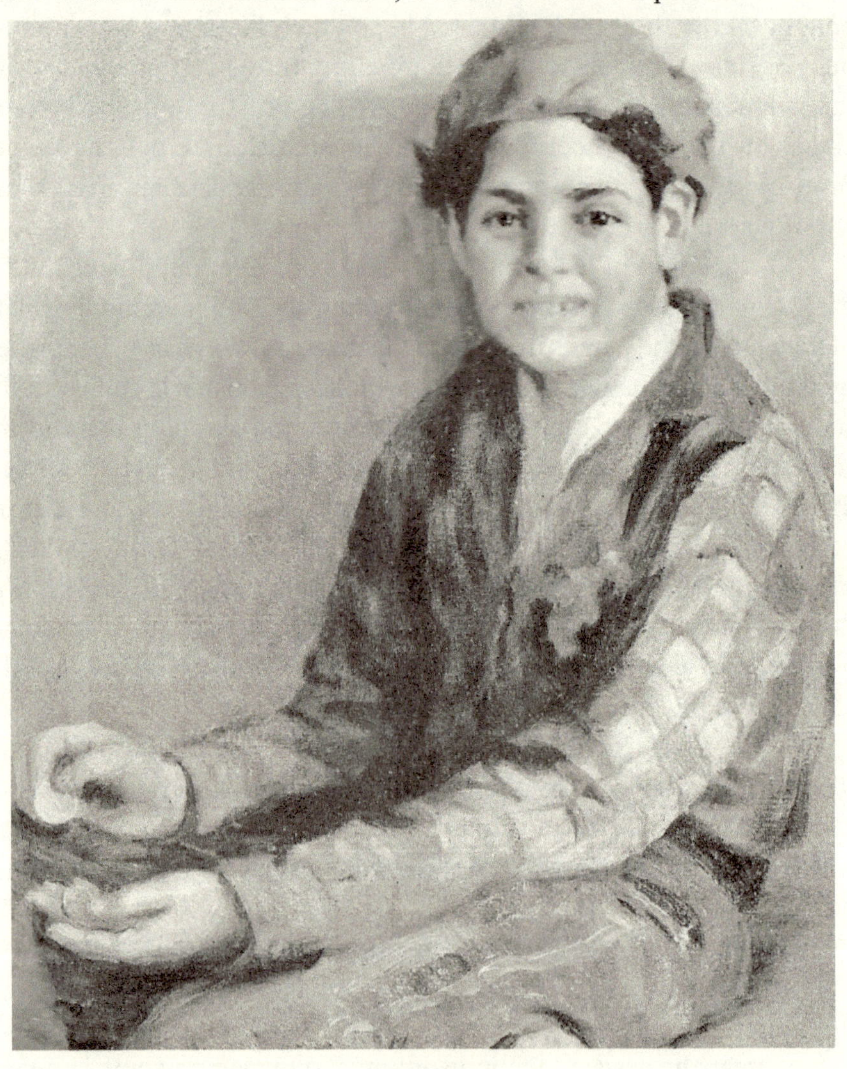

Four Bits

Clarence Arthur, a twin of Adrian's, artistic craftsmanship. He performs the exalted duty of carving fine frames for the four painter members of the "Brewery," as the bunch are sometimes dubbed, and others of the art ilk. For years he has labored to develop a style of wood carving, which is not only unique, but wonderfully beautiful. It would be hard to find the equal of the designs ordered for the Justices Butler and Van Devanter and other portraits in Washington and throughout the country.

* * *

There was Arthur Allie—Arthur, the dear old Socialist—an artist by nature as well as technique. He had read all the Marxian literature outside of Russia, constantly talked the Henry George "single land tax" theory, and sneered at rights of property. "The Government should own all lands and all real property and decide on a scale of equal pay for everybody. No man has any more right to this world's goods than anybody else, whether he be bootblack or the manager of a railroad." He said, "Shrewdness in manipulating natural resources is a vice, not a virtue." Allie was a creature of self will. Nobody could do anything with him, nor could he do anything with himself. He was full of ideas that would turn the world upside down—if they could only be put into practice. He said no honest man could ever be a success financially, but only the rogue. He had so much respect for his own inclinations and ideas that he never could adopt those of anyone else. In the art class he was adamant against the instructor's advice. A quaint vein of humor, however, always made his presence agreeable. Whenever an idea or opinion on a subject of common interest was expressed, he countered with an opposing one, and when he found himself worsted in an argument, he made a joke of it all, and we would laugh it off. One winter he invented a tent with a stove in it. Through a small window in the canvas, he looked out while working. The harvest of his labors was one very fine winter landscape that hung at some of the exhibitions.

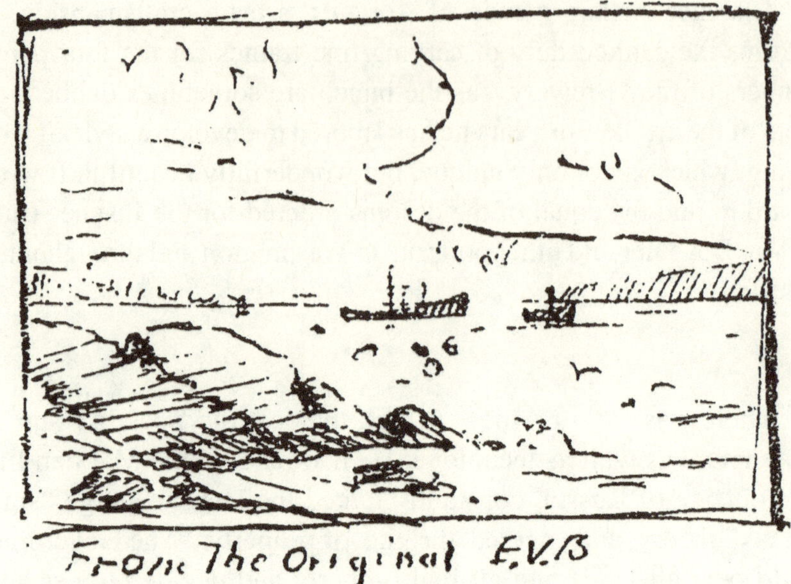

When he had saved two hundred dollars, he married a very sensible girl—at least sensible in everything except love. But that is where nearly everyone falls down and if matches turn out happily it is either an accident or the grace of God. Perhaps God steps in to make the affair look like wisdom on our part. There was never a truer saying than "Love is blind." At least, all these were our surmises when she married Allie, but marriage for him proved just the right kind of a tonic, although he courted it and rebelled against it at the same time. I cannot say that his wife ever used the rolling pin on him, but he showed great fear of displeasing her. When their first child came, he grumbled at having to rock the cradle or walk the floor nights with "the squawking thing." Mrs. Allie, by making her husband hold his job at sign work and saving his money for him, in time was able to make the first payment on a house they bought. Then she rented out rooms, thus contributing largely toward raising the money to meet the payments on the house as they fell due. Recently I learned that they had paid up in full. Now he is a real landowner and never speaks of "single land tax" or "government ownership" anymore. When I saw him last, he said, "Well, if a fellow manages right, he just can't help getting rich." I am inclined to think the wife did the managing, even if she did not pop the question.

Long before the dream of an art institute for St. Paul had germinated in the minds of certain ladies, I had interested several St. Paul men in the project of an art association of some kind for the purpose of holding exhibitions and forming an art school. In answer to my appeal, quite a number of men met one evening at my Seven Corners studio. Among them were Judge Flandrau, Chris O'Brien, the now famous architects Cass Gilbert and Alan H. Stem, also other architects, lawyers, and artists—but no financiers. Three of us had appointed ourselves an invitation committee and sent a formal invitation to Mr. J. J. Hill, Commodore Kittson, and other outstanding men of finance, none of whom attended. Only a group of talented, ambitious dreamers who could have done wonders for the worthy cause with financial backing responded to the invitation. Judge Flandrau was appointed chairman of the meeting.

In the course of discussion, the president made a famous speech in which he said we should not be too ambitious in an art movement. "The city is too young. The Northwest is yet too crude, not ready for art. We could not function for lack of interest among the people." In reply, I referred to the example of the businessmen of our then smaller neighbor, the city of Minneapolis. In forming their Exposition Association, over one hundred thousand dollars had been raised for art culture to make the Mill City an art center talked of throughout the nation. After all, our meeting resulted in nothing but "hot air," and the movement soon died.

A few years later, a group of women organized the St. Paul Art Association. They opened a class and the movement dragged along for several years, until the holding of an art loan exhibition and its resulting success, which all agree was caused by the women. They formed a comprehensive organization, to be known as "The St. Paul Institute of Arts and Sciences." About that time the late C. W. Ames, that remarkably clever and enthusiastic art promotor, took over the executive reins and made it a notable institution of the Northwest. He inaugurated an annual exhibition of the works of art of seven states and sent the collections to other cities throughout the country on educational missions. The death of Mr. Ames was a stunning loss to the country. Since his passing, the local art exhibition spirit is again lagging, but the substantial basis upon which the institution rests, with its notable achievements, will not be forgotten, and someday another Ames will arise to carry on the good work.

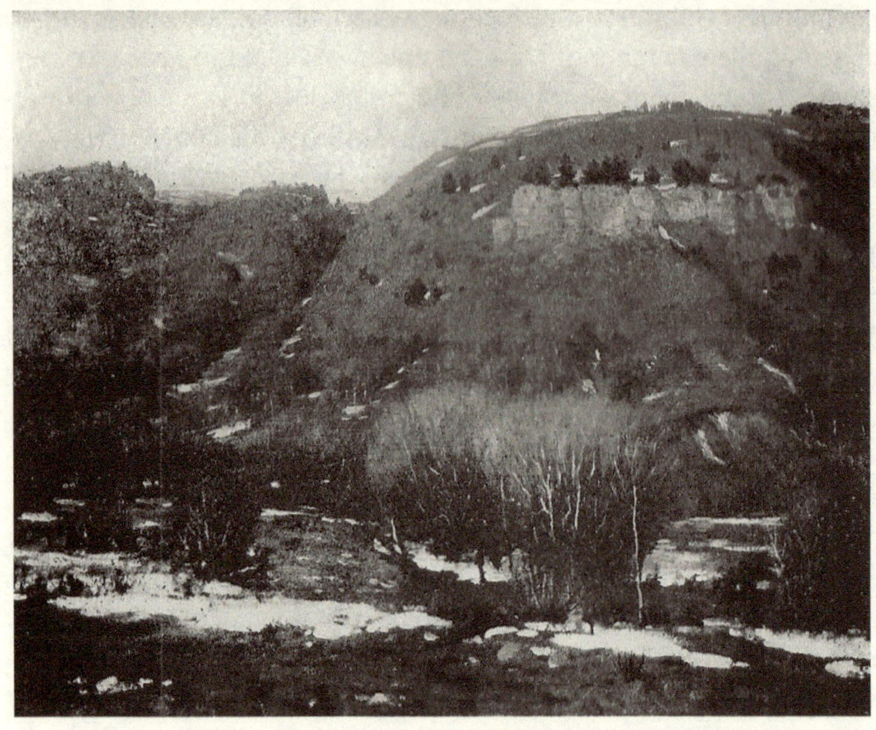

Hills of The Little Iowa, Purchase Prize, Northwestern Artists' Exhibition, 1915. Courtesy St. Paul Institute.

When I first went East to paint the portrait of Mrs. Wm. Sprague, I sublet my studio to another artist. Only a few years ago I met a gentleman who began to tell me how pleased he was with a picture of mine and knowing that I had never sold him one, I asked where he got it. "I bought it," he replied, "of Cohen, the pawn broker." Of course, I had never been in Cohen's place, in fact, had never seen the man, and I was curious the know how he came by it, and went to see him. I asked Mr. Cohen, "Have you any paintings by Mr. Brewer, the artist?"

He said, "No, I used to have a good many, but I have sold them all. I put a good deal of money into them, but I got it out again."

"Whom did you buy them of?" I questioned.

"Oh, Mr. Brewer," he said.

"What kind of looking man is Mr. Brewer?" I inquired.

"He is rather sandy and quite large. He used to come in frequently and want some money, and offer me a picture."

I said, "Mr. Cohen, have you ever seen me before?"

He looked at me scrutinizingly, and replied, "No."

"Well," I said, "I am Mr. Brewer."

"Oh," he said, "you are not the Mr. Brewer that I bought the pictures of, for I have never seen you before."

The fact was the man who had rented my studio had copied some pictures of mine, put my name on them and sold them as originals, or forged my name to his own pictures.

For many years it was my pleasure to take the family and my pupils to the country for a time in the summer. We usually rigged up a camp, with tents, cots, cooking utensils, sometimes at Lake Minnetonka or Pike Island, or elsewhere. Frequently we would rent a cottage at White Bear or Bald Eagle Lake. One time at Pike Island we had a most enjoyable time. We had the island all to ourselves and could paint anywhere, free from the intrusion of curious people. We had invited several amateur artists beside the pupils. There were Dr. Goodrich, the dentist, who painted persistently; McKelvey, the skeptical sign painter and landscapist; Sid Ewing, Arthur Allie, and several others. We all painted in the open, some badly and some only half badly. We had a negro cook, as black as your hat, who had a Roman nose. Every afternoon he would row to the mainland and go to town, only to come home half stewed and unable to cook the evening meal. Then my wife would take pity on him (she always takes pity on scalawags, finding some excuse for their behavior), and would prepare the meal herself.

One afternoon a storm arose which developed into a cyclone. As trees began to crash about us, I called to the boys to help me make more secure the guy-ropes of the tents, while the women and children huddled inside. Finally one tent went down, trapping them within. Then away went the kitchen tent and the pots and pans were scattered everywhere. The screaming of wriggling youngsters and women, the downpour of rain, amid thunder and lightning, made a jazz medley of sound! What a mess it was! Fortunately, it was as short in duration as it was violent, and in fifteen minutes the sun was again shining.

One day the class was painting on the eastern point of the island and after luncheon, the girls, my wife, and some other invited ladies, came over to where we were working and strolled about until suppertime, when all returned to camp. The cook, as usual, had evaporated, and we were startled to find the camp in possession of a herd of cows bent on satisfying their bovine curiosity and messing things up generally. Standing inside the kitchen tent door, head out, was a fine Holstein, with her neck stretched forward and up, chewing something and lapping her lips while the foamy liquid streamed from the corners of her mouth. She was chewing the last bar of the cook's laundry soap. So abstracted by its flavor that a punch in the ribs by one of the boys was needed to make her leave the place. In turning about, she upset the long plank table with all our dishes and milk bottles—the proverbial "bull in a china shop." From the door of the other tent emerged another cow, chewing something also and it was not soap either, but one of the ladies' stockings. She had the foot end down her throat while the leg of it flapped about. The stocking, when rescued, was a "holey" show, to the regret of the owner. A calf put his foot through one of Doc Goodrich's canvasses and drank all the water in the pail brought from the Fort for drinking purposes. But such is camp life, and how we did enjoy it!

In the meantime, through correspondence with Wack, I had kept him acquainted with our maneuvers. He had gone to London, where he became manager of a large manufacturing concern at a very worthwhile salary. Before leaving New York, however, he met a charming black-eyed girl, the daughter of a well-to-do family of West Eighty-ninth Street. Asparkling bit of sunshine, she was the life of every gathering. She had no lack of attention from the young men and no one knew or guessed where her preference lay, until Wack up and married her! Harry induced me to go to New York and paint the bride. When the picture was finished, Wack took his bride to London, where they lived for eight years.

Since then, Wack, who was educated for the bar, has become an author, artist, lecturer, editor, and traveler, with a record of many distant objective sea voyages and overland tours in quest of literary material and adventure. He is a life fellow of the Royal Geographical Society of London, and a fellow of the American Geographical Society. He has written a number of inspiring books on outdoor life, among them three recent volumes on organized camps for boys, girls, and adults. He was the founder and first editor, thirty-odd years ago, of *Field and Stream*, our largest sportsman's magazine, and is an ardent angler, game hunter, and camper of long experience in many parts of the world. Just now he is the associate editor of several magazines and the travel editor of one. Mr. Wack has long been a frequent radio speaker for the city of New York and leading broadcasting companies, on many topics—among others, nature and outdoor life, sportsmanship, art, civics, travel, exploration, and the privileges and problems of daily life. He is a member of the Bar of New York, and president of the Brooklyn Society of Artists.

Chapter XIII
Joseph Jefferson and Margaret Anglin

The birds sing, the brooks babble, the trees move and flowers have their odor—things which the painter cannot paint.

—Joseph Jefferson

We lived for three and one-half years in Ridgewood Park. Each winter I returned to New York, still hoping to establish myself there and eventually have my family with me. One winter, I had the same studio Tryon had occupied when I was in his class. Later, a cheaper place was found on Twenty-fourth Street near Sixth Avenue.

For several months no commissions came in and my finances ran so low that I was unable to furnish the studio with a long wished for comfortable bed. A couple of boards across dry goods boxes, covered with a quilt, formed my sleeping place. Indeed, it was hard and my bones often ached in consequence.

Father Ducey was then a well-known and popular priest, whose church was on Twenty-eighth Street. A friend suggested my getting acquainted with him. Consequently, I wrote Archbishop Ireland for a letter of introduction. When I called, Ducey was suffering from a severe cold and was in bed. He requested to see me in his room. I noted the striking features, the wonderful flesh color, sparkling blue eyes, gray, almost white hair, of a man sixty years of age. Motioning me to a seat, he read the letter I handed him. The Archbishop had mentioned in the letter that perhaps Ducey would let me paint his portrait; to which he replied that he was a poor man and he had always been opposed to showing his own likeness, but that he would come to see me. The next day he called at the studio and reluctantly consented to pose for me as I told him I would not consider it a business proposition.

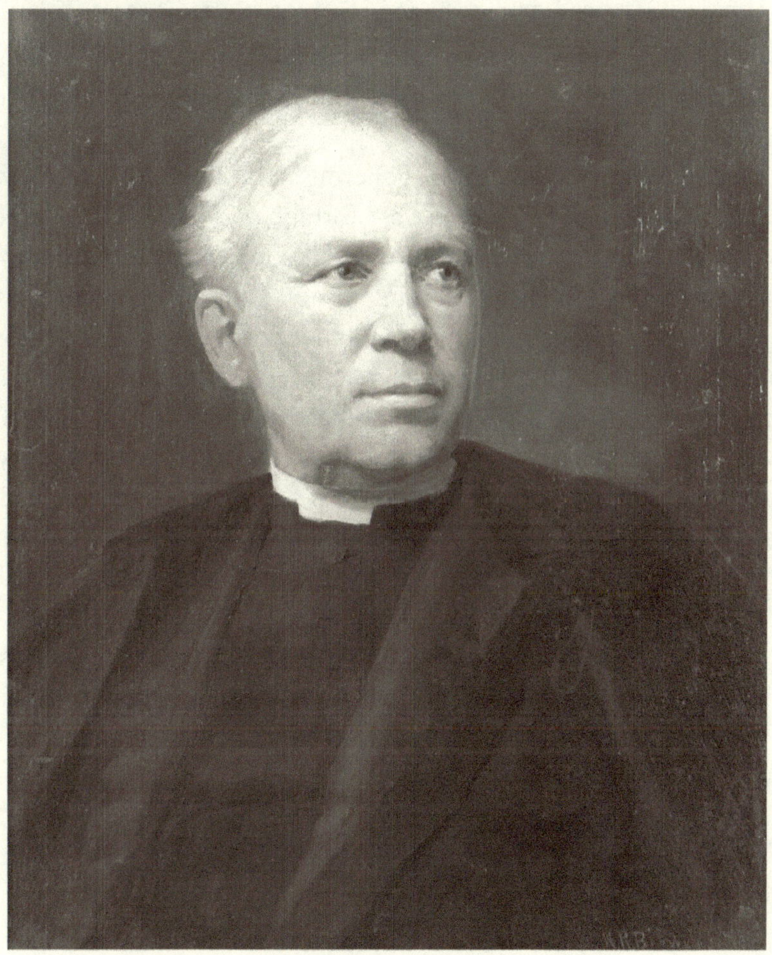

Rev. Father Ducey

He asked about my family in the West, and doubtless surmised that my financial condition with a family on my hands was none too good; but, of course, I could not tell him the real facts. A couple of days later, His Reverence, on leaving the studio, remarked that a lady had sent him some money with a request that he place it where he thought it would do the most good and he thought he could do no better than to give it to me—and threw the envelope on the table. It proved to be a check for fifty dollars—enough to pay a month's back rent, a laundry bill and buy some food. A few days later, he repeated the kindness, but when I opened the envelope this time there was Ducey's own check for fifty dollars more. This I mailed to my wife. A third time he left a check, but when I went to the bank to cash it the teller smiled and said Father Ducey had no funds there at present, but if I would keep the check it would be good later he was sure.

Ducey was one of the most generous souls I have ever known. It was said that he had inherited a vast fortune and had literally given it away—often times to wholly improvident subjects. The beggar would get his last penny, whether deserving or not. Ducey was a learned man with a positive socialistic leaning. His theories were frowned upon by his superiors in the Church and he was, no doubt, under surveillance, owing to the fact that he was an intimate supporter of the late Doctor McGlynn of St. Stephen's Church, who had been unfrocked by the Bishop for insubordinating the use of his pulpit for the propaganda of socialistic doctrines. Dr. Burtsel, another cleric, socialistically inclined, with McGlynn and Ducey formed a trio which must have caused the hierarchy considerable worry.

McGlynn was a powerful orator, a broad-gauged man who sympathized with the laboring people and was extremely popular. When he was silenced and another priest sent to replace him, the congregation threatened to mob the new appointee. McGlynn's case was referred to Rome, and he was requested to appear there and state his side of the question. This request he entirely disregarded but continued to lecture every Sunday night, with Henry George and others of that school, at Cooper Union Hall. In his speeches he showed an attitude of rank rebellion against the policy of the Church. Finally, a peremptory order came from Rome, warning him that if he did not appear there within six weeks, he would be formally excommunicated. Again, he defied the authority. His popularity began to wane, however, and for several years he lectured in various parts of the country and then fell out of sight. Becoming ill and facing his last end, he requested to see the Archbishop, who, on receiving the telegram, hastily took the train and saw him in time to receive his recantation and plea for restoration to the high office of the priesthood.

Ducey never openly preached socialism, but at heart he was a socialist. He had a most likeable personality and a keen wit. He was brilliant in conversation and generally sympathetic. He lived frugally at home, having an old cook whose Irish brogue and pockmarked face with dark, piercing eyes and white hair were more attractive than her food. I made a head of her, draped in a black Spanish veil, which was quite a hit at some of the exhibitions.

Almost every day, Ducey would call before noon and invite me to lunch with him—not at his own home, but always at one of the best dining-rooms—the Waldorf, Sherry's, Delmonico's. He said he felt he was entitled to at least one wholesome meal a day. Never would he allow me to pay the bill—for obvious reasons.

One day Father Ducey walked into the room, followed by Joe Jefferson, whom he had invited to look at his portrait. Joe was very complimentary in his criticism. He particularly spoke of the quality of my blacks in the draperies. I remember his saying that black was not black in light. He said, "If that is black," pointing to the light on the sleeve, "what is this?" referring to the dense shadow under the sleeve. As the world knows, Jefferson was a real artist, not only as an actor but in many other ways. He was familiar with the brush, having painted many landscapes. He was not academic, nor did he value truth in his rendering of forms and color, yet his observation and judgment of things was extraordinary. This was manifested in his rare discernment and choice of works of art for his private collection. When it was placed on exhibition after his death, everybody was surprised by its exceptionally high quality. Ducey said, "Joe, I would like you to let Mr. Brewer paint your picture." "All right," said Joe, "but I haven't much time. Tomorrow is Sunday, and that is about the only time I can give for a sitting. How much time will you want for a head?" I told him I could make a sketch in an hour or two and the following day he appeared promptly. In a short time, I slapped out the head, which is here illustrated and of which Mrs. Jefferson declared, "Well, Joe, that is the best you've ever had. We must have it." Joe afterward bought the picture. Before leaving town, Jefferson gave me a cordial invitation to visit his summer home at Buzzard's Bay. He said,

"Come right along; you don't have to bring any paints or canvas—I have plenty of them. Come right up there and make yourself at home, and I'll be glad to sit for you for a larger picture." I told him that I would be delighted to paint a full figure of him in his character of Rip Van Winkle.

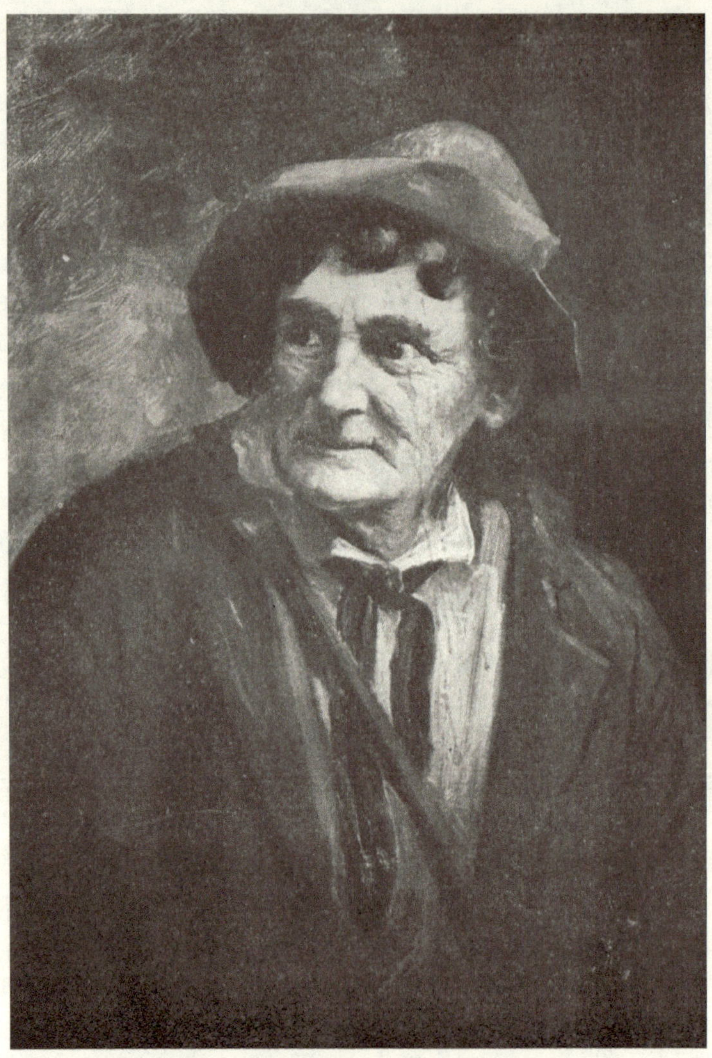

Joe Jefferson as Rip Van Winkle (sketch).

The summer was on and I returned to St. Paul where several matters came up that absorbed my attention so completely that I neglected to accept Mr. Jefferson's invitation until September. He wrote me then that he would have to postpone the sitting as he had to go out on a tour, but proposed that I come to Chicago in November where he would be playing, and do the work there. This I did. Before I began the picture, he suggested my seeing him play. "Come to the theatre. You should see the play from the audience and from behind the wings; come to my dressing room and familiarize yourself with Rip Van Winkle before you start the picture." He gave me a chair on the stage where I would not be observed by the audience. When it came to the last act, where Rip awakens from his twenty years' slumber, I saw him put on the most wonderful makeup. His long white beard and hair completely covering the Jefferson locks, intensifying and multiplying the lines, made the most perfect disguise I have ever seen. Presently he emerged and lay down on the floor back of the drop curtain. Instantly the curtain was raised, soon a slight bend of his head in my direction told the audience that Rip was waking. "Oh! Is that my arm?" he questioned as he moved the member stiffly. "Is that my foot?" His voice and movements suggested a squeaking of joints that had not moved for two decades, eyes that glared as they stared about as if on a strange world—but always coming back to me. Lifting one knee and clasping his hand to his back, he groaned realistically, then slowly staggering to his feet and with his left hand clutching his heart and the other hand shading his eyes, he gazed about upon an unfamiliar landscape. Stooping, he lifted his gun, but the wooden stock having decayed fell in pieces, while he gripped the barrel alone. "Where is my Falling Water—my home?" he asked, and he stared at me as though questioning me. He seemed oblivious of the tense, expectant audience, but was playing for me, for this was the act he hoped I would portray—his favorite act of Rip Van Winkle. This act, however, did not appeal to me as much as the former one, in which he is driven from his home by his irate wife for his shiftless, drunken habits—when he wandered into the woods in the storm and paused beneath the trees, saying, "Oh, how I love these trees! They have so often sheltered me." His dog, Schneider, had disappeared, and seeing the hobgoblins coming with a keg of brew, he was startled, and gun in hand, stood ready to shoot. That action in the forest I thought more capable of artistic interpretation.

The next day I made a sketch in pencil and showed it to him, saying, "This is my conception." With something of a disappointed look, he exclaimed, "Oh, I thought it was the old man Rip you would prefer to paint." He gave me sittings in the studio of J. Francis Brown in the Fine Arts Building. Each evening I saw the play and became more familiar with its variations and dramatic features. When the picture was finished, Jefferson was very much pleased, saying, "I think you have caught the spirit of Rip Van Winkle as no other artist has." We concluded to postpone the painting of his favorite act until he reached Palm Beach.

When I called on Mr. Jefferson at Palm Beach, Ex-President Cleveland was there, and they were out fishing together. That evening I found Jefferson in. When he took me in and introduced me to Mr. Cleveland, he immediately brought up the subject of the picture and suggested to Mr. Cleveland that he sit for his portrait; but Cleveland had already been painted and was not interested in the proposition.

I had just completed arrangements with Mr. Jefferson for sittings, when I was taken suddenly ill and was confined to bed for several days. My recovery was slow and peculiar. Sudden dizzy spells would come over me, which completely incapacitated me for work. The doctor advised my taking open air exercise and walking in the sun as much as possible. While out, a spell would come on, and I would have to seize the first lamp post or coconut tree available. I fancy some people thought I was enjoying a morning jag. My recovery was much retarded, and Mr. Jefferson had to leave for the North, so we decided to do the work in New York.

That summer, before I went West, Ducey suggested my taking a better studio uptown, near his church, on Twenty-eighth Street. "Why not pull your things out of here now and store them in the basement of the church until you return in the fall?" he questioned. "But," said I, "I hardly feel that I can afford to pay the higher rent for a studio in your locality." "Well," said he, "if you can get the patronage, you can afford to pay the rent, and I will see that you get the business." So it was in my new studio on Twenty-eighth Street the next winter, that I finally painted Jefferson as the old man Rip. On one occasion, wrestling with his long beard and hair, I felt that I had lost some spontaneity of touch. "Do you know how I would paint that hair, Mr. Brewer?" he asked. Seizing a rag on my table, he dabbed it into some thick, heavy white paint, muddled it around, and slapped it on the hair. It was a clever touch and splendid in its effect. I have never worked over that spot on the picture.

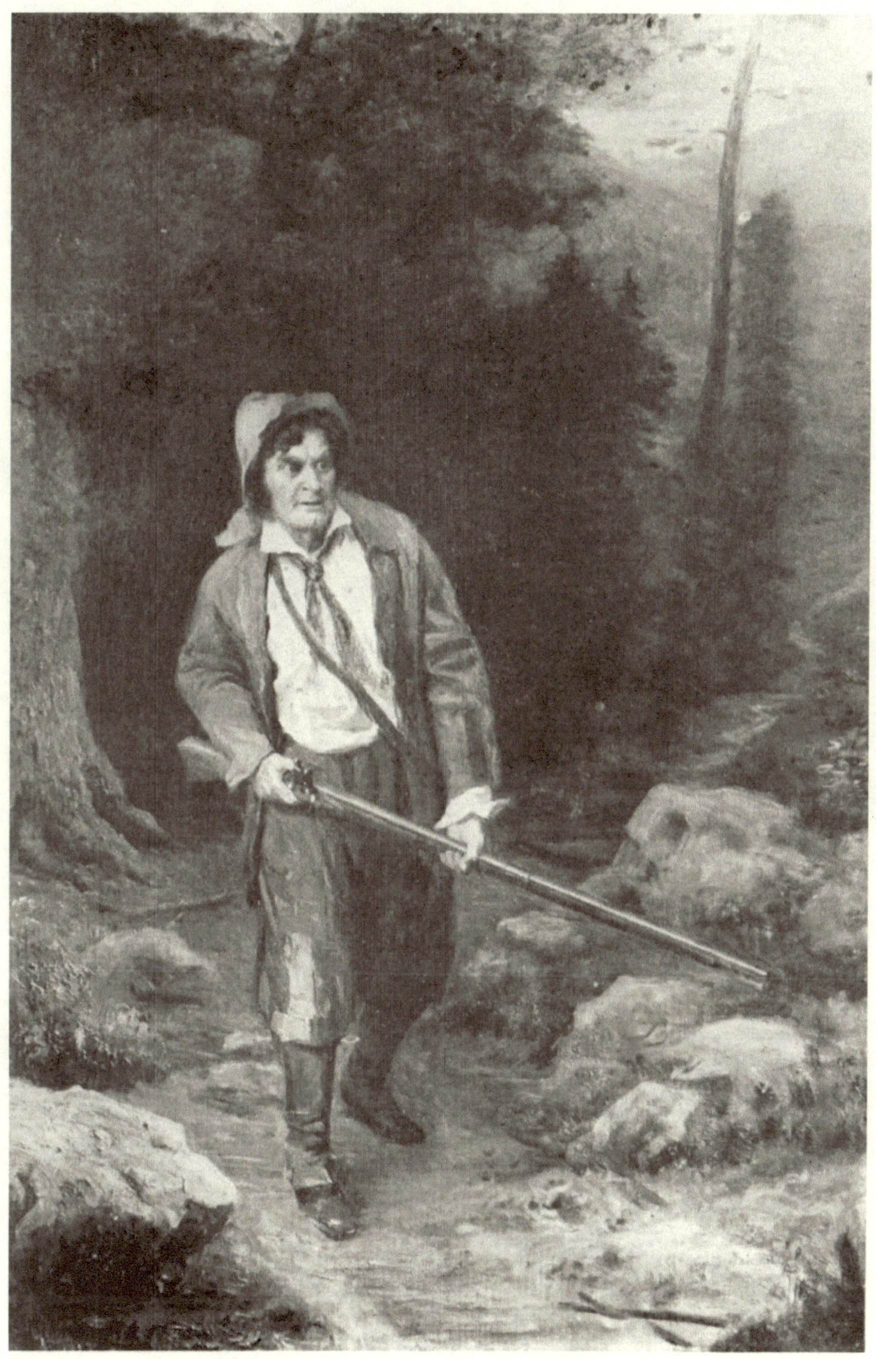

Joe Jefferson as Rip Van Winkle.

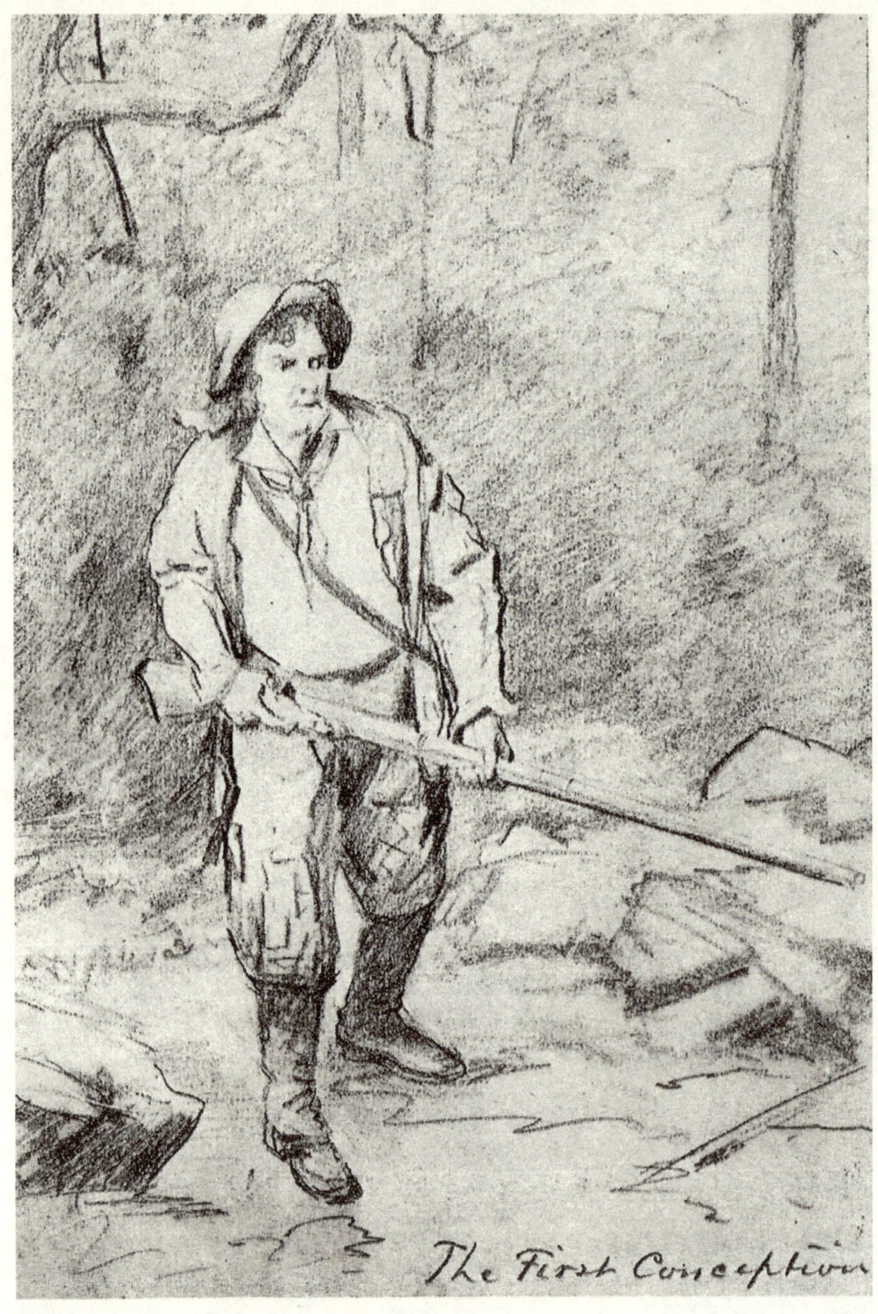

The first conception.

Mr. Jefferson inspired me as no other sitter did. He was keenly alive to everything that could help an artist to do his best and his appreciation could be discerned by his mobility of expression. In posing for Rip Van Winkle when the hobgoblins are near, he would seize his old gun, take his position and call out: "Now I am ready! I feel the part." At other times he would cry out in his well-modulated voice: "No, no, this will not do! I am not Rip Van Winkle—hold up a while!" He would then walk around with his gun a few minutes, go back to his place and say cheerily, "Now, I'll try it again." Then, in his quiet, inimitable way, he would put his right foot forward and become the living personation of Irving's unique character. "Ah, now, this is better. It is all right. Have you got it?" he would exclaim.

In posing he never failed to have his valet come to the studio with him and assist him in making up for his part. I could well understand how he became such a great actor; he never omitted details and heartily entered into the spirit of every pose he attempted. I discovered that Mr. Jefferson was an admirable critic and few things escaped his artistic observation. He remarked one day that he did not consider artists alone the best judges of art, because they are apt to be absorbed with the technique and fail to grasp the spirit of the subject. Occasionally, while posing, he would relate an anecdote and his eyes would twinkle with genuine merriment. During the many times he posed for me, I never heard him relate a story that had a sting in it, or indulge in disparaging remarks. I could not help thinking of the poet Holmes' expression that he was "so many years young," while I painted Mr. Jefferson, for he had that cheerful exuberance which indicates health and good feeling.

We had discussed the trees in the first painting and one morning he brought me a watercolor sketch. Handing it to me, he said, "This is the way I paint trees." I still have that precious little picture. Jefferson painted a great deal, but always in a frenzied, imaginative way. His valet told me that while painting he frequently forgot to put on his smock and in his enthusiasm often muddled his picture with his fingers, wiping them on his best trousers. He had to be watched to prevent his ruining them.

My friend Wack, who then lived in London, came to New York on a business trip and was present at the final sitting. He said, "Mr. Jefferson, we will be glad to see you in London, and if you should come, we'll be delighted to entertain you." Jefferson's face assumed a thoughtful expression, and he finally shook his head and said, "No, thank you, Mr. Wack, it is too late now." His health had been failing, and no doubt his years were telling on him.

Joe was always Rip Van Winkle, in manner and speech, off the stage and on. For instance, in talking with him one was reminded of Rip's accent when telling of his bride's falling off the bridge on the way home from the wedding, of how he nobly plunged into the water and pulled her out. He was asked, "Would you do that now?" His face took on an expression of deep thought, and he answered slowly, "I believe I'd go home and think about it." His long years of characterization of Rip had become habitual. His manner was simple, frank, courteous, always lacking anything that savored of assumed dignity or self-consciousness. In overalls he would have been a typical farmer or mechanic; and no one would guess that he was a master in dramatic art, a painter, a writer, a financier, par excellence.

In his memoirs he tells of his earliest recollections. When a child of six he was with his father's troupe and took part in the plays. In those days they had to build their own stages in halls, and sometimes barns, paint their own scenery, as they traveled about in covered wagons from city to city. Jefferson was wont to appear between the acts of Rip Van Winkle and address the audiences, grown to manhood and womanhood, to whom he had played when they were children. Jefferson was playing in Minneapolis on one occasion, when our son Ed and his wife Mamie met him after the play. Mamie, when in a playful mood, had a little habit of pointing her finger at the person to whom she was talking. Mr. Jefferson caught the finger and held it upright, saying, "Look out, that might shoot!" He had many little humorous informalities, pleasing and intimate.

Between the sitting for old man Rip's picture, Jefferson left the costume in my studio. My wife had come to New York and was ill at the home of Dr. Coggswell in Brooklyn. Mrs. Coggswell was also confined to her bed with la grippe, an ailment, which is now called "flu." (When I was a boy the doctors dubbed it "epizootic.") To make old ailments appear like new and mysterious diseases, the doctors re-christen them every decade or so, giving them different names. I had an attack of the flu in 1930, and my symptoms were identical with my "epizootic" of sixty-five years ago.) By way of entertainment for the convalescing invalids, I thought of putting on Jefferson's costume and cutting a few Rip Van Winkleian capers. Taking the costume, I told the doctor of the plan and he helped me makeup, down in the basement. Then he went to my wife's room and told her that a strange demented old man who lived in the neighborhood and whom everyone knew to be harmless, frequently entered the houses and spooked around in an amusing way and that he wanted her to see him. So, he led me into the room. In a bent-over attitude, one hand on my back, I maneuvered about the room, looking into the vases, the beauty box, smelling of perfumes and the like and came up close to the bed and peered down at the invalid. She was eyeing me with apprehension. As I came close, she drew back, saying, "O Doctor!" The doctor assured her that I was perfectly harmless and told her not to be alarmed. Then he led me to his wife's room. Mrs. Coggswell had a Collie dog that lay at the foot of her bed. At once, the dog arose, looked at me for a moment and began to wag his tail. Mrs. Coggswell exclaimed, "Well, that is somebody Collie knows, and I guess I do, too." I returned to my wife's room and pulled off the makeup, to her utter surprise. "Well," she said, "I thought I had seen those sparkling eyes before!"

On one occasion Jefferson gave a large exhibition of his landscapes in Washington. Of course, the academic painter, the believer in the Claude Monet theory of broken color to achieve sunlight, or the rigid draftsman will not agree that Jefferson attained very high qualities in his work; but anyone looking at that array of canvasses must observe that he has stamped them with an individuality unlike that of any other artist. He once said to me, "I have always had a burning desire to be a painter, but I presume I shall die in the harness as an actor." Is this not true of many great men who imagine they have failed to find themselves in some other sphere than that which circumstances, perforce, have compelled them to follow for a life occupation? I am no stranger to that feeling, for it was necessity that first led me into making crayon portraits and from that to the painting of portraits from life; and today I would rather paint the landscape or the dramatic figure. The greatest incentive for me in the painting of an average portrait is the financial consideration. Seldom do I finish a portrait which gives the satisfaction that I hoped to enjoy in the beginning of the work. I believe I can readily see why the actor, going over and over the same play for thirty or forty years, as Jefferson did Rip Van Winkle, fails to enjoy that keen mental exhilaration that comes with the creative spirit in the doing of a new and original thing. All great art is creative—never reproductive. Beethoven's symphonies and Wagner's operas were original creations; every great picture or poem or sculpture is the product of a new conception. In fact, to me it would be a dreadful bore to have to repeat the great plays over and over again.

Joe and I hobnobbed together a great deal. He seemed to like me—and who could fail to love him! We visited the galleries, studying pictures and discussing various art themes. One needed to spend only an hour with him among the works of great masters to discern his keen appreciation and his wonderful understanding of the great problems which the artist must face and solve for himself. One day, speaking of the works of various artists, I referred to Chartran. Chartran, a Frenchman, had become the vogue among New York's Four Hundred. His price was twenty-thousand dollars a portrait. Everywhere you heard him spoken of and saw his pictures. He lived at the Waldorf and assumed high airs. Even President Theodore Roosevelt was captivated by him and had his own, his wife's, and Alice's portraits painted, only to be criticized for his lack of judgment; for they said he could have easily employed a far better painter among the American artists. "Do you know," Jefferson remarked, "I think Chartran should spell his name 'Charlatan,'" and a merry twinkle flashed into his eye.

Referring to the work of Sargent, he said, "Sargent made a head of me—it is at the Players' Club. Sargent's brush work is all right, but," placing his hand to his heart, "he doesn't touch me." I can understand that Mr. Jefferson's nature called for something more emotional, more dramatic, perhaps; and after all, we judge works of art often with the heart as much as with the head.

In Mr. Jefferson's memoirs we read:

"When I first saw the works of Constable and Corot, I did not like them. They seemed to be devoid of subject matter, and there was an unfinished look about them that gave me the idea of mere sketches carelessly painted. As I became familiar with these pictures, I gradually began to understand what they meant. I then discovered that it was I, who was at fault, not the artists, and I felt ashamed to think that I had seen so much and knew so little."

Jefferson will long be remembered as the greatest comedian America has yet produced. The last time I saw him, he called at my studio for a short chat before going to Florida, where he was stricken with his last illness. The actor's reward—fleeting acclaim and a purse of measured gold—could scarcely be said of Jefferson, as his life was so full from other sources. His brush and his pen will probably prevent the oblivion that comes to others of lesser genius. Jefferson has gone and in the years that have passed no one has taken his place; nor in this age when so many are clever but few are great is it to be hoped that his sceptre will ever rest in the hand of another.

* * *

Good Father Ducey never missed an opportunity to further my interests and acquaintance with his friends. We went to see Margaret Anglin in her play "In the Wilderness." In one of the acts, the character she impersonated having received a proposal from her sweetheart wanders into a wilderness in doubt and uncertainty and stands amid the trees by a pool in which she gazes abstractedly, picking off the petals of a flower and dropping them into the water. I thought I saw in this a theme for a picture and incidentally remarked about it to Ducey. A few days later, he called with Miss Anglin, ostensibly to see his own portrait. She was a member of his church and he knew her and the family well. As in the case of Jefferson, he suggested her posing for me for a picture and referred to the subject of the girl "In the Wilderness." This resulted in Margaret's coming for sittings.

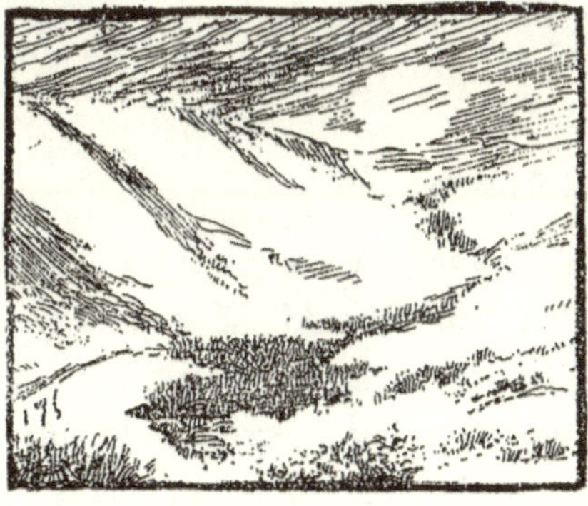

Margaret lived with her widowed mother and sister, Eileen. They were Canadian people, and Mr. Anglin had been a member of Lord Dufferin's Cabinet. I understand he was a better statesman than financier and left the family in modest circumstances. It is said that Margaret occupied a hall bedroom while fighting her way up in New York. Her success had been marked, and she was enjoying great popularity. When I met her, her theater was packed nightly and critics showered her with praise. Most natural and unaffected in manner, beautiful and gracious, she threw herself into the work of posing with the sympathy and tact natural to most actresses, knowing well how much the artist depends at times upon his model for incentive and help. Every attitude she struck was picturesque. She could not be otherwise. As Sarah Bernhardt stated, "Margaret Anglin is the greatest emotional actress of America," and this estimate by the greatest emotional actress of France can well be accepted as correct. Frequently I had to employ Margaret's sister Eileen as a substitute, since Margaret's work was extremely exhausting and left her little time for posing. The following letter stresses her application to her work:

> My dear Mr. Brewer: Indeed, I am sorry not to manage today, but I simply can't! I have a splitting headache—and pages of verse to learn before noon tomorrow. Pity me! I shall try to get in tomorrow for an hour. My maid will explain about the pictures. The framed head I am crazy about—I mean the expression of course, and the little costume picture, too.
>
> Very sincerely,
>
> Margaret Anglin.

One evening after work, we went to the Waldorf for dinner. The time passed so quickly that I feared she would be late at the theatre. I offered to get a cab, but she insisted upon the necessity of walking for exercise. The wind was blowing a terrific gale and it was bitterly cold. In accompanying her to the stage door, I noticed her dynamic energy, for I was out of breath trying to keep up with her.

One day she brought in her friend, a Mr. Jones, a Canadian who had been mayor of St. John, New Brunswick, and who then lived in New York—a fine elderly gentleman. He gave me a commission to paint a portrait.

Returning to my studio one very cold night after a heavy storm of snow and sleet, I found a couple of little ragged urchins hugging the hall radiator for warmth. They were pathetic in their tatters and had been crying from the cold. I said to them, "What are you doing out in such a storm as this?" "We have to sell papers for Mamma. Papa is sick and will die," said the older one. At this statement, they covered their faces and cried more pitifully. They told me they had three little sisters; that their mother had cautioned them not to come home until they had received thirty cents, at least, from the sale of their papers; but that it was so cold they couldn't stay on the streets to sell them. I took their papers away and gave them money and got their address, thinking I would investigate their story, which later I found to be literally true. When I gave them the bill, the eldest one said, "Oh, Mister, we will pray for you." Then they scampered away in the storm. Two or three days later, as I came into the studio, I again saw the boys in the hall warming themselves. I learned that their father was better, and the doctor said he would get well. I asked them if they had prayed for me as they promised. "Oh, yes Mister," came from both, "we pray for you every night."

"Who taught you to pray?" I asked.

"Mama—she sends us to church, too," was the answer.

"Where?" I questioned.

"To St. Stephen's."

"Every Sunday?"

"Yes, every day."

"Every day?" I asked, eyeing them doubtfully.

"Yes, every day. When we get through selling our papers we go and give a penny to God. We put it in that little box there by the pilla', where Baby Jesus is, and then we kneel down and say a prayer."

And the smaller boy added, "A prayer for 'oo, Mister."

I told them to bring the paper to my room every evening, and I'd give them a dime for it. One day the little fellow said he could sing. He had a sweet, childish voice of unusual power and in his natural phrasing, as he stood on the model stand gazing about the walls, he presented an appealing picture. The children came to the studio every day at the same hour, and as if he considered that he had not adequately repaid me for the dime he received, the little singer always insisted upon giving me a selection from his repertoire.

At this time, I was working on the Anglin portrait. One day I told Miss Anglin the little newsboy story. At that moment the two boys walked in and the little fellow offered to sing for her. Whenever he sang, he insisted on standing on the model throne and in this instance he felt the importance of his entertainment. He opened his mouth to a dangerous size, and the little chest swelled, while his eyes roved about the room and back to the listener, never losing sight of the effect of his music upon her. The shrill voice mounted the roof; then he would lower it to a little more than a whisper and shake and shudder for expression. After a pause, with something like a hiccough, a high note would pierce the air and then drop to a groaning basso. The words were not intelligible, but now and then, something like a word would come out with tremendous emphasis. When he had finished, Miss Anglin opened her purse and took out a bill, placed it in an envelope, and pinned it on the inside of his coat pocket. She asked him to pray for her as he had done for me. The lads promised surely to do so, and they bowed themselves out of the door.

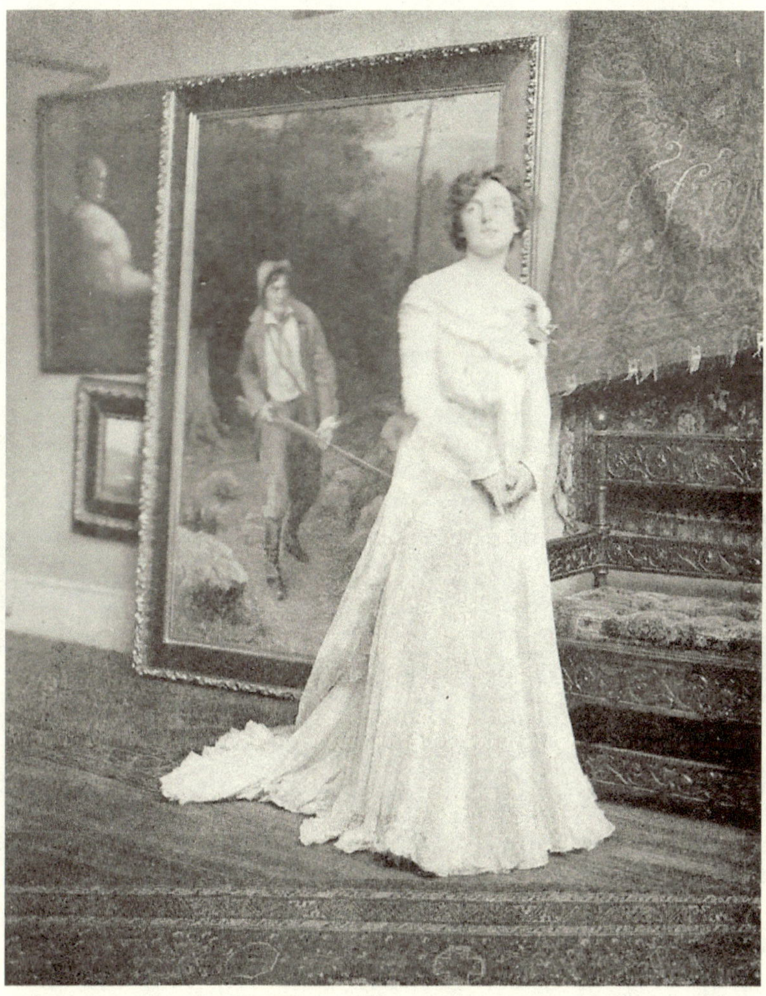

Margaret Anglin in the studio

One day Mrs. Charles M. Freeman called to see the Jones portrait. She was a handsome lady with large, beautiful eyes, a wealth of gray hair, and was a subject for an elegant portrait. Looking at the Anglin picture, she said, "If I thought I could get a thing like that, I might try it myself." Later I painted her in a gray costume with furs and an English walking hat, standing on the steps of her home as though waiting for her carriage. I improvised a background of buildings in gray tones to harmonize with her lovely attire. This portrait was favorably commented on by Mr. Jefferson. "The break in the sky," he said, "is a pretty note in the whole scheme and enhances the effect of the picture, while it does not in any way weaken the strength of the figure." Jefferson's criticisms were always brief, but to the point.

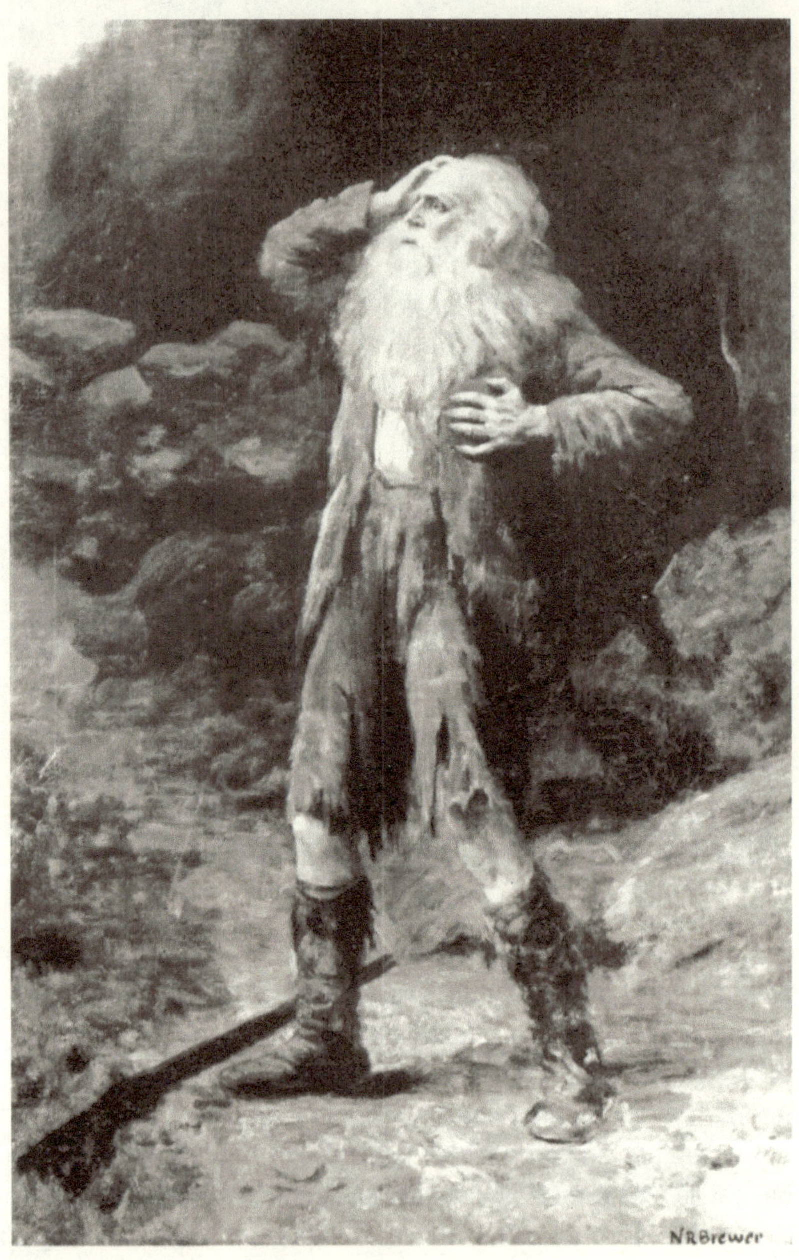

Rip van Winkle, awakening

Again, my mentor, Ducey, came in—this time bringing J. Carroll Beckwith, the courtly, handsome, cultured gentleman, able painter and writer. Beckwith was always kindly. He spoke highly of the dramatic quality of Ducey's portrait. Of course, Ducey was dramatic in reality. Wearing his long cape, in a humorous mood he would mount the platform, strike a McCullough attitude, and with a Shakespearian phrase, produce a telling effect.

When I showed Beckwith some of my landscapes, one in particular that I had painted indoors from a carefully made sketch from nature, he remarked that I should never paint a landscape indoors. "Now," he said, "your sketch is a ten times greater work of art than your finished picture. No one should work that way."

"How, then," I ventured, "did Inness, Corot, and many of our greatest painters do their finest things indoors?"

"It is true," he said, "they have done so, but it is not a safe practice for younger men."

In this Beckwith certainly voiced the school of the realist, but Beckwith was not a landscape painter. Homer Martin and Wyant would not have counseled the same course, for they believed that a great landscape was an interpretation of nature rather than a realistic and servile rendering of facts and impressions. In making my sketch for this picture, I had caught enough of the realistic on which to build a more interpretive expression of the scene.

During the conversation, Beckwith suggested my joining the Salmagundi Club, saying it would be a great help to me to know the artists there and to become identified with their activities. "All the best artists of New York, you know, belong to it and they give a series of exhibitions every year, which would bring your work before the profession," he said, and offered to propose my name and find someone to second the nomination and act as one of my sponsors. A few days later a couple of artists from the membership committee came to my studio to select the membership picture, which each artist is required to contribute to the Club's gallery. Thus J. Carroll Beckwith and Joseph Hartly were responsible for my membership in the highest technical art body in America.

Beckwith and I became fast friends. One day, together we called at Chase's studio on Tenth Street and I shall never forget the impression made on me by both the studio and the man. Chase at that time was at the height of his popularity, both as a painter and teacher and his receptions at the studio were crowded with admirers and students. I longed to be in a position like this man and to be able to maintain such a studio. It is a well-known fact, however, that even Chase, with his wonderful popularity and personality as teacher and painter, ran upon the rocks of bankruptcy and had to abandon perhaps the most attractive studio at that time in America.

Chase was one of the outstanding characters in American art; many of his creations will live and add luster to his name. He was a born teacher, giving too much time to his pupils. The conscientious teacher thus weakens his vitality, which he should hold in reserve for more important creative work, and the effect of this is seen in many of Chase's paintings, especially toward the latter part of his career. Some of his portraits, when compared with those of an earlier date, are pathetically inane. Chase once said to me, "Brewer, I think your work is too uneven. One would hardly think it was done by the same person. I admire some of your heads, still life pieces, and landscapes very much, but your large portraits are not so fortunate. In them you appear too eager to please somebody. You should not allow your sitters to influence you." I felt like saying, "It is not the sitter but the necessity of getting his check that influences me." To paint people as they want to be painted degrades the artist to the level of the tradesman. To be a tradesman when necessity demands is not necessarily dishonest, but you cannot disown your paintings, and your artistic sins will follow you.

One day Father Ducey brought Mrs. Frederick Neilson and her party to see my portraits. What he said to Mrs. Neilson to interest her in my work I do not know, but later she called and suggested my painting a portrait of her granddaughter, little Miss Kemp. She was a spoiled and very irritating child, and to paint her was almost an impossibility; nor could the grandmother compel her to behave. I had to resort to a substitute and a photograph to get anything of her at all. This work was followed by a portrait of Mrs. Neilson herself, in a Worth salmon-colored velvet gown with a long train. The two pictures were exhibited that fall at a loan exhibition of portraits at the American Art Galleries on Twenty-third Street and Madison Square. Before beginning the latter portrait, I opened the door early one morning in answer to a timid knock and there stood Miss Kathleen Neilson, bearing a huge box containing her mother's gown. This was only a few weeks previous to the Vanderbilt-Neilson wedding, which took place in Newport where Reginald Vanderbilt was then living. Their wedding was the great event of the year in the social world, and they went abroad for their honeymoon.

Mrs. Neilson invited me to be her guest in Newport during the summer, where I spent three months, during which time I painted several prominent Newport people—Mrs. C. M. Oelrichs, Mrs. Woodbury Kane, Mrs. Hollis Hunnewell, Miss Natalie Schenck, and others. The following winter I gave a one-man show at the Salmagundi Club, New York, with forty canvasses, which included Jefferson, Anglin, and Freeman portraits. The prominence of many of my subjects called forth a great deal of comment in the press. The *Herald*, the *Times* and the *American* each devoted a whole page to reproductions and notices of the pictures.

Chapter XIV
Abandoning the Atmosphere

The East draws its neophytes from the West and is careful in its picking—for those alone whom destiny marks heeds the call and climb the rungs of fame.

One can readily understand how an artist may cease to grow when he leaves a great art center like New York to establish himself in the West, where culture is yet embryonic, art is scarce and artists few.

Mr. Douglas Volk had achieved much distinction in New York with his Puritan girl subjects and was considered an artist of great promise. Then he accepted a position as instructor in Minneapolis. Four or five years later, Dwight Tryon questioned me regarding him. "What is the matter with Volk? The things he sends to the Academy and the Society of American Artists are so poor we hesitate to accept them." In six years, Volk gave up the position and returned to the metropolis, where he soon regained his artistic vigor and produced many good things. Robert Koehler, likewise, stepping into Volk's Minneapolis position, began a technical toboggan slide and never recovered his former strength.

I think I am safe in saying there cannot be found a great painter in all the Middle West who does not retain a hold on New York and live there at least part of the time. Every artist who does not feel the urge of the East may as well content himself with mediocracy. The East draws its potential talent from the West, and it is careful in the picking—only those who measure up can tread the rungs of fame. As to recompense, the western artist draws his reward from narrow confines, while the genius who captures New York has America at his feet. From the day I first landed in New York I have felt this urge; but somehow, I was not able to break the thongs that bound me to the West. There were family and property ties acquired before my first trip East. St. Paul was my wife's birthplace and the sacred attachments of a large family circle made it impossible for her to content herself in New York. She declared when we first lived there, that she realized the truth and pathos of Payne's "Home, Sweet Home:"

> "Mid pleasures and palaces though we may roam,
> Be it ever so humble, there's no place like home."

Five times we moved to New York and back. Then we began to be called nomads. In fact, the moving habit got so bad we could not quit even after we finally abandoned the East. For eight winters following I lived a bachelor's life in New York trying to carry on—but I did not—carry on—as some bachelors do. There were no wild studio parties about my place; for I was always too busy. I maintained my studio in the dear old Van Dyke studio building for eight years, but spent the summers with the family in St. Paul, where I then found interest in building a house, which proved to be quite a pretentious affair. That occupied over a year of time when I scarcely touched a brush except as a house painter. This put me back where I was when Mike upset the pot of black paint on Mrs. Monfort's sidewalk. And, too, I was using the spade as of yore. Even cracking rocks for our driveway with a ten-pound sledgehammer in the hot sun, until I acquired a bad case of neuritis and called Dr. Rees. After I told him what I had been doing, he said, "Well, Brewer, I never knew you were such a damn fool." After all, there was lots of fun in it. In fact, I have always been able to get great pleasure out of any kind of work, so long as it culminated in permanent achievement. You know, handling the spade is quite an art. I have built seven houses, none of which pleased the family, and got rid of them. I handled the tool a great deal in digging, grading, gardening. I have lived on farms where I had to dig post holes, root cellars, and all kinds of holes, so I consider I am entitled to a spade man's diploma. I have hired many men to work for me. These men never did any other kind of labor, and yet only two out of the whole bunch knew how to handle the spade. Send a man to transplant an evergreen or a shrub, and if you don't stand over him and tell him how, he will kill the thing as sure as he would a rattlesnake.

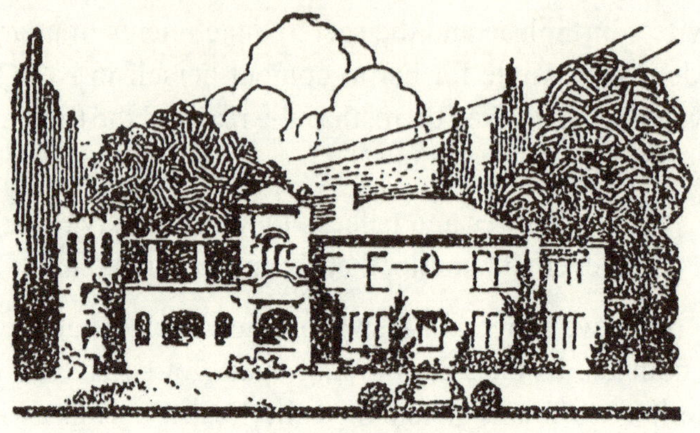

Casa del Rio

Casa del Rio sketch

The house was built on a high bank at a curve on the Mississippi River Boulevard, commanding a view of the river for several miles—one of the most romantic sites between the Twin Cities. Shortly after we took possession of the new house, our son Reuben, who had always made a hobby of prize chickens, had a fine flock, which he kept in the new chicken house. They had to be locked up, as all chickens do when transplanted from the old coop to the new. You may take your pets from an old, leaky coop and put them into a nice new one, high and dry, but just as soon as they are released, they will hike right back to the old roosting place. And how like chickens humans often are! They have to accustom themselves to new environments before they are content. A neighbor who kept several purebred dogs, seemed to think it was the privilege of the dogs to wander hither and yon, whether murder was in their hearts or not. One morning I noticed a prize Airedale scamper out of my yard. I hurled a stone at him, which he saucily ignored, and then he slowly trotted in the direction of home. I found that he had gone into the coop and slain twenty-one of Reuben's fine Plymouth Rocks. I did not know to whom the animal belonged, nor did Reuben; but that day, unknown to me, Rube started out to discover the owner of the dog. He met our neighbor's gardener and told him about the tragedy, swearing vengeance and death upon the marauder, could he ever find him.

That evening my dog-fancying neighbor called. With fire in his eyes, he opened on me, "I understand, Brewer, that you have threatened to kill my dog. Now, I want you to know that that is a valuable dog, a very valuable dog and if you injure him in any way, you will have to take the consequences." Not knowing the cause of this sudden outburst, I was greatly surprised. I had previously signed a petition for the vacation of an alley in the block and thus far had neglected to pay my assessments. He continued, "And I understand, also, that you have not yet paid your assessment for the vacation of this alley." He prolonged his arraignment until my ire arose, and I became excited as he was and said, "Now, Mr. —, I want you to understand that my payment toward the alley vacation is none of your damn business," shaking my finger at him; "furthermore, I want you to go out to that coop and see what your fine thoroughbred Airedale has done. There lie twenty-one valuable hens, thoroughbred hens, fully as valuable as your dog, and if that cur ever comes into my grounds again, as sure as you are standing there, I will kill him. Now it is up to you to take care of your ugly beast if you want to save his valuable life. Don't come around here threatening me with anything, after your dog has maliciously entered our coop to do his murdering." On that I went into the house and slammed the door in his face.

Two days later I received a very apologetic letter, saying that he regretted that anything unneighborly had arisen, but he valued his dog so highly that he didn't want any harm done him. He would see that the offense was not repeated and offered to pay for the chickens. Of course, I had to acknowledge his apology and replied that I, too, regretted anything unneighborly had happened, but the loss of twenty-one thoroughbred chickens—valuable chickens—was a considerable annoyance. However, we could not accept his offer to pay for them.

A year afterward our son Wallace, who had been one of the engineers on the Panama Canal and on the Medina Dam in Texas, came home with his family. They had with them a thoroughbred bulldog they called "Snooks." Snooks was a quiet, peaceable animal, a splendid watch dog, and when told to guard a car or piece of property would do so until officially relieved by his master, and no one ever dared come near it in the interval. One day while I was planting some rose bushes in front of the house, Snooks stood watching me when this neighbor's Airedale put in his appearance in the street. Snooks pricked up his ears but made no move until the Airedale ventured to trespass upon our grounds. Then he walked slowly toward him as much as to say, "Let me get hold of him." The Airedale was a fighter and a little larger than Snooks. In a moment, there was a set to, and Snooks' jaws landed just back of the Airedale's ear—and there he hung. The Airedale was game, and there was about as vicious a canine scrap as I have ever seen. The Airedale did all the yelping and all the barking. Snooks landed him on his back at times. When he released his hold; the Airedale came back with intense ferocity, and again the bulldog jaws brought forth more yelps. In vain, the Airedale tried to shake off his antagonist, but the squatty bulldog was not one to let go.

I feared my neighbor's valuable dog would be badly injured and concluded I must part them. I shouted at Snooks, but he misunderstood my language and shook the Airedale all the more viciously. Seizing a broom handle that lay nearby, I determined that a clubbing of one or both was necessary, but every time I directed a blow at Snooks he dodged and fought all the harder. In fact, my efforts were understood to mean that he must murder the Airedale. The scrap took both of them into the street and to the sloping bank on the other side. I followed them over the crest of the bank and for a good fifteen minutes failed to make Snooks understand that murder must not be in the game. Not wishing to be in at the killing, I left them and returned to the house. Sometime later Snooks walked up to me and looked up at me as if to say, "Well, I did it." Weeks later I met my neighbor and he began to tell me that something dreadful had happened to his dog. He was so badly damaged that he had not been able to walk for a month. I did not tell him that I had tried to save the life of his valuable dog or that he was mighty lucky to be alive.

Chapter XV
Pioneer Exhibitions

A South Dakota Brewery—A North Dakota Barber—A House by a Dam Site—A National Gallery Dream—The Zigzag Trail of My Propaganda

The first winter after the house was finished, I took a crew of men into the woods and dug up great trees forty feet high with six or ten tons of earth on the roots. We let the earth freeze, hauled them to our grounds, and dumped them into great holes that had been previously dug. Thus, we planted huge elms, maples, and ash. Ninety percent of those trees lived and are beauties today. My men said I was foolish—that I should plant smaller trees. I retorted that I was already nearly sixty years old, and if I had to wait for a sapling to grow, I would never enjoy its shade.

I soon found my bank account exhausted, with large bills unpaid. Something had to be done, and that soon. A lady from Aberdeen, South Dakota, whose portrait I had painted the year before, urged me to take some of my portraits to Aberdeen, promising to show them with her own at a parlor tea, feeling sure I could get some orders. Of course, she said, I could not get New York prices, since Aberdeen had no millionaires. In a few days I was busy. One week I finished three study heads by Friday night.

One of the most interesting persons I painted was Ike Lincoln, who was a very unique character, tall and portly, red faced, and weighing at least two hundred and fifty pounds. He was a native of the state of Maine, but left home when a mere boy and worked his way westward. First he was a mule driver; then he was promoted to a mail carrier across the bleak prairies from Yankton to Aberdeen. The towns were little more than groups of shanties. Lincoln eventually became State Senator and banker, and married a refined lady. That happy incident, however, did not refine Mr. Lincoln's language. From the backwoods of Maine, he retained the native dialect, and no doubt, added to it some of the mule driver's vernacular. Yet Mr. Lincoln was a most praiseworthy citizen whom everybody esteemed. Without knowing anything about it, he had great respect for art and all cultural things. One day he said, "My brother back in Maine has a 'pitcher' up in the old attic by some fellow that signed himself Stuart. Don't guess it 'mounts to much." "What is the first name?" I asked: "Gilbert?" "Yes," he replied, "somethin' like that. It is a pitcher of my grandmother." I told him if it happened to be a real Gilbert Stuart and he could euchre his brother out of it, I would paint his wife's portrait in exchange for it. It would have been a bargain, but I never heard anything more about it.

Doane Robinson, South Dakota State Historian, dropped in when I was painting Senator Ike Lincoln and wanted me to go to Pierre, the capital city. He said he had long been thinking of creating a gallery of memorial portraits of prominent builders of the state for the large rotunda on the first floor of the new Capitol, that many had promised him they would have their portraits painted when they found a competent artist to do the work, and that he would put me in touch with such people all over the state. So, after six weeks, I went to Pierre and did three half-lengths. One of these was of the present United States Senator Norbeck, before he ran for Governor, and while he was still in the well-drilling business.

In Pierre I formed the acquaintance of that most delightful gentleman and jurist, Judge Smith, a member of the State Supreme Court. He was not only an able lawyer but made a hobby of the study and collection of old violins. From him I acquired two fine old fiddles in exchange for a picture. The state of South Dakota had spent a large sum of money on the new Capitol building and had obtained several paintings by the great mural painters of New York to decorate the building. One of these canvasses represented some treaty negotiation or other transaction with the Indians, in which a high government official is seen in a friendly gesture, extending his hand to the chieftain of the tribe. One day when Judge Smith and I were looking at the picture, he said, "The only fault I find with the picture, Mr. Brewer, is that the artist forgot to put a lemon in the white man's hand."

My venture into South Dakota netted me ample funds to meet my obligations and enabled me to spend several months decorating, gardening, and landscape painting. For two years Robinson kept sending me to different towns throughout South Dakota to do portraits for his gallery, until the canvasses numbered more than twenty, most of which were hung in the long corridor of the beautiful Capitol. South Dakota has always been a staunch prohibition state—yet they now have to endure the humorous appellation "The Brewer-y," which is applied to their Capitol.

My success in South Dakota tempted me to take a try at North Dakota. In 1914 I went to Valley City to paint the portrait of Ex-Governor White for the State Capitol at Bismarck. It was just in harvest time and the fields of ripening grain seen against the beautiful sage green hills offered many tempting subjects for landscape work. The Governor's son, just back from college and with nothing to do, often took me out in his car to make studies.

One Saturday a circus was to give an afternoon performance. About nine o'clock in the morning we parked close beside the road, painting a wheat field a few miles from town. A stream of farmers was coming to town to go to the circus. The procession differed from that leading to the first circus I ever saw, at Rochester forty-eight years before, only by the fact that they came in automobiles instead of by horse or ox-teams. They did not have to rise at four o'clock to make a twenty-mile trip to see the parade. Half of them had Fords; others had large cars, some of which were very expensive. A man with a badly trimmed, rawboned span of plugs came along and stopped. On the board seat with him was a woman in a Shaker bonnet, and a bareheaded girl of about ten. In the rear of the wagon box, they had a lean pig in a crate. They were curious about my work and asked several amusing questions. The girl said they were taking the pig to town to sell so they could go to the circus.

When we got back to town about noon, the streets swarmed with people. It was a gala day for Valley City. I went into a barber shop to get a haircut. I had been wearing my hair quite long and full, and I instructed the barber to shorten it not more than half an inch. He sailed into me with his shears, as I fell into a brown study and did not observe what my man was doing. When I woke up, I found he had mistaken half an inch for half a foot. I looked like a baboon. I remonstrated and scolded him for his stupidity. He apologized and, to smooth things over, became very talkative; told me how much better I would look with my head clipped nearly to the crown, the way it was being worn; and to add seeming insult to injury he finally asked, "I s'pose you are traveling with the circus?" "Yes," said I, "I am their clown." "Oh," said he innocently, "that is a great honor. I s'pose they pay you big money."

As luck had it, Senator Little of North Dakota was looking about the Twin Cities for an artist to paint his portrait, and a banker friend of mine, to whom he had spoken, recommended me. Mr. Little came to the new house, which we had named "Casa del Rio" (house by the river), giving it a Spanish name because of the suggestion of Spanish architecture. It happened to be on the river near a broken government dam, which formed rapids in the Mississippi. In searching for a name for it, one of the boys said, "Let's call it a house by a dam site."

And thereby hangs another tale. This broken dam was the sad relic of a once perfect dam built with government funds obtained by Minneapolis politicians to make their city, instead of St. Paul, the head of navigation. The dam cost several million dollars, and as there was no navigation on the river, a watchman was placed there and paid a salary for over twenty years to guard the government's property. Finally, the politicians declared that the dam was useless because there was not water enough in the stream. The only way to carry out their original plan was to build another dam four miles below, high enough to raise the water thirty feet in the channel. At last, a small packet, its deck laden with furniture, was sent through the new locks to assure people that the scheme was feasible. There was a brass band on the boat and another on the Lake Street bridge. The banks were lined with crowds to see the opening of navigation. The newspaper said that two hundred thousand dollars would be spent for docks to receive the piles of freight. Withal, it was the celebration of an event prophetic of future traffic. That was the last boat that came through the locks for five or six years. Then Henry Ford, realizing that water power was going to waste, succeeded in getting a franchise and built an automobile factory. The raising of the water in the channel has made a cesspool of the river for over six miles, since the sewage of both cities empties into the stream. This the State Board of Health has determined to rectify, but it will require another expenditure of millions to undo the mistakes politicians have made.

This points to a moral. Dr. Holmes, Director of the National Gallery of Art in Washington, and other influential and public-spirited people have been striving for twenty years to get an appropriation sufficient to build an adequate gallery for the housing of the nation's art treasures. Dr. Holmes told me that each year from five to seven million dollars-worth of paintings and sculpture had been offered by patriotic citizens for a public gallery. These offers had to be declined because there was no place to put them. Gifts of one year, he said, could be sold at public auction for enough to erect a building, yet Congress repeatedly declined to make such provision for the housing of these contributions of immeasurable educational value to the people of our country. When Mr. Chas. Lang Freer, of Detroit, wished to give to the nation his five-million-dollar collection, the committee took the matter to President Theodore Roosevelt and stated that there was no place to put it. The President, in characteristic fashion, brought his fist down upon the desk and said, "Accept it anyway; we'll find a place." But no place was found, and Mr. Freer declared that he would not allow his collection thus to go begging but would erect, at his own expense, a building suitable to house his gems. At a cost of millions of dollars, that beautiful gallery now on the Smithsonian grounds was completed and endowed. European countries, bankrupt as they are, are appropriating money for the purchase of works of art for their national galleries. They point with pride to their great museums as indicating the degree of their culture, while we with all our money use it for building useless dams and other schemes for political graft. Lately, however, Chief Justice Charles Evans Hughes has voiced an urgent plea for an appropriation to build an adequate gallery to house the nation's treasures. He said,

"Many collections of rare importance and great value now in the hands of private Americans would undoubtedly be speedily added to those already in the custody of the institution, should a suitable building be provided." In this way, the nation may hope in time to gather a collection of art treasures second to none.

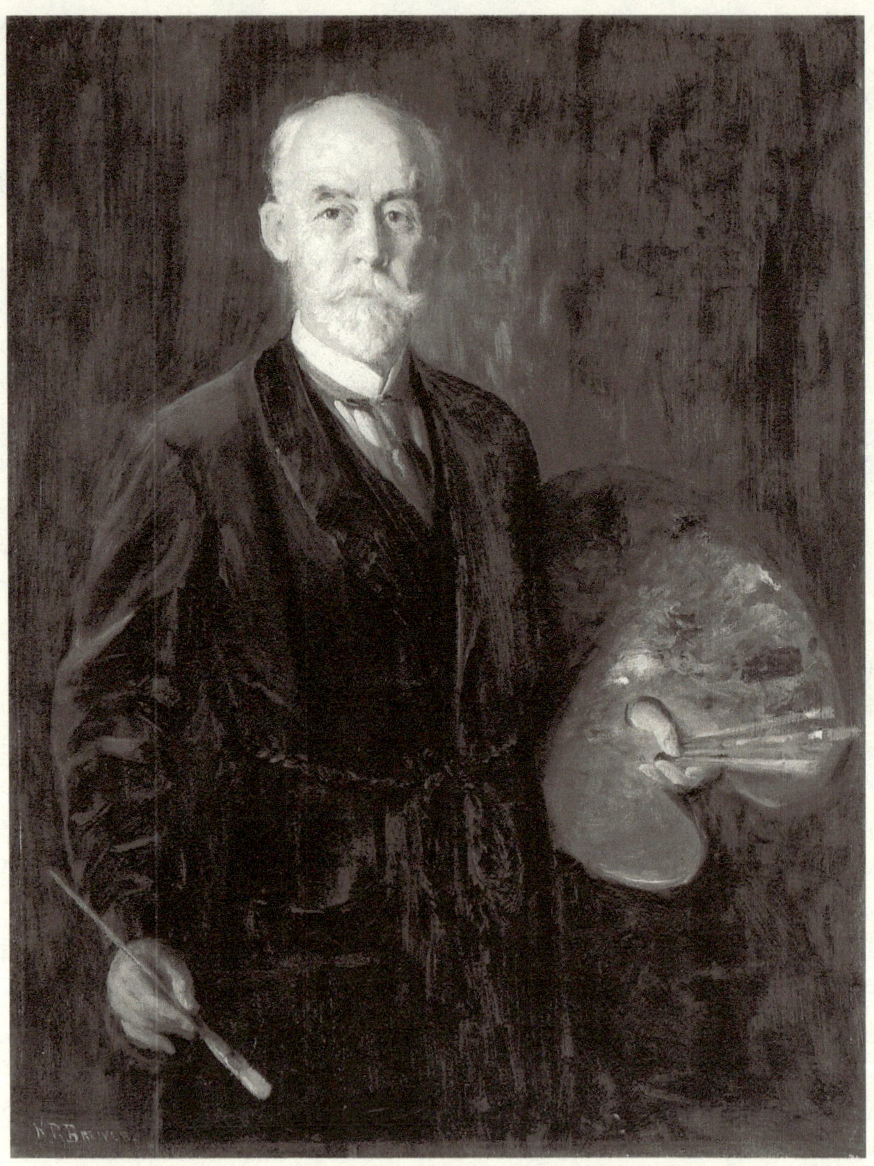

Dr. W. H. Holmes, Director, National Art Gallery, Washington, D. C.

The portrait of Senator Little was also intended for the Capitol at Bismarck. He suggested my going out there to paint one or two of his friends, which I did. A lady told some of her friends in Fargo of my presence in North Dakota, which led to my going there and painting five or six portraits at better prices than I ever received in South Dakota.

My eldest son suggested a new scheme. He was in favor of forming a collection to be offered to various art associations for educational purposes. He got appointments for exhibitions in Sioux City, Omaha, Cedar Rapids, Mason City, LaCrosse, Winona, and other cities. These exhibitions were given by the local art leagues. In all cases the leagues defrayed the expenses of shipment and gallery cost. Most of the leagues were formed and conducted by public-spirited women; only occasionally was a man at the head of those institutions. The ladies would give a program and a tea at the opening of the exhibition. Most women, I have found, like their tea sweetened with sociability. They would gather in great crowds to view the pictures, hear a gallery talk, and enjoy themselves generally. I soon found that my exhibitions were well advertised.

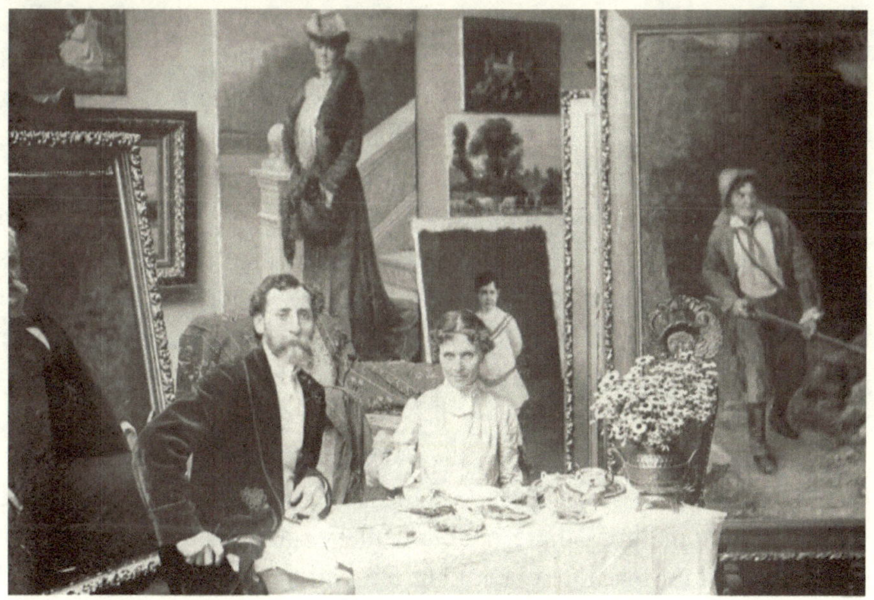

Tea time in the studio

In every city in this great land, I find a genuine hunger of the masses for art knowledge, a desire to see pictures, to hear lectures, and enjoy the best music. America is awakening. This is particularly true of the younger generation. High school students, and even those of the grade schools, crowd the art exhibitions. Women's clubs can always be depended upon to do their share in the promotion of art study. Even the commercial bodies are no longer indifferent to the value of art in civic life, such as city planning, encouragement of better tastes in public and private architecture and furnishings, and providing parks and boulevards and things, calculated to make "The City Beautiful." In spite of my passion to ply my brush, it was the observation of those conditions that inspired me to become a part of the uplifting forces and to aid in the formation of a circulating exhibition, which might be used for educational purposes in these towns and cities.

Possessing a number of works by contemporary artists of note, and adding several of my own pictures, the collection numbered about forty canvasses. I have offered this group for exhibition purposes to many struggling art associations. The zigzag trail of my brush has led to practically every large city west of New York, including Pittsburgh, Youngstown, Dayton, Chicago, Milwaukee, Evansville, Knoxville, New Orleans, San Antonio, Austin, Amarillo, Lincoln, Wichita, Sioux City, Houston, Beaumont, Dallas, Duluth, Oklahoma City, Kansas City, Little Rock, Memphis, Birmingham, Nashville, Atlanta, Miami, and many others. The enthusiasm created by this collection and its accompanying lectures was most gratifying and everywhere registered a large attendance. A special effort was made to enlist the aid of schools and colleges and this effort met with a hearty response. Frequently it was in my heart to exclaim, "God bless the women!" I found, on their part, a ready willingness to take advantage of this opportunity to learn something of art and pass it on to the younger generation.

In one town over eight thousand attended the exhibition during the two weeks it was shown. Many of these were pupils from the public schools and sometimes three or four gallery talks were necessary in a single day. I find that interest among the children is greatly stimulated by requesting a vote on the favorite picture, and it is pleasing to note the deep interest taken and even the disputes and controversies that rage over some of the favorite canvasses. In gallery talks it has been my aim to define in as few words as possible the broad principles of art criticism in order that the amateur and layman may have a simple basis of judgment in his solution of the problems in the pictures and his comprehension of the artist's message. I quite agree with G. K. Chesterton that the ignorance of the learned is often obscured by an excessive flow of words that only befog and mystify the questioning student. In the final analysis, the value of art may be judged by its effect upon the public mind, and any art that remains incomprehensible to those who seek earnestly to understand it fails to be an unlifting factor in human life and remains more or less an enigma, if not a positive deterrent to further inquiry.

We must make it clear to the searcher by some form of demonstration that art is a language and that the artist in his work is presenting a message that is not of the spoken word. It is his interpretation of beauty, his conception of the poetry of life and all that relates to it. This can be accomplished best when the instructor has before him a varied group of works wherein the various technical methods, the color demonstrations and arrangements can be discussed. The intelligent layman is not slow to grasp the general principles and formulate a correct basis for judgment when aided by a lucid and intelligent direction. Unfortunately, today there is a class of instructors, superficial and sensational, who exploit the ultra-radical, that blatant incongruous splashing of color without form or sense, meaning or understanding, that ignoring of fundamental art truths.

I recently heard a glib discourse over a group of such rubbish that seemed but an effort to mystify and mislead. When the speaker was through, a gentleman who had listened attentively remarked, "I wonder if he knows, himself, what he is talking about—I don't; If that is art, I want none of it." Not long ago I asked the head of an art association who "fell" for this artistic rubbish if he really thought he was helping the cause by exploiting such art. He replied that shocking the public into guessing what art really is would bring them out of their lethargy and create a desire to know more of the subject. And I think it opportune here to quote from comments by Thomas Craven in the Los Angeles Examiner, Nov. 28, 1934—these remarks evidently refer to the Carnegie International Art Show at Pittsburgh.

"The exhibition, as an art showing, deserves no consideration. It is a reflection of the tastes and temperamental loftiness of Homer-Saint-Gaudens, who, when requested by the people of Pittsburgh to explain his selections, had the effrontery to reply that 'art is the idiomatic, stylized expression of visual eccentricities, which give satisfaction only to those capable of understanding them.'

"That is typical of the cultivated superiority of museum dwellers."

What is needed in America is more circulating exhibitions of high-grade works. In this the American Federation of Arts is doing a great work, and it is gratifying to know that many of our best artists are "on the road." Every vagrant artist who shows his handiwork in the new towns in quest of a livelihood is a missionary spreading the gospel of beauty and leaves in his wake a certain subtle influence that lives and bears fruit. The field is practically untouched outside the larger cities. There are thousands of towns in the Middle West that have never had an art exhibition and their people's knowledge of art is limited entirely to what they read and hear from others. It is my opinion that they can readily be interested in art if they can only be reached.

These shows have been the means of my meeting so many fine people and of forming friendships I shall never forget, that, after all, the compensation in a moral sense has been well worthwhile. I have painted many of the distinguished people of the country—governors, princes of finance, ladies of high and middle station in society, authors, musicians, and ecclesiastics of high rank in all faiths. Seldom have I sojourned in any city that I have not carried away with me recollections of one or more acquaintances, women especially, whose appreciation, understanding, and love of art have made knowing them a delight, and whose conversations I find myself in later years recalling with keen pleasure. I commenced the exhibition "racket" twenty-two years ago and am still at it.

While in Evansville I saw a woman with her child come into the gallery. She was dressed plainly, evidently of the working class, an Italian type, though fair. The child was only a few months old, fat, chubby, staring about with wide, curious eyes. The mother wore a loose shawl drawn about her shoulders. The tender manner in which she carried that child, hugging it close to her with the absorbing love of a devoted mother, suggested a splendid subject for a picture, and I painted her. The picture I named *Motherhood.*

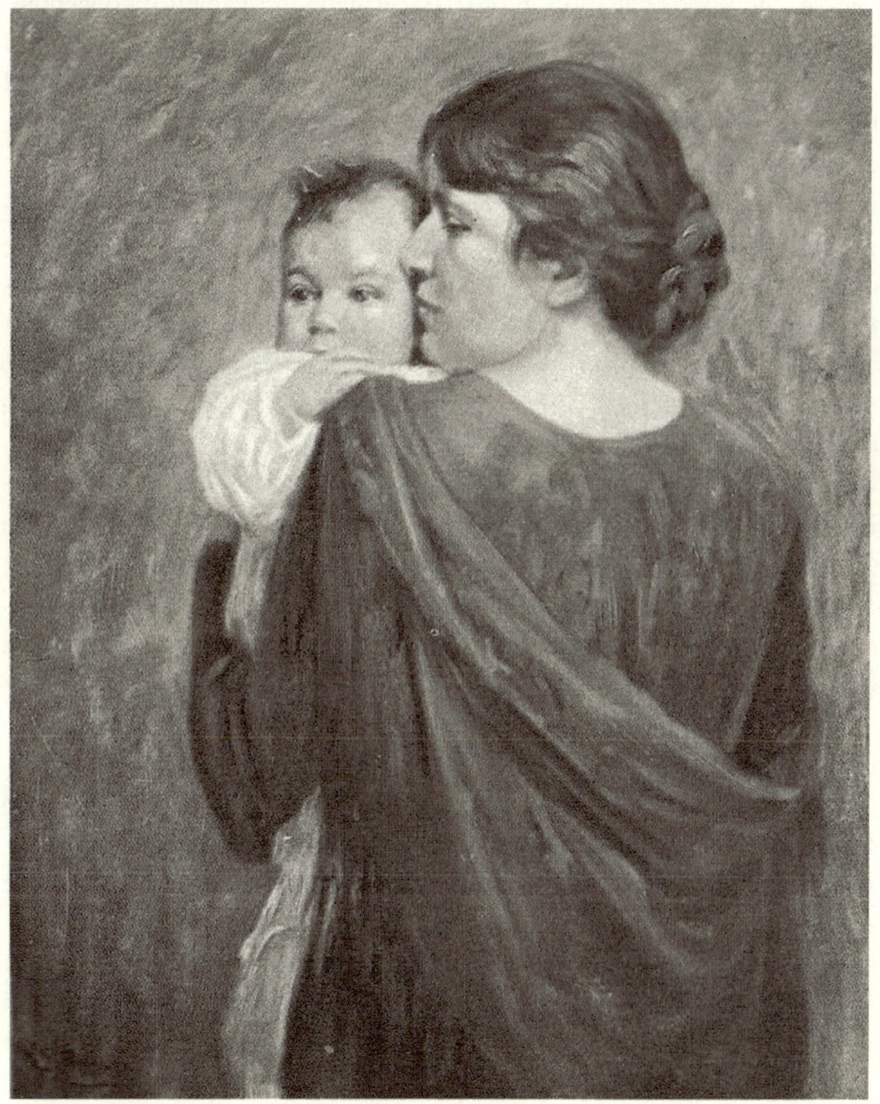

Motherhood

A few years later I sent the picture to the Art Institute of Chicago. During its display there I gave an exhibition in Pittsburgh. One day I received a telegram wishing to know if I would allow my picture to be entered among four others from which group the prizewinning picture for the municipal art purchase prize would be chosen. The picture would eventually be placed in the Municipal League collection. Of course, the honor was not one to be spurned, and I readily consented. I had decided to spend some months in California and on my way, I stopped in Chicago for a couple of days. An anonymous criticism of the entire exhibition that appeared the day before was mailed to each exhibitor and all art patrons and dealers throughout the city and country. It was printed on beautiful and expensive paper and evidently was written by someone not only of keen artistic judgment but who had the means to publish it. His purpose in concealing his name, no doubt, was to give him greater latitude and liberty in saying what he thought without incurring the animosity of the exhibitors. Never have I read such a scathing arraignment of the mediocre things; nor did he show much mercy for many of the stronger painters. Every picture in the exhibition was reviewed, some with three or four words, some with a line. Lucie Hartrath, John Stacey and his wife, Pauline Palmer, Carl Krafft, were all handled without gloves. The criticism of my *Motherhood* ran thus: *Motherhood*, by N. R. Brewer—a sentimental subject handled without sentiment. For clear academic drawing and painting, about the best thing in the whole show."

The artists of the Tree Studios were congregated in the halls, cogitating and guessing who this unmerciful critic might be. Since my picture had received complimentary criticism, I was told the suspicion centered upon me as being the author. As I passed down the hall, I noticed suspicious looks darting in my direction and they began to ask me who I thought might be the author. Cameron volunteered the statement that I had the best criticism of any, and I surmised he was trying to draw me out as to whether I were guilty. I was in a hurry to catch my train for the West and was told that the decision awarding the Municipal Art League prize was to be made that day. I was not looking for a prize, did not expect one and in my rush to get the train forgot all about it. Our son Adrian went with me to the station. He suggested my calling up Mrs. Grower, president of the league, from the station before I left, to ascertain if possible who was the winner. As soon as I mentioned my name over the phone, Mrs. Grower said, "Why, Mr. Brewer, I have been trying to get your studio. I want to compliment you for having drawn the prize." She said many nice things about the comments that had been made by the judges. Adrian, in bidding me goodbye, said, "Well, Dad, that may make your trip a little more pleasant"—and then the great Northwestern train pulled out of the station. I was told after my return from California, some four or five months later, that the members of the Chicago Society of Artists, to which I belonged, had petitioned the Municipal Art League to rescind their decision on the ground that I was a nonresident and nonresidents were not eligible for a prize. I had maintained a studio in Chicago five years. Two winters my wife and I had lived there. The management, knowing this fact, replied to the petitioners with a rebuke, mentioning my eligibility and saying that such a petition did them more harm than good and that the decision of the judges would stand.

J. Francis Brown at one time remarked to Fournier that the artists of Chicago should get together and devise in some way to "disbar all those Eastern fellows who come out here and pick off our prizes." This instance only voiced a general narrow feeling which characterizes so many workers in creative fields—a petty jealousy and selfish rivalry—but since the crumbs that fall from the table of Dives are so few and the Lazaruses so many, I presume we have to put up with it.

My exhibitions at Moulton & Ricketts' gallery and at the Art Institute and the portrait of Joe Jefferson exhibited at the Anderson gallery had won considerable notice in the press and among the artists, and, while I had not exhibited for several years at the Institute, when I sent four large canvasses at one time, three of them were accepted and hung, including my large "Valley of the Missouri." This same picture was solicited by the director of the Iowa State Fair exhibition, when an important display of invited works was held. Later, again it was invited by the Art Institute of Chicago for a special exhibition of landscapes representing American scenery. My pictures, *The Sculptor*, *Magdalene*, portrait of Alexis Fournier, *The Dotted Veil*, and others appeared at the annual exhibitions. In view of all this they may have thought me a dangerous rival!

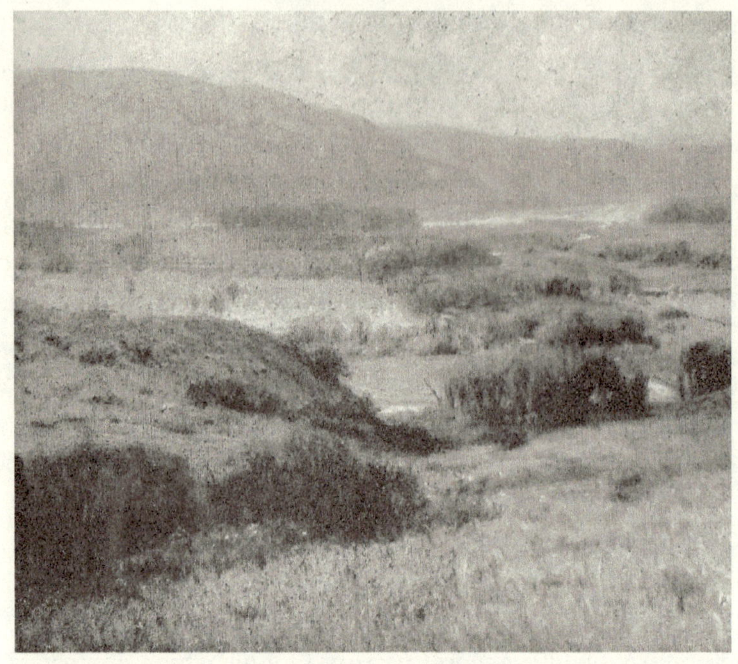

Valley of the Missouri

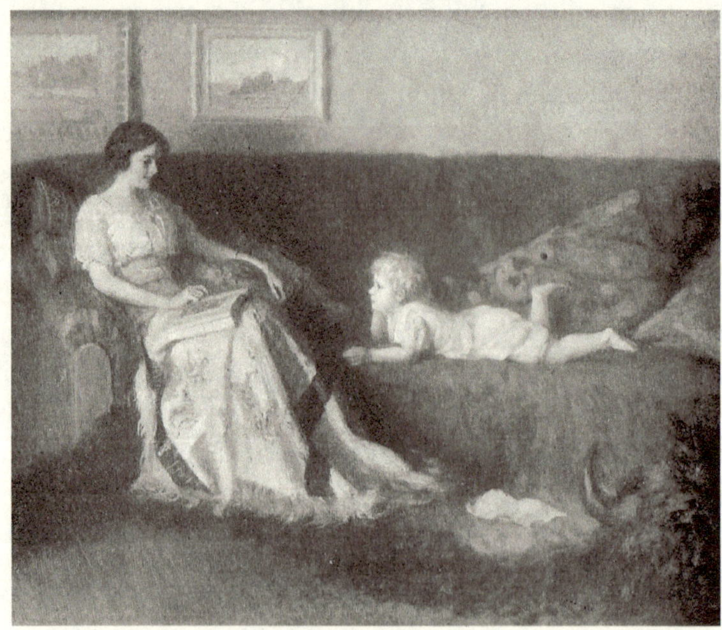

The Story Book

It is measurably gratifying to me to be spoken of as a pioneer in giving one-man shows; yet I was not such, for mine was an exhibition representing the works of a group of artists. Several prominent artists asked me how I managed to do it all. O. D. Grover of Chicago said to me, "My God, Brewer! how do you do it? Wherever I go I hear of your exhibitions and the crowds that attend them." I answered, "I let the ladies do it for me. I merely superintend the hanging and do some talking; they do the rest." The noise they made in the press must have reached Paris, for H. O. Tanner, one of the foremost painters of Europe, wrote me the following letter:

> Paris, Feb. 23, 1923.
>
> Dear Mr. Brewer: Someone sent me a clipping about your New Orleans exhibition. I notice you have a picture of mine, Rachel. I presume you are its owner.
>
> I hope you had a real success which you deserve for the great educational work you are doing.
>
> Very truly,
>
> H. O. Tanner,
> 5113 Ru St. Jacques.

The colored maid who had charge of my room at the hotel in Dayton, Ohio, was in interesting type. She was a mulatto with an Arabian nose, high forehead, fine mouth, and chin—a tempting subject. The housekeeper was willing, she should pose for me for a head. I draped her with a lemon-colored headgear and a green shawl, seated her by a table, looking down, one hand resting on the edge of the table. It was satisfactory as a mere bit of drawing and painting but lacked something to complete a picture. Those who saw it were not impressed except by the technical work, and it kicked about my studio for several years. One day I pulled it out and had a happy thought. Why not put a fishbowl on the table close by? It completed the composition and added a bit of narrative, which seemed necessary. The Vanderpoel Art Association had repeatedly requested me to contribute a picture to its memorial gallery, and, since I had known Vanderpoel intimately, I had this picture framed and sent it to them, receiving the following acknowledgment:

> My Dear Nicholas Brewer: The "Fish Bowl" arrived in time for the meeting on the evening of the fourteenth. If your ears didn't burn, they should have as Dudley Crafts Watson spreadeagled a good deal about your contribution and well might he. We are all so delighted that anything I would say or could say would be inadequate to give you any idea of our appreciation.
>
> Please accept our sincere thanks for the part you played in making this meeting the most successful of any we've ever held.
>
> Cordially,
>
> Vanderpoel Art Association,
John A. Campbell,
9250 So. Robey St.

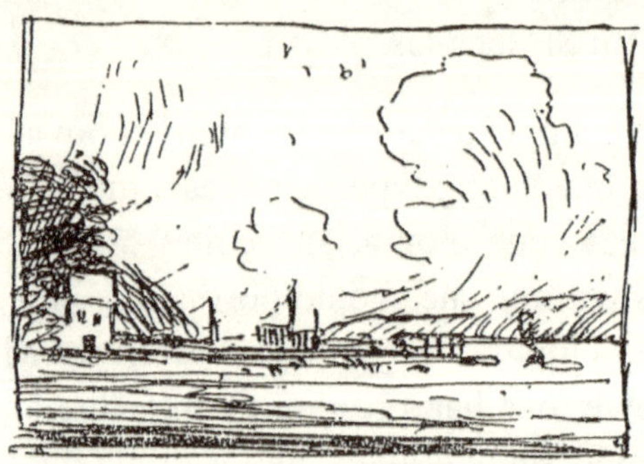

While in Dayton, I painted the portrait of Mrs. P—, wife of a widely known man of vast wealth. Mrs. P—, a charming woman, had many lines and a somewhat jaded expression which I tried to modify a little. But when her husband saw the picture, he insisted that it must show every line, as he felt they were necessary in a delineation of her character. Having steered as much as possible from extremes, I finally produced a picture with which she was entirely satisfied and wished it hung in her home. It fitted very nicely into the end of the room and she awaited, with some anxiety, her husband's return that evening. On seeing it, he declared it did not express her age and he was not pleased with it. She declared that if another line were added or any change made she would not tolerate it in the house. I suggested taking it back to the studio and doing a little more work on it. I noticed the thing was working mischief between them and felt that if I persisted the responsibility for domestic trouble might rest on my shoulders. I finally kept the picture and the more I look at it the more I am convinced that it is one of my best. It was reported that the couple separated recently. Perhaps I was one of the causes.

The one outstanding thing that I recall about the Atlanta show was the great interest shown on the part of the school authorities. The high school pupils were sent to study the pictures and write their impressions of them in letters to the principal of the school. Later she sent me forty or more of these letters, which I still treasure. One day two thousand pupils of the seventh and eighth grades were sent in, in four squads, to visit the gallery and I was asked to give them a studio talk. As this has been a customary thing at my exhibitions, I have always been deeply impressed with the manifest interest of children in pictures. One would think that the subject matter or the story in each picture would be about the only thing with which the young would concern themselves; but I have found that technique, the laying on of the color, the drawing and the quality of light and shade are noted and studied quite as much.

I have encouraged the asking of questions to call out discussion and some of the queries were very surprising, showing a capacity to go deeply into the subject of art expression, as well as a keen enjoyment of the beauties of nature reflected in the pictures. They will crowd about me while I am talking, with their eyes wide open and ears listening, and when some leader asks a question, every word of my answer seems to go home to young hearts hungering to know something of the artist's wizardry—for many look upon an artist as a super-being, gifted with some mysterious power to make things live over again on canvas.

Again and again I meet older high school and college students who want to know all about art as a life's vocation and how and where to study. Some have been drawing, painting and reading for a long time—many under incompetent teachers. They show me their studies, many surprisingly good, others hopelessly bad. Some say, "I don't know that I have talent. Would you advise me to continue?" I believe in encouraging everyone who hopes or wants to be an artist. I tell them if one has a sense of proportion, a fairly accurate vision, an obedient hand to set down what the eye sees, a great love of natural beauty, an instinctive fitness of things or natural taste, good commonsense judgment, and a dynamic application with determination to surmount obstacles he can become an artist. If not a great one, an artist, nevertheless. Art is said to be the product of "twenty-five percent inspiration and seventy-five percent perspiration." It is natural love of the beautiful and the capacity to work it out. "Can I make a living at it?" is a common question. Out of my own experience, I answer, "Yes." In modern life so many avenues for commercial artwork have opened that the student is enabled to live while applying himself to the study of higher art, and if he fails to arrive in that, he will still be better off than one who measures calico behind the counter.

How often we meet people who seem to have missed their proper calling. While seated in one of the galleries of the Fine Arts building at the Pan American Exposition at Buffalo, an old man in rustic garb who had been attentively studying the paintings took a seat beside me. Turning toward me, he asked, "Are you looking at the Acropolis?"

"Yes," said I.

"Well, to get a view of it," he said, "one must go out into the other gallery and see it from a distance. It is one of the most beautiful paintings I have ever seen and there is another below it, that girl with the goldfish. Oh, I think those hands and the face are wonderful! Do you know the artist who did it?"

I replied that it was the work of Julian Story, husband of Emma Eames, the singer, and that there in a row were three pictures by the same artist. His wife was the model for all of them.

"Oh, yes, I recognize her face in each," he said. "Aren't they beautiful? See that farther one where she is singing, what a tone it has!

See the expression on her face! It makes one feel the power of music. And that cattle piece above it—how true it looks! Those animals are well drawn. I have one nearly like it. Oh, my!" he said with a sigh, "I have spent three days in these galleries and cannot tear myself away from these beautiful things. My time is limited, and I must go home to attend to my work. I wanted to see the other great things in this show, but I guess I will have to pass them up."

His enthusiasm over the pictures was so marked that I ventured to ask if he were an artist and he replied, "An artist? Yes, in mud. I am a farmer, a milk raiser for the New York market, but I have loved beautiful pictures better than cows all my life. I don't expect to see many more after this. I am getting old, you see," and he stroked his white beard.

We had a half hour's conversation. When I told him I was a painter, he grabbed my hand and questioned me regarding the kind of work I did. Then he said, "My farm is in the Mohawk Valley. I have a fine place and would like so much to have you come and stay there as long as you like. You will find much around there to paint. We will give you a fine large room to yourself, and my good wife will do everything to make you comfortable. We have the best Jersey milk and cream and good plain food. Won't you come? Then I will have a good chance to see how you paint. That is something I have never seen, for I was born right there on that farm."

The earnestness of his plea seemed like a soul's cry for a better understanding of beauty and art, for under that farmer's exterior dwelt the spirit of an artist. He had surely missed his proper vocation. Many times afterward, I thought of him and how much more pleasure art, as a profession, would have yielded him during life, than the raising of milk for the New York market!

There is keenest joy in feeling the urge to create a thing of beauty! I have been so thrilled with anticipation after having started something, that sleepless hours preceded the dawn, and I would arise restless under delay until my model came. What joy can there be in answering merely to the beck and call of the maddening crowd or in driving pegs at the cobbler's bench? The sad part of it is that the aspiring student in rural places must make a great renunciation. Home ties, old friends, and scenes of youth must give way to the call of a career in some great center where environment is so different. Nor will the change be only temporary. New interests, new friends, new struggles will make the days on the farm or in the small town but so many memories never to be lived over. The great centers are constantly sapping the country of its talent because it provides nothing on which the artist may live and learn.

At many of my exhibitions I had the lady in charge keep a register for every child to sign on entering and instruct them to study the pictures carefully and on leaving to set down on the register opposite his or her name the catalog number of his choice. The Indian picture, *Fading Glories*, was always most popular with the boys and *Motherhood* with the girls. Another noticeable thing is that up to twenty or more years boys and girls show about equal interest in art and pictures. At forty, what a difference! Perhaps the habit of commercial grind, the starting of a business career, is so absorbing that men are weaned away from cultural things—in many cases hopelessly—while wifehood and motherhood stimulates the calling together of moral and aesthetic things for the home and the family, which reacts upon the woman and makes her a sweeter companion and friend.

My exhibition in Macon, Georgia, was better attended than in any other city of its size. The average for three weeks was about five hundred callers daily, and the last day, Sunday, between one and six o'clock over one thousand came. Weekdays the exhibit was open during the evenings, and almost every night I was asked to give a gallery talk. Professor Joseph Robinson wrote a lengthy interview and description of the display for the newspaper and daily flattering articles appeared commending the Macon Art Association in bringing it here. They had commissioned me beforehand to paint a portrait of Harry Stillwell Edwards, the novelist, for their gallery, and the canvas was hung with the others shortly after the opening night. The writings of Edwards are well known. His ten thousand dollars prize novel, *Sons and Fathers*, is a notable work and Edwards was an interesting subject. We became fast friends. He would call late in the afternoon nearly every day for a short chat. A staunch Democrat, an ardent admirer of President Wilson, he frequently spoke of the injustice heaped upon the President and the tragedy of the close of his career.

One day a lady was seen carefully studying the pictures in the exhibit. Three different days she called and whiled away the time, frequently stopping before *El Capitan* and other western subjects. Her great interest led my son Angelo to open conversation with her, and he found she had been in California and would like to know the price on those subjects. She asked to be allowed to hang a few of the pictures in her home so she might live with them to make her choice easier. It resulted in her buying four of them. One was a study of Old Baldy, whose white cap was peeking over the San Gabriel Range. I had made the study on a particularly happy day going from Riverside to Pasadena under most fortunate and auspicious conditions. The study was a joyous reminder of a glorious day: it had been admired greatly by many artists, all of which made it a valuable keepsake, and it was like breaking heart strings to part with it. But at Angelo's solicitation and because Mrs. Walker had been so entranced with my work, I consented to let it go. Mrs. Walker called frequently in the evening when I was giving gallery talks and stayed till closing time.

She asked us to dine at her home one evening and we were never more royally entertained for she was a conversationalist par excellence. Left a widow quite young, with ample fortune to indulge her tastes, she had turned to literature, art, and music. She had purchased the house where Sidney Lanier, the southern poet, was born, lived, and died and in the dooryard she had erected a monument to the poet's memory. After dinner, we went into a room adjoining the drawing room. There was my *Old Baldy,* not a large picture, hanging within easy reach. I paused and lifted it off the hook. A flood of memories renewed the regret of consigning it to the gentle mercies of someone else. I abstractedly ran my hand over its surface and said, "Oh, the day when I did that!" and hung it up again, not realizing that she was observing me closely. When we were seated in the large room, she excused herself and went into a rear room and closed the door. It was some time before she reappeared. She stepped to the picture again and looked at it a few moments, then joined us and led in the conversation. Next day she came to the gallery while I was out and told Angelo she was filled with remorse for having bought *Old Baldy*. "When your father tenderly ran his fingers over the canvas and said,

'Oh, the day when I did that,' it broke me all up and I feel guilty for taking it away from him, for I know it means more to him than we imagine." He quieted her fears by telling her I would soon forget it. One night she asked us if we would like to go to a meeting of prominent citizens, called to consider ways and means of raising funds to erect a suitable bronze monument to the memory of Sidney Lanier. We reached there late and took seats in the rear, as the discussions were under way. Committees had been appointed and the working forces organized. At the right time Edwards, who had observed us enter, arose and addressed the meeting, saying there was a gentleman in the room he would like to call upon for a few words—and mentioned my name.

I have never tasted any kind of liquor that made me shake at the knees quite so quickly, as when suddenly called upon to speak in public. I have always been subject to stage fright on the slightest provocation. What did I know about Sidney Lanier? What could I say about this movement to honor his memory? These thoughts flashed through my mind rapidly. As I did not rise, Mrs. Walker, at my side urged me to say something. "You can do it nicely," she said. Angelo said, "Get up, Dad, you are elected." The audience began to clap. I arose and they motioned for me to step to the front. I tried to think of something to say. I must compliment the townspeople in this worthy work, I thought. I got through that part all right. Then I thought of Ruskin's words, "We build the monument where we failed to crown the brow," a pretty little saying and it might be opportune. I found myself in deep water. Had people of the sovereign State of Georgia failed to crown the brow of Lanier, letting him nearly starve to death while writing his enduring stanzas? Or had they, on the contrary, showered on him the plaudits of a popular hero? I was decidedly ignorant of everything connected with the life of the poet. I knew some things about the colonial development of Georgia culture, and said a few words about that, letting Lanier alone, and wound up by saying that "doubtless sometime in the distant future, the citizens of Macon will call another meeting to consider the placing of a monument on yonder hill to honor the memory of their great living poet and literateur, Harry Stillwell Edwards." Edwards bowed and smiled his approval and the meeting broke up. I felt that I had been stupid, but dear Mrs. Walker delicately complimented me, and Angelo bluntly said, "You have done worse than that, Dad," which relieved me of some of my chagrin.

Next day I asked Mrs. Walker if she would allow me to use her sketch to make a larger picture of Old Baldy to have in my exhibitions. To this she readily consented and when it was done, she came with her sister in the evening to my studio in the hotel to see it. She said she was now relieved of her compunction for stealing away my pet study, since I had a larger and better one. She was infatuated with California and as we both had, at different times, ransacked that fair country from sunny San Diego to lonely Sonoma by auto, whiling away azure days in the Yosemite and forest of sequoias, we had much to talk about. I showed her over a hundred fine photographs I had taken en route, scenes she was familiar with and we prolonged the conversation past midnight, while her sister dozed comfortably in the big rocker. I apologized for keeping them so late. "Oh, no, Mr. Brewer," she said, "I could enjoy talking here with you all night about our wonderful trips through God's country, as you call it." The next year the South Shore Country Club of Chicago had my whole collection on their spacious walls the entire summer and at the close they bought *Old Baldy*, their choice of the lot. It now hangs over the mantel in their extensive library.

Before leaving Macon, I was commissioned by a descendant of an old family to paint copies of two portraits by Sully. They represented a handsome young couple who had their portraits painted in Philadelphia in 1831 while they were on their honeymoon trip. These were the finest Sullys I have ever seen and surely he had an exceptionally handsome couple as models. The man, with full, curly black hair and burnsides, handsome brows and eyes, wore the high collar and stock of that period, with a cape slightly loose on his shoulders. The bride was in white and had the sweetest, most intelligent and benign countenance I believe I have ever seen. The cultured southern people of Macon displayed a sincere and wholehearted interest in art and made my month there a happy one. Their beautiful old homes are perfect examples of colonial architecture, but no more beautiful than the gracious hospitality dispensed within their doors.

Chapter XVI

The Trail Leads to Little Rock and Hot Springs

In the fall of 1919 the Art Association of Little Rock, Arkansas, gave an exhibition of my paintings on the top floor of the magnificent new Court House, which they had secured for a permanent gallery and exhibition room.

Our son, Adrian, had just been mustered out of the airplane division of the Pacific Coast, and was groping about for something to do along art lines, for his inclination lay in that direction. He displayed not only marked enthusiasm in his work, but unquestioned talent in landscape painting. So, I thought it well to take him to Little Rock with me as a helper, to assist the ladies in charge of the display and to see that the pictures were properly hung and handled. Besides, if he were to become an artist, the experience would be valuable.

The exhibition was opened with a reception, which included speeches on the part of the Governor, Charles H. Brough, the president of the State University, and myself. While waiting on the platform, during the musical selections, the Governor whispered to me, asking the names of several of our great American painters and some of their individual characteristics. The time was so brief, I could mention only a half dozen of our leading painters, giving a few of their traits. When the Governor rose to talk (and an eloquent speaker he is), he juggled the names I had given him in a most learned fashion, and wound up with a peroration that should go on record, with many of his other speeches, as a compendium of well-intentioned misstatements. However, no finer character, no truer patriot, no abler educator, and diplomat than the Governor could be found. He had me paint his portrait, which has been placed in the State Capitol.

Nowhere in all my experience in giving exhibitions, have I had such hearty encouragement and patronage as I met with in Little Rock. Extracts from a letter to The Little Rock Mirror indicates the Governor's hearty cooperation:

"Parallel with our commercial renaissance should grow a renaissance of the fine arts. A great French critic has said that every nation must acquire commercial supremacy before it acquires a supremacy in the aesthetic and cultural side of life. This was true of Greece, in the age of Pericles; of Rome, in the age of Augustus Caesar; of Italy, in the days of Venice, Pica, and Genoa; of England, France, and Germany in the heyday of their prosperity.

"Reasoning by analogy, therefore, the forward-looking citizens of Arkansas have a right to expect a generous patronage of the fine arts and a recognition of the value of the trivium and quadrivium will follow in the wake of the golden age of our economic prosperity.

"Four years ago, a number of the cultured ladies of Little Rock organized the Little Rock Fine Arts Club, which now has a membership, active and associate, of approximately eighty. Recently there has been exhibited, under the auspices of this club, at the County Court House, a magnificent collection of paintings, valued at approximately $100,000, the property of Nicholas R. Brewer, one of America's great artists. That a genuine interest is being taken by our cultured people in the development of the fine arts, and the establishment of a public gallery, may be seen from the generous patronage, which has been accorded this collection within the past ten days. Nothing could have reflected more eloquently the desire of our people to advance along cultural lines than the praiseworthy patronage recently given this notable exhibit, and also the substantial patronage just accorded grand opera in our city.

> Let us emulate the example of our greater cities and of our sister commonwealths, in establishing in our capital city a public art gallery, open to all people, in order that our children and our chil-

> dren's children may cultivate the fine arts and recognize the cultural value of life. It is high time that we realize the value of making a LIFE, as well as the value of making a LIVING.
>
> Governor Charles H. Brough.

Immediately after the opening of the exhibition two ladies approached me, wishing to arrange to have their portraits painted, and the people of Little Rock kept me busy filling their orders until the following January.

That summer I painted a picture I called *Armenia*. Adrian, like my other boys, always felt in duty bound to bring Father up and never missed an opportunity to criticize my work—and sometimes even my behavior. One's offspring are often inclined to be more fastidious about their parents' manners than their own.

When *Armenia* was finished, Adrian, looking at it, said "No, Dad, you haven't got it; it is neither flesh, fish, nor fowl; it might, though, be called foul." That and other comments cooled my enthusiasm over the picture, and I was about to junk it—cover it over with paint and use the canvas for something else. But the day after the opening of the show, the president of the Little Rock Fine Arts League bought the picture for her own private collection.

A prominent artist and collector who has much to do with the selection of paintings for an eastern museum happened to be at the hotel, and hearing of the exhibition went to see it. He was so impressed with *Armenia* that he was sure it would be considered a valuable acquisition and offered to buy it, but the lady would not consider selling it. I said gleefully to Adrian, "Ah ha! He who laughs last, laughs best."

A large landscape was purchased by D. H. Cantrell, who had his wife's portraits painted. A couple of years later, when Cantrell planned to build a new mansion, he told his architect to plan a spacious drawing room around the landscape, so the architect built a unique mantel above the fireplace, with paneled walls around the painting. The picture was mounted with a carved wooden border, touched with gold. When they were about to move in, Cantrell called me in San Antonio over long distance, to know if I thought the heat from the fireplace would be apt to injure the painting. I told him I thought not.

In cleaning up, the fireplace had been choked with papers, shavings, and other combustibles. When they touched a match to it, they discovered the chimney had no draft and the flames and smoke belched out in great volume. There was a scramble to get the picture off the wall, and the beautiful paneling was ripped to pieces. Further tests proved that the flue was faultily constructed, due to carelessness or the ignorance of the architect. Most of the chimney had to be torn down and rebuilt. The picture was not damaged.

My manager, Ben Greene, arranged for an exhibition in Hot Springs the next January. There I met and painted one of the notable steel magnates of the East, Mr. James A. Campbell, President of the Youngstown Sheet and Tube Company. About a fortnight after our arrival in Hot Springs, I received a summons to appear at the City Hall and pay my tax for the privilege of "doing business in Hot Springs." It did not occur to them that an extensive exhibition of paintings, with lectures on art, could be educational instead of commercial.

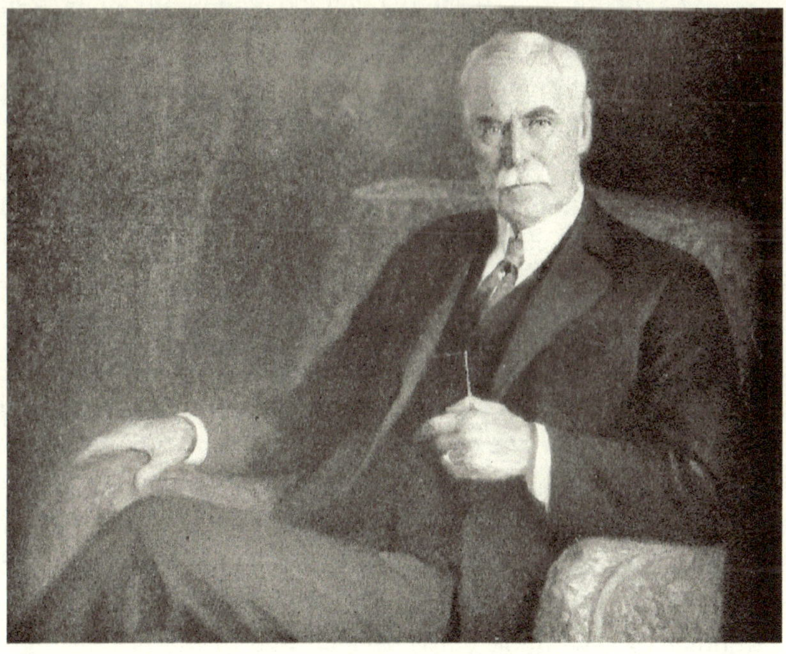

James A. Campbell, Courtesy Butler Art Institute

Adrian had launched out for himself in serious landscape painting and did several pieces, which completely surprised me with their fine technical qualities. He showed splendid feeling for color and composition and no small ability in drawing, but to sell landscapes in Hot Springs was difficult. One previous winter, while in Minneapolis, Adrian sneaked down on the Mississippi River's edge in the dead of winter to sketch the gorge of snow-covered broken ice with frigid water showing in the foreground. His feet and fingers were nearly frozen. He worked up a thirty by forty winter scene, sent it to the exposition of works of artists of seven Northwestern states, at St. Paul, and captured a medal prize. The jury was composed of Wuerpal and Berninghaus of St. Louis. A critic, in an interesting and intelligent review, said this: "The Brewer picture is a remarkable bit, its ice probably as wonderfully painted as ice can be. I shall borrow a chance remark from one of the jurymen, who said, 'Thaulow?' when he looked at it, and Thaulow can paint ice that makes one cold in the summertime."

The next year, Adrian did nearly the same thing, painting the Washington Avenue, Minneapolis bridge, with the city buildings in the distance. He called it *Flood Waters*—a good name with the broken ice and foam below the Falls of St. Anthony.

While Adrian was in the service, I sent both these pictures to the Art Institute, Chicago, where they were well received and won his election to the Chicago Society of Artists. The chap never sent another picture to the Institute, nor did he continue to pay his dues to the Society. Before enlisting for war service, he painted with me in Chicago where he found good subject matter along the smoky Chicago River. Many of the sketches he made there were, indeed, remarkably strong. One day Adrian rushed into the studio, besmeared with paint after a mishap that might have proven serious. To get a good view of the river and buildings, he had climbed on the top of a freight car that stood idle close by the water and was so absorbed in his work that he did not observe a switch-engine that was about to bump into the car upon which he stood. The impact was so sudden and fierce that he went headlong over the side of the car, his easel, picture, and kit following him.

Another day, while at work beneath one of the bridges, he was suddenly startled from behind by a policeman who demanded to know what he meant by making such sketches. Suspecting that he might be a German spy or something equally devilish—for it was war time—the policeman hauled him to the station for questioning. When he was finally released and back at the studio, he told me his interesting experience—"I had the scare of my life. Those mutts were not at all inclined to accept my explanation. I told them my innocent intention and purpose, who I was, who you are, and all about us, referred them to the Art Institute and everybody I know, to no purpose, it seemed. I have just been put through a third degree, and all to prevent the blowing up of the Chicago bridges with this innocent stick of dynamite," and he held up a tube of paint.

In Hot Springs he met Miss Edwina Cook and married her. When their first child was born, Adrian was out of funds, out of work, but not out of debt. I was painting a portrait in Memphis when he wrote me for money. I was slow to respond because of former experiences.

While traveling on a train he had met a former editor of Hot Springs, who now owned the newspaper in Texarkana. This man, on learning who Adrian was, suggested our bringing my collection of paintings to his city and urged Adrian to go there to make the arrangements. He also mentioned several prominent people who he was sure would be interested in having portraits painted. Adrian immediately wrote me to send him sufficient funds to make the trip. In a few days I received a letter asking me to come immediately, as Mrs. Buchanan, of that place, wished to have a portrait painted.

My work was nearing completion in Memphis, the weather was beastly hot, and I was preparing to take wing for the north, but Adrian must be helped out somehow. In Texarkana the weather was hotter than ever and there he was, with only a heavy northern winter suit, without means to buy cooler attire. Mopping his face, nervous and fidgety, he loaded me into a taxi to see the prospective patron. He knew that upon that order rested his financial salvation, as he asked a thirty percent commission. Leaving me to talk to her alone, he walked about the lawn, inspecting the flowers, but I knew he saw nothing but his troubles in every leaf or rosebud he nervously plucked. When I emerged and told him that I would begin the portrait on the following day, a ray of sunlight passed over his face that illumined the gloom within, and a happier kid I never saw. "Now," he said, "I will be out of debt, with something ahead."

He closed an arrangement with the Woman's Club to give an exhibition in the fall. When the portrait was finished, we started north.

The custodian of the State Capitol in St. Paul sent for me to inspect the condition of the numerous fine oil paintings and portraits in that handsome building. I found them in a deplorable state from neglect. All those hanging on outer walls were badly bloomed, the canvasses wrinkled, some of them cracking from over varnish. The State, he said, was willing to stand the expense of having them properly looked after. Adrian, who had made quite a study of pigments and varnishes, knew more about such work than I, and, going over them together, we concluded to accept the job of restoration.

A large room with good light was assigned us, and works by America's greatest painters, for which the State had paid several hundred thousand dollars, were removed from the walls. The careful removing of varnish, which had bloomed, involves no little labor. Many of the old portraits were badly cracked. The job took most of the summer, to Adrian's great satisfaction and relief. When the pictures were rehung, an entire new system for lighting them was installed. Ever since, those priceless masterpieces have been seen to the best possible advantage.

That fall, Adrian, according to appointment, put on a display of my paintings in Texarkana. He continued with me as business manager and erstwhile landscape painter. He was clever in giving gallery talks and demonstrations. Meanwhile he became interested in painting Texas landscapes, especially the blue bonnets and wildflowers. We both went to Austin in April to see the wonderful fields of blue bonnets and were beguiled into making numerous studies. The first few attempts took the conceit completely out of us, for those sunny hills of waving blue and purple presented problems we had never tackled before. There was no such thing as painting the blue bonnets individually, not even as close up still life studies, and Adrian was the first one to realize it. He said that Onderdonk was the only man who had painted a blue bonnet field with any degree of consistency.

After reviewing our studies, made during a couple of weeks of hard outdoor work, we came to the parting of the ways. I gave it up as a hopeless task. He continued according to his convictions, and the following year produced some very lovely things. In 1928, he carried away the Edgar B. Davis first prize of twenty-five hundred dollars, with his *In a Blue Bonnet Year*. He was living in Little Rock when the wire came, informing him of his good luck. That night he called me on long distance to tell me of it. His presence was desired at the prize winners' banquet, and requests came from two or three other cities for exhibitions of his pictures. Raking together all his pictures and studies, some fifty odd in number, quite a creditable display was available. After three months, but fourteen remained on his hands.

At this writing, 1930, in compliance with a request from a New York gallery for pictures enough to make a special display, he is working hard on some of his finest things, which will be shown there next fall. Three lusty youngsters now romp and play around Adrian's home—Betty, the eldest, a bright, precocious child, and two redheaded twin boys, Adrian and Edwin. They have nicknamed them the "Wrecking Crew."

Chapter XVII
Finance—Religion—Art

Ignace Paderewski—George M. Reynolds—Cardinal Mundelein—Maude Powell

While touring through California, we stopped at Paso Robles, where I painted the portrait of Ignace Paderewski. Until then, I had never met the world's greatest pianist—that man who had enthralled the music lovers of two continents, hobnobbed with royalty, been the guest of the greatest painters, poets, and statesmen, and who has helped shape the political destiny of his beloved Poland in her emergence from the recent conflict of nations. His views on the art of government have called out expressions of respect from the ablest leaders of the day; yet he is every inch a great musician. Paderewski came promptly at the appointed hour for his sitting, dressed in a cream flannel suit. After the necessary preliminaries, we commenced our work, throughout which an animated conversation was kept up between my traveling companion, Father O'Sullivan and Mr. Paderewski, which I occasionally joined. He seemed entirely willing to discuss topics of general interest.

"I presume you have had your portrait painted before?" I asked. "Oh, yes, several times," was his response. "By Sargent?" "No, Mr. Sargent has asked me to sit for him, but I was unable to keep the appointment at that time, and somehow, we have not been able to come together since, and now I believe he has discontinued painting portraits, has he not? He must have made a vast sum of money in his long career. But Burne-Jones, Alma Tadema, Bonnat, and Jerome have painted me, likewise Princess Louise, daughter of Queen Victoria. Of course, as she was of royalty, I had to be agreeable and sit for her, but she was very slow. At the Versailles Peace Conference I sat for an American who was painting some portraits, but the picture was rather a failure." "You are, then, not an amateur at sitting," I said. "Oh no, I have known many great artists. I knew De Newville. Benjamin Constant, Carolus Duran, and many others." Upon being asked whether he knew Bastien-Lepage or Marie Baskirtscheff, the Russian, he said, "No, but I knew Tony Robert Fleury very well."

The conversation then drifted to the political situation. I asked a few leading questions of the former Premier, regarding the European situation in general and the Polish question in particular, a subject which I thought would inspire the animation so typical of him and which I wanted to portray.

"The world is in a bad way," he said with a sigh. "You refer to the Bolshevik tendency?" I asked. "Yes," he replied positively, "it is everywhere, even here in America. It is radical socialism with all its horrible revolting doctrines. I have reasons to know. I was Premier of Poland for eleven months and I know something about it. I know the awful conditions there and elsewhere, too."

He now began to warm up. His face assumed a serious, agitated look, and he forgot he was posing for me. I had selected a profile view of his face. He started to turn and look straight at me while talking, which made it impossible for me to continue work. Father O'Sullivan, who had been standing behind me, observed my predicament, took a seat in front of the Premier and asked a question, which caused him to turn around and again assume the correct pose. The real purpose of Father O'Sullivan's adroit move was not observed by the Premier and only caused him to go deeper into the subject and what he termed the religious phase of it.

He said that when a young man he once read Karl Marx's work on Capitalism, and on being asked what he thought of it, said, "I would call it the fifth Gospel of Marx, and I am right, because it is the gospel of the socialists. It is their religion and it is unnatural. For instance, the Christian religion, Mohammedanism, Confucianism and other religions are based upon the supernatural, but Bolshevism is built on the unnatural and, therefore, it is wrong. It is horrible." On being asked if they did not deny Christ, he said, "Yes, they hate Christ, they damn Him. In one city they tore down all the Christian monuments and erected two in place—one to Karl Marx and one to—whom do you suppose? Judas Iscariot!"

He dwelt upon the horrible conditions of the famine, when human flesh was sold in the shops for food, repeating similar conditions that have occurred in China. "Napoleon saved France by killing twenty thousand—Russia would have to kill six hundred thousand."

Then he referred to the awful slaughter of the "Flower of the Russian Army," in the Pripet marshes, through the treachery of General Rennin, who was of German descent; also to the policy of placing German families in Russia for political reasons.

Then turning to the League of Nations: "A league for the preservation of peace had already been established and the American people were anxious and willing to support Wilson's idea, but antagonistic propaganda soon changed public opinion, and now America is the only country which refuses to accept the League. Wilson was outwitted by Lloyd George and Clemenceau, who demanded surrender of one thing and another, which further supported the antagonism to the League in this country." Asked his opinion of the League, his reply was, "The Articles of the Covenant is one of the three greatest documents ever written: The Magna Charta, the Constitution of the United States, and the Covenant of the League of Nations."

I asked, "Could Ireland bring her case before the Council of the League?" He replied, emphatically, "Yes, she could. The League was formed to settle just such questions. It would unanimously vote for absolute autonomy, perfect self-government, but not complete independence, because granting complete independence would establish a precedent that would cause turmoil and trouble all over the world, for many nations have similar situations of their own. For instance, Spain has the same trouble with Catalonia, which has its own language; France has Algiers. Not that the nations do not sympathize with Ireland, for they do, but they could not afford to vote for Irish independence. The Irish have lost favor with the allied nations, on account of the unfortunate affair of Sir Roger Casement and the matter of submarine bases, for no doubt there was assistance given Germany in that way."

Referring to the matter of disarmament, he said that disarmament would work in regard to the army, but not the navy.

When asked if he ever tried to paint, he said he had not, but added, "My father was an artist, principally a sculptor, and his religious statues are in many of the churches of Poland."

In criticizing his portrait, he suggested that the face appear less fleshy, but that he liked it better than any of the seven other portraits that had been painted of him. He did not make the usual statement, "There is something wrong with the expression," but went on to say that it is unfair to the artist for the subject to suggest criticism, since a portrait should be the artist's characterization of the sitter.

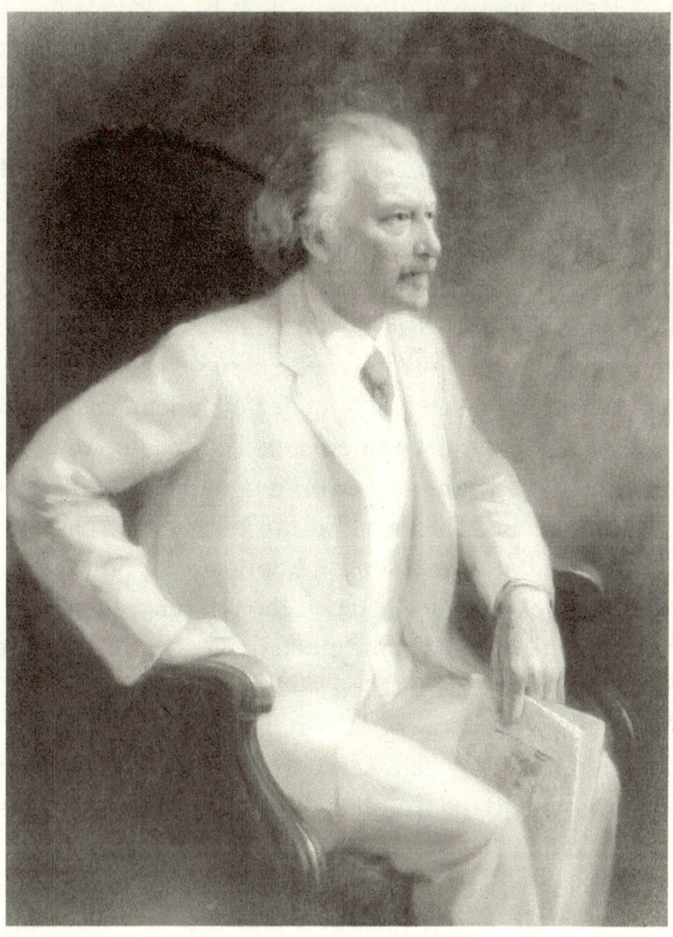

Ignace Jan Paderewski

As the days taken up in the sittings were replete with interesting conversation on varied subjects, both Father O'Sullivan and I jotted down in our notebooks, in the evening, what each could recall of the sayings of this remarkable man. In comparing our notes, we always found that both of us had forgotten a good many things of interest in the day's talks.

One day Father O'Sullivan, in his characteristic meekness, asked me if I thought it would be all right to tell Paderewski that he had a brother who was a musician and who lived in Berlin, where his operas had been played at the Royal Theatre. When he mentioned it to Paderewski, he said, "Well, if your brother's operas have been accepted in Berlin under the approval of royalty, that is, indeed, a great honor." O'Sullivan asked if he would care to see some of the scores of them. Upon being answered in the affirmative, he had them sent to Paso Robles. Paderewski played them and spoke of their high quality.

Paderewski was not an early riser, seldom appeared until noon, but spent many hours in the evening at his piano. You can imagine our delight on hearing the most wonderful improvisations, when that instrument became a living thing; it moaned and it laughed; it sang with the joy of life and the sorrow of the dirge, under his magic touch.

Paderewski is a man of dynamic energy, profound thought, and great nervous tension, but always under complete self-control. Mrs. Paderewski, on the contrary, is tremendously excitable. One day she brushed into the room when I was working, without even saying "good morning," but launched into a rapid-fire outburst of pantomime and language, whether Polish or Italian I know not, of quite some length, then a pause. The ex-Premier listened thoughtfully, then uttered decisively three or four words, which settled the matter and quelled the agitation of his excited wife. She then said in broken English, "You must excuse, Mr. Brewer; it was very important."

Paderewski's mind, when weary from overstrain, flits momentarily from the profound to the frivolous. When the tones of his instrument after hours of action have died away, he will be seen with his wife almost daily going to some nearby movie for a little relaxation. He stands aloof from all social functions and is almost a recluse. Great men, artists, statesmen, creators seldom find social pleasures as rich in satisfaction as that of introspective contemplation that leads to outbursts of creative power.

To be able to find great joy in one's own thoughts and in the things we do is indeed a priceless heritage. Some of the most unhappy people are the jaded devotees of frivolity. They have so little within themselves to make life worth living that they plunge into the social whirl to escape ennui. And therein lies the merit of early discipline, the discipline of necessity, toil, even hardships and suffering. It has been said that no great poem was ever written, no great picture ever painted nor great role ever acted that did not grow from the bitter dregs of suffering. The cradle of luxury is not the birthplace of genius. And Paderewski has gone through it all from his early Polish boyhood struggles to the renown he now enjoys.

* * *

To have headquarters nearer my field of operation, in the middle states, I opened a studio in Chicago. Before that time, however, Mrs. George M. Reynolds commissioned me to paint her portrait. She wished to surprise her husband on his birthday with the picture, and since it could not be painted in the home, I was obliged to paint it at my hotel. When the canvas was nearing completion, she told me that the directors of her husband's bank had engaged Mr. Louis Betts to paint his portrait for the directors' room, and that Betts would shortly begin sittings in the home. It was generally known that Mrs. Betts was her husband's very efficient manager. The fact that the picture would be in process of work when my picture was sent home and presented to Mr. Reynolds, placed me in an extraordinary position, bringing me into direct rivalry with one of the strongest painters in this country today. I did not know what might arise from it to prejudice Mr. Reynolds against my picture, especially since Mrs. Reynolds had also said that should my likeness of her prove satisfactory to her husband, she wanted me to paint a companion portrait of him.

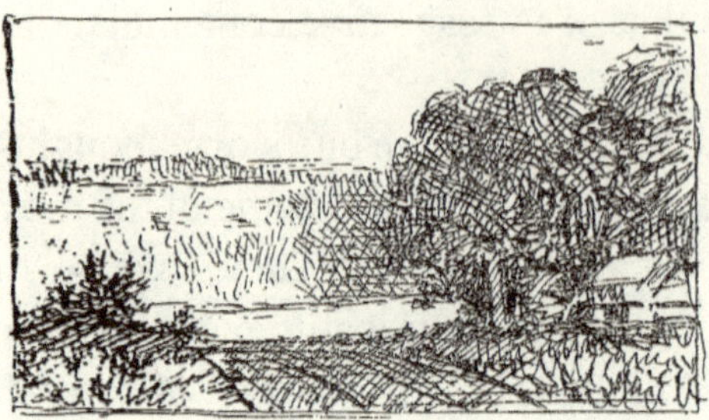

The unusual circumstances caused me some concern, and I was at a loss to know how to handle the matter. I finally concluded to take Mrs. Reynolds into my confidence. I told her that while I had the greatest respect for the work of Mr. Betts, I knew neither him nor his wife personally; that owing to the spirit of competition existing, I preferred not to place myself in an embarrassing position—possibly to be damned with faint praise, or have Mr. Reynolds prejudiced in his judgment of my work. Mrs. Reynolds, a clever and high-minded woman, readily grasped the situation and said, "I understand your position, Mr. Brewer. I'll tell you what we'll do. I'll simply put this picture in the library, lock it up, and I'll fix it so Mr. and Mrs. Betts will not know that it has been painted."

The following day Mrs. Reynolds told me that Mrs. Betts had already spoken to her and Mr. Reynolds about Mr. Betts painting both their portraits and suggested that she have a new gown made. "I want to go with you to help select it," Mrs. Betts had said. Mrs. Reynolds turned it off by saying she was too poor a subject for a picture and had not thought of having Mr. Betts paint her portrait.

The following Sunday, being Mr. Reynolds' birthday and the time appointed to give him the portrait, Mrs. Reynolds asked me to the house in the afternoon to meet Mr. Reynolds and to see how he liked the picture. As I entered the drawing room, Mr. Reynolds, who was there alone, greeted me saying, "I presume this is Mr. Brewer. My wife is upstairs and will be down presently," and cordially shook my hand. He continued, "I want to tell you how well I like your portrait of my wife. It was a perfect surprise to me." Then he proceeded to tell me that Mr. Betts was painting his portrait by order of the directors of his bank. "My wife wants me to sit for mine for the home, to match this one. Mr. and Mrs. Betts have solicited the order for both pictures for the house.

But I shall wait and see how Mr. Betts' picture of me turns out and on my return from California in about two months, I will decide in favor of the artist whose picture I like best. I must say I like this picture of Mrs. Reynolds very much. The likeness is good, and the coloring is superb. Mrs. Reynolds has already told me you did not wish Mr. and Mrs. Betts to know that you have painted this picture at the present time. I can assure you that we shall say nothing about it, nor shall we let them see the picture." With this assurance I awaited his return from California.

In the meantime, I saw the Betts picture at the bank and admired it very much. It was an excellent likeness of Mr. Reynolds and beautifully painted.

Later a letter came from Mr. Reynolds requesting me to call at his home, as he wished to discuss the matter of his portrait. He told me that he had finally decided to employ me to paint the picture, giving as a reason, "I think I like your style of brush work a little better than that of Mr. Betts. The reproductions you have shown me of people I have known are excellent likenesses. Now, I am a very busy man. I believe my wife said that you had painted her picture in less than five days. Mr. Betts kept me in the chair for over two weeks. That is a great amount of valuable time. How long will it take you to do mine?" "Well," I answered, "if you can give me Saturday and Sunday from ten o'clock on,"—days I knew he would not be busy—"I think that will suffice."

Mr. Reynolds is chairman of Chicago's only billion-dollar bank. It was said he declined a seat as Secretary of the Treasury in President Harding's Cabinet. Born in Panora, Iowa, in 1865, he began as a clerk in Guthrie County National Bank, of Panora, on a salary of twenty dollars per month. In 1893, he became cashier of the Continental Commercial National Bank of Chicago, rose to its presidency, and engineered a merger with the Illinois Bank and Trust Company, the largest bank outside of New York.

He is a man of keen, positive, determined judgment. When seated he remains erect, never slouches or lolls, is quick in action. He is dear and lucid in his definitions and sees through things at a glance. A conservative, competent advisor, he inspires confidence and respect.

My portrait pleased him and now hangs in their beautiful library in a niche specially built for it, while that of Mrs. Reynolds fills a space in the large drawing room to the left.

* * *

One day Mrs. Anderson, of the Anderson Galleries, Chicago, sent me a request to see them about a portrait that was wanted, and acquainted me with the fact that the subject was the man who at that time was called "His Grace," but now, "His Eminence," Cardinal George W. Mundelein. After learning that I was available, Mrs. Anderson informed His Grace that I would be glad to meet him at the gallery to discuss the matter of a portrait. It resulted in my painting his picture at his home.

I found in His Grace the sweetest, most benign character I think I have ever met in a man. He was every inch a gentleman, kind, considerate, unostentatious, with dynamic energy devoted to the general uplift of his people and the building up of the various forces of his vast diocese. His having been elevated to the high office of the cardinalate is proof that responsibility rests upon unbending shoulders.

He also had me paint a portrait of his predecessor, Archbishop Quigley. He said he wanted it as nearly in the style of Healy's as possible, since several of Healy's portraits of members of the Western hierarchy were in his collection. The Cardinal is a great lover of art and a collector. He once said, "All my salary goes for books and art," and in his collection he had many noteworthy canvasses.

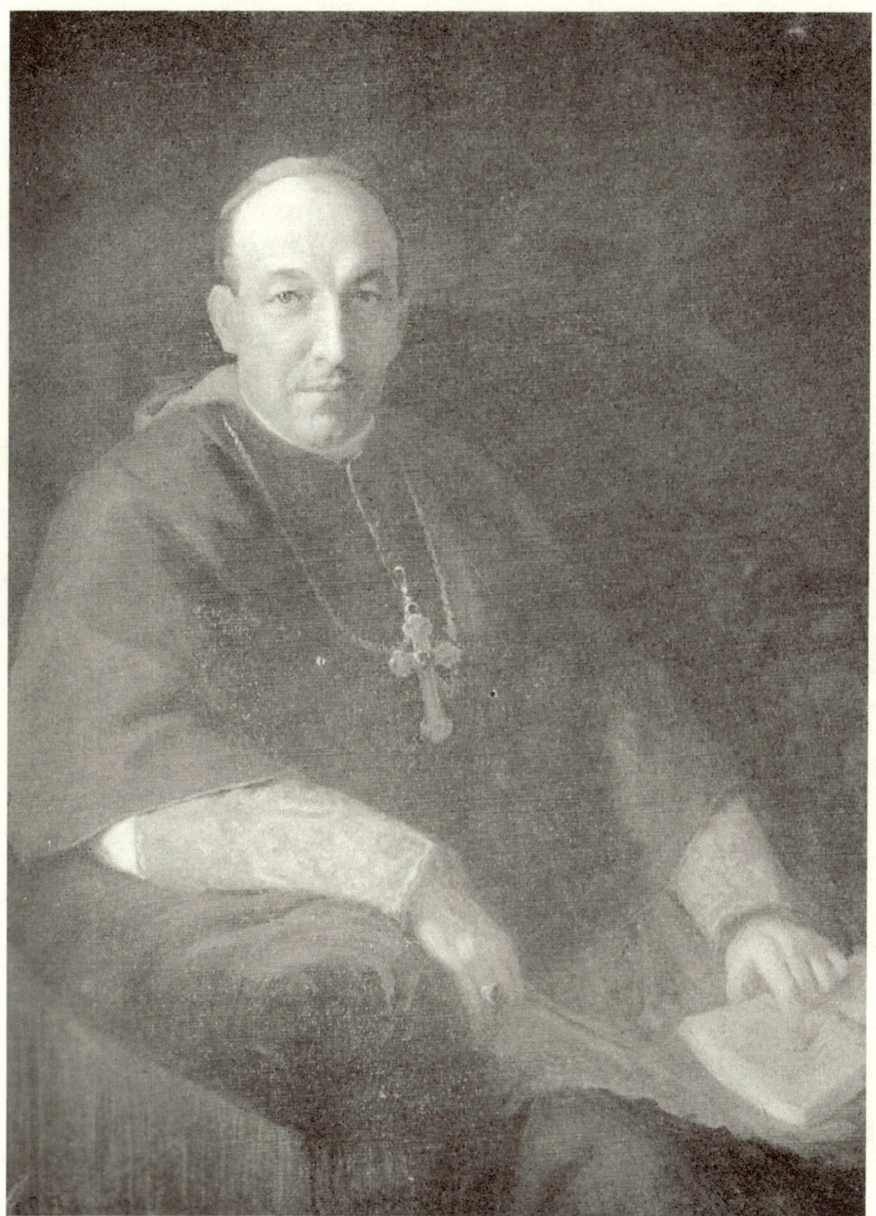

His Eminence George Cardinal Mundelein

At the Anderson Galleries, at that time, they had on display one of my paintings, which I called the *Star at Bethlehem*. The Archbishop was very much interested in the subject, no doubt on account of its religious character, and expressed his admiration. The day before Christmas I sent it to his house as a Christmas gift and shortly afterward received the following letter:

> Chicago, Ill.
> Dec. 27, 1916
> Mr. N. R. Brewer,
> Auditorium Hotel,
> Chicago, Ill.
>
> My dear Mr. Brewer,
>
> One of the first acknowledgements being sent out after Christmas day is to you. I want to thank you for the beautiful painting of the *Star at Bethlehem,* which arrived here just as I was leaving to celebrate the Pontifical High Mass on Christmas Day. It is, needless to say, that I am pleased with it, for I consider the conception and the carrying out of the idea very fine. Moreover, it is certainly a brilliant piece of coloring. I am at a loss to know, at present, in what place I am going to put it, but most likely in one of the reception rooms downstairs. I would prefer to have it in my own room, however, but I am not going to be selfish and keep everything for myself but will share it with others who come into the house. As I am to preach on the subject of the Epiphany on next Sunday week at the Cathedral, I think I shall sit down and contemplate the painting for a little while and see if I cannot get some good ideas from it. Perhaps if the sermon turns out to be a good effort, the painting may have contributed somewhat toward this effect.
>
> I trust that your Christmas has been very pleasant, and I hope that the new year will bring you an abundance of blessings from the Lord, and that

all of your works will prove as acceptable to those who possess them as the three pictures from your brush that hang in this house.

I beg to remain,
Sincerely yours,

George W. Mundelein,
Archbishop of Chicago.

* * *

Maud Powell was as well-known throughout America as any concert celebrity of her time. Famous as a violinist and possessed of great personal charm, she counted her friends by the thousand, wherever the tones of that priceless instrument of hers were heard. Her violin was veritably a part of herself, for not only was it the medium through which she sang and brought to her enraptured audiences the melody that dwelt in her own soul, but it was her daily and hourly companion, whose strings she caressed in marvelous improvisations or difficult scores. She had little time for purely social functions, often declining flattering engagements, which most people would esteem an honor to receive. But the fullness of her joy in making music made easy the labor and concentration that was necessary to develop her facility and round out the technique that beguiled her charmed listeners.

Arrangements had been made at the close of one of her tours for her to come to Chicago to sit for her portrait. Consequently, one fine morning, in answer to a knock at my studio door, I met for the first time the lady with the violin case under her arm, about whom we had heard so much. At our first greeting I perceived the invigorating charm this woman possessed, which, coupled with her musical talent, made our acquaintance delightful.

When it came to planning the picture, she suggested my arranging an unconventional costume. From a chest I pulled a gown, which had belonged to a grand opera star. I had picked it up in New York for studio use because of its cut and color. She was charmed with it and soon put it on. Of course, the violin with its beautiful red color had to be in the picture. Seating herself on my Roman divan of purplish red, amidst pillows of varying tints, she fell into a characteristic pose, holding in her right hand the instrument which formed a centralizing note of color. I flung about her shoulders a long purplish gray scarf that streamed to her feet forming graceful lines and partly concealing her left arm.

With a temperament innately artistic, her sympathetic grasp of my requirements, and her delightful conversation rendered the sittings a pleasure and the work a success. At every rest interval she seized her violin and played.

Ten years after I finished the portrait, and Maud Powell had passed away, I had the pleasure of once more handling that Guadagnini. The instrument had been a gift, in recognition of Powell's talent, from the King of Italy, and bore on its back an ivory inset with the coat of arms of that Royal House. Maud Powell, at the time of her death, had three great violins—the one here mentioned, a Stradivarius, and one other of the same class.

While in Tulsa a short time ago, Enrique Rasoplo paid me a short visit. He is a famous violinist, having played for English Royalty, in the private apartments of the King and Queen of Spain, and in the Royal orchestra of Madrid. His father was a Mexican of great wealth, living in Mexico City, and his mother an Italian. Enrique was educated in Italy and Spain, where his mother's family dates back far beyond the days of Guadagnini, holding many names distinguished in music and art. Hearing I had painted the Powell portrait, he came to acquaint me with the fact that he was the proud owner of Powell's famous Guadagnini. Opening the case to identify his ownership, he handed me the violin. Yes! there it was, the Royal coat of arms ornamenting its bright-hued, enameled back.

Rasoplo, handsome and courteous, of Italian type, is married to a lovely American girl from Nashville, who considers her dark eyed husband the greatest and best man in the world, as all good wives should.

No artist believing in the principles of the modern radicals could ever draw or paint that violin, for it is as difficult to limn as is the hand that plays it.

The human hand is the most wondrous instrument by which every man-made thing has been builded, ever executing, without hesitance, the dictates of the intellect.

Watch those hands of Paderewski as they sweep the keyboard, obedient to the behest of the master's emotion; or the quivering graceful action of the hands of Maud Powell, sensitive to the subtlest shading of tone as felt in the soul of the artist, as she drew those entrancing strains from the heart of her Guadagnini.

I had a photograph made of Maud Powell's portrait, which she was anxious to have as soon as possible. In a short time, I received this characteristically cordial note from her:

> May 28–18.
>
> Dear Mr. Brewer—I have been waiting patiently, or maybe a little impatiently, for the photographic copy of the portrait. But I dare say, you have been busy with your Red Cross lady and others besides—so quickly do you work. I wrote you from the train on my way home. The address of my cousin is: Chas. A. Dean, 740 Cass Ave., Detroit. Another cousin, Walter W. Davis, will probably go West to meet his wife, in which case he would stop off to see my portrait, at my invitation and your consent! I am very busy and shall be till about July 1, when I hope to get away to the mountains. I still recall, very pleasantly, our being four days at the studio. Your photograph is placed among those of my most distinguished artist friends on the wall near the piano. With kindest remembrances,
>
> Sincerely,
>
> Maud Powell.
>
> P. S. I have hung the moonlight scene in just the right place where the light is favorable. It is charming.

And the following letter a short time later:

June 10–18.

Dear Mr. Brewer:

The photograph, which is very good, came just after I had written, but I failed to acknowledge it as I was just off for three days at the Norfolk Festival. People seem to like the portrait immensely. Even my maid said, 'Mrs. Turner, them photographs don't make you look graceful and *a lady* like the painting does,' which if you think it over is a tribute to the artist. Please don't belittle the compliment, for the truth comes from such people—I know I value their point of view.

I am writing to Mr. Carrington today, but if you expect me to part with my copy of the picture to those people, I must have another one for myself. Did you want me to send to the 'Art News' and the 'International Studio,' or were you going to do that?

I have a lovely light on the little picture. Don't fail to invite Mr. and Mrs. Phelps over to St. Paul, if you happen to have the portrait with you.

Mr. Edmund J. Phelps,
2323 Park Ave.,
Minneapolis.

With kindest remembrances and hope to have the pleasure of meeting Mrs. Brewer, I am,

Always sincerely,

Maud Powell.

This was the last word I ever had from her, for her sudden death occurred not long afterwards and cut short in its prime the career of one of the world's greatest women musicians.

Chapter XVIII
Sketching Under Sunny Skies

Pasadena—Capistrano—Santa Barbara—Carmel by the Sea

Just California

'Twixt the seas and the deserts,
'Twixt the wastes and the waves,
Between the sands of buried lands
And ocean's coral caves,
It lies not East or West,
But like a scroll unfurled,
Where the hand of God hath hung it,
Down the middle of the world.

Sun and dews that kiss it,
Balmy winds that blow,
The stars in clustered diadems
Upon its peaks of snow;
The mighty mountains o'er it,
Below, the white seas swirled—
Just California stretching down
The middle of the world.

—McGroarty

The call of the West had been ringing in my ears for a long time. After my exhibition in Pittsburgh, I decided to visit the Land of the Setting Sun. Moreover, Mrs. Reynolds had frequently urged me to go there and paint some of her friends. On the way I scribbled down a few notes.

"And now we are rushing toward the great salt sea and the city founded by Joe Smith and Brigham Young, who wished that they might remain young and live forever with their many wives, whose beauty was so aptly described by Mark Twain in 'Roughing It.' 'I wonder if I shall get a glimpse of any of these ninety-year-old damsels.'"

"Now we are coming into a stretch of country white with alkali. The fields and hills look like snow."

"Was awakened at four o'clock. The moon is shining brightly, making visible the rugged, bad lands of Utah. The great crevices of the hills catch the moon shadows, filling them with weird mystery. The ceaseless clickity-click of the car wheels counts away the weary miles until the dawn shall break, and while I lie awake, I get to wondering what kind of spirit inspired Joe Smith and his wives to grope their way through vast and cheerless hills, arid and desolate, to establish their colony at Salt Lake. Perhaps they thought the devil would not have the courage to follow them."

"After breakfast, seated in the observation car, we study the mountains. Blink! we are in a tunnel and no lights in the car. Ah! the porter has come to our rescue and we can see again. This is a long hole in the ground. St. George's Dragon could easily crawl in and pull his long tail in behind him. At last we see the sun again and what a mountain view breaks upon our vision. Here everything is covered with pure white snow, save the solid clumps of red, orange, and gray willows along the river. Beyond rise the foothills, dotted with cedars, then the mighty crags of red stone or shale, and higher the purple peaks resting among the morning clouds. Oh! what color! If only this d—engine would break down and leave us here awhile, I might carry away a sketch, but it all changes too quickly and leaves the mind confused with a multiplicity of impressions."

"Since 9:30 a.m. we have passed through Echo Canyon, Devils Slide, and Unitah. Ogden is in the mountains.

"I shall not try to describe the beauty of Echo Canyon, or the great hills at Devils Slide. They are artist's mountains. They are paintable, they compose and come within the possibility of color. Seen in their winter dress of snow, they are entrancing—especially so, at Devils Slide. There is a hotel at Echo, a cement mill at Devils Slide, and perhaps a place one could board. I would travel a long way to find such a field for a month's landscape work.

"I cannot say that Salt Lake City is beautiful, but certainly her situation between two great ranges of mountains at the southern end of the Great Salt Sea is exceptional and interesting. On a level plain, she is fringed on three sides with mountains that rise to five thousand feet! Steep enough to puzzle the Rocky Mountain goat in their venturesome climbs."

The following night in passing through Rainbow Canyon, I was awakened by a creaking and slow jerking of the train. I raised the blind and peeked out at the moonlit mountains. I discovered the curves in the road were so abrupt that the train could only crawl along. Then, as the sun arose, we passed through the most gorgeously colored peaks, blue, pink, orange, and gray. Next we saw the great desert, with hundreds of miles of drifting sand and sagebrush. In another two hours we were following the bed of a dried stream, with only the sand drifts left by the vanished waters. As we pursued its course through occasional small pools, a little stream struggled into the ocean of sand, ever growing larger toward its source. Rivers usually grow larger toward the mouth, but this charitable one is trying to slake the thirst of the blistering, hungry sands—but in vain.

"Now we are in a rolling country, sand hills covered with dwarf pines, cactus, and yucca. Ay! there is something ahead. The white capped Sierras. There has been a snowstorm somewhere up in the heavens, touching only the highest peaks. Eventually, we shall descend to that valley way down where the alfalfa fields and blooming peach orchards look so pretty. We are a long time winding about. The great, white pyramids peek at us over the dark green foothills. It is but a shortchange from arid sands, winter snows to blooming orchards, but God does not seem to care how he juggles the seasons in painting his great pictures.

"There looms ahead a towering mountain, its base lost in the deepest purple. Leading down from the white apex, the crevices resemble forked lightning. Oh! the beauty of this valley! It looks like June on the banks of the Missouri, blooming orchards, grazing herds, alfalfa, and then on and on to the foothills.

"Aboard again after a platform promenade at San Bernardino. The city is gaily decked, flags everywhere. I asked a bystander what this all means and was told it is the National Orange Festival. 'Do they raise oranges here?' I queried. 'Do they!' he exclaimed. 'Which way are you going, stranger?' 'To Los Angeles,' I told him. 'Well, before you get there, you'll know!' and for fifty miles past Riverside, orange groves seemed endless! Millions of trees, bending down with the burden of golden fruit, mingling with the blossoms of the future crop. Seen against the white-capped mountains, they present a fascinating picture.

"A fellow has just sold me a Los Angeles newspaper, but the beauty of peach blossoms and eucalyptus will not let me read it. Nor will Old Baldy, off to the north, poking his nose up ten thousand feet. He seems three miles away, but in reality, is thirty. Now we are near Los Angeles, and Old Baldy has followed us all the way from San Bernardino."

* * *

My first night in California I spent at the Great Huntington Hotel at Pasadena—Pasadena the Lovely, which should be called Paradisa. For six weeks I painted there and occasionally made a trip to Los Angeles, where I met Jack Smith, the marine painter, and his lovely wife; also William Wendt and his wife, who, by the way, is an able sculptor. Orrin White, who was doing delightful mountain pictures, was giving an exhibition in Pasadena. I have seen few mountain painters whose work I liked quite so well. His handling of those vast subjects gleaned from the high Sierras showed skill and promise.

I met Benjamin C. Brown, the landscape painter, and we formed quite an intimate friendship. I met Edward B. Butler, the millionaire artist. Butler has a studio on the banks of the Arroyo Secco. I became acquainted with Alson Clark, who has a delightful studio near Butler's. Mr. Butler invited me to paint in his studio. It was from his window I made my *Cloud Shadows* —a picture of that wonderful range with shadows gliding up those colorful slopes.

Ben Brown, quite a remarkable character, a man who has been handicapped by ill health most of his life, was born near Little Rock, Arkansas. I had seen some of his portraits. Brown, today, would admit they were the bungled efforts of a sick man striving to make a living. But portrait painting was not his forte. He is a most prolific worker and has painted many beautiful landscapes of California scenery. Erratic, impulsive, and high tempered, he is gifted with a pronounced vein of humor, an altogether delightful fellow to know.

His studio is on North El Molino Avenue and he claims to have there a couple of thousand canvasses in all stages of work, from mere sketches to completed pictures. With gray hair, which streams down over his forehead, he presented a splendid subject for a portrait, so I prevailed upon him to sit for me for a head. It proved one of my best and most spontaneous things. He liked it; but his mother did not. She found "something radically wrong with the mouth." Of course, I was painting the picture for myself, so to myself I said, "I don't give a damn whether she likes it or not." I sent it to the Los Angeles exhibition, where it was well received and hung. It was in my studio in Chicago one summer when the place was occupied by a man as sub tenant. He had lived in California and knew Brown. The picture disappeared and I have never seen it since. I am not accusing anybody of having taken it—it might have fallen out of the window—but I regretted losing it, because I think so much of both Brown and the portrait.

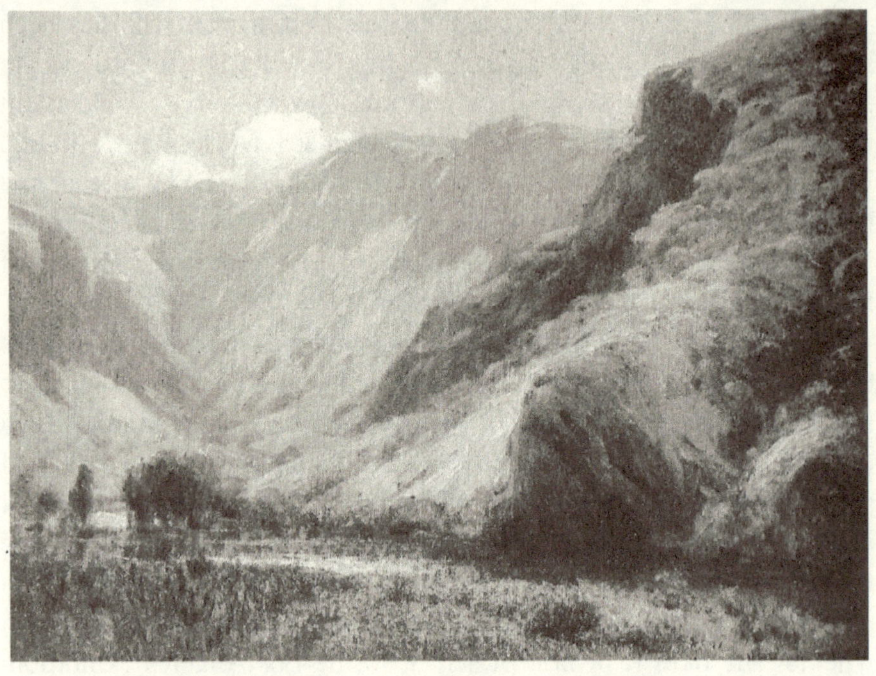

Aliso Canyon, Courtesy Decatur Art Institute

One day, after work in Butler's studio, Butler said, "Let's drop in on Ben and see what he is doing." Ben had just brought in a fresh sketch he had been making out in the valley somewhere. Butler was primed for an argument, and he said, "Ben, you've got a nice sketch there, but your sky is entirely too dark." In my judgment, many of Butler's skies were entirely too light, hence the difference between them. Ben protested that the sky was truthful. An argument ensued and feeling began to rise. Seizing the picture, Ben shouted, "All right, if you don't like the damn thing," and he brought it down over the corner of a chair, ripped it to shreds, and threw it at Butler's feet. After leaving, Butler expressed regret for having "got such a rise out of him," but he still protested that Brown's skies were too dark.

Butler was not more fond of an argument than was Brown, however, for if Brown could not stir up one, he would begin to ask, "What color is this or that patch or spot?" and if told it was blue, purple, or green, he would contradict it and start an argument to prove that he was right—that the other fellow's eyes were defective.

Jack Smith had invited me to visit them at Laguna Beach where he was painting, and when my work was done at the hotel, I found rooms with a Mrs. Curtiss, where Jack and his wife boarded, and there I painted for several weeks along the marvelous coast with its rocky cliffs.

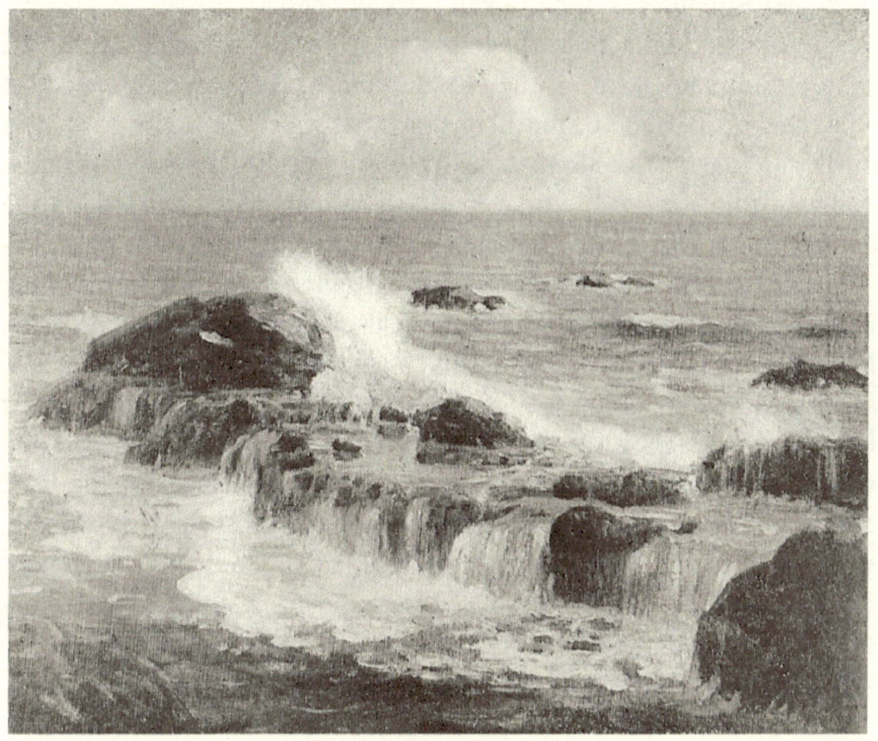

Wave-washed

From Laguna we could hear the cannonading of the battle fleet from San Diego and the roar of the guns, though the ships were far away and out of sight. The concussion was so powerful it caused the windows to rattle.

Gardner Symons had a studio nearby and so did William Wendt, Jean Mannheim, and several other well-known California painters.

Jack Smith is a vigorous painter of the sea and many of his pictures rival those of our best American marine painters. Most of his work is done in the open, and when the wind is so strong that he needs shelter, he works on the leeward side of the house or garage. In Los Angeles, however, he has a fine studio where he spends the winters.

Mannheim, likewise, paints the open sea, though he has painted many fine portraits.

Alson Clark was fond of painting the ruins of the old missions, especially San Juan Capistrano, of which he has made twenty-five or thirty large pictures, some of them prize winners.

Smith had frequently spoken to me about his friend Reverend St. John O'Sullivan, pastor of the old mission of San Juan Capistrano, of what a wonderful and beautiful character he was, how he loved art and music; and Jack assured me that if I went there, I would not only enjoy knowing this remarkable man, but I would want to paint around the ancient ruins. One day he volunteered to drive over there, from Laguna, some twelve miles, with Mrs. Smith, Mannhein, and myself. Father O'Sullivan was not at home, but the housekeeper at the mission, Mrs. McArthur, urged me to bring bag and baggage and stay there as a guest, as long as I liked, telling me that Father O'Sullivan would approve her invitation. Gathering up my things at Laguna, I did as requested and was given a room close to the administration building, facing the front corridor. The housekeeper was an intelligent woman, a semi-invalid, who had been in the employ of Marshall Field as a buyer for the house. She had contracted tuberculosis and was trying to recover in the balmy climate of California. She was handling the domestic affairs of the mission household with extraordinary skill, assisted by an Indian maid, and one or two other helpers. I think the maid's name was Marie. This girl was an educated Indian with all the traits of her people—distant, reticent, but clever.

We were standing in front of the mission when Father O'Sullivan came around the corner of the long corridor after several days' absence. He had under his arm a beautiful live peacock. The moment the Indian girl saw him, she uttered a real Indian whoop, and screamed, "Oh, there is Father!" Running to him, she threw her arms about him and patted him on the shoulder. He let her take the peacock and then came to greet us.

Mrs. McArthur explained my presence, and he hospitably invited me to be his guest, saying that he had heard of me and hoped I would find something there to paint.

O'Sullivan was born in Louisiana and graduated from the University of Notre Dame. Shortly after his ordination, he developed tuberculosis. For many years he lived at various sanitariums in the southwest, New Mexico, and elsewhere, seeking recovery. It was a long, tedious fight.

After ten years of this discouraging condition, O'Sullivan, leaving the sanitarium, went to Los Angeles to see the Bishop, who told him to go down to Capistrano and rest and see how the climate affected him. Shortly he became interested in attempts to restore or check the decay at the old ruins. He began to move about in the open. In course of time his doctor told him he thought the disease had been arrested.

At the time I visited him, however, his doctor had given him a poor report and advised him to discontinue work and to rest.

After I had been there a couple of weeks, Mrs. McArthur told me that as a surprise for Father O'Sullivan, she wanted to have a dinner and invite a number of artists—Gardner Symons, William Wendt, Jack Smith, Mannheim, and two or three others from Laguna, also Alson Clark from Pasadena, and many others. There in the room where the padres had partaken of their frugal fare, on the same old tile floor and the same old furniture, we were seated at a tempting dinner, and His Reverence at the head of the table was acquainted with the surprise. That evening, ladies and gentlemen of thc village came in, who added to the merriment of a most delightful time.

Old Capistrano is known far and wide for its historic, as well as artistic interest. Many a picture has been painted of it and several motion pictures have used its crumbling arches as location. After the Mexican political vandals had seized and secularized the twenty great missions of California, Capistrano, with all its lands and buildings and its wealth of tile, was sold to a relative of the governor for the miserable price of seven hundred dollars. It was then used as a roadhouse or ranch and its magnificent corridors stabled horses. Where once the padres and their neophytes knelt in prayer, wanton revelry reigned.

The spacious patio surrounded by buildings, where over fifty useful branches of study and craftsmanship were taught the Indians, is now but a square of broken arches. Under the magic influence of Father O'Sullivan's direction, the mission presents a different aspect from that of fifty years ago. Flowering vines climb the great arches, and order and beauty are everywhere. While there I made sketches and painted my picture, *Shadows of Capistrano*, also the long corridor, which I named *The Cloister*.

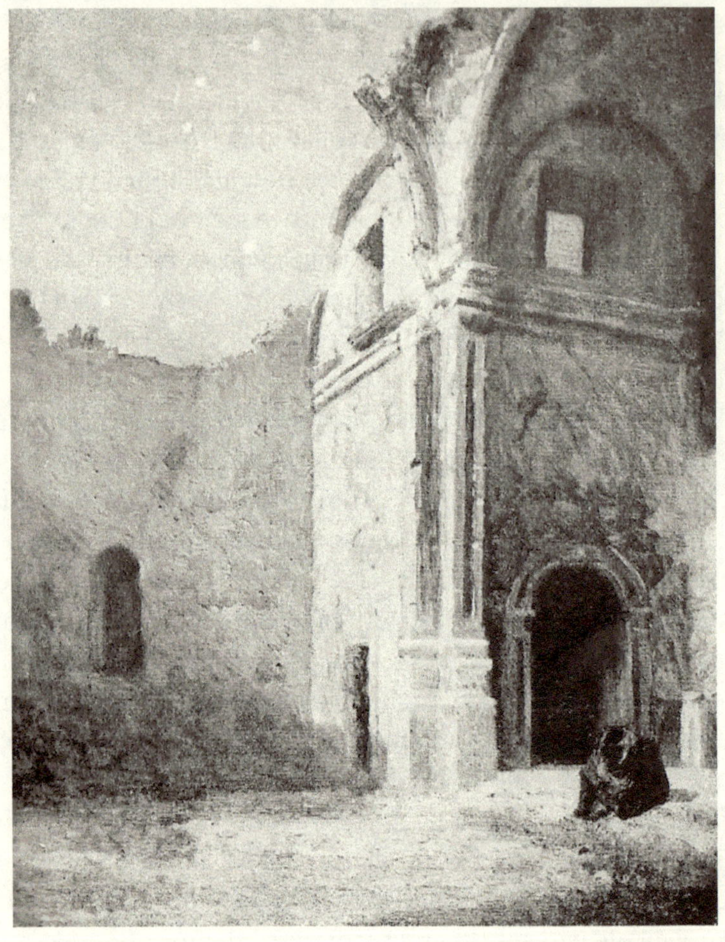

Shadows of Capistrano

The original floor tiles made by the Indians about 1772 are still in use. In one of the tiles there is a fresh footprint of a little child; in another, that of a dog.

I remarked to O'Sullivan about the similarity between the chancel of the fine new Church of St. Mark erected in St. Paul, and the ruined sanctuary of Capistrano. I mentioned the name of the architect—John T. Comes. "Why, he spent three weeks here a few years ago," O'Sullivan said. Evidently, Capistrano was responsible for the architect's inspiration.

One day O'Sullivan returned from Los Angeles and stated that his doctor had given him a very discouraging report, and he might have to go away and rest. I suggested our taking a pleasure trip in his car, that I would sketch and paint, and he might idle away his time in the sun, eating oranges. After some thought, he concluded it might be an advisable and enjoyable thing to do, so we started on a nomadic tour that lasted for more than four months, wandering hither and there, San Diego to Riverside, back to Los Angeles and up the coast to San Francisco, down the Joaquin Valley to Merced and the Yosemite.

At San Diego we spent some time with lovely friends of his. I made several studies in the neighborhood—one of the old missions of San Diego, which was built in 1769 by Father Junipero Serra, the first of all the missions of California. Little is left of the ruins of this old mission. From it I painted the canvas I called *Night*. It represents the ruin against a blue, starlit sky. A faint light gleams from one of the windows, signifying the occupancy of a keeper. The picture has been in several important exhibitions. A writer in the Washington Evening Post, in a review of the Art Club's exhibit, made the brief remark: "*Night*, painted in oils by Nicholas R. Brewer, a work in which the artist conveys surprisingly well the sense of the nocturnal."

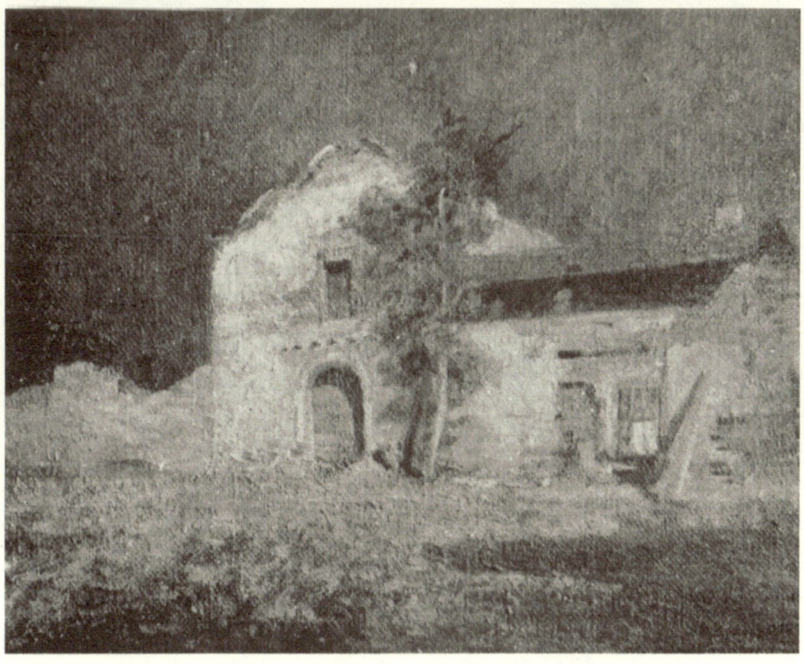

Night, first mission built in California, San Diego, 1769.

The first night after leaving San Diego, we stayed at Elsinore, a beautiful little town in the mountains near a placid lake, as pretty in its setting as is the name "Elsinore." Next morning, we got an early start and passed through the hills in the direction of Perris. Looking back from the lofty slope, the Santa Anna mountain range stood out in the charming blue, and on the hillside were some beautiful eucalyptus trees. We halted to make a sketch. Climbing the steep hill to get a better view of the trees and the mountains, I spent an hour or two with my pastels, while O'Sullivan, who was a camera enthusiast, spooked about and made several close ups of the eucalypti. He prided himself on reproducing the bark and twist of the trunks. From the pastel study, I afterwards painted my *San Gabriel Range*, now owned by the Progress Club at South Bend, Indiana.

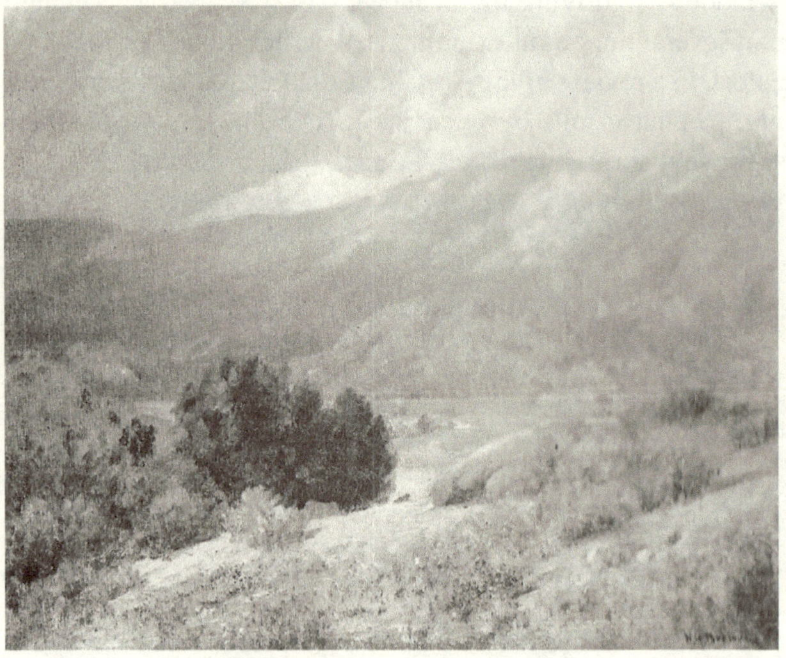

San Gabriel Range, Courtesy Progress Club, South Bend, Indiana.

We arrived late that day at Riverside and went to the Mission Inn. Father O'Sullivan was well-known there, being an intimate friend of Frank A. Miller, Master of the Inn, one of the outstanding characters of California. As we entered the grounds, Mr. Miller was seen standing some distance away, with a huge green parrot resting on his shoulder, and surrounded by a group of ladies. As he saw us enter, recognizing O'Sullivan, he immediately left the group and came to where we stood, heartily greeting us. Presently, he led us to the office and said to the clerk, "Give these two gentlemen the best there is in the house, for as long as they wish to stay."

A more fascinating personality than Mr. Miller's is hard to find—a man of great wealth, of varied travels, a collector of art, who had built this remarkable hostelry, which he named "The Mission Inn."

It was designed to resemble, in its architecture, a medieval monastery. Everywhere in its vast corridors and galleries and chapel are objects of a religious character—antique furniture, rare tapestries, and rugs. Miller is a great lover of the missions of California, a broad-gauged liberal Congregationalist in religion, who is yet a great admirer of the Catholic history of California and has done much to promote and perpetuate those remaining tokens of that wonderful crusade by the Sons of St. Francis, in the cause of the evangelization of the Indian.

On one occasion he told us of the beautiful Congregational Church in the next block, toward the erection of which he had contributed no small share. When it was finished, he said he told the committee there was but one more thing to be added and that was a large painting of the Virgin, to be placed high over the pulpit. They objected strenuously, accusing him of being altogether too much of a Papist. He said, "Gentlemen, that makes no difference; the picture has got to go up there," and it did.

One day while going through the cloisters, enjoying the beautiful specimens of art, I came across a very large photographic reproduction of my picture *The Worship of the Magi*, which I once did for one of the churches in New York. O'Sullivan was with me and I called his attention to it. Later he mentioned to Mr. Miller the fact that he had in his possession a reproduction of one of my paintings. Miller rushed down to the room and, seeing the reproduction, exclaimed, "Did you paint the original of that, Mr. Brewer?" "There is the name on it," I replied. "Well, I am delighted to know the artist," he said, and grabbed my hand. "I bought that picture because I liked it and thought it a remarkable presentation of the subject."

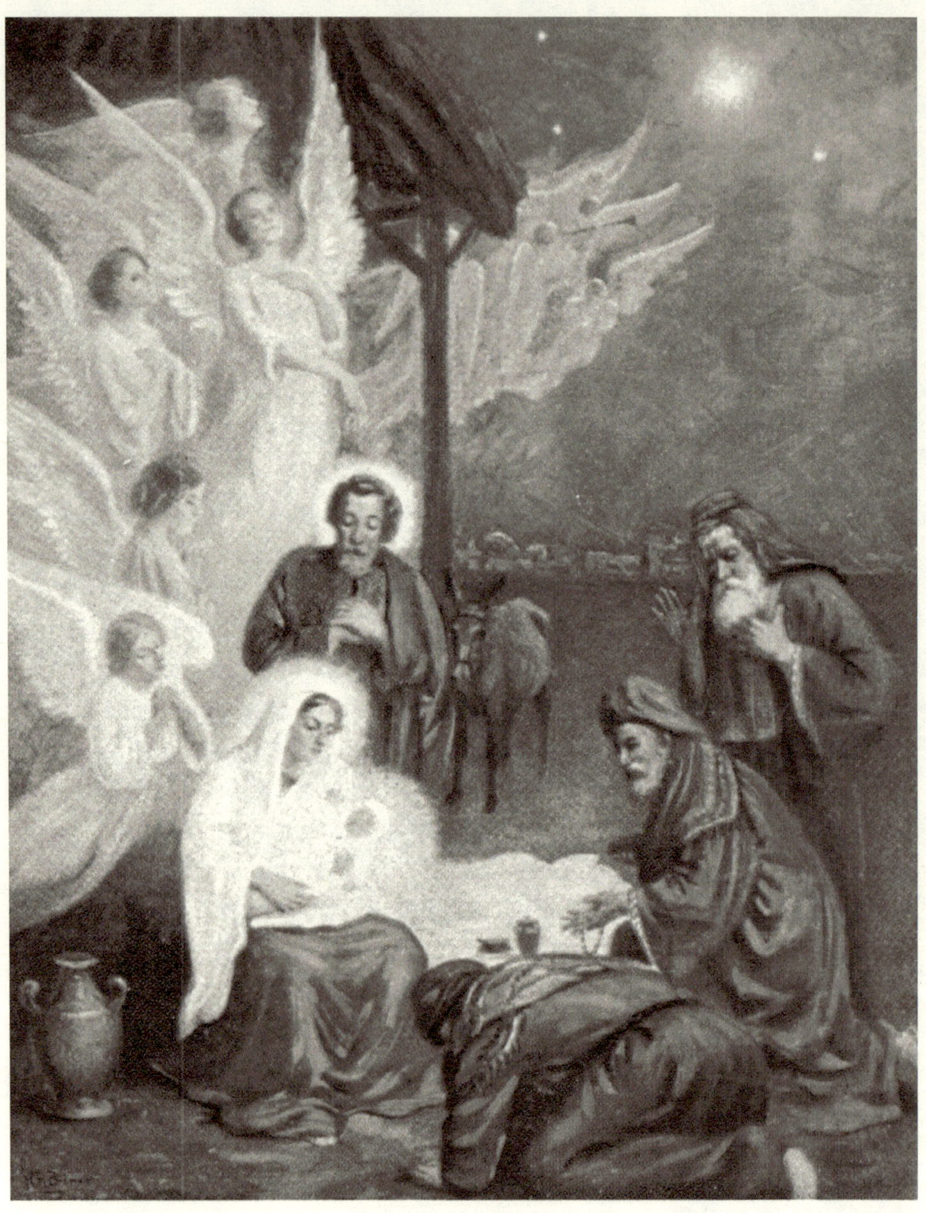

Worship of the Magi

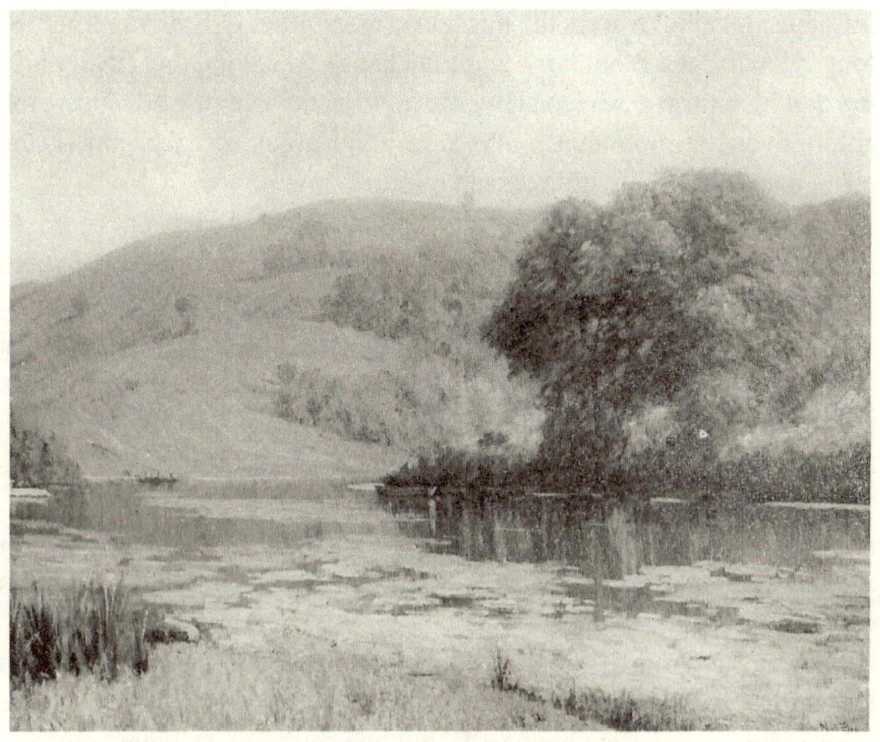

Waters of the Cheyenne

The first evening that we were there, O'Sullivan came and said to me, "I have something to show you; we will go and take the car." After a few blocks out of the suburbs, we began to climb Mount Rubidoux. I knew not where we were going, nor would he tell me, but as we spun around the mountain that rises like a pyramid to a height of some fifteen hundred feet, in the Santa Anna Valley, we got a view in all directions, with the glistening stream far below and beyond the San Gabriel Range. Mount San Antonio, commonly called "Old Baldy," white capped and gray, was in the distance. Its summit was surrounded with light fleecy clouds that seemed to cling only near the sparkling snow. We finally arrived at the top, where the good people of Riverside, and from all over Southern California, meet at dawn to worship on Easter morn. Here, tens of thousands bow their heads in prayer, as the first days of light creep over the mountains and flood the valleys with misty shadows upon the annual feast of the Resurrection. Here, President Taft unveiled that beautiful tablet in honor of Junipero Serra, founder of the missions. Over all towers the mission cross. Father O'Sullivan lingered long, viewing the mountains and the change in colors, and finally told me that his purpose was to show me how, as the evening advances, the colors over the mountains vary from vivid green to deep purple, the change taking place within fifteen minutes time.

After a visit to San Bernardino and the Sunset Drive, our return to Los Angeles and Pasadena was by way of the foothill road. We spent the entire delightful day loafing along the short seventy-five-mile drive, and I made two important sketches. One was the sketch I afterward sold to Mrs. Walker in Macon, Georgia, and the other large picture purchased by the South Shore Country Club of Chicago. To me, it was a wonderful day, balmy, clear sky. Mountain and foothill rose in a marvelous purple to the azure above.

We stayed two or three weeks in Los Angeles, where I met John McGroarty, author of the Mission Play, and one of the editorial writers on the *Los Angeles Times*.

John McGroarty—the smiling, genial Irishman!—No artist could know this man intimately without wishing to paint him, for his is not only an interesting type pictorially, but he is an artist by nature and one who can fully appreciate art in every form. On our first meeting, Father O'Sullivan suggested that he sit to me for his portrait, which he readily consented to do. He proposed that I do the work in the studio of a friend of his near the Playhouse, where he had his office.

McGroarty suggested my painting the Indian Chief Lux Oshy, who takes the part of Capitajeno, chieftain of the Indians of Carmelo and Monterey, in the Mission Play. Lux Oshy is a full blooded, educated Chicasha chieftain and a typical Indian, in spite of his perfect English and citizen's dress. Never for a moment does the dignity or immobility of the Indian chief depart from him; it emanates from him like an atmosphere. His stage attire is a full feathered bonnet and wolf skin robe, with a bow and quiver of arrows strapped to his back. During the second act of this wonderful drama, he stands at one side of the stage, arms folded, gazing into the future, with an occasional disdainful glance at the white man's revelry. It was this phase of his acting that gave me my motive for the picture I have called *Fading Glories*. Painting from sketches made on Mount Rubidoux, I arranged a background befitting the theme. The hour is twilight; on the mountain side he gazes over the hazy valley with an expression of sad contemplation, for he not only views the fading glory of the day, but the fading glory of his bygone race.

Indian Summer

Over the hills and the valleys
Hangs a veil of mystic blue.
'Tis a haze called Indian Summer
That comes each Autumn anew.
A bit of the smoke from the camp-fires
Of Indian tribes long gone,
But it lingers on until evening
Like the echo of a song—
The song of a race fast fading
Like the sun sinking low in the west
For the soul of the Indian warrior
Will never, never know rest.
So his spirit returns each Autumn
As the year fades to its close
In a haze called Indian Summer—
Whence it vanishes no man knows.

—Ethel M. Franklin

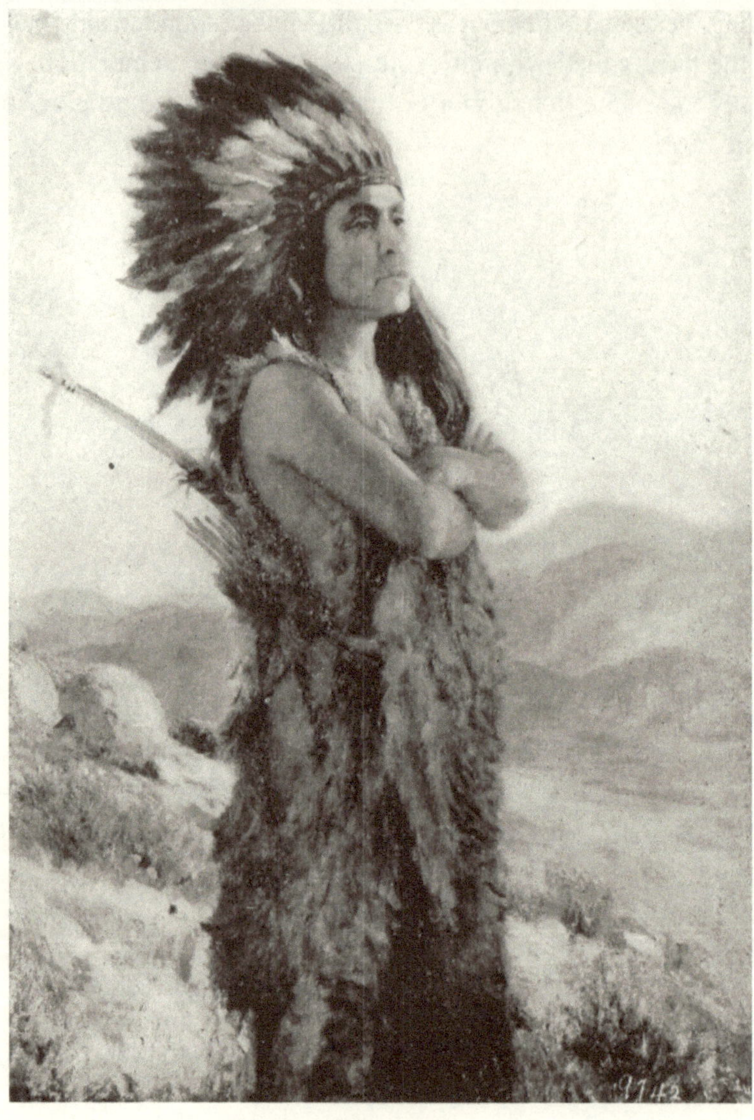

Fading Glories

McGroarty has a beautiful home in the Verdugo mountains and insisted upon our visiting him there, where we met his charming wife and several guests, most delightful people. The McGroartys took me up some distance on the mountain side to his private sanctum, where he did his writing. It was a steep climb, indeed, but from the lofty site, the lofty Verdugo valley and the distant mountains were truly a delight to see. Here, this genial man of letters, gave me a most urgent invitation to come and spend the summer. “You may take possession of this den of mine,” he said, “we will give you all you want to eat, and you can paint to your heart’s content.”

It was my regret that I had to return to the East and could not avail myself of this most cordial and hearty invitation of the McGroarty’s, and it is yet my hope to be able to return to that land of poesy and romance and to the company of these interesting characters, whom it was my pleasure to meet there.

Restive to continue our journey, O’Sullivan and I again took the road to the North. At Ventura, we spent the night before a trip through the Ojai Valley. The little town of Ojai is unique, in that all of the buildings, practically, are of the Spanish mission style. The shops open in front onto a corridor like the missions, where their wares are displayed.

We made a circle of the valley, some twenty miles, and returned to make Santa Barbara that night. There we stayed for a time, and I painted a portrait of Friar Zephyrin Engelhardt, the historian. The aged Franciscan had been a prolific writer and his histories of California are today regarded as the most authentic and complete in existence. He had traveled throughout the state, visiting the old missions and the few remaining descendants of the Indian tribes, many of whom had cherished historic relics and documents of the times when the missions flourished. He had collected many volumes and manuscripts of the padres.

In his brown robe of the Franciscan Order, his flowing beard, prominent brow, and skull cap, he presented a picturesque figure. Seating him as I first saw him, on a bench far more ancient than himself, in the rear cloister of the mission, I painted him against a background of broken plaster and adobe brick, stained by time. Beside him is a pile of musty old books, one of which he is perusing with deep interest. When the picture was dry, I rolled it and brought it with me in my trunk. When Paderewski saw it, after looking at it thoughtfully, he exclaimed, “It has the atmosphere of history, it is beautiful.” I called the picture *Records of the Past*.

Showing me through the vast library, the Friar pulled out a musty old book. It was the record book of San Juan Capistrano by Junipero Serra, founder of the missions of California. There was the veritable handwriting of this wonderful man whom all California, regardless of religious creeds, venerates today. His monument may be found in every park of the important cities. Most of the book was written in Latin, the rest in Spanish. Father Engelhardt translated several passages for me. One was the story of an accident the venerable missionary had with a mule when his leg was badly injured. He called the hostler and asked him what he did with similar injuries to the mules. The man said, "I have a liniment which I use." "Well, bring it to me; I must have you put it on my leg." "Padre," he protested, "that liniment is only for mules." "Well," said the padre, "that is just the reason why you should bring it to me."

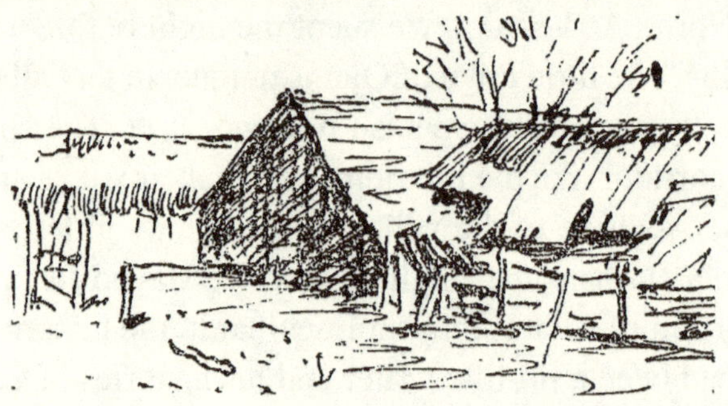

I made a number of sketches in the mission garden and in the mountains, some of which I have since used in my exhibitions. After our departure from Santa Barbara, we stopped at Pasa Robles where I painted Paderewski.

Leaving Monterey, we went to Carmel-by-the-sea. Carmel is one of the most important of the several artists' colonies of the Pacific Coast. Near by the quaint village is the old mission of San Carlos de Carmel. It was Junipero Serra's headquarters and it is there, within the walls of the old church, that his honored dust is laid. Catholic pilgrims, kneeling at the communion rail, look down on the marble slab that marks his resting place.

This is one of the most artistic of the many missions and has been sketched and painted by hundreds of artists. The arch that leads from the main church into the baptistry, which is now a museum, is one of the architectural wonders of the Pacific Coast and has been studied by many architects. One of the interesting things displayed there is the cot on which Serra slept. It consists of a stretcher with four posts, over which is tacked stoutly a raw cowhide, tight as a drum. It was as hard as the earth.

On the grounds close by are some remaining adobe walls, showing the rooms once occupied by the padres and teachers and in one stands a cross marking the spot where Junipero Serra died.

A local pastor, who had been collaborating with O'Sullivan in the art of restoring the missions, had undertaken to restore Carmel. They were baking adobe bricks and tile in the sun and laying plans for the restoration of the mission to its original state.

Here I made the acquaintance of Mr. Joseph Mora, the sculptor, brother of Luis Mora, who was designing a sarcophagus to be made in bronze and placed over the tomb.

We decided to rest in Carmel for some time and cast about for a studio. Mrs. Laura Maxwell, the artist, owner of a cottage and studio all equipped for housekeeping, was glad to let us occupy it during our stay. There was much sketching in view and I soon became engrossed in work.

We intended to remain there a few weeks even though we could not find a cook or housekeeper. Under the protests of O'Sullivan, I volunteered to perform the duty of cook and pot washer, if he would be the errand boy. So, we went to Monterey for a load of provisions. O'Sullivan had a way of dumping everything helter-skelter into the tonneau of the car. After securing our load, I stepped aboard, when my errand boy handed me a paper bag saying, "I think you had better carry these eggs to prevent their breaking." I carefully carried the supposed eggs, but on leaving the car I discovered they were lemons instead. O'Sullivan had dumped the eggs in behind and thrown parcels on top of them. A slippery floor of the car was the result.

Mrs. Maxwell, a most pleasing and cultured woman, one day offered to show us the way to Point Lobas, the only place in the country where the cedars of Lebanon grow. It is privately owned property and we had to pay a toll to go through the gates, but the day was well spent. There I made two sketches from which I painted my picture called *A California Marine.*

At the Highlands, a few miles farther to the south, we called on William Ritschel at his fine studio on the cliffs. He came over occasionally where I was working. Ritschel is one of our ablest marine painters.

We spent several days in San Francisco. The impression one gets there is that it was a misfortune to have stopped the great earthquake conflagration at Van Ness Avenue. A vast portion of the city still remains an ugly reminder of that period of decadence in American architecture following the Civil War, when all semblance of real art in domestic construction was submerged in an overelaborate gingerbread display of cheap woodwork. What a blessing, from an aesthetic point of view, it would have been had the flames swept on from Van Ness Avenue to the Golden Gate! After all, in time, when these ugly buildings shall have disappeared, San Francisco will be one of the most beautiful cities on the coast.

One morning we ferried across to Oakland and took the highway south through the Joaquin Valley to Merced, and the next day climbed the foothills to the Yosemite National Park.

It is difficult to describe one's impression on entering the great Sequoia forest of redwoods and sugar pine. As we drove down a little decline to a stream we had to ford, we had our first view of the oldest living things in the world. There, on a mound some twenty feet above, stood a tree, a mighty giant! A grizzled Patriarch three thousand years old before the pyramids of Egypt were built or before Moses received the Tablets of Stone. To one side, in a hollow or declivity, stood another, measuring twenty-eight or thirty feet in diameter, twelve or fifteen feet above the ground, and towering three hundred or more feet toward the clouds. Their hoary bark and outstretched arms seemed to call out to the ages, for the span of the longest human life is but a small fraction of that interval of existence dating back even before the dawn of human history. Think of it, one of these mighty trees stands on a mound some twenty feet higher than the other, which shows conclusively that the surface of the earth there has not changed, nor has the bed of that little stream dried while their gnarled limbs were reaching out as if to stay the storms of the high Sierras.

We halted and sat in wonderment, for nowhere else in the world can such a phenomenon of nature be found. Driving deeper into the forest, we found the redwoods more numerous, as were the sugar pine. These latter are also giants, often taller than the redwoods, but more slender in girth. Some of them measure fourteen to fifteen feet in diameter, with a beautiful bark that resembles the pattern of the alligator skin.

A little way farther on we passed another, a giant among giants, majestic in its mien—the "General Sherman Tree." It is estimated that this tree was 3,000 years old when Christ was born. At the time of the Trojan Wars and the Exodus of the Hebrews from Egypt, this great Sequoia was a flourishing sapling. It towers 279.9 feet into the sky; its base circumference is 102.8; its greatest diameter 36.5, and it has developed a diameter of 17.7 feet at a point 100 feet above the ground. It was named in honor of General William T. Sherman.

Driving to the Government camp, the home of the mounted police, who patrol this most wonderful of all Uncle Sam's National Parks, we passed "the fallen giant." How long he has lain there, no one knows, but on his bark fifteen feet above the ground, twenty-six horsemen have posed on their mounts, for a photograph. Farther along, we have "the telescope," a tree whose heart has been burned out and only the bark, or that containing the sap remains. One hundred eighty feet above the ground the top was broken off. We walked into the aperture and looked through the largest telescope in the world to the blue vault above. All that is left of the tree alive is the sap flowing bark with spreading green branches and limbs. In another place, the road passes through the heart of a tree.

I think that I shall never see
A poem lovely as a tree
A tree whose hungry mouth is pressed
Against the earth's sweet flowing breast;
A tree that looks at God all day,
And lifts her leafy arms to pray;
A tree who may in summer wear
A nest of robins in her hair,
Upon whose bosom snow has lain;
Who intimately lives with rain.
Poems are made by fools like me,
but only God can make a tree.

—Joyce Kilmer

A little sign by the roadside read, "Do not fail to see Wawona Point." We climbed higher along the hillsides and when we could go no farther with our car walked up the promontory. Suddenly an entrancing view burst upon us. A thousand feet below was Wawona Valley across which the mountain rose in the direction of the Yosemite. I painted Wawona Valley from this point.

Chapter XIX
From El Portel to Miami

Mount Shasta—The Canadian Rockies—The Granary of the World—The Bryan Family

In the blue haze, miles away, a phantom-like stream of silvery mist revealed Wawona Falls, adding solemnity to the solitude of that wondrous valley. Dusk had begun to fall so we turned about. In front of us rose the gilded summits of the Sierras with glowing snow and purple shadows in the last rays of the dying sun. The ground in places was covered with snowdrifts and up through the mantle peeped beautiful crimson blossoms.

We drove back through the forest and lodged at Wawona Inn. The chill of the altitude, though already June, made us shiver under our topcoats. The next morning, the sun warmed the atmosphere as we started on our thirty-mile journey over almost impassable mountain roads, so narrow that only at places could two cars pass. Here, at times, we could look below us a thousand feet and a little further on a thousand feet above. It required nerve and skill to drive the Buick on this trip, but good Father O'Sullivan had both.

After passing Chink O Pin we arrived at the checking-in station, where the agents start the stream of tourist cars down the incline past Artist Point and Inspiration Point, leading to the Yosemite Valley, several thousand feet below. It was at Artist Point that Albert Bierstadt made sketches for his famous Yosemite Valley painting, spoken of in previous pages, with El Capitan in the middle distance. At the checking-out station below, an awaiting train of ascending cars was held until our group was released. Nearby were the Bridal Veil Falls, which scatters spray nearly eleven hundred feet in one glorious leap.

The Yosemite Gorge has an apparently level floor-bed, with beautiful drives and bridges crossing and re-crossing the Merced River for a distance of nearly six miles. This river was formed by the numerous wonderful waterfalls that spill over the cliffs—some of them two thousand feet or more. June is the time when the falls are most beautiful and the one called "Widows' Tears" is said to be the highest single leap in the world. After the snows have melted the stream dries up. Words fail to describe the beauty of this marvelous valley, fringed by rocky cliffs and peaks almost perpendicular, rising to a mile in height. El Capitan, which has so often been painted, is a sheer ledge thirty-six hundred feet high.

Several hotels offer accommodations to thousands of tourists. Campers' tents are used by many travelers. We had a tent and spent many days in sketching and driving. We balked at mountain climbing, though we were somewhat tempted to take a muleback ride, fourteen miles up the mountain to Glacier Point, where guests at the Glacier Point Hotel have the advantage of the grandest scenery of the whole Valley.

My affairs in the East were pressing and I felt that I must conclude the most delightful vacation I had ever had. I call it a vacation because for months I had flitted about in a comfortable motor car, basking in the sun and sketching hither and there, but as my portfolio of sketches numbered fifty-four serious works, it proved that I had used my time in more than idle pleasure. I decided regretfully to part with my traveling companion, whom I had learned to love dearly. Father O'Sullivan said that he would get some books and while away more time before returning to Capistrano. He afterward wrote me that on the day after our separation he met an old classmate whom he had not seen for twenty years, the pastor of an Eastern church. Together they continued for another month the wanderings O'Sullivan and I so happily began four months previously.

I boarded the bus, which travels the road that descends through the narrow course of the gorge close to the roaring cataracts of the Merced, as they plunge over the rocks that have tumbled down in times past from the cliffs above, to El Portel, the highest point reached by the railway. There I bought a ticket for San Francisco. The line from this point courses the mountain sides once scaled by the gold seekers in the days of '49. Everywhere you see the remains of the hydraulic pressure used to wash the sides of the hills or to gather the gold dust or nuggets. At San Francisco that night I stepped aboard the Pullman for Portland, Seattle, Vancouver, and through the Canadian Rockies to Chicago and the East.

Next morning through the dining car window we saw, far in the distance, the glistening white cap of Mount Shasta. She seemed to be playing hide-and-seek with us; first appearing to the right of the train and then to the left—and so we continued until noon time, when we were opposite her ten miles away. All the afternoon she accompanied us. At 5:39 we entered a tunnel and said, "Good night, Shasta." We were still in the State of California, after a twenty-four hours ride from San Francisco, which is over seven hundred miles from the southern border of California. Another night's ride and we arrived in Portland, where the famous rose show was being given; but the roses of Southern California pleased me more, for there I had seen a vine covering a bungalow, with over seven thousand blossoms big as one's two fists. On to Seattle, then aboard the ship to Vancouver. At that time (1921) Vancouver impressed me as the most desolate city I have ever visited. After the World War the city seemed too near dead to revive. Next I enjoyed two days ride from Vancouver to the town of Field, The Great Divide, Lake Louise, Banff and through the Canadian Rockies, which gave use some of the most glorious mountain scenery in the world.

No words can describe the grandeur of this rugged country. We rode for a day in an open flat car, through the valley of the ten peaks, that we might see without hindrance that glorious range. Toward evening, illumined by the golden sun, the glistening glaciers green in the lights, purple in the shadows, presented pictures no brush can paint, and when seen reflected in the placid surface of Lake Louise, one realizes the inadequacy of words to describe them.

I saw the mountains stand
Silent, wonderful and grand,

Looking out across the land
When the golden light was falling
On distant dome and spire;
And I heard a low voice calling,
'Come up higher, come up higher,
From the lowland and the mire
From the mist of earth desire,
From the vain pursuit of pelf,
From the attitude of self;
Come up higher, come up higher'

—James G. Clarke

Leaving Banff at night, we awakened at the west border of that flat, level plain, which we traversed two days and nights. Through the most wonderful wheat fields in the world we traveled down through Saskatchewan, North Dakota, Minnesota, with her ten thousand lakes and cultivated fields—Iowa, Illinois, Indiana, Ohio, to the smoky hills of the Alleghenies. This vast fertile region is called the granary of the world. For thousands of miles it is but a sun-kissed ocean of waving grain. Millions of heads of cattle, swine, and sheep dot the fertile pastures.

A few months later several artists of Chicago, led by the ambitions of a visionary woman who thought to establish an art colony on the Gulf of Mexico near Pensacola, Florida, organized a party to make the trip to investigate the locality and asked me to join them. They were going to hold an exhibition in Pensacola and were going to buy a large tract of land and do a great many other ambitious things. The day was set for our departure and pictures were sent ahead for the exhibition. We had a jolly good trip, despite my convalescent condition after an illness, but when we landed at Pensacola and started to explore the territory, the whole scheme fell flat. In disgust everyone returned to Chicago except myself.

The principal of a high school asked me to talk before the class one day, after which, I casually remarked that they had a bright looking crowd of pupils. "Yes, indeed," said the principal, "every one of 'em is a hundred percent American—not a fo'ehneh among 'em." I asked, "Where do the foreigners go to school?" "We don't have 'em down heah."

I wanted to get a certain book from the public library and started out to locate the institution. I made several inquiries before I found that the public library was in a certain business block. When I asked the elevator girl if that were the case, she did not know, so I had to inquire of one of the offices and was told on which floor the library was located. When I got off the elevator it was with difficulty that I could find anything that looked like a library. In an office room about 14 by 20 a pile of books was stored along the floor, without shelves, and a sleepy looking woman sat at a desk. I asked where I might find the public library. "This is the public library," she said emphatically. And the book I sought was not there.

I continued my journey to Jacksonville, Palm Beach, and Miami. In the latter place, the Woman's Club wished to sponsor an exhibition of my pictures and a show was put on, which resulted in my painting several portraits, one of which was of the Hon. Ruth Bryan Owen, then president of the club, whom I found a most delightful subject.

The first time I met her father, the late William Jennings Bryan, was at his residence in Coconut Grove. As I entered the grounds with his distinguished daughter, he was standing talking to a gentleman some distance toward the seashore. Upon observing us he immediately came to us. Mr. Bryan impressed me as being a man with a forceful personality, his handclasp demonstrating great cordiality and physical vigor. After the usual formalities he took me into the house to show me a picture of himself by Irving R. Wiles, which hung in his library. It was certainly a very creditable picture, distinctly characteristic of Wiles' excellent style. We had a long, pleasant conversation. Later I painted the portrait of Mrs. Owen. The sittings were made at the place where I was staying. Clad in a plain white Canton crepe shawl against a dark colorful background, one hand resting on a chair, she made an effective picture.

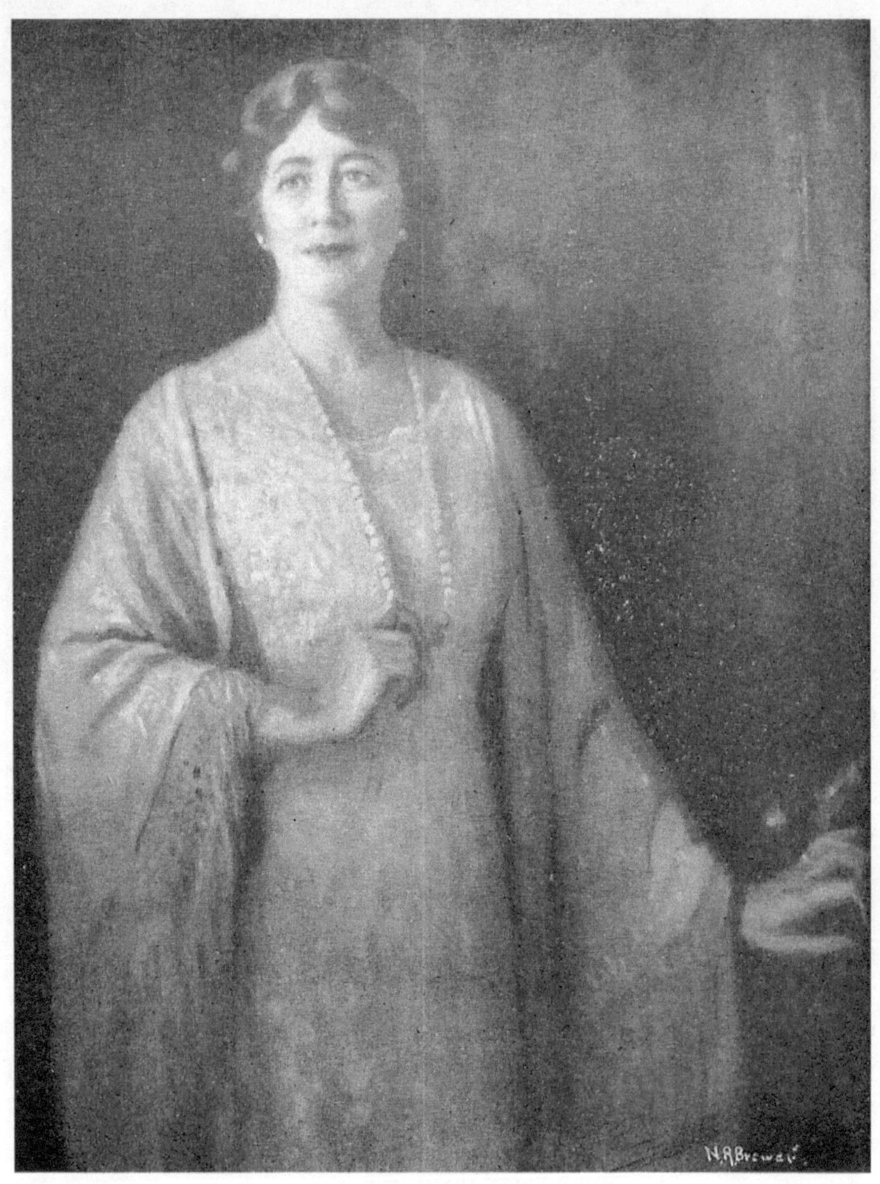

Hon. Ruth Bryan Owen

One day on the street I saw a man with a bundle of loose canvasses under his arm, entering a certain building. I took him to be an artist and immediately spoke to him. He was a Boston painter who proved to be too versatile for his own good. A wood carver, collector, illustrator, portrait painter, landscape painter, writer, and student, who associated intimately with Sargent, having made many of Sargent's frames. With it all he had a sort of Simple Simon manner, was a clumsy, untactful, gawky type of person. When he learned I was painting Mrs. Owen's portrait, he was very anxious to see the picture. Scrutinizing it very critically, he stepped close to the picture and stood for some time without speaking. Finally, he stammered, "Well, they say Sargent is the greatest painter of today—but I think some other people can paint, too." Another pause, as he smelled the canvas. Then he wheeled about and frankly asked me, "Don't you think that is as good as a Sargent?" "Yes," I said, chuckling, "and a damn sight better." And he took me seriously.

Major Owen, a typical Englishman, was a most reticent and unassuming gentleman. His charming wife seemed to take the initiative in the Owen family. Of their several children, the oldest daughter was the most beautiful girl, I think, I have ever seen.

The Owens entertained me at their lovely home in Coconut Grove. The war was still on between England and Ireland. At the table one day, I sought to draw out an expression on the subject from my conservative English host. Every reference to the subject failed to elicit more than a quizzical look or a Biblical "Yes" or "No"—never a smile. A remark from the lady gave me a chance to tell an applicable story.

Two Irishmen, Mike and Pat by name, were returning home after dark one night and passing through the woods, they heard a disturbance in a tree overhead, which proved to be the movements of a large wild cat. Not knowing the nature of the animal Mike said, "Pat, you climb up and push him down and I'll catch him and we'll take 'im home." The higher Pat climbed the higher went the cat. Presently, Pat began to yell, "Help! Help!" "Do you need help to catch him?" called Mike. "No," shouted Pat, "I want help to let him go."

I followed up by saying it reminded me of England's predicament in determining how to let go of Ireland. The burden of war with Ireland was poking John Bull in the ribs, and Lloyd George was scratching his wits to find a way to get rid of Ireland; but the snarls and growls of Ulster at such an attempt at relief placed England between the Devil and the deep sea, as it were, and the Prime Minister's cries were heard afar.

In spite of my simile, the Major seemed to slump into a reflective mood of indifference, and to this day, I am guessing his attitude on the burning question of Ireland's liberation.

Shortly after I completed the Ruth Bryan Owen portrait, I was taken severely ill and called in Dr. Jones. After his diagnosis he said "You are a very sick man. You must remain quietly in bed and have a nurse. I will send one." After several days, in a letter to my nephew Bill Fritz, I innocently described my ailment and said the Doctor had put me to bed with a nurse. Bill has a great sense of humor and consequently advertised my scandalous conduct among his friends. In fact, he will not allow them to forget it.

Chapter XX
Self-Examination

Patronage of the Arts Growing Less in the Church—Art's Judges—The Cottonwood Seed

My exhibitions and experiences have called for a good deal of public discussion. At first, I considered my talks tremendous failures and felt so ashamed of them that I lay awake nights thinking what a fool I had made of myself. I then started to write out what I wanted to say and memorized it, but invariably when I got up to speak, I would forget everything I had written and my talk would be entirely different from what I had originally intended. When I considered that the people really wanted to hear something about art, I began to be natural and spoke more fluently about the subject that dominated my life.

Once I was asked to respond to a toast at a banquet of the Cretin Alumni of St. Paul. The subject was to be "Art and Religion." I had no idea of the importance of the occasion or the distinguished men who would be there, but I wrote out something I thought would answer the purpose and intended to memorize it but could not get to it before the time. When I arrived at the banquet room at the Windsor Hotel, I found a gathering of educated men: Archbishop John Ireland, three or four other prominent clergymen, a host of noted attorneys and businessmen, with Judge T. D. O'Brien as toastmaster. I was sure that I was going to make a fool of myself again.

A friend, who had brought the request from the Alumni for me to speak, sat at the table next to mine. Realizing my predicament, I whispered to him that I had not had time to memorize my notes and had forgotten to bring them with me. He said he would go and get them and would prompt me, but I knew that would confuse me all the more. As the time for my speech drew near, I felt like a criminal about to be led to the gallows.

This was a temperance crowd and the smell of liquor on a fellow's breath would be considered nothing short of a sacrilege; but I remembered the delightful "I-don't-give-a-damn" feeling I had once after drinking a glass of grog, so to "steady my nerves" as Pat said, I stepped into the bar of the hotel, got two good swigs of Bourbon, and went back to the table before the speaking began. The tonic had the desired effect. When it came my turn to respond to the toast, all that I had written came back to me, word for word.

In the course of my remarks I said, "It is not my wish to arraign the Church, but it is evident that in these days she no longer is entitled to be called 'the Mother of the Arts.' In the ages of faith when those imperishable monuments of art the great cathedrals of the old world came into being, when such masters as Michelangelo, Leonardo, Titian, Murillo, and hosts of others flourished, their fame was due to the patronage of the Church and the religious fervor enkindled by her fostering care. Today art must seek its livelihood at the hands of multimillionaires, railway magnates, and princes of finance, in consequence of which it has taken on an entirely secular, materialistic character. Art has come down from the pedestal of exalted idealism to cater to the mundane tastes of crass social adornment or commercial utility."

I must have covered my subject with credit, for after the festivities were over, His Grace came over to me and, grasping my hand, said, "Mr. Brewer, I want to compliment you on what you said. It is all right to say those things about the Church, but you know the spirit is sometimes willing, but the flesh is weak." And a year later he referred to my speech in conversation with a mutual friend and spoke of my excellent choice of words, as well as my courage in saying what I did.

This was, of course, enough encouragement to tempt me to drink, but the Volstead law went into effect shortly after, which saved me!

I tremble in my boots whenever real artists look at my pictures. For the opinions of the average layman I care little. But the judgment of my professional equals or superiors impels within me profound respect. Many literary art critics only arouse disgust with their pedantic conceit. And we might include many higher authorities, heads of museums and art institutions. These disabilities are spattered throughout the pages of art history. There are few great creative artists of the past who were not ignored or openly condemned by the authorities of their day.

Rembrandt, Rousseau, Millet, Corot, Dupre, Daubigny, and Whistler labored, half fed, in the creation of works that, today, are priceless. Gericault starved before the *Raft of the Meduza*. Millet's *Angelus* was offered by the artist for five hundred francs and refused. Corot was fifty before he made his first sale. All because the critics did not know.

America today is repeating history. Prizes are given where there is little or no merit, while better things are refused. In fact, were Michelangelo, Andrea Del Sarto or Velasquez to return today, under new names, their works would be rejected at the Corcoran or the National Academy. They would be termed "Old Stuff," in spite of the fact that their kind has come down through the ages and belongs to the everlasting sea of beauty and cannot be cast about on the changing crests of vogue. Not that art is not a mutable thing, changing with conditions. It is an expression of changeable things, but through an unchangeable language based upon the beauties of nature.

I had always had the mistaken notion that, if a man once becomes a great artist and can deliver the goods, the world will chase after him. Consequently, I was content if I could only support my wife and educate our children and keep on piling up better pictures. At fifty, I began to figure things out. I had all along thought myself a young man with the major part of life before me, but lying awake at four o'clock one morning, something told me. I had just passed the two-third mile post. It came like a thump. The thought saddened me for a long time. I saw that, at the rate I had been going I would need about three lifetimes before the world would know that I had arrived. I realized I was on the wrong track, and I began sending things to exhibitions with quite a measure of success. At the same time, I began giving my one-man shows far and wide, always in the hope of soon being able to quit the road and settle down in New York.

My exhibitions, lectures, and teaching throughout thirty states have resulted from motives half philanthropic, half selfish. I have had the altruistic idea of helping the world to better see and enjoy as manifested in art.

Like many other artists, I've never been fully satisfied with my work. I would paint most conscientiously out of doors on my landscape studies, then carry them home and begin larger pictures from them. Somehow the result often seemed unsatisfactory, and that dissatisfaction was sure to be increased by the smart critics who thought it necessary to advise me how to improve them. I would paint them over and over through several years, then finally obliterate them.

One day I gathered about twenty unsatisfactory canvasses and with a big brush and white lead I gave them a respectful burial. Exhausting my white lead, I let one canvas escape. A few days later an artist friend seeing it on the floor, said, "Brewer, why don't you send that picture to the exhibitions? I think it is the best thing you ever did." Acting upon his suggestion, I have sent it to eight or ten important shows, and no jury has yet rejected it. Are the juries dumbbells, or am I?

Pope's famous lines: "Know then thyself, presume not God to scan; The proper study of mankind is man," state the hardest lesson in the world to learn. But why preach? The world will wag on through endless ages, and human nature will ever be the same.

I wonder if I may be pardoned for indulging a sense of satisfaction on receiving a voluntary bit of praise from an artist whom I highly respect for his better knowledge of technicalities? About 1915 an exhibition of the works of artists of seven Middle Western states was held at Omaha. I have an artist friend, Robert Gilder, who lives at Omaha. He had a cabin studio in the woods some miles out, where he gets some delightful landscape bits. One day while we were sketching in a shady nook shortly after the close of the above-mentioned exhibition, Gilder spoke of a visit he and Charles Gruppe made to the gallery.

"Your picture," he said, "hung near the door in the first room, and we spent some time before it. On passing out, after inspecting the pictures in the other rooms, we again paused before your canvas. Gruppe, tapping the picture with his knuckles, said, 'After all, this is painting.' I mention this, Mr. Brewer, because I thought it might please you to hear it." And please me it surely did, for here was an unsolicited expression of opinion of a prominent and able painter.

* * *

While we were in church in Duluth one delightful Sunday morning, something floated through an open window and soared up and down slowly over the congregation. At a distance it appeared like a small puff or ring of smoke, but as it came closer, we saw it was several cottonwood seeds hanging together. It came nearer and lower, and was about to light on a lady's lap, when she seized it and cast it on the floor. The priest was preaching, and a fairly good sermon, too—something about a certain Biblical character. What he said was good, yet somehow my thoughts wandered back to the cottonwood seed, which seemed to carry a lesson, a whole sermon, more lasting and convincing than did the sermon from the pulpit.

Why was that seed given wings to soar so beautifully on the slightest zephyr, even through the windows into the sanctuary, and descend among the worshippers? Here was a tiny seed, heavier than air, incased in a mesh of tiny darts, feathery, ethereal, gracefully swayed by the breeze, born along for an indefinite distance, sometimes for miles, where it might bury itself in fertile soil and spring up and become a tree. Without that buoyant substance to carry it away, it would, of course, have fallen to the ground under the parent tree, where there would be millions more—too many to take root and grow. Here was a beautiful example of design in nature, purpose, thought, a plan by which the forest might be extended and perpetuated. And this is only one of a million instances that might be found, showing equal purpose or plan in nature. The rubber tree sends out a tender new leaf, covers that leaf with a cloth-like sheath that protects it from the hot sun, the wind, and the rain. When it can endure the elements, the sheath loosens, unfolds, and falls off. The covering was invented for a purpose. And this shows plan—design.

Plan is the offspring of thought, intelligence. Mere matter has no intelligence; consequently, it cannot devise or invent design. Scientists call it a law of nature, but they do not seem to answer the question—Who made this law of nature, and who sustains it? If all this material world is an accidental coming together of atoms, of various forces, whence the plan, the design? Accidental happenings are necessarily chaotic, irregular, without repetition; but this cottonwood seed was just like every other of its kind that ever ripened on billions of trees throughout millions of years—and will so continue. Heredity is a part of its design. The cottonwood tree will never be anything else, and the rubber tree will never change its character or habits.

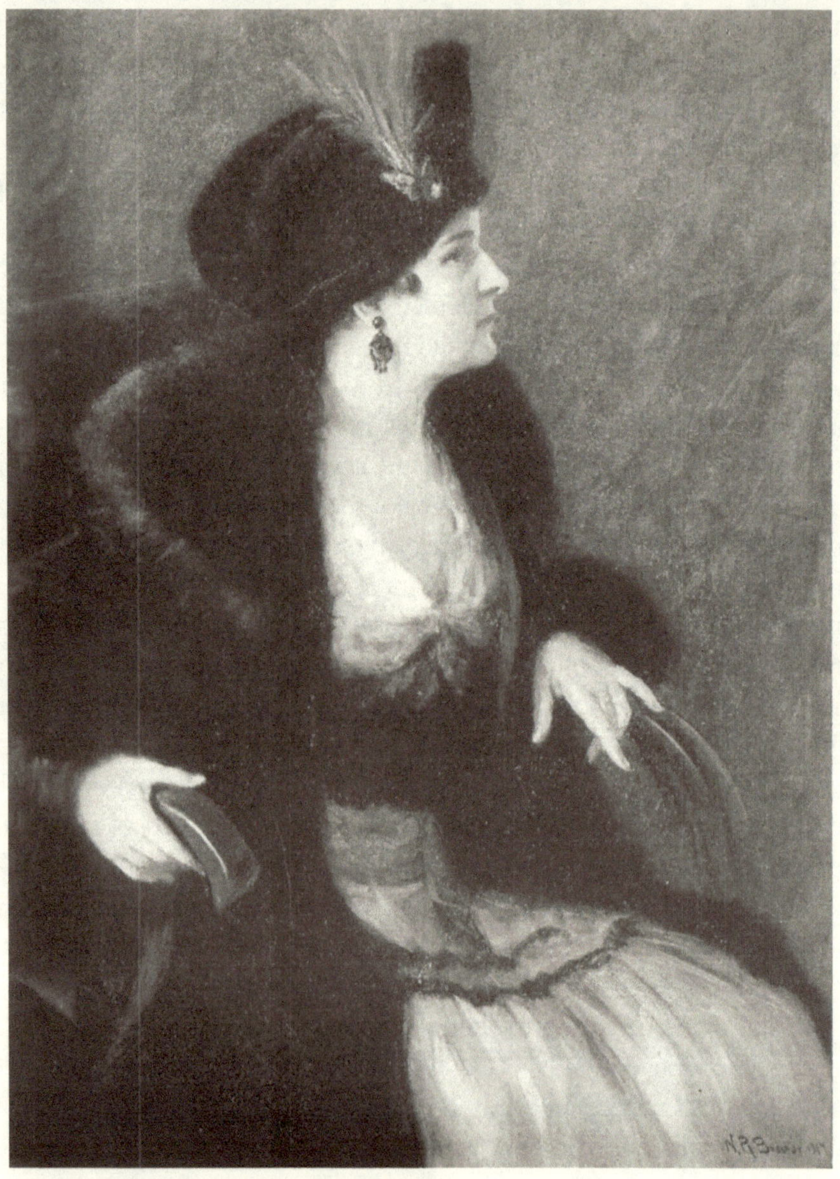

The Purple Coat, First Prize, Illinois State Art Exhibition, 1917.

But it is an amazing thought that man is the only animal that ever works out a new design or lays a plan. Every nest-building bird, every insect, reptile, quadruped, or crawling creature that builds anything at all, does it out of pure instinct without reason, never varying from the manner of his forefathers of millions of years, while man seldom repeats, that is, in his creative efforts, and all his works are prompted by a sense of the beautiful and the perfect and the useful. Does that not seem to argue that man possesses the prerogative of a creator; that he reflects something of the likeness of the Infinite Architect of the whole, limited and finite in his powers, yet bearing the stamp of divinity in his soul? And as the service concluded, I bowed my head and said, "Our Father Who art in Heaven, Thy greatness and power are mysterious and awe inspiring. I bow before Thee in reverence and love, knowing that I am Thy son, made in Thy image with the power to create enduring things. Amen."

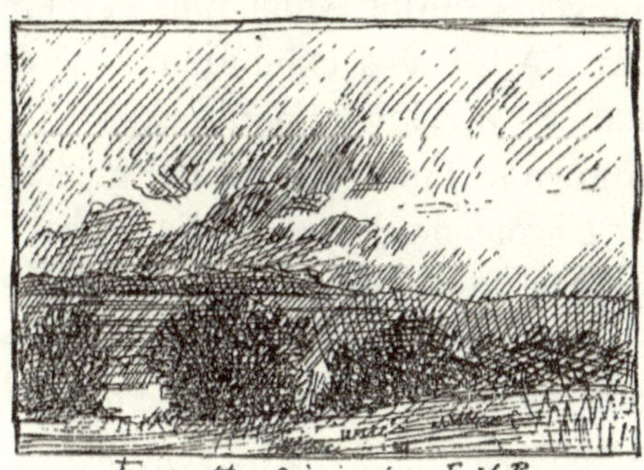

From the Original E.V.B.

Chapter XXI
Portrait and Landscape Painting

The painted portrait is the voice of the soul spoken through the features.

I gave up the studio in New York and never set foot upon that sacred ground for ten long years, during which time I sent pictures to the Salmagundi and National Arts Clubs' exhibitions, where they were usually well received, but they were *not* my portraits.

It is a well-known fact that some of our greatest portrait painters fail to please their patrons on the score of likeness. During my exhibition in Newport, Mr. Joseph Weidner had Sargent paint his wife's portrait. He caught her in a laughing position, with her head and hands up, and mouth wide open. Mr. Widener came to see the display of my Newport portraits and mentioned the Sargent picture. I asked him if it were a success as a portrait. "Well," he said, "as a likeness it is a failure, but it is a Sargent you know." He was big enough to understand that a great portrait need not be what everybody terms a striking likeness. The commonplace photographic expression familiar to the relatives is a personal thing. Apart from the generally pleasing likeness there must be an expression of the artist—his conception and description of the character of the subject. If it is that, it is a creative thing and a real work of art, whether or not it pleases Aunt Jane or Uncle Dudley.

In the judging of a portrait, there is a psychological phase of mental action, which is personal to the one passing judgment; a composite impression often colored by one's own temperamental choice of expressions, which few portraits can satisfy. The impressions are gleaned from real live flesh and blood, while the painting is but an abstract analysis of the external and mental characteristics as the artist reads them. Consequently, the best portraits are frequently unsatisfactory to intimates of the subject.

There are few people who realize that the artist should be given *carte blanche* to express himself and that they should refrain from trying to influence him. They will ding away with comments and suggestions, all the time declaring that they want the artist to use his own judgment, that they are not artistic and know nothing about it—"but don't you think this change or that would help it?" It requires extraordinary will power on the part of the painter to set his foot down and ignore completely all the suggestions expressed by otherwise charming people, and the more charming, the more difficult to resist. Then there are some who in their hearts want a picture that flatters them beyond recognition and seem never to be pleased. I have of late years resorted to a certain ruse with such people, and when the portrait is about finished, I have them go with me to a photograph gallery and have a dozen or more snapshots taken, with varying expressions, out of which I tell them some one or two will have the desired look. Then I can easily achieve what they want. Invariably, on seeing the unretouched photographs wherein all the lines are emphasized, they become suddenly very much pleased with the painting and decline to have me do any more work on it.

While my pictures were being shown by the Art Association in Duluth, I was commissioned to paint a portrait of a handsome mother holding her four months' old baby. This lady was in her own estimation something of an artist. In Chicago she had tried to earn her living by commercial art and newspaper work. Meeting a good-looking young doctor from Duluth, who had inherited a great fortune, and was considered a coveted catch by the Duluth belles, she married him and was installed as mistress of a mansion overlooking Lake Superior. This fact, of course, caused jealous tongues to wag, and when a stranger asked how she stood in society, the reply was, "I don't think she stands." She seemed to like her portrait very much, and the doctor was quite enthusiastic about it.

A year later I again landed in the Arrowhead city. I called the lady on the phone to say, "How-do-you-do." She told me she had been working the portrait over, that "after the romance of the sittings was over" she began to form a dislike for the expression in the picture. The doctor thought she had spoiled it. In consternation, I asked if I might see it, but she said she was going to do more work on it; after that she would be glad to show it to me. I had thought it one of my best pictures and wanted to have it photographed. I asked her if she would have done the same thing if they had employed John Sargent or some other renowned artist to do the work instead of me.

"Yes," she said, "if the expression did not suit me."

With many people who have portraits painted, the kind of expression to be acquired is the chief consideration. Give them what they like in that way, and they will accept the very worst kind of a daub. Whistler's answer to a lady who asked if she would be obliged to take her picture if she didn't like it, "You reverse it Madam; if I am not pleased with it, you will never get it," means nothing to them.

The mischief comes when the person ordering the picture feels that he needs the advice of some of his friends to enable him to decide if he is going to like it and asks to be allowed to have them look at it. I find that about half of those so impaneled as a jury will shake their heads on first sight. The others will heartily approve, and some will be emphatic in their praises. Once a lady asked, "Who is it supposed to represent? I would not know it."

A few moments later, the nursemaid brought in the subject's little two-year-old girl, who ran to the picture, pointed at it, and gleefully shouted, "Mamma! Mamma!"

I used to be very much disturbed and worried by the adverse snap judgments sometimes expressed, but experience has taught me to await the psychological change that almost invariably comes on their getting acquainted with the painting. Some will say, "Well, as one looks at it, it seems more like you," and in half an hour will pronounce it a splendid likeness. Some must come to see it two or three times before discovering it to be a truthful representation of the sitter. A common remark is, "There is something wrong about the mouth, but I can't tell you what it is." It is almost always the mouth that troubles them. It is said that John

Sargent's definition of a portrait was, "A picture of somebody, with something wrong about the mouth."

Mrs. G., of Fargo, was very well pleased with her portrait and gave a tea and unveiling, when everybody spoke their praises of my work except one lady, who picked very severely at the mouth. It had no life in it, she said. Mrs. G. vehemently defended the picture and said, "My dear, I wish you to know that my mouth is not a moving picture." (That is just what her mouth really was—it moved so rapidly no instantaneous lens could ever catch it.)

Upon my finishing the portrait of Mrs. Farrington, of Minneapolis, she asked permission to bring an artist friend to see it. The picture happened to be exposed on the easel when they entered. The artist, a girl not over twenty-two or so, instantly said, "No, Mrs. Farrington, it isn't you," and sailed into the picture mercilessly. I had been working and still had my palette on my arm. She then picked on the mouth, the ear, and hair, and particularly the lack of definition in the mesh of the Spanish lace shawl about the shoulders. Thumping at the face again, she said, "Now, I will tell you, Mr. Brewer, how to fix it. You have a dark shadow on one side of the nose; if you will take some Prussian blue and rose madder—plenty of rose madder—and put a dark shadow on the other side of the nose, it will make it all right, I am sure."

I had been getting madder and madder at her brazen egotism, but this last remark was the straw that broke the camel's back. Ignoring her madder advice, I threw my palette down and said, "There, Mrs. Farrington, is your picture. I am done." And done I was. Nothing but the thought of the youth and ignorance of this would-be artist could extenuate what many would have taken as an insult.

It is strange how rapidly some people will grow into liking a portrait they at first could not consider a good resemblance, especially if they are left under the impression the artist is still laboring with it. Seeing it again the next day, they will remark, "You have greatly improved it."

In my early days, I remember I had to make a crayon portrait from a photograph, for a lady whose husband had recently died. The photograph was a poor one, taken several years previous to his death. In my enlargement from it, she could not see a likeness. I worked on it long and faithfully. On her second or third call I concluded I should never be able to please her but told her to come in again after I had worked more on it. I turned it to the wall and did not touch it. When she saw it again, she said, "Well, that is very much better, but it is not right yet." Again, I turned it to the wall for a few days, and again she said it was much improved. I repeated the ruse six or eight times, until she finally said, "Now it is perfect, Mr. Brewer; don't touch it again."

On a few occasions when some tantalizing patrons were very insistent on changes about the mouth, I have used a dry brush, pretending to charge it with color. As I drew the brush over the part mentioned, they thought immediately they saw an actual improvement, and bade me not to work further on it lest I injure the expression.

In many cases the painting of a portrait is to me a worrisome and disagreeable task. A lack of intelligent sympathy and understanding on the part of the patron or family, combined with prolonged and unreasonable criticisms, causes a feeling of relief when it is finished. This was not the case, however, when I painted the portrait of a Mr. Zeitlow, owner of the Aberdeen Telephone Company. He had reaped a fortune from his business and had two lovely daughters. One, whom he had educated in Europe, was musical. The other, a bright, practical girl, was his private secretary. Painting the face of his portrait involved a whole afternoon. The latter daughter was so interested in my work that she sat close by me and observed every touch, glancing at her father to see how accurate my modeling was, until the likeness was complete. At the close, she exclaimed, "Why, Papa, I never really looked at you before today."

This suggests the question, *Why do most people, when criticizing a portrait, not base their judgment upon actual observation of the subject's features, instead of on impressions received casually theretofore?* I have known husbands who could not tell the color of their wives' eyes, although they had been looking into them for years.

Some of the happiest times of my life I have had painting one or more portraits in a family circle. I recall with the keenest pleasure having to paint seven portraits for the Priddie family in Beaumont, Texas—father, mother, son, two grown daughters, and two grandchildren—all delightful people to know. Never was there a request made as to how they wished to look or what they preferred to wear in the picture. I was assured that any way I painted them would be most agreeable. One or more persons at a time would ask to sit and watch me work, when the light conversation would be most agreeable and reassuring. All were excellent subjects with decided characteristics.

Likewise, the painting of Mrs. William Stark, of Orange, Texas, and her beautiful daughter-in-law, Mrs. Lutcher Stark, both cultured and appreciative women, and both art collectors. Mrs. William had given her collection, which contained many fine pieces, to the University of Texas to be placed there after her demise, and she wanted her portrait to go with them. In this case, the only one who tried to pick flaws in my work was Mr. Lutcher Stark. To him, his mother's portrait was perfect; but the idolizing husband saw something in his wife, I am sure, no brush could paint. I, myself, was so enamored of my wife's beauty that when I once painted her as I saw her no one liked the portrait. They all declared it did not look a bit like her.

And there was dear little Mrs. Elizabeth Jordan Gilliland, in Memphis. This was before her marriage. The only daughter of devoted parents who lavished upon her every comfort, gratified every whim or desire, yet she grew up so naive, gracious, and sweet it was a joy to know her. With a mind attuned to the finer things of life, she came to the task of posing for a painting, with an understanding of the requirements of art far above the average. I posed her seated on the arm of a divan near a fireplace, the fire throwing a faint glow on one side of the figure, climbing to her lovely neck, cheek, and hair. If I may compliment my own accomplishment, this portrait was the nearest to a real work of art I have ever reached—at least of a beautiful woman. Elizabeth was not only highly pleased with it, but said she liked the artist even better. The Jordans were so hospitable that during my stay in Memphis I whiled away many pleasant hours in their home. When the picture was finished, Mrs. Jordan gave a tea, and nearly three hundred guests crowded into the beautifully decorated drawing room. The picture was hung just above the receiving line, and before it stood the blushing subject in the same dress and throw she wore while posing.

In the early days, when I was still doing crayon portraits from photographs, a French laundryman, who had been doing our family wash, lost his wife. This misfortune broke the old man up badly. I had never seen such a case of real grief and we all thought he would lose his mind. His name was Lefevbre. To soothe his heartache, Lefevbre commissioned me to make a life-size crayon portrait of his late spouse from a tintype. I happened to be very busy at that time and had to delay the work about three weeks. One morning he came in all spruced up and looking like a different man. I began to make excuses for not having begun the portrait and told him I would start it in a few days.

"Well, Mr. Brewer," he said hesitatingly, "I sink I will not have you make a portrait of my fus' wife; I will have a picture of my secon' wife." He had married again!

In a southern city, I was asked to paint a portrait of an outstanding dry good merchant by the name of Dinklespliel. He had come to town years ago with his "all" in a carpet bag. Now there was danger of his absorbing about all the business the town had. He had a decided foreign accent, was tall with rugged features and black eyes, a forcible talker who usually got the best of a bargain. When his picture was finished, he was so well pleased with it that he wanted one of his wife. She first asked for a reduction in price on account of my doing the two of them. But since she was so short and fat, altogether ungainly, and not at all to my liking as a subject, I declined. A coarser personality could scarcely be found, both in manner and language.

She said, "Vell, Mr. Prewer. I dun't vant to be painted in a tress; I vant you to make me in a trape. I dun't like yello, I like levindy better."

"Well," I replied, resigning myself to the tortuous task before me, "Mrs. Dinklespiel, go to the store and select something you like and let me see it."

She bought a gaudy colored figured drap of lavender shades and we started to work. Speaking about the kind of facial expression she wanted, she stepped before the mirror and made several contortions no artist could ever catch. It is my habit to disregard such requests until my work is nearing completion, and then consider them, only if they are reasonable. As time went on, the lady continually harped on how she wanted to look in the picture, until my nerves were on fire and my temper tried to the limit.

There are certain people one cannot insult. Their skins are as tough as that of a rhinoceros. I began to make rather brutal remarks to her. She retorted with equal vehemence. In fact, for several days we hurled verbal rolling pins and bootjacks at each other.

She would say, "I dun't like dat 'spression. I dun't vant to look like dat." Then going to the mirror, she would resume her contortions, dimpling her fat cheeks and squinting her eyes as though smelling Limburger cheese or asafetida, and remark, "I vant to look like dees."

With all patience exhausted, I would reply, "Mrs. Dinklespiel, I will never paint you that way. I shall paint you the way I see you. Furthermore, I want you to bring your husband and daughter in to see the portrait for I know they will like it."

"I dun't care if dey like it or not, I dun't like dat 'spression, and I dun't got to take this thing wat I dun't like."

"Well," said I, "you have got to take this thing whether you like it or not. You can put it in the cellar or in the attic as a rat-killer if you like, but you will send me a check for it just the same."

The next day she brought in her married daughter who was a woman of good sense. When her eyes fell upon the portrait, she exclaimed, "Well, Mamma, I think that is a good likeness of you and a very pretty picture." (I had relieved my subject of at least fifty pounds of her avoirdupois and shaved her double chin down).

Just then the door opened, and her husband entered. Looking at the painting he said, "Vell, Mamma, that is a very fine pitcher of you, but vere is my pitcher?"

I had turned his canvas to the wall. When I showed it to him, he almost shouted, "Oh, I got a crate pitcher of me! You know, Mr. Prewer, vat I goin' to do mit dat pitcher? I goin' to hang it on de balcony in de shtore. You must put your name on—put it on pig so everybody sees it. You know ven you paint Mr. Tootmilder he hangs it in his home and only a few people sees it; but I put mine in de shtore vere a huntred tousand sees it. Dat will be goot advertisement for you, hein?"

With the approval of the family, the "levindy" woman offered no further objection regarding the facial "spression" in the picture, but the climax of humor came when Mr. Dinklespliel, before writing my check, tried to induce me to accept one-half the agreed price because of the advertising I would get from the display of the "pitcher."

I once painted a beautiful gray-haired lady in Lincoln, Nebraska, much adored by her husband, who wished her to be "immortalized in oils," as he said. She had a superb figure of statuesque charm, which he wished clothed in scant diaphanous draperies, low at the bust and with a train, which he insisted on arranging to suit himself with a view to revealing the wonderful form beneath. When I first saw the lady, I was impressed with the great possibility she presented of my making an exhibition portrait. I said I would like to send the picture when finished to the Chicago Art Institute display. The idea appealed to them forcibly.

The man pestered me so much during the course of the work offering not a single expression of approval that I was made to feel I was pleasing neither him nor myself. I finally told him I was at the end of my rope with the portrait, and I expected him to reject the picture flatly.

"Are you sure that you can do nothing more?" he asked.

Throwing down my brush, I replied emphatically, "Yes."

"Well, then," he said, "I shall go and write your check." When he handed it to me, he said, "We are delighted with your work, Mr. Brewer; I think it is the finest portrait I have ever seen.

They boxed the picture and sent it to me in Chicago for exhibition. When the case was opened, I looked at it with rested eyes and ordered it put back in the box and returned to him. I shall always be ashamed that it bears my name.

As I have advanced in years, I have fallen into a course of procedure in the doing of my portraits, which is something like this: Before laying on color I settle upon my composition, the pose, lighting, masses, the construction of the head and features, and the spacing. I then sketch them in with charcoal leaving the smaller divisions and details to be worked in with the brush. Then I cover the large spaces first in color as nearly as I can approximate the general scheme; the dark masses are swept in thinly, the lighter ones with a heavier impasto of paint. When most of the canvas is covered, if I have the time the head comes next. The light portions, half tones, and shadows are brushed in with ample pigment, then the truing up on the construction and general modeling with attention to smaller features and details until the semblance in form begins to look like the subject.

The simpler the list of colors possible on the palette, the better. I never employ more than thirteen or fourteen colors, in addition to black-and-white. With these, I produce every effect I wish, whether outdoors or in. There are nearly a hundred colors manufactured, many of which are fugitive and not chemically dependable. Many art students use them for their brilliancy, not knowing their deleterious effect on other colors. For instance, all colors with a lead base should be avoided. All the whites, except Zinc, Permalba and Phillips, are lead whites, all the chromes likewise. The student should obtain a manufacturer's list giving the chemical compounds of their colors. I use only turpentine or kerosene as a diluting medium. My list of colors is: Oxide of Chromium, Emeraude Green, Cobalt, and Ultramarine Blue, Yellow Ochre, Raw Sienna, the cadmiums, any Vermilion (except American), Alizarin Crimson for glazing, Indian Red for flesh shadows, Burnt Sienna, Raw and Burnt Umber.

When whipping in dark masses in portrait work I use considerable turpentine in a color wash, or what the French call lavis, sufficiently heavy to be left without further working, provided I happen to hit the color I want for that particular passage. Dark colors will grow less dark over a light canvas if washed in thinly than when used heavily. It is well to go over all light passages, such as flesh and light draperies, two or more times, until the desired effect is secured. Keep the whole picture in as light a key as possible. If certain parts or the whole work cannot be completed *premiere coup* (that is *in one go*), let it dry, then use retouching varnish, and when that is dry repaint the unsatisfactory places about as before. Other parts may be glazed with thin washes for the final tone desired.

I have been requested by an artist friend to say something in these pages for the benefit of art lovers and students about the modes of attack while sketching outdoors, ways and means of covering the canvas or the panel quickly, what to see in nature and how to see it, what to omit of the clutter in a landscape before the artist, the essential planes, and the theory of genuine pictorialization in a work of art.

For outdoor work one saunters forth to find a subject in the hope that when painted it will be a picture. Finding an eligible composition depends upon the picture sense of the finder. Millet said, "He who finds is formed to find." Some individuals tramp for miles, missing many a delightful subject and return with a daub, which on more reflection will be cast onto the scrap heap.

Pictures stare at us from back alleys, goat yards, wood piles, old sheds, and crumbling walls, and from the streams and fields. One need not go to the Fiji Islands or Halifax to find new subject matter. Beauty abounds everywhere, in homely as well as majestic scenes. A stump, a sapling, a pool, with the distant plain and sky may serve for a creative work that will challenge admiration of intelligent people as long as it shall live. The more comprehensive the subject the more difficult to handle and the oftener less satisfying.

Outdoor sketching requires technical facility and speed to catch the passing mood, the fleeting gleam, the changing day. Who can overestimate the value of mood in landscape? The most thrilling and delightful effects we see are usually evanescent, fleeting. They are nature's smiles. But, unlike the human smile, once gone they never return. The blue shadow of the cloud sweeping the mountain side may be the only one that day.

Facility comes with practice. Students should practice persistently and get all the fun out of it they can for the harder they work the better will be the color-makers' business!

In sketching from nature, half close and squint your eyes so as to see only the big masses without the multiplicity of little forms. A painting should not be a photograph, exact as to every unimportant detail. Exactness as to the placing of the large masses is even sometimes unnecessary. Create a work of art by building a picture out of the *suggestions* nature offers you. Corot said, "It is more what one leaves out than what one puts into his canvas that makes a picture."

Be sure of your values, the planes, the foreground, second foreground, middle distance, extreme distance; and the sky, its gradations, color, and relation to the earth. Get the lay of the land; find or create lines that will establish the level, especially of waters. Don't let people feel that your river is going to pour out of the side of your picture. Make nature serve your creative instincts. By using her larger aspects, truthful to her relations and tints, your work will ring true, yet it will be a poetical creation, a song, not a mere mechanical prosaic description.

Today people prate loudly of the *decorative*—the pattern—as an all-important quality in every picture. All forms must be rendered in flats with proper spacings they maintain. The purely decorative, however, is muralesque, serving the purpose of decorated walls to match and complete a room or a building. The landscape is a thing in itself to be framed and to serve another purpose as different from the merely decorated wall as *Gray's Elegy* is from a legal document.

But the main thing to the art lover and the student is not to lose much time on isms and pseudo-philosophies of so-called art. Just paint, paint, paint! And think, observe, and dream. When you have come to know nature in many of her moods, caprices, and brainstorms and have acquired a mastery over your keyboard, that is, your palette, like Paderewski you can sail off into a world of extemporaneous dreams and improvisations and tonal symphonies. And that is art!

After I had made over five hundred outdoor studies, I began to paint my landscapes indoors from impressions preserved by field sketches, hastily, joyously, lovingly made. And I will say that not until then had I painted a landscape worth looking at. All the world's great landscape painters have adopted that procedure. You can get your raw material outdoors in the presence of an incidental landscape. Memory of things seen and felt is a part of human imagination, and all creative work must be imaginative and dramatic, often poetic. There is no talent so thrilling as that founded on *creative genius!*

From a standpoint of technical excellence, I seldom improve a work by going over it a second time. But back of all technique must be the great motive, the urge, the inspiration. At least so it is with me. Science, knowledge—they are one thing; inspiration is another. One is a means to an end; the other is the message, the concept. However well drawn and painted work may be, without something more than technique the result is empty and pedantic. One should paint only when inspired by some great inner prompting born of life, nature, plus the paintable, the picturesque, the beautiful.

Once I was painting in the studio of Mr. Walter Clark in the National Arts Building in New York. Clark had frequently spoken of a young woman he knew, a musician, who hoped to make her debut in grand opera soon. He said he would like to see me paint her; she was such an excellent subject. She had a dress designed and dyed by herself in which she was to dance. He felt sure if I could catch the swing-and-go of her action it would be a great picture. I told him to have her come in with the costume and I would look at her. Next morning, I was detained, and they were waiting at the studio when I arrived. She wore the dress for the inspiring dance. For half an hour she pranced about for me to catch an action. There was a lot of action, but the girl's face and figure did not impress me—I could not see that it harmonized with the spirit of the dance and consequently, felt no urge nor enthusiasm. Without conception I could get no inspiration to paint and the dancer began to tire. Clark impatiently said, "There is a canvas; why don't you get busy?"

I could not say that I did not see anything to paint so replied, "I haven't got a conception yet."

After a little more dancing she sprang upon the model throne where a piano bench stood with the telephone directory hanging over one end. Seating herself sidewise and with her hands clasped and stretched upward she laid her head down on the book. The light streamed down on her shoulders, arms, and back. The sweep of line in the figure and arms was immense. Her profusion of red hair threw the face into the shadow. The massing was superb. She closed her eyes, resting. I shouted, "Don't move!" Nearby was a plain blue drape. I seized it and threw it about the lower part of her figure, all of which was more or less in shadow.

"There," I said, "is my picture."

With charcoal I quickly sketched in the lines and action, the hands clasped together. Clark disappointedly said, "I thought you were going to paint a dancing figure."

I could no more have painted her dancing than the man in the moon. When the picture was finished, they were both disappointed and suggested that I label it, "When the Cook has Went." I now call it *Magdalene.* Somewhat old-fashioned but it is Magdalene. It expresses the spirit of introspection, repentance, sorrow—quite a contrast to the original intention for the picture, which was to depict the action of joy, abandon of the dance.

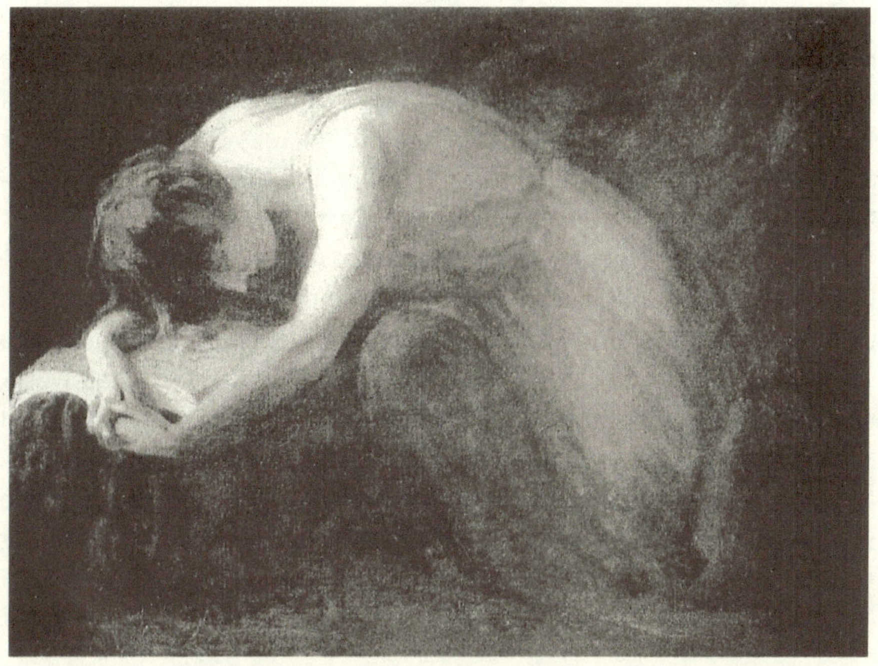

Mary Magdalene

It is one of my best pictures, so some artists say; but people who have never repented, or those whose consciences prick them do not like it. "It is religious, sentimental, conventional," they declare. Dr. Holmes, Director of the National Gallery, suggested my giving it to the gallery, saying he would hang it in a prominent place. It has been accepted by several critical juries and well hung.

In portrait painting I would always like to feel the same impulse, to be able to arrange my composition so that light and line and mass would be telling qualities in the finished work, but many subjects have not been paintable people. One's personal choice of type always asserts itself. One will prefer a pug nose, another a Roman one; some prefer a corpulent figure, others a slender one; some like a peachy, rose-like complexion, others a skin like a vinegar pickle.

I usually prefer that my subjects engage in conversation while posing, provided they hold the posture until I release them. There are few people indeed who can be made to realize that in portrait painting the artist must draw and model the features under a given light and from one point of view. A portrait is nothing more or less than a careful rendering of forms as they appear in immobility. The slightest change in the position immediately changes the entire expression of the face. What people see in faces is animation, not features. That is why I talk to my subjects while I am painting. A busy mind, stimulated by conversation, affords animation, and a portrait must have life.

Nine out of every ten notable characters I have painted have behaved about the same. They either forget themselves or have the notion that by seeing them in every conceivable position I can construct a composite portrait expressive of all the occult characteristics and workings of the gray matter back of their features. They think the artist must read the soul, however obscure it may be, and transcribe it into enduring color. They think he is a sort of wizard who creates flesh and blood in a mysterious way, when in reality, he is only a craftsman who draws what he sees.

Chapter XXII

False Philosophy

Things are fit for art so far only as they are both true and apparent.

—Poe

Truth is ever old and ever new. A statement embodying truth needs no revision as to facts. Anything that needs revision is not the truth. The multiplication table needs no revision nor improvement. Five times five is twenty-five—six times nine is fifty-four—are truths no man can add to or take from.

The American Constitution is not a collection of truths but a device for the regulation and government of human society. It may be revised and improved upon.

"Thou shalt not covet thy neighbor's wife" is not a truth but a commandment, the breaking of which may involve three people in a divorce trial or murder; and this last statement is a truth, believe it or not. Truth is always harder to find than fallacy. The latter is everywhere. Men are bred on falsehood from childhood. Confront a man with a truth which he does not see and you at once arouse his prejudice, and if you are not careful, you will have an argument on your hands. If you are too persistent you may even come to blows. There is nothing harder to uproot than prejudice, yet truth is a demonstrable quantity. It may be distinguished from the false if we will but forget what we have learned about a thing and with an open mind start all over again.

Recently an article appeared in one of the papers in which an instructor of a well-recognized art school said:

"The old academies of Europe are dead, and the old systems of standardized instruction are gone. The effort in the modern schools is to teach the student to look upon his material with his own eyes and to record things as he *individually sees them*. Education in art, like education in all other fields, is seeking to develop the talent of those who have new ideas to express. It is not content merely with giving them unpliable technique made up of hard and fast rules."

Pretty words but they contain both truth and fallacy. From my half century of experience, I cannot see wherein modern instruction should differ fundamentally from that of the great masters of all ages. To see and record things as we "individually see them" has ever been the essence of art instruction. Art is but an expression through the medium of form and color of the artist's impressions of life. It is not a perfect copy of nature. It is an interpretation, a semblance of her forms only. Bacon defined art to be "*Homo Aditus Natura*." (Man added to nature). If absolute realism is the end and not the means only, there is no need of higher thought and art is useless because we cannot improve upon nature.

> To gild refined gold, to paint the lily, to throw perfume on the violet, to smoothe the ice, or add another hue to the rainbow, to seek, with taper light the beauteous eye of heaven to garnish, is wasteful and ridiculous excess.

* * *

It is related in ancient history that a certain Roman comedian was wont to please his audience by imitating the cackle of a goose; a peasant thinking he would add to the entertainment brought a live goose under his toga and at the proper time made it cackle; the audience hissed him. What they wanted was not the real cackle of the goose but the human rendition of it. Man's ideal of the real makes art.

I do not understand all this talk about new ideas in the modern curriculum. Rembrandt with his fine loose brush work, his broad masses of chiaroscuro, his unique conception, was wholly new—so were Rubens, Van Dyke, Frans Hals, Velasquez, and Whistler. Everything creative is new, a new conception with the individual technical characteristics of the artist in the use of his means.

The article reads further:

"The technique of modern painting begins and ends with feeling, but between the first impulse and the final achievement there must, of course, be a highly developed craftsmanship if the work is to be distinguished."

That craftsmanship is nothing more than the old-fashioned academic drawing to produce a semblance of form. The old schools cannot be accused of neglecting to place value upon feeling, but no school can give the artist personal, temperamental emotions. One must have those in his nature. All the art school can do is to train the student to see form and color in their big, simple masses, and to eliminate or avoid "the over-heavy, ornate, sweet, and elaborate."

The great masterpieces of Rubens or Van Dyke are examples of these simple truths that have survived the ages. There has been a multitude of artists who have departed from the principles of the great masters and have degenerated into platitudes of over-elaboration, minute and photographic details, mere prettiness, tiresome narrative, and other meaningless things. These qualities are worth little, but are they worse than the utterly inane, idiotic splashes of many of the moderns?

In every age there have been a few who stood out from the masses and who have produced the things that live. J. F. Millet once said, "When a genius has once unearthed a treasure, we come for centuries to scratch at the same hole." The many follow; the few lead. How many of the followers of Cezanne, Matisse, Van Gogh, will ever be mentioned in the history of art?

In that immortal work of Rubens, *The Descent from the Cross*, do you perceive a "slavish imitation" or a lack of "the simpler, more direct standards" of what this writer calls the "swift age in which we live"?

The modern conception seems to be rather a distortion of form than a simplification of it, and to be quite different from that ideal, which inspired Michelangelo or Andrea del Sarto. It appears to be an illogical effort to be "different," a confusion of warped minds that produce gruesome images. The fact that we moderns paint our faces and lips or fly in the air, navigate under the sea, or broadcast our speech does not indicate that human nature has changed one whit. Not until the human heart and temperament have undergone a complete transformation will the great motive impulses that find expression under the artist's brush change.

Art in every age has had its lapses. Modernism, it seems to me, is an ephemeral expression of impulses arising from the deception, distortion and lack of harmony that is characteristic of our day. In my method of work, I have tried to shun Charybdis and avoid the danger of Scylla, thereby keeping in the safe road between extremes. It is not my wish to tread on the toes of the moderns or to worship at the shrine of decadent classics, but to take the best from all, mold it into a harmonious philosophy of beauty, and forge ahead.

Many of the moderns will tell us that to try to interpret nature at all is old-fashioned, and that we must evolve something from within ourselves. That "something" they produce, and which so frequently finds its way into our galleries is so vague and mysterious that its message remains an enigma. They say, when we exclaim, "I don't get it!" "Wait, it will come to you after you have given it more thought."

In that famous cubist picture *A Woman Coming Down Stairs*, where the canvas is strewn with cubes and triangles or what not, in one place a woman's eye, in another an ear or a part of a foot, I would defy anybody to find a woman coming down stairs. She must have fallen and broken completely to pieces.

A story is told of some Paris artists who wished to test the intelligence of a jury that was hanging works so radical that their meaning could not be deciphered by anyone. They concluded to send the worst picture that could be produced. They backed a docile jackass up to a table on which were a number of pots of different colored paint and placing a canvas where his switching tail would hit it, they punched him in the ribs. Each time his tail, covered with paint, would splash the canvas. Then smearing some of the splashes together to do some blending, they coined a new name on the picture and sent it in. When it came before the jury, members rose to their feet and critically examined the new and wonderful production, the like of which had never been seen before, even the name was new, and they voted it a prize!

At an exhibition assembled by the Art Club of Chicago some years ago, there appeared a number of cubes shaded up all over a canvas like lumps of sugar. The title of the picture was *Nativity*. In another room almost the identical thing was hung but in a different scheme of color, called *Jazz*. These with works of Matisse, Van Gogh, and numerous other extreme radicals were written up as "a magnificent display of the new art."

Edward Allen Jewell, in an article in the *New York Times* on the proposed American Luxemburg, a museum of modern art, says:

"Modern art now rides the crest of the waves," to which Mr. Albert Sterner replies: "Possibly, at the moment, so-called modern art does ride the crest of the waves, but is it not well to remember that all waves very quickly turn their crests, merge their waters, and disappear in the great and everlasting sea? It is not necessary to found a special museum for the exhibition of the peculiar modes and mannerisms of 'self-expression' which have always been manifested in the gropings and experiments of artists through the ages. As opposed to these experiments, great expression in the arts has invariably remained impersonal and striven through its exponents for clarity and sanity. Think of the futility and the huge space that would be needed if we were to exhibit the myriad unrealized and purposeless experiments of the world's inventors. That such experiments in the fine arts are eagerly sought, appraised, classified, and offered for sale for the special consumption of the dilettante collector hardly gives them the right to be accorded that mark of distinction that a place in a museum has hitherto donated and conferred."

The New York papers recently startled the public with the statement that the jury of the National Academy had awarded a major prize to a picture after it was hung wrong side up. From such procedure one is led to think that there must be something wrong with the intelligence of the jury making the award.

The vagaries of human reason are many, and false philosophies that haunt the schoolroom, studio, drawing room, and salon are distilled everywhere. Arguments of all viewpoints, harangues and bickerings, sometime fistic encounters, black eyes, and sore noses result. One shouts, "This is the right way"; another, "Here is the correct theory," when in fact there is no truly right way. If there is, it is every one's own way.

Oh, the critics! Oh, the art writers! Oh, the museum directors! Many of the latter tried to be artists but finding it an impossible job, dropped the brush and adopted art politics. They are eloquent exponents of crazy radicalism, the kind that some people hang bottom side up, because nobody can guess heads from tails; the puzzlers, the abstractionists, the crazy quilt patternists who call it the new art.

Oh, the art writers! who prate most profoundly and mysteriously about the good or bad drawing of Rubens or Rembrandt while they could not draw a pig's tail if they tried. Writers of articles for the dilettante millionaire buyers' consumption; glorifying art to make it look like a good investment; books no real artist ever cares to read; criticisms with ambiguous phraseology so profound as to conceal the ignorance of the bombastic critic.

Oh, the new age—"The New Deal"! It deals with everything from politics and potatoes down, even religion. It pervades the masses below forty years of age and often above. Soon there will be a new dictionary from which the words, manners, modesty, propriety, etiquette, and many others may be eliminated because they are old fashioned.

Oh, the nudists! in both high and low life. Young women coming to dinner in less than bathing suit raiment, unless the weather forbids.

Oh, the distortionists with their stretching of necks and noses and all the parts of the figure.

Will the "human form divine" be able to survive at all?

The standards of truth and beauty are smashed to smithereens.

"A thing of beauty is a joy forever" is a silly saying. Truth and beauty are as individuals see it. Individualism is the watchword. Individual interpretation of all rules and laws.

In one of our great universities there is a club whose purpose is to develop a super race, physical and mental, who will redeem mankind and produce a millennium, a perfect state of society wherein everybody will be supremely happy.

Their policy is to chloroform all the invalids, all the weak, all the defectives, even those with poor hearing or too fat to waddle, and everybody else at sixty years old. Then there will be no need of breeding by selection, for all will be perfect.

But since the ages have had their lapses down to social indecencies, rebellions against constituted authorities, communism, degrading decadence, and all manner of evils, may we not hope there will be a return to the sane and truly progressive along all lines, especially in art?

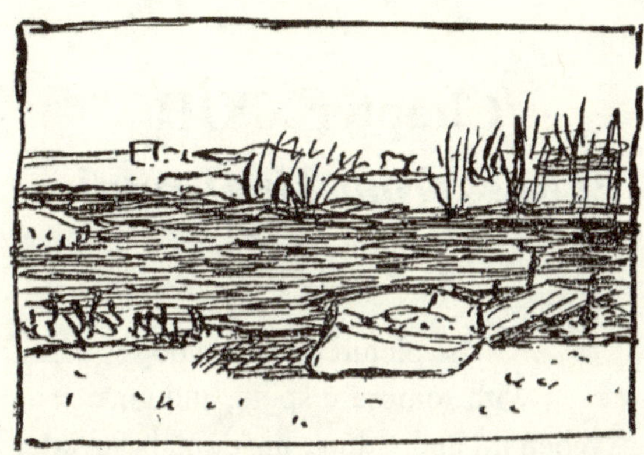

Through form and color every painter reveals his message and that is his individual concept of the beauties of the world in which he lives, the things, the phases of nature that impress him, and the doing of it is his art. The world in time will assign him his niche according to the perfection of his ideals, the loftiness of his soul, and many who have made much noise and clatter while spoiling good canvas will not be found in any niche at all.

Chapter XXIII
Echoes from The Frontier

The picturesque cowboy
with sombrero spurs, and gun,
When art and culture his domain invade,
Will turn about and run.

When giving an exhibition with the Waco (Texas) Art Association, I received a letter from Mrs. H. G. Hendricks of the Amarillo (Texas) Art League soliciting a display of my collection in Amarillo. I replied that we were booked ahead but that we might be able to engage with Amarillo later in the season; Subsequently, I wrote her that I would suggest giving the display after I had completed an engagement with the Duluth Art League in October. She complained of their not having much money to pay for a loan of pictures but that they would pay express charges, local gallery expenses, and would give a tea.

By way of encouraging what I thought to be a body of women struggling in the cause of art, I volunteered to pay the express charges and our personal expenses and give a couple of lectures. Consequently, the pictures, including some twenty works by contemporary artists, which I own, were shipped to Amarillo.

Advance publicity was ample. The reception was attended by all the women in town. The pictures elicited much favorable comment. It proved an event. People declared they had never seen such a show.

The Art Association had a president, vice-president, secretary, treasurer, and board of directors; but I never saw more than three or four women who had anything to do with the institution. One of these seemed to be the leader. She directed all the president's activities, at least she said so. The other ladies merely sat and looked on and nodded assent to whatever the leader suggested.

A night or two after the opening of the show, a man and his wife came in who wished to have their portraits painted. Before the pictures were finished, another order followed. Each patron, however wealthy—and all were spoken of as millionaires—was determined to make his bargain and would set a price above which "he would not go." This seemed to be the Amarillo custom.

One evening the wealthiest man in the Amarillo section came into my room with his daughter-in-law to get a "wholesale price" he said on six portraits. I had heard of this man. It was said that he had more cattle on his several ranches than any other cattle raiser in the world and that one of his tracts of land extended for ninety miles in one direction; also that he had many oil wells. Cattle were bringing top prices then; yet he wanted wholesale prices on three pairs of portraits of himself and his wife.

At once I saw as in a dream my canceled debts. I said, "My dear Mr. —, since you are such a handsome man, and having heard your wife is very beautiful, I will cut my retail price for you right in the middle," naming the amount. He looked at me with a sphinxlike stare. His was a face over which varying emotions played no more than on the Satanic gargoyles of Milan Cathedral. He neither blushed nor whitened nor twitched a hint of disdain or look of surprise but rose and walked out of the door saying, "I'll see you again."

After I waited several days for him to appear, a man who knew him advised me to go to him about the matter. Time was fast approaching when I simply had to have some money. If I could only get his order, I could arrange with my banker to take care of my real estate troubles, so I went to his office. I waited quite a while before I could see him.

As I entered, he gave me a vacant stare. He neither rose, nor asked me to be seated, nor did he address me. Using my accustomed brevity, I broached the subject at once and began to discuss my "wholesale price" of portraits.

"Well," he said, "I expected not to have to pay more than $—," naming a sum so ridiculously low that I was disgusted. I rose, picked up my hat, and was about to leave. I hesitated and thought to try a little commonsense argument. He listened with that same inexplicable look. I mentioned the much higher prices he would have to pay in New York besides the trouble of having to go there for sittings, to all of which he listened without moving a muscle

Perceiving that I was getting nowhere, I wavered, and finally offered to make a reduction below my "wholesale price," frankly saying I would not accept the offer he had made. For some time neither of us spoke. At last he said, "Well, I'll call you up tomorrow."

Two, three, four days passed. I decided to end it one way or the other by going to see him again. I knew his family wanted the pictures for his daughter-in-law came in twice to know what progress I was making with his portrait.

He had not "closed the door" as diplomats say, so I felt that I could with full self-respect renew the negotiations. I called at his house in the evening and found him alone. He took me into a backroom and closed the door. Seated by the fire he opened the subject himself "I never buy anything except at a bargain and I must have a decent price or nothing doing. I'll give you $— and no more."

I saw there was nothing more to be said, so I rose to go. Above the mantel was a large portrait in oil of a Texas steer, a longhorn. It was a horrible daub. He called my attention to it. "I only had to pay fifty dollars for it," he said.

"Well," said I, "that was one time when you did not get a bargain."

"Did you ever paint cattle?" he asked.

"Yes," I answered, "in my early career I painted a great many cattle pieces."

"I suppose your price for a herd of cows would be pretty steep," he said. I replied that it surely would.

We drifted momentarily back to the subject of the portraits, and I began to figure mentally that the amount of his offer, humiliating as it was, would just about save my real estate. I questioned what the effect of the reduction would have on my other patrons and he volunteered secrecy, condescendingly saying, "I'll give you a gentleman's agreement that no one but ourselves shall ever know the price." Then I wilted like a whipped dog. The heart for the work was taken out of me.

Returning to the hotel, I pondered over the situation. My resentment was at high pitch. That primitive instinct lying within the nature of every man who has made a measurable success of his life prompted better thoughts. I went to sleep determined to cancel the whole arrangement. Sleep cooled my heated brain and when morning came more reasonable thoughts prevailed. When my secretary came in, we discussed the case. She urged me to go on with the work saying we would soon leave that part of the country and it would be easy to forget the humiliation in the realization that I had redeemed my lots that proved such a good investment. The work of completing the man's picture proved tantalizing. His sphinxlike face and manner reminded me of a sketch I once made of a jumbo bullfrog that I caught in the shade of some weeds where he thought he was securely hidden and lay watching me, never even blinking an eye while I worked.

I tried to interest the man, tried to flash some animation across his stony visage. I spoke of the wonderful progress of culture during the last thirty years and of its reflection in the arts in our country. The only answer to my statements was a shade of quizzical curiosity in the staring eyes. The tight-set lips remained the same. After I had prophesied a glorious future for art in this country when men would come to know that art is quite as valuable to the human race as cotton and pork, my sitter ventured to say, "But I guess people don't buy many pictures. They cost too much."

"The cuss!" I said to myself. "I'll give him something to think about."

I reviewed the millions and millions spent by cultured rich men annually, the vast bequests to art museums and schools, the great private collections being formed, and the fabulous prices paid for pictures, especially portraits, running into hundreds of thousands of dollars each.

"The million-dollar portrait has arrived," I said. "The greatest drawback in the progress of culture is the attitude of so many wealthy men who are entirely indifferent to the cultural and"—a knock at the door—a caller to see my subject on business. My work and my eloquent speech were ended.

As the portrait was about completed, I dismissed the cowman to calm my agitated nerves. I was surprised next day to learn that he had left town, without notice, for a prolonged visit to his ranches. I sent the pictures to his home with the bill and later received a check for them. A week or two later, the newspapers announced his sudden death from heart trouble. I thought of the words of Holy Writ: "Thou fool! This night thy soul shall be required of thee and then whose shall all these things be?"

Several days later, the committee of the Amarillo Art Association called and said their treasury was completely exhausted, intimating that since I was enjoying a whirlwind of business they felt that I might be willing to pay them a liberal commission on all the orders I had received in town. Of course, I was surprised. I thought that as I had given them a painting and born all the expenses of the display, I was doing more than we had agreed upon and told them so.

They called again the next day. This time they demanded a commission on every order I had received. I evaded their demands as best I could. An ugly spirit began to develop in the contention and all the ladies began talking at the same time.

When a man tries to talk down four glib women, he invariably proves a failure, and discretion dictates that he beat a retreat. But in this case, it would never have done for me to have absented myself from the general powwow. Because of defective hearing it was impossible for me to distinguish one word from another in the hum of piping voices. In a frantic moment I said, "Well, ladies, since you all persist in talking at the same time, I must discontinue any further discussion of the subject. If one of you will talk at a time I will try to listen."

At this remark the eyes of the aforesaid leader flashed resentment, which was reinforced by the glances of the balance of the group. They rose to their feet and started toward the door. My secretary, who stood close by and had been listening, overheard the leader say, "We will just make him pay us a good stiff commission on every order he has taken."

That afternoon an attorney-at-law employed by the Art Association came to see me to present their demands. He frankly admitted they had no legal claim as they declared I had never agreed to pay them a commission on orders taken.

"Then how can they collect?" I asked. "I doubt if they can," he replied, "but they can make you a lot of trouble by obtaining a writ of attachment, which will tie up your pictures and keep you here until the case can be heard in court. It will involve the expense of a lawsuit and cause you lots of trouble and loss of time, and I would advise you to effect a settlement with them."

He was extremely apologetic, expressing regret that a man of my standing should be placed in such an embarrassing position.

"Your misfortune, Mr. Brewer, is that you are dealing with a body of women who have set their minds on getting something for their treasury and you cannot reason with them." This appeared like nice legal advice and I saw that there was nothing to do but yield to demands so I got a settlement agreement and wrote him a check.

This man's bearing was one of affable determination. I do not know if he carried a gun then or not as he did at a later date when he shot his son-in-law who had secretly married his daughter. The son-in-law went to his office one day to confess and obtain fatherly pardon when the father-in-law shot him dead. The criminal went to prison to await trial. Through technicalitics of law and the powerful influence of his profession he was acquitted of a most dastardly murder.

* * *

The night before the presidential election a great political rally was staged by the Democrats in the Amarillo auditorium. Excitement was running high in Texas although we heard little of the Republicans in Amarillo. Hoover Democrats were plentiful in the Lone Star State elsewhere. My secretary and I went to the auditorium to listen to assurances that Al Smith was going to be swept into the White House by a big majority the next day. There were several speakers on the stage including three women. We were seated well up on front. A woman came out of a side hallway leading from the stage and beckoned me toward her. Back of the wings I was told by two gentlemen that I was wanted to tell the audience why I had been a backslider from Republicanism. I protested that I had never made a political speech in my life. Protests meant nothing to them. They took me by the arms and dragged me out to a seat with the orators.

One of the speakers was a lady possibly sixty years of age, though guessing a woman's age at first sight is uncertain. Her gown, unlike the current style, was nearly down to her ankles. The upper part, collar, and sleeves were in the fashion of twenty years ago. Scanty gray hair was drawn back tightly into a Grecian knot. She was tall and very thin. Expecting to be the next on the program, she fidgeted about nervously. When she arose to speak a high-pitched, piping voice carried over the vast audience. At first, she halted as if breaking down, then recovered quickly, never losing her train of thought and never using the wrong word. As she progressed she had the audience with her and at times the applause was deafening, especially when she used her sleeve for a handkerchief. Her arguments were clear and forceful. She declared herself a Baptist. Her combat of the ministers and bigots in their war on the Catholics showed her broadminded justice. When she sat down, they called for more, and the applause died slowly.

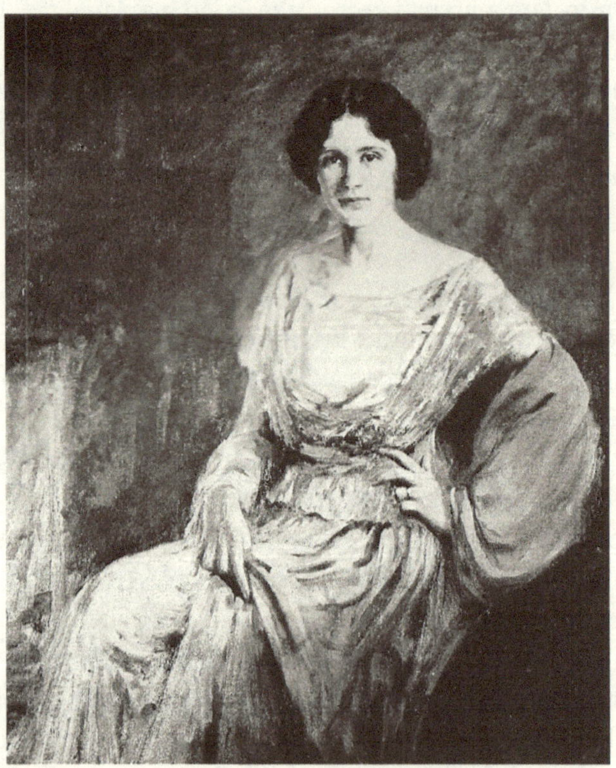

Mrs. Elizabeth Jordan Gilliland

I was then introduced as the most famous artist in the world. I was also acclaimed famous for having discovered that Republicanism was rotten and that, at last, light had come to my wonderful soul and I was going to tell them why and how! Of course, I was wholly unprepared, but an audience, an occasion, and a subject like that, were really inspiring.

I started by telling them a story I once heard of an Irishman who boasted of a meritorious act in converting a Jew. One day as he was about to pull Ikie out of the water by the hair to save him from drowning, Pat demanded, "Do you believe in Jesus Christ?"

"No," said Ikie, so Pat soused him down again. He pulled him up and asked him a second time.

"Yes," said Ikie, spitting out water. Then Pat put him down and held him under the water for fear he'd become a backslider.

"Well, I am a backslider, and I am here tonight because no one held me under," I said.

I was just getting warmed up telling the "why's" when the chairman pulled my coat tail and choked me off. He said Al Smith was about to deliver his famous speech over the radio. My wife wrote me later that she knew why Al Smith was defeated. She had heard about my speech!

* * *

Gene Howe is owner and editor of the *Amarillo Globe-News*.

Before we left Amarillo, Mr. Howe came to see me about painting the portrait of his father, Ed Howe, who lives in Atchison, Kansas. The father was spending the winter in Florida, but it was arranged that I go through Atchison on my way north in May or June and deliver Gene's request that the Sage of Potato Hill give me a sitting for the picture.

Everybody knew Ed Howe, not only for his splendid books on travel and other subjects, but especially for his autobiography, *Plain People*, which had recently appeared in book form after running serially in the Saturday Evening Post.

The eminent writer received me cordially. A well-preserved man at seventy-six, he reminded me greatly of Joseph Jefferson. Smooth faced, about the same build, alert in his movements and sprightly in conversation. On being acquainted with the object of my visit, he demurred at the idea of sitting for his portrait, but when I told him that his son earnestly desired to have the portrait, he acquiesced, saying, "Gene is a good boy and I love him, and for his sake I think I will do it."

In our conversation I referred to Gene's recently published scathing comment on the art of Mary Garden and the Chicago Grand Opera incident in Amarillo, which has been so widely spread abroad by the Associated Press. "Well, what does Gene know about art, anyway?" he commented. "You know as well as I, he has a woman reporter, whose opinion he reflects, and you know how little the average reporter knows. I have always had music in me. I feel it and have heard so much of the best that I think I could write a half intelligent comment—but Gene, never! He is mighty clever, though, in other ways."

That afternoon I started the portrait at my room in the hotel. Howe conversed continually during the sittings. At the finish of my work, he insisted that the right eye was entirely too small, but his delightful niece, who was present during most of the time, protested any change and declared that his eyes were by no means alike in size. I made no change, and he finally accepted our judgment.

In our arrangement, Gene insisted on my pleasing his father in the matter of the likeness and if I failed to do so, he would not be obliged to accept the picture. I took the portrait with me to do some final work on it, and then sent it to Gene at Amarillo. Gene wrote me the following letter:

> Dear Mr. Brewer:
>
> I received the portrait you painted of father and have sent it to Atchison for his approval. In my opinion, it is a striking likeness of him and it pleases me very much, but, as I explained to you, he is the one who has the final say, and when I hear from him as to whether he approves it, I will send you a check.
>
> If Father likes it, we will hang it in the Globe office at Atchison.
>
> Yours truly,
>
> Gene Howe.

A day or two later I received this characteristic missive:

Dear Mr. Brewer:

The portrait has been hung in the Globe office and this is the universal verdict: From the nose up, perfect; below the nose, faulty.

Won't you come this way again and look at me below the nose and put in a speck here and there? The howling makes me nervous.

E. W. Howe.

Ed Howe said he is not an art critic; that he knew no more about it than his son Gene did, "which was damn little."

I wrote him I would stop on my next motor trip South and look at him "below the nose" and that I would satisfy the critics, very likely, by using a dry brush. All they want is to know that their criticisms have been noted, tabulated, and recognized as wisdom. In their minds, the picture needs correction about the mouth and when touched a little they fancy a change has taken place and are satisfied that they have enabled the artist to produce a great masterpiece.

In Howe's mind, the one and only purpose of a portrait is to produce an expression called "a likeness" that will please everybody who has never really looked at the shape of his mouth as the artist must; and mind you, the mouth of that versatile "Sage of Potato Hill" has no extraordinary quirk about it but is just plainly a moving picture. A portrait of anyone should primarily be the artist's reading of that person's character and an expression of what he sees there. As long as it is readily recognizable and measurably pleasing, the purpose, in so far as the likeness is concerned, has been served. All this talk about smiles or frowns or the age expressed is out of place. One moment there is a smile, another there is a scowl, then a look of surprise, of thought and a thousand other things, out of which the artist must choose what he considers most consistent in the depicting of human character.

In five years, Ed Howe will look very different from his portrait. In twenty years, the picture will be unrecognizable, and in a hundred years nobody will care about it unless it has those elements of art, which will command the respect of the REAL critics.

Chapter XXIV
Architecture

In the elder days of Art,
Builders wrought with greatest care
Each minute and unseen part;
For God sees everywhere.

—Henry W. Longfellow

You may travel the full length of the average residential street in any city and you will see scarcely one house you would look at a second time for its architectural beauty, but you will find a thousand monstrosities, buildings much uglier than the tepee of the aborigines; in fact, the primitive man, in his natural way, is more artistic than we are.

The pioneers hacked down trees and cleared fields to grow crops. They split the trees into rails, which they piled up on zigzag fashion to make the snake fence. To hold the top rider in place, they drove long stakes at each joint, allowing them to stick up above the rail like the horns of a caterpillar. Neither rails nor fence had a straight line in them. Then they built cabins of logs, filling the chinks with mortar to keep the cabins warm. A large fireplace of stone or adobe bricks was built, and the broad chimney outside broke the square surface of the cabin. They split shingles two feet long and eight inches wide and when laid they were nearly as handsome as Spanish tiles. Seen on a hillside against a forest of stately trees, with other sheds, a grain stack or corn shocks, these cabins make a picture. I love to look at those mute remains of pioneer days.

Then our forefathers developed sawmills and plaining mills to make the straight posts and weather boards. Later came plastering, and glass for the windows. Everywhere were straight, long lines, the effect of the machine. Now practically everything we use is made by machinery—our shoes, food, clothes, tacks, and lip sticks. The hen is the only remaining naturalist; she absolutely refuses to use machinery in the manufacture of our breakfast fry. Even the spade is becoming obsolete. Only the backwoodsman recognizes the axe, and fewer people know how to handle it.

But many men can now better estimate the distance between the earth and the sun—or lecture to us on evolution. The world is humming with machinery and labor-saving devices, with the consequence that craftsmanship is vanishing.

The main purpose of the ancient guilds was skilled workmanship, many of the great creative artists developing therefrom. Today, art is seldom considered by the factories; the quicker and cheaper a thing can be joined or carved, the more money there is in it. Money to a mad nation is like oats to a racehorse—a spur for more money-action, more greed.

At one of the ruined missions near San Antonio there still remain specimens of stone carving that challenge the admiration of the world. It is said that a young cutter was sent from Spain to carve and decorate the facade of the Church and that he spent eighteen years in stone-labor on that one building. The elaborate front with numerous pedestaled statues of saints, magnificent doorways and windows, gargoyles and cherubs, apart from the historical interest of the place, forms the attraction to tens of thousands who visit the mission annually. One of the windows was removed intact with its heavy masonry, crated, and sent to one of our World's Fairs, where it was declared by architects to be one of the most beautiful specimens of architecture in America. An artist on visiting the place was heard to say, "It is marvelous what a faith will cause men to do!"

Today we have stone made by machinery with perfect uniformity of design and ornament but lacking the human touch. It cries aloud in its stereotyped sameness. Art has no place in a building though its top story pierces the clouds when the basic question has been how cheaply can it be built for the returns it will bring on the investment.

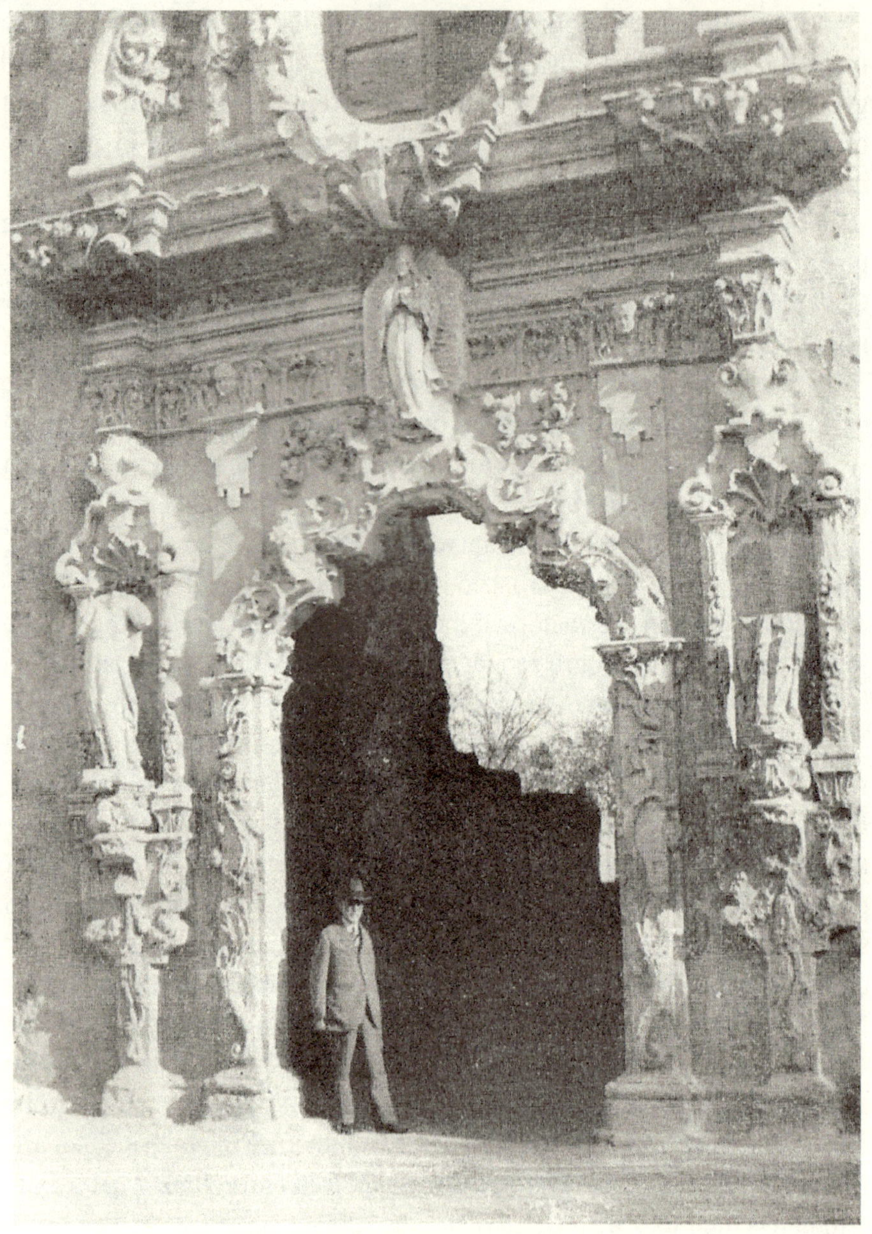

The Broken Portal of San Jose, the most beautiful ruin in America.

Many people rail at the idea of spending a great deal of money in building beautiful churches. Why not donate that money directly to charity instead? They do not realize that the raw material used in church construction was worth comparatively little before human labor gave it its value—the marble in the quarry, the wood in the tree, the iron deep in the bowels of the earth, the glass only grains of sand. Human hands shaped it all and put it together. The building has been a medium of distribution of the money, mainly of the rich and well-to-do, among wage earners. What a blessing if in this 1930 economic depression when millions are crying for work the millionaire and the billionaire would offer more of their vast holdings toward the creation of imperishable things of beauty for edification and example to succeeding generations.

On the subject of church building Dr. Fosdick says: "If we did not do this, the lover of his fellow men, who feels the tragedy of unemployment, the agonies of poverty, the need of agencies that minister to the broken bodies and minds of men, and who sees millions of dollars put into a gorgeous church graven and beautiful with stone and glass, would have the right to protest.

"I was a young man before I saw my first cathedral. The impression of that hour has never left me. Caught off my guard by its unexpected loveliness, I was surprised into unbidden tears. Beauty does something to you. Here in this mechanized city, we need what beauty can do to us, especially when it is directed to spiritual ends."

But much more can be said for the purpose and the source of inspiration that called the world's great cathedrals into being. They are not the offspring of one mind, one architect. They represent the creative force of centuries of men. They express the ideals, the faith of multitudes that strove to erect an enduring monument to their living God. To this end, no labor was too hard, no sacrifice too great. In olden days, the young man's ambition was to acquire rare skill in order that he might dedicate his art to the building of great cathedrals. The artist did not sign his name to his work nor work for personal fame. He did not care if his merits were merged with those of the many so long as he wrought well and to the honor of the Deity.

The architect built his great heart into these
sculptured stones,
And with him toiled his children, and their
lives

Were builded, with his own, into the walls,
As offerings unto God.
—Henry W. Longfellow

It was art inspired by lofty ideals that created those marvelous monuments of another period, the ages of faith. And it was faith and the spirit of worship that gave birth to Gothic architecture. Many artists have declared that Gothic architecture never has been and never will be equaled.

The main purpose of architecture is its usefulness. It may be ornate or plain, but it ends with the purpose for which it was created. Over and above all other styles, Gothic is preeminent in that its purpose, which is worship, is expressed in its clustered columns, its pointed arches, its pinnacles, and spires pointing to the sky, bidding man to raise his thoughts to the eternal, the everlasting.

Dr. Fosdick, in speaking of the beauty of his church, referred to what beauty does to us and the church's usefulness as a center of religious activities. He did not speak of that one transcendent thing in Gothic architecture—its spirituality, its soul.

America, while leading in many of the sciences and mechanical discoveries, has been a borrower of art. As the Greeks borrowed from the Egyptians and the Romans from the Greeks, so we have borrowed from all Europe. The Pilgrims brought no art with them to our shores, and left no monuments of art. Their minds were of a different cast. In Newport there is an ancient tower with origin unknown. Many scholars think it antedates the landing at Plymouth Rock, perhaps built by the Norsemen centuries before.

On the contrary the Spaniards brought to New Spain their art. The padres knew well the usefulness of art in their religious propaganda. The ancient Church has ever held that art and beauty are the handmaidens of religion. One can understand that the peal of the mission bells told the aborigines there was something beautiful in the white man's religion.

In San Antonio the note of the same Angelus bell that floated on the air seventy years before the Liberty Bell was cast, before Washington was born, still carries its message to the faithful and the unfaithful alike. Everywhere in Mexico, California, Texas, and wherever the Spaniards planted the cross they left their art. Much of it is gorgeous and beautiful, and its influence is still felt in our modern buildings, ecclesiastical, civic, and domestic.

Colonial architecture, found at its best in the Southeastern part of the States, is perhaps the nearest to an original type; yet traces of its ancestry also extend across the seas.

There was a time in the development of our great country when architecture degenerated into hideous discord. Everywhere we can see the remains of that cheap, gingerbread, wooden ornamentation, smothering every other idea and making many of our new, rapidly growing towns bedlams of ugliness.

An outstanding example of that period, which I have mentioned in a previous chapter, is found west of Van Ness Avenue in San Francisco, where they stopped the great conflagration. I repeat that it would have been better if these old buildings had burned.

I know a lady in St. Paul who bought a house of this type because the location and rooms suited her. Then with ladders and axes she set men to work smashing off the gingerbread ornaments. When finished, her house was much improved.

In the last thirty or forty years, however, our architecture has made wondrous strides toward recovery and real development. Modern radicalism has not yet shown its blighting hand in architecture, except spasmodically, as it has in the other arts. Perhaps it does not adapt itself so easily to such contortions, wild goose rhythm, or lack of balance. Many of the new buildings of today are marvelous improvements over those of bygone times and bode a glorious future for America's architecture. While government architecture, since the best period of colonial development, has been neither good nor bad, it has had its high lights of notably fine examples. Our domestic types between 1830 and 1880 can be called nothing less than deplorable.

But looking back at the beginning of the present-day renaissance and contrasting our recent development in domestic, commercial, and ecclesiastical buildings with what has gone before, one is amazed at the speed of our strides toward a more distinctive type.

The late Leon Bakst said during his recent visit to America:

"It is this dare-devil originality which has made the one art which is America's specific contribution to the art of our century something superb and unique which the world has never seen and but for America may never have seen—I mean American architecture."

Architecture, like the other arts, must draw from the developments of the past. Yet we have no distinct American background to speak of to furnish our architects materials that may be embodied into plans fitting the new requirements of modern life. Our rapidly changing domestic and economic conditions call for new designs that tax the skill of the architect and make more uncertain the coming day of a glorious national architecture. As to the skyscrapers, most of our examples are as yet but practical piles of brick and steel with a decided capitalistic twang, although a few exalted examples seem to bode the coming of an American type that may yet be classed as monumental.

Gazing up at a fifty-story office building with a thousand windows, one like the other, each one emitting light into an office that rents for a certain amount of money, one receives an impression of commercialized architecture difficult to endow with artistic beauty. Contrast this example, if you please, with one gleaned from the facade of an ancient Gothic cathedral, and then say which you think the greater as creative art. Suffice it to say, however, that our past achievements and national genius point to a growth that will be "The glory that was Greece, the grandeur that was Rome."

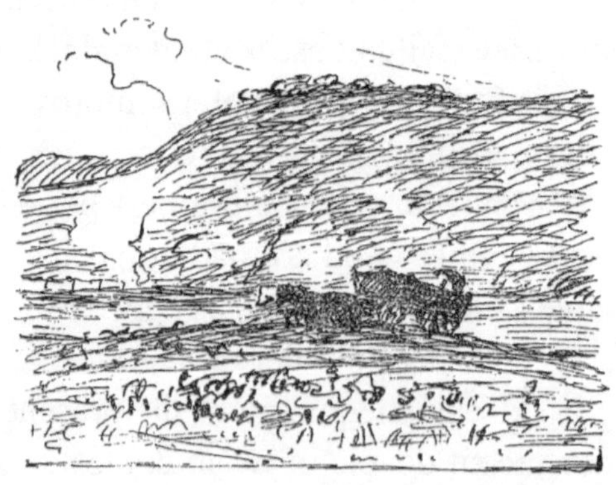

Chapter XXV

The Growth of Art in America

> Art follows only in the wake of material development. America is awakening to an appreciation of beauty; pari passu should grow a renaissance of the fine arts. This was true of Greece in the age of Pericles, of Rome in the age of Augustus Caesar, of Italy in the days of the Medici, when at the height of her prosperity. America is in the midst of her renaissance.
>
> —*Charles H. Brough*

In the great Middle West sturdy and enterprising men and women have been engaged in building an inland empire of wealth; a material world that in time will grow beautiful when enlivened by the spirit of art. This vast empire has nearly been built. Frontiers are no more, and the traveler from his car window sees over the thousands of miles of fertile fields growing towns and cities bustling with active human life. He realizes that this is a land of promise. Here the corporal needs of mankind have been fulfilled lavishly in reward for toil; and here is the base and the foundation for an intellectual and spiritual growth that bodes well for the future of the arts.

To one who observed midwestern conditions of the early seventies, when Chicago was regarded as the end of the trail, the change seems marvelous indeed! Today great universities thoroughly equipped in every department of learning, and countless voluntary social organizations for aesthetic development are preparing the coming generation for a fuller appreciation of art in all its forms.

In the brief span since the passing of the bison, the great art museums of Chicago, St. Louis, Minneapolis, Detroit, Indianapolis, Toledo, Cleveland, Cincinnati, Pittsburgh, and Buffalo have come into existence. All over the land are privately owned art collections representing the expenditure of millions upon millions of dollars. Art leagues and schools impart instructions in many of the larger cities, enabling the student to get his art education near home. No longer are Paris and Munich the mecca for technical training. There is a spirit in America, bred of material prosperity and liberal opportunities for education, that stimulates the growth of art. Material well-being has first to be acquired, and then with consequent leisure and reflection, yearnings for cultural things are indulged.

A brief review of the gifts and bequests of public-spirited American citizens to art centers, published in the American Art Annual, reads almost like a fairy tale. California received as a bequest from Mr. Henry E. Huntington his collection of works of art valued at fifty million dollars, together with a fund of eight million for maintenance. In his collection are Gainsborough's *Blue Boy*, acquired for approximately two hundred thousand dollars, and Lawrence's *Pinky*, for three hundred eighty-eight thousand five hundred dollars. That gallery was opened to the public in October 1928.

The Toledo Museum of Art received by the will of Edward D. Libby twenty million dollars in 1928. The Institute of Fine Arts, Cincinnati, received two million seven hundred five thousand in a drive to secure two and one-half million to meet the condition under which Mr. and Mrs. Charles P. Taft gave their home, one million dollars in cash, and a collection valued at three to five million dollars. The sum was contributed by nearly four thousand individuals. The will of the late Mr. Emery bequeathed to the Cincinnati Art Museum the famous Edgecliff collection valued between three and five million dollars.

The building fund for the proposed Nelson Art Gallery of Kansas City was further increased by a bequest from the late Irwin R. Kirkwood, editor of the Kansas City Star. A fund of six hundred fifty thousand dollars also became available to Kansas City during the year for the purchase of the museum site by the will of the late Mrs. Mary Atkins.

Mr. Edwin S. Balch of Philadelphia bequeathed two million dollars to that city to build a museum to house his art collection, which was also left to the city.

The Cincinnati Art Museum received one hundred thousand dollars from Miss Mary Hanna for an addition to its building. During the same year, the University of Chicago received a gift of one million dollars from Mr. Max Epstein, art patron and philanthropist for the establishment of an art center. The sum of five million dollars was subscribed as part of the preliminary cost of ten million dollars to Chicago's Century of Progress for 1933. Included in the plan is an international exhibition of art to be assembled.

An art collection valued at several million dollars was presented to the National Gallery of Art by Mr. John Gellatly of New York. The collection is especially rich in works by American artists. Director Holmes of the National Gallery in Washington informed me that the gallery is offered annually from five to seven million dollars-worth of art works by public-spirited citizens, which cannot be accepted for lack of building space. These are only a part of the donations to the cause of art throughout the country in a single year.

This subject should not be left without mention of the great collectors who have formed galleries of priceless works and who finally bequeathed these collections to various art museums and the National Gallery at Washington. The high value of these aggregations of works has been determined by the taste and discretion displayed by those whose munificence has already contributed so much to the stimulus of taste throughout the country. There was a time within the memory of the writer when the works of our American artists went begging for patronage. About 1880 interest began to be manifested by a few collectors—Evans, Hearn, Freer, and others, in the creations of our outstanding native painters. Dealers are slow in handling the works of artists who are not widely known and in public demand. Consequently, the pictures of some of our best artists were ignored by the dealers, and the American buyers bought only foreign art. They stressed the Barbizon and Dutch schools, which were exploited far and wide. Later there arose a group of buyers who realized the value and merits of American art and bought liberally.

Many of these paintings have already found a permanent home and are open to public view. Notable among them is the collection of the late Mr. Freer, which is now the property of the nation and housed at the expense of the donor in a magnificent gallery on the Smithsonian grounds. Here we find grouped individually the works of Tryon, Thayer, Dewing, Whistler, and others.

Aside from a few collectors who prided themselves on owning only works of the great foreign masters, most of the late collectors have been more catholic in their selections and have hung the great foreign works side by side with those of Inness, Wyant, Blakelock, Martin, Tryon, and the later masters; even many others whose reputations have not yet been subjected to the test of time.

With few exceptions, these collections in the course of time are either dispersed under the hammer or donated collectively for the cultural interests of the people. We have reviewed the vast donations of such men as Huntington, Taft, Libby, Balch, Kirkwood, Dunwoody, and hosts of others who have so left their priceless treasures that they have become the property of the people. All praise is due to the magnanimity of these promoters of culture who have contributed so largely to the potential glory of American art.

From Henry Rankin Poore in *What Europe Thinks of American Art*, published by the National Arts Club, New York, I wish to quote authorities of all major countries:

"Constant struck a clarion tone which rang out with no uncertain sound at a dinner given to the masters of Paris by the American Art Association of Paris, a pronouncement, which was received with a slight wave of incredulity by Parisians and Americans alike. It was in 1891 that he prophesied, 'In fifty years the center of the world's art will be America, probably in Chicago.' Forty years have elapsed; there are ten in which to turn prophecy into fact. An initial step was taken some years ago when the Collectors' Association of America arranged an exhibition of foreign and American art so hung that every other canvas was native or foreign. The even quality of this display was frankly conceded by every collector of exclusively foreign paintings....

"Said Laura Knight, one of England's most virile painters, a member of an International jury at Pittsburgh: 'I am amazed at American

Art. I had no idea of its scope. I am going home to tell my people about it and what it signifies in the world's art.'

"In an editorial from 'Il Giornale d'Italia,' upon the International Exposition at Rome, entitled 'The Strong Peoples', the writer says: 'When coming out of the rooms of the American pavilion, you have the feeling of respect imposed by respectable persons. It is an honest people producing honest art. It is a strong people producing calm art. It is a people seeing its aim and knowing how to reach it without artificial exaltations. It is the triumph of good government reflected in art.'

"'La Vita' of Rome declares 'North American Art has a strong characteristic of its own. It is a sane and solid art. These works are rendered by the American artists with manly and noble exuberance; in no wise by nervous, exalted, or sick people. They are the kind of people who use the brush with the same dexterity as the oar.'

"Henri Matisse, having viewed a few of our museums remarked, 'An American artist should learn his *metier*, develop his faculties and work in America. He can learn it in New York, as well as anywhere in the world; better in some respects. Consider how much fresher are the subjects for a painter in this country, the scenery, the architecture, the people. Let him go to Paris for occasional visits but an American artist should express America.'

"Said the late Sorolla, while visiting this country, 'I realize, as I look about me, that in several points I am outclassed by what I frequently encounter here.'

"The recent exhibition of American Art at Budapest elicited the following comments: 'America today has in nearly every respect a peculiar significance different from any other and is characterized in everything by the superiority of wealth and the courageous clan of youth. It has the force and courage of initiative with all the requirements for taking the lead, and its aptitude provides an individual type in the society of men and a new era in history in which it is first among all nations today and will be even more so tomorrow and the day after tomorrow.'—*Nemzetiujsag*

"'In one word, the art of modern America may look to a great future. Its development is even more astounding and, apart from the great number of artists of foreign origin, it has an excellent staff of artists of purely American antecedents.'"

* * *

"'The art of the United States is just as young, healthy, and realistic as the huge country itself. Though it derives most of its artistic impulse from Europe, its young and marvelously developing culture is not affected by the spiritual crisis of the old continent. America's art is based on visible reality.

"'Both painting and sculpture are under the influence of a conservative and realistic spirit. Their technical ability is impeccable, be it plain air impressionism or the result of form and coloring within a studio. Their correctness may serve as an example to our painters who, after giving the outlines of their more interesting and more individual visions, are on a larger scale. This is the difference between Hungarian temperament and American accomplishment.'" —*Budapest Review*

"From Stockholm we hear this: 'The artists who present American art to us in this interesting exhibition are closely united with the aspirations and sentiments of the community of art to which our best also belong, from which they started and to which they return. In their works, we discover beauties, which deeply affect us as they remind us of our good artists and of what is similar in the artistic development of good art in all countries.'—*Pester Lloyd*

"'The artistic life of America, its production and the appreciation of its works has reached a very high level, especially since the war. Not only its authors, theatres, and films often greatly surpass the best European production; the painters and sculptors, too, have reached the foremost ranks. The new generation of artists of America has not only learned much, especially at Paris, but became originally linked to the exceptionally quick development of American art; they speed along the old road. It is a real pleasure to walk past their well-balanced works and to drown one's self in the special beauty of their portraits and landscapes.—*Magyarsag*

"From Minister Lindskog, opening the American Exhibition at Stockholm, March 15th, 1930: 'I express a strong hope that from the American art, which we shall see here, at once both free and rich, free from the sometimes too burdensome traditions, rich in mighty concepts from a proud and independent culture, will come to our own art valuable impulses and enduring profit.'

"Under the caption 'U.S.A. is more highly developed culturally than is generally believed,' the critic of the *Dagens Myheter* writes: 'I am convinced that this exhibition will give an entirely different conception of America from a cultural point of view than that which generally prevails in Europe . . . Now that the hanging of the Exhibition is finished, do we first get an impression of what a really imposing collection of representative art there has been sent from the other side of the Atlantic to Sweden. In America, the project has awakened the greatest interest, and it is possible that when the Exhibition closes in Stockholm, representatives from other European countries wishing to borrow the beautiful collection will meet with a favorable response.'

"Another review states: 'It is a collection that demands time and more time, it is so comprehensive, so varied, so rich in style, in periods, and artistic personality and understanding.'

"'There can be no doubt that the American exhibition, which opens today with proper solemnity in the Academy of Art, is one of the great events in the art life of Stockholm in recent years. After a first view of the well-arranged exhibition, one gets a feeling, which I presume he who comes to New York for the first time also gets, a feeling of something new, richly faceted, and bewildering. But an appetite has been awakened and a wish to know all about this thing of which we get an idea, and which is so different from the, somewhat stagnated, art within our own horizon. We come to a great banquet, become shy and confused before so many strangers, but little by little we joyfully meet acquaintances.—'(*Carl Asplund* from *Svenska Dagbladet*)"

These quotations are published by the National Arts Club.

* * *

A few years ago, Mr. Edgar B. Davis of San Antonio inaugurated an annual exhibition of paintings representing the wildflowers, cotton fields, and ranch life of Texas. He offered large prizes available to two classes of contestants—national and state. The magnitude of the prizes and the publicity given to the movement inspired a most pronounced interest, not only to the artists and students of the Lone Star State, but throughout the whole country. Many artists of the East, as well as of California, Arizona, and New Mexico, entered the contest, which made the displays notable in point of merit. But the happiest result, perhaps, was that it brought home to the common people of the South the importance of art in the community. The prizewinning pictures were displayed in most of the larger towns of Texas, also New York. Among these pictures appears Adrian Brewer's twenty-five-hundred-dollar prize picture, *In a Bluebonnet Year*, and my *Cotton Harvest* that won a twelve hundred and fifty-dollar prize the following year. In 1929 the cash prizes given by Mr. Davis aggregated thirty-four thousand dollars.

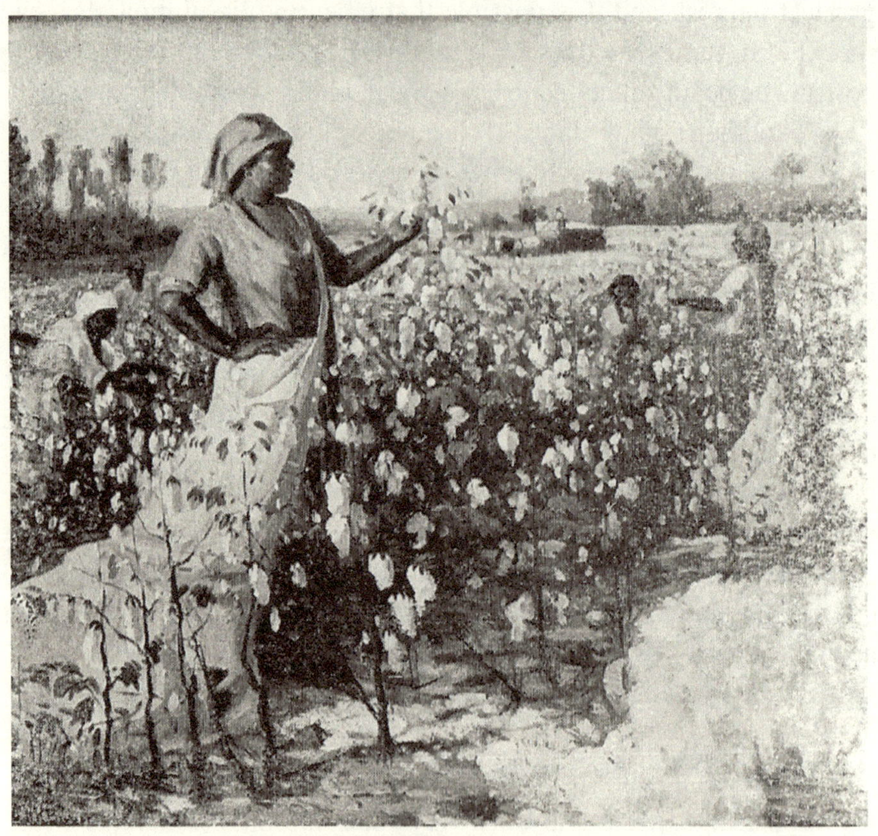

The Cotton Harvest, Edgar B. Davis Prize, Courtesy Witte Memorial.

The Rocky Mountains and the Sierra Nevadas no longer divide that endless producing region from the shining lakes of the North to the billowing gulf on the South—the great Middle West—from that wondrous land of promise, the Pacific Coast. Nowhere can there be found such an aggregation of commonwealths of modern structure, so young, so youthful in new enterprises, so yearning for the finer things of life, so proud of their history and their achievements as California and the bordering states of the coast. Here the artist finds everything to satisfy his ambitions in the way of subject matter. Scenes unparalleled for beauty, whitecapped mountain ranges, blossoming orchards, foothill and meadows spangled with blue lupines, waves of wildflowers, and a rugged coast where the blue Pacific rolls in, placid or tempestuous, against rocks of picturesque grandeur.

Here is a land of wealth drawn both from her native soil and imported from the East. Her coast and foothills are dotted with the mansions of retired millionaires who have gone there from the less agreeable climates elsewhere. Millions made in the congested marts of the East are spent lavishly there, reacting upon the arts. Her growth has been marvelous. Little did the gold diggers of '49 dream that the gold they were carrying away would be returned a hundredfold, or that those barren, semiarid valleys that greeted their eyes would be transformed in a lifetime to endless fruiting orchards and gardens, yielding millions of carloads of fruit that are shipped East. Nowhere on earth has any country added a million in population to a single city in less than a score of years as has occurred in Los Angeles.

California has a group of strong painters whose pictures are seldom seen in Eastern Exhibitions. They seem satisfied with their own local shows and the patronage given them by patriotic people in their own state. Artists' colonies are scattered along that beautiful coast from Santiago to the Golden Gate. California is paving the way for a glorious future in art. We can visualize the time approaching when that land of beauty and poesy will rival the East as a center of creative art.

* * *

In answer to my question regarding art in America, Ignace Paderewski said, "There is no part of the world, Mr. Brewer, where art and taste have advanced so rapidly during the past thirty years as in America."

Another significant indication of the awakening of a wholesome sentiment, in relation to art in the commercial and industrial world, is the businessmen's art clubs in many cities. These clubs are formed of professional and businessmen for the purpose of actual art study in the open. Often have I seen groups of their members sauntering with their sketching kits to the woodlands in pursuit of subject matter, sometimes with an instructor, more often alone, where they set up their easels and paint with a rousing enthusiasm. Many find this combination of intellectual and physical diversion more fascinating and invigorating than golf or horseback riding. These clubs usually give annual exhibitions of their works, and it is surprising to note how meritorious are many of their productions. Many have not thought of this kind of amusement until they were past fifty or sixty years of age. Yet several outstanding names—Vezin, Butler, DeWolf, and many more—are a credit to the genii who can turn from habits of economic grind to the study of art. Some are born with all the innate elements necessary to become artists, but owing to adverse conditions in youth are diverted into more mundane channels in the struggle for a livelihood. They develop a business or professional character instead. They hanker for the work of the painter all along until they can lay aside the less agreeable occupation for the joys of the artist's work.

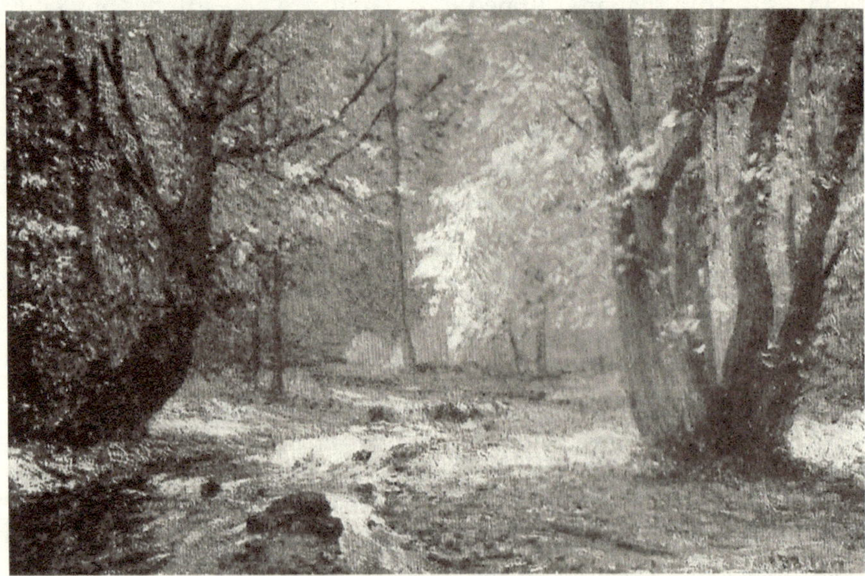

The Woodland Brook

It is a singular fact that women are not so heroic in indulging their tastes, considering that in later years they have had more leisure than men, and need not throw overboard altogether a life's occupation in order to do it. I have often suggested to women's art bodies that they organize sketching classes and pattern after the procedure of their brothers and have offered to help them in their endeavors. But they seem to lack the enthusiasm necessary to make a success of it.

Chapter XXVI

Washington, D. C.

The most interesting city in the United States to me is the Capitol of our nation with a population of more than 420,000. When the colonists landed at Jamestown the wildest figment of imagination could not have pictured what today confronts the traveler who wends his way from the remotest part of our vast national territory through populated plains and bustling cities to the center of our government, the beautiful city of Washington, named for the Father of his Country.

And Washington is yet in the making. If today one projects his imagination a hundred years ahead, it is likely he will be far from the mark as to what yet will be accomplished in the making of a city beautiful from an artistic and historical point of view.

History has been made in many parts of the new world but nowhere to the degree as in Washington. From the days of Thomas Jefferson down to the present time, the National Capitol has been the scene of world events, social and political triumphs, and heart-rending tragedies. The formation of a "Government of the people, for the people and by the people" that has stood the test of one hundred and fifty years, with a Constitution that challenges the admiration of statesmen of the whole world, is not likely soon to pass. Here was written the Emancipation Proclamation, and here the great Emancipator fell victim of an assassin's bullet. One reverently treads the steps leading to the modest bedchamber where Stanton, after laying down the lifeless head, exclaimed, "Now he belongs to the Ages."

The visitor wanders among the stately buildings—To the Lincoln Memorial and views Daniel French's masterpiece, the sculptured Lincoln. Then across the Potomac to beautiful Arlington Cemetery, once the home of General Robert E. Lee, the Tomb of the soldier "known only to God" and among the thousands of monuments commemorating America's loyal sons and daughters, her worthy dead.

During the Civil War, several battles were fought near Washington between the contending armies. Recently I painted a picture of "Old Stone Bridge" under which flows the waters of Bull Run, and over which the Rhode Island forces retreated towards Arlington after a disastrous defeat under command of my friend, the late Gov. William Sprague, which I have described in a previous chapter.

Over this bridge the forces of General Polk likewise retreated after the second battle of Manassas in 1862. It is not the mere fact that both armies passed over this bridge that makes it worthy of mention but its artistic stone arches, built to stand a thousand years, reflected in the amber colored waters, which to me seemed a subject worthy of good canvas and paint.

East of the Potomac River at what is now Georgia Avenue is the Battleground of National Cemetery. Here was repulsed the raid of the Confederates under Lieutenant General Jubal A. Early with 15,000 men who sought to take the Capitol, which was poorly defended, on July 12, 1864.

Major Edward R. Campbell, the last surviving veteran, who was a youth of 20 years when the battle was fought, tells this story:

"Me and the Old Vermont Brigade was fighting down at Petersburg, Virginia.

"On the evening of July 10, 1864, we got word that General Early had defeated General Wallace at the battle of the Monocacy and that old General Jubal Early and 15,000 Johnny Rebs were advancing on Washington.

"Lordy, but there was some excitement. We got out of Petersburg in an almighty hurry and marched 20 miles that night to City Point, on James River. A transport took us down the James and up the Potomac to Washington, where we arrived ready for action about 6:30 on the morning of July 12.

"President Lincoln met us personally. He told us that Johnny Reb was camped in the shadow of the Capitol. Citizens who weren't too scared, lined the street and cheered the Old Vermont Brigade as we marched up Seventh Street to Brightwood, where we deployed as skirmishers on the right flank of Fort Stevens.

"Minnie balls from sharpshooters were hitting all around and killing a few. Shells from light artillery were whining over our heads and kicking up dust in front of us.

"We waited for the order to advance. Other troops were brought up on our right. To our left was Fort Stevens. To the left of Stevens was a detachment from New York.

"There weren't any trees near the fort like there are now. I was watching the fort where cannons were blazing away. And there was President Lincoln. He was standing on the parapet, cool as could be. He was the only President of the United States to direct troops under fire. And I was mighty proud to be fighting for him that day.

"It was a mighty dangerous place for the President of the United States. A medical officer standing beside him threw up his hands and collapsed. A minnie ball from a sharpshooter cut him down.

"General Wright, in command of the fort, ran up and dragged the President of the United States right down off that parapet. He didn't care if Lincoln was the President, the Commander-in-Chief, or what—General Wright was in command of that fort and he knew he was supposed to protect the life of the President.

"Then came the command to advance. We did. And when we unfurled the pennants of the Old Vermont Brigade, General Early knew what he was up against and cleared out. He remembered us from the Battle of the Wilderness.

"Early left some sharpshooters in an old house (6404 Georgia Avenue, which still stands). They held us up for a minute or two, but we drove 'em out and continued to drive the Rebs for about another mile.

"I was in the party sent back to bury the dead. We picked them up from where they lay, scattered over the field—most of them killed by sharpshooters.

"We had about finished the job, and who do you suppose came driving up? It was Lincoln again.

"I'll always remember what Lincoln looked like and what he said. He looked sad. He didn't say anything for a minute. We all stopped working. Mr. Lincoln held up his hand and said, 'I dedicate this spot as the Battle Ground National Cemetery.'

"Then the President and his aides rode away.

"No, that wasn't the end of the war. We kept on fighting. We chased General Early for a couple of days on out through Rockville, Maryland, and Poolesville, and on to the Potomac River, where he crossed above Leesburg and escaped into Virginia."

* * *

In 1923 I received a request from the art committee of the Arts Club of Washington to give an exhibition of my paintings in their gallery. The Club now occupies and owns the spacious old building once owned and used by President Monroe as his home. The rooms are reminiscent of that period with large high ceilings; the same old board floors, walked on by distinguished men and fair women of that day. The drawing room is now an art gallery with hanging room for thirty or more paintings.

Entering the gallery one day I noticed an elderly man intently scrutinizing my paintings. An attendant introduced me to that able and highly respected artist, the late Dr. W. H. Holmes, Director of the National Gallery. Dr. Holmes was not only a splendid painter in both oil and watercolor but a man of various attainments. He had devoted many years to the study of natural history, geology, ethnology, and anthropology. He was elected a member of the National Academy of Science, which is the foremost scientific body in this country. Therefore, he was an efficient director of the National Museum, which also embraces the so-called National Gallery, although the word "gallery" is something of a misnomer since there are but six rooms that are used exclusively for paintings while along the halls and rotundas pictures are scattered, mingling with stuffed animals, quadrupeds, bipeds, boa constrictors, buffaloes, bears, beasts too numerous to name. It would take a year to see them all without trying to name them.

It would not be so difficult to name all the pictures or the artists in those few rooms, and that is all we Americans can point to as evidence of our national culture. Dr. Holmes and his co-laborers tried for twenty years to impress our Congressional lawmakers of the civic value of art to a nation and to secure an appropriation for a suitable art temple to house the treasures offered annually to the nation by retiring wealthy collectors who have been despoiling the galleries of the old world of priceless gems.

After living some time in Washington and coming in contact with many of the Members, one is forced to conclude that to most of these dignitaries the highest art is vote-getting and political intrigue, that quite a few could not tell you who Shakespeare or Phidias were, that they have never gone past the title pages of classic literature, and as for art—why, that is merely something to cover your walls or to amuse women and children. This governmental apathy weighed heavily upon the sensitive soul of Dr. Holmes to such an extent that he said he had lost all hope that America would ever be classed as a cultured nation. I saw him but a short time before his passing and when I asked about the prospect of having a gallery building he slumped in his chair and shaking his head said, "No, it will take a hundred years to educate those fellows on Capitol Hill and then we will not be here."

Yes, they appropriate billions without a blush but to appropriate fifteen million for an art gallery would cause them to gasp at "an unheard-of folly."

Chief Justice Hughes recently published a strong article maintaining that the Government should pay more attention to acquiring works of art and should erect a suitable building to house the numerous gifts in the way of rare and costly collections of art that are frequently offered to the nation. He said, "If we had such a building we would, in a few years, have a national gallery equaled by none."

* * *

In 1933 I received a commission to paint a portrait of Mr. Justice Willis Van Devanter of the Supreme Court. I had engaged a studio in the Corcoran Gallery of Art, which had a most excellent skylight. This room has been used by many famous artists. Some of the Presidents and many cabinet members have posed there for their portraits. Justice Van Devanter, far past his three score and ten, a profound lawyer and active golf and gun sportsman, presented an interesting subject. He never failed to keep his appointments and lent himself beautifully to the work as a model.

As the sittings progressed, my distinguished subject never offered a suggestion or hint as to how he wished to be painted. He would say in answer to an occasional remark I would make to draw him out, "This is your picture, Mr. Brewer. I am not the artist. I know nothing about the work." Nor would he permit any of his friends to intrude upon my time or attention. But when the portrait was nearing completion and I suggested his bringing Mrs. Van Devanter to see it he resorted to an entirely different procedure. He not only brought his wife but every day and on Sundays, sometimes several times a day, he would come in followed by one or more friends, whom he commissioned in the peremptory tones of a court judge to state their opinion of my work. When they hesitated, as they often did, he would help along their criticisms with various suggestions. He would always say "Do you think so?" never "I think so." In all his remarks about the picture, the Judge never once stated his opinion of it to me.

During two or three weeks following the completion of the portrait, my esteemed patron had invited into the studio Chief Justice Hughes and Mrs. Hughes, Mrs. Taft, all but one of the Associate Justices, nearly all the Hoover Cabinet officers, the Attorney General, Mr. Frederick A. Delano, and about twenty more notables. All this was done ostensibly to secure various criticisms but back of it all I believe Van Devanter's real reason was to advertise my work, for I am sure that under that rugged and blunt exterior of his is a great, noble heart of sympathy and humanity.

Mrs. Van Devanter, however, seemed equally desirous of having her friends see the picture and assist me by their suggestions in improving the likeness. One day after I had considered the canvas finished and it was thoroughly dry, she brought in a lady, the wife of one of the Associate Justices, whom I had heard was very hard to please. This pseudo-critic at once found fault with both sides of the cheeks. "There was not jowl enough; the cheeks were too narrow." "Can you not touch it out a bit?" Mrs. Van Devanter asked. I tried to argue the necessity of their looking at the distinguished jurist first but this had no effect; they had been looking at him for years and were sure of their observations. I concluded to try a ruse. Knowing how easily I could remove all the fresh paint, I proceeded to obey orders, and painted the cheeks larger.

"Does that improve it?" I asked. "Yes, but a little more." And more, and more, until I had given him as beautiful a pair of mumps as any physician had ever seen. Then they declared it "perfect." It was a stunning portrait, the best of them all, and satisfied with their hour's labor with me, they departed. Presently my secretary, Miss Irene Macauley, came in. She was a clever, observant girl and had watched the progress of the portrait from the beginning. Staring at it with a startled look she inquired, "What have you been doing with that picture? You have ruined it."

"Oh, no," I said, "the picture is all right. The ladies have helped me to make a masterpiece." At this juncture in walked my son, Angelo, who shouted, "What the Hell? You have spoiled that face."

"Oh, no," I said, "It's perfect now." Mrs. Van Devanter and Mrs.— helped me and they have declared it perfect. Angelo and Miss Macauley protested vehemently. To prolong their disgust, I argued awhile. Then throwing the canvas on the floor I poured kerosene on the fresh work, and with a clean rag wiped away every particle of fresh paint leaving the canvas as it was before.

A few days later, the same ladies came in again to admire the result of their able assistance, and again they declared it a masterpiece. None of them noticed that I had made them the victims of a practical, but necessary joke, for again they declared, "Now, it is perfect."

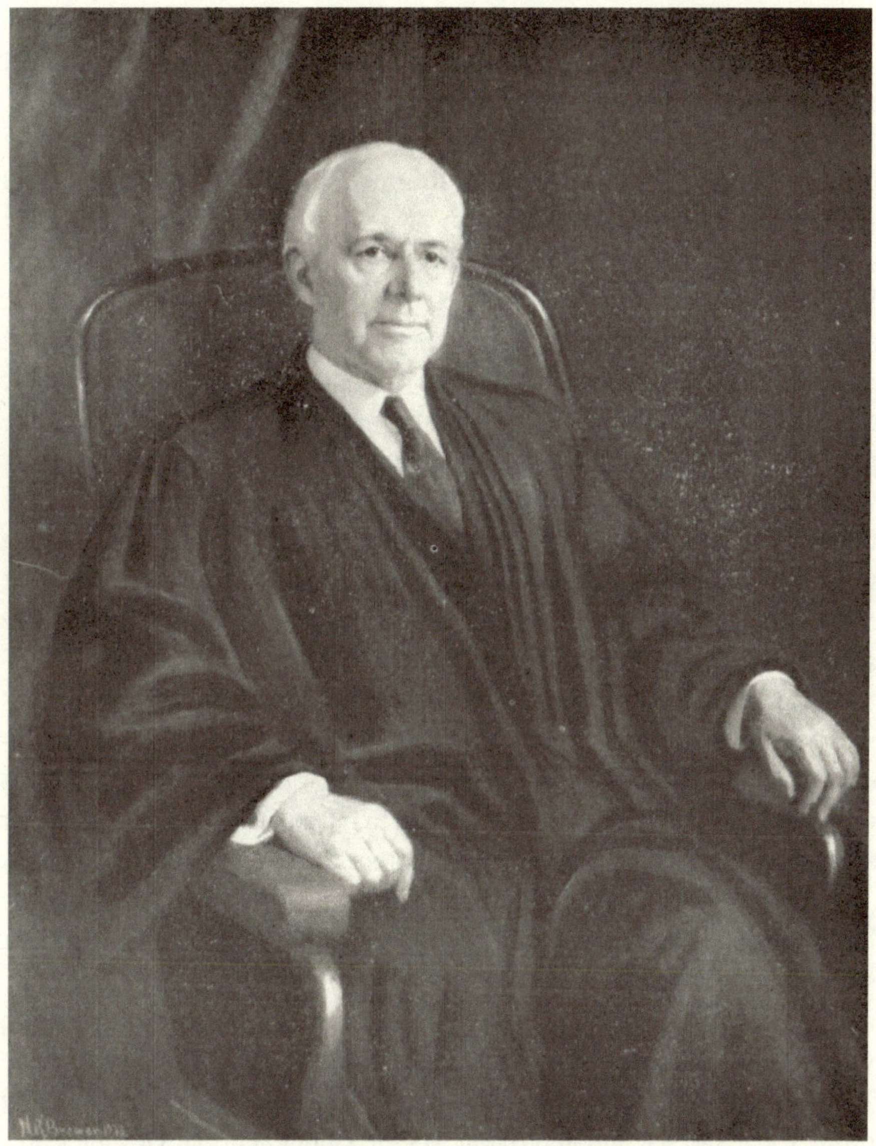

Mr. Justice Willis Van Devanter

* * *

While occupying the studio at the Corcoran Gallery, I painted for the second time a portrait of Mr. Justice Pierce Butler. I had painted Justice Butler shortly after his appointment to the Supreme Bench by President Harding in 1921 or 1922, but the picture was not owned by the Justice. I had painted it for my circuit exhibitions and western shows. However, I had never felt quite satisfied with it, and after the Richmond exhibition, it was discarded.

When Justice Butler saw my portrait of Justice Van Devanter, he gave me an order to paint another of himself. I took the old canvas and plastered it over with a heavy coat of paint of a light, warm flesh tint about where I wished the head to be, and with darker paint elsewhere. When it was dry, I drew the outlines of a new picture. I like to work on an old canvas in this way that has been heavily charged with pigment. Should the covering coats of paint be applied too thinly however, after a lapse of many years the first picture may finally emerge to be quite perceptible. This may have been the case with some of the old masters where three legs or two heads are seen on the same body. Well, if the first Butler should ever appear under the second Butler, this portrait will surely show a Dr. Jekyll-Mr. Hyde combination, for a ten-year development of even a profound lawyer past the age of fifty is readily seen by those who read the human countenance.

Butler has grown more stern, more reticent, and dignified under his present responsibilities although his old-time humors often broke out under a piquant quip or bristling epigram, when a hearty laugh follows his own wit. Nor is he willing to wait for you to return the humor in a phrase or short story but is apt to interrupt with another and another of his own gems.

However, the story of an Irishman in a town where the law forbade spitting in the streets and the man had stumbled about with dark streams of tobacco juice oozing from the corners of his mouth until he met a policeman, whom he asked, “Say Mishter Cop, will you tell me where I can schpit?” arrested his attention and caused a hearty roar.

When the Butler portrait was finished, he likewise brought in many of his friends to see and approve it. As the Butler and Van Devanter portraits stood side by side in the studio they fell to comparing the merits of the two and the friends of each would favor the one of their heroes, whereupon we dubbed the two bodies the Van Devanter and the Butler Clans.

This all shows how the subject matter affects the judgment of the average layman. He does not venture an opinion of the art quality of the work. As I have said before, if the likeness in a portrait is pleasing, people will accept the worst kind of a daub. However, there was one of the

Butler Clan who assumed the position of critic of the artistic qualities of the portrait. She feigned to have little respect for her distinguished father's picture and dubbed it "a likeness, but old stuff," so the report came to me later. Should I meet her again, I would feel like asking her if she thinks some of the "new stuff" will live down the ages as has much of the "old stuff."

Later in the year, we rented a house on Q Street where there was a large studio. It was there I painted Justice George Sutherland, a splendid subject and a charming character. Mrs. Sutherland would not permit but two or three of their friends to see the picture before approving it. The Justice said when his wife was satisfied that was all there was to it; outside opinion was not solicited.

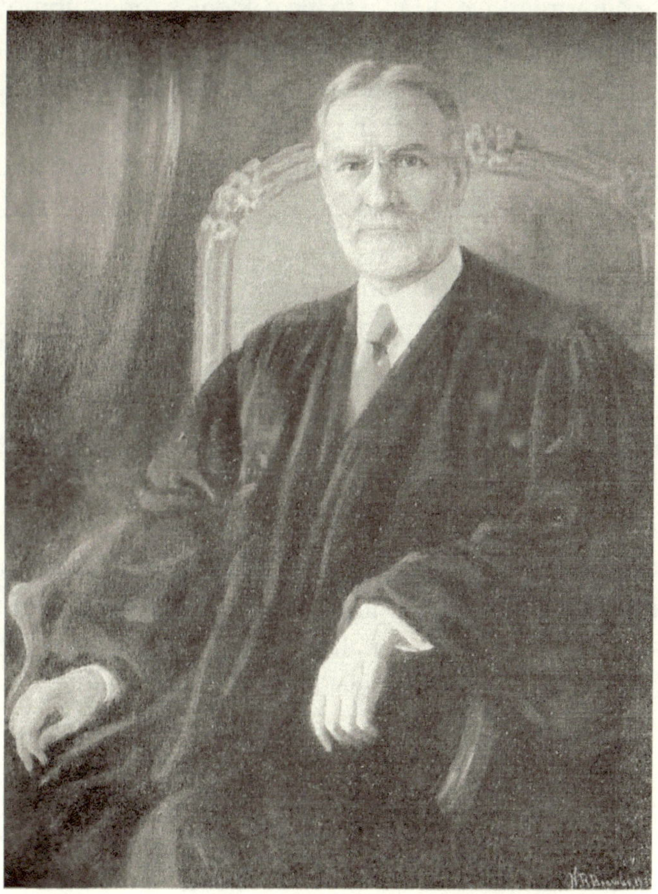

Mr. Justice George Sutherland

Of all my winter's work, my most pleasing subject was Mr. Frederick A. Delano, uncle of President Franklin D. Roosevelt. Delano was a tall, erect, handsome man bordering seventy years, with large eyes, dark brows and strong, kindly features, gray hair, what there was left of it. He is a gentleman one cannot know without loving him; kindliness and consideration emanates from him like atmosphere on every turn, and though a very busy man, he always finds time to consider the interest of his fellowman.

Because of his remarkable type and features, I was greatly impressed on his first visit to see the Van Devanter and Butler portraits. When he called a second time, he made a closer scrutiny of my work. I referred to his own features and asked if he would not favor me with sittings for a portrait I would like to have and use for exhibition purposes. Mr. Delano replied that he was not a rich man and could not afford to have a portrait painted. I replied that I did not intend it that way, that I would not consider him obligated in any way. On the contrary, it would be a great favor to me to be permitted to paint so excellent a subject for my own purposes. With that understanding he consented and gave the sittings.

When the picture was finished, Mr. Delano was much pleased with it and said that sometime in the future he hoped to buy it. As I considered the pleasure of knowing him ample reward for my work, I asked him to accept the picture as a gift from me after I had exhibited it a few times. To this, he demurred, but I persisted, and there the matter rested.

Later the picture was shown with the three portraits of the Associate Justices, one of the Right Reverence James Hugh Ryan, and several other Washington subjects, at an exhibition and reception at the Mayflower Hotel in Washington, which was attended by a large gathering of distinguished friends of the subjects I had put upon canvas.

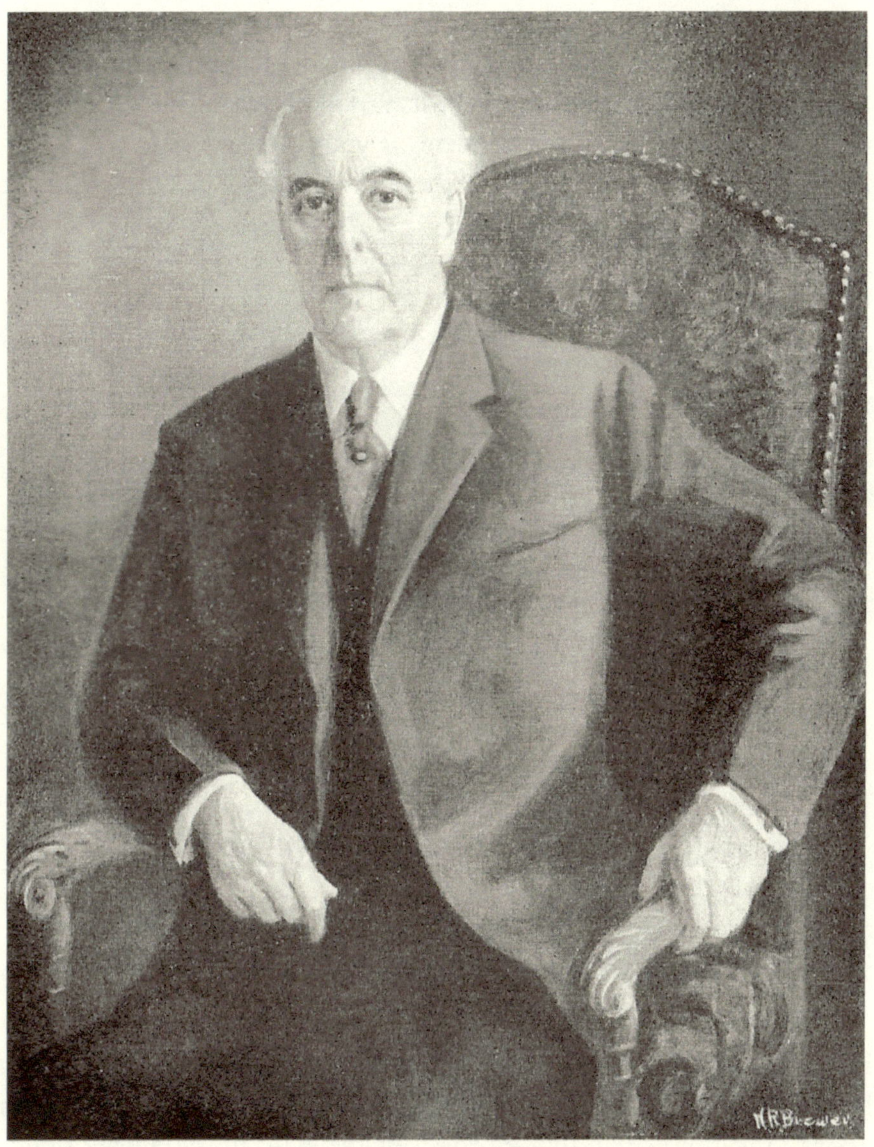

Mr. Frederick A. Delano

A year later I received from Mr. Delano the following letter:

> My dear Mr. Brewer:
>
> Ever since you painted that portrait of me and presented it to me as a gift, I have not felt quite comfortable at accepting so much of a gift. For this

reason, I am making a tardy acknowledgement in the form of a check for part payment. I hope you will receive and accept it, not as payment but as partial acknowledgement of your gift and as evidence of my appreciation of it.

Sincerely yours,

Frederick A. Delano

My reply:

Dear Mr. Delano:

Your very nice letter with enclosure was received.

I did not expect it, and I want to say that it was your remarkable personality that made me want to paint your portrait, and I felt that I had been fully repaid by knowing you.

Let me again express my appreciation and respect, and I trust that when we shall have passed on, my humble brush-work will remain an expression of a man of whom everybody speaks with the highest praise.

Very sincerely your friend,

Nicholas R. Brewer

During the winter I was commissioned by Senator Joseph T. Robinson, Majority Leader of the Senate, to paint two portraits, one of himself and the other of Mrs. Robinson. To do this work the Senator assigned to my use an unused room of his suite in the Senate Office Building. The room was large and well-lighted with all the furniture necessary. I only had to move in my studio paraphernalia. The large front window faced the park in front of the Capitol. A number of commissions followed which kept me there two winters.

My portrait of Senator Robinson proved a great success, at least from the viewpoint of his numerous lay friends. Many came to see it including the Secretary of State, Mr. Cordell Hull, and Mrs. Hull. Mr.

Hull asked me to see him at his office as he wished to consider one of himself. At the mention of my price, however, he seemed to balk. Later he sat some young student I was told, with consequential regrets.

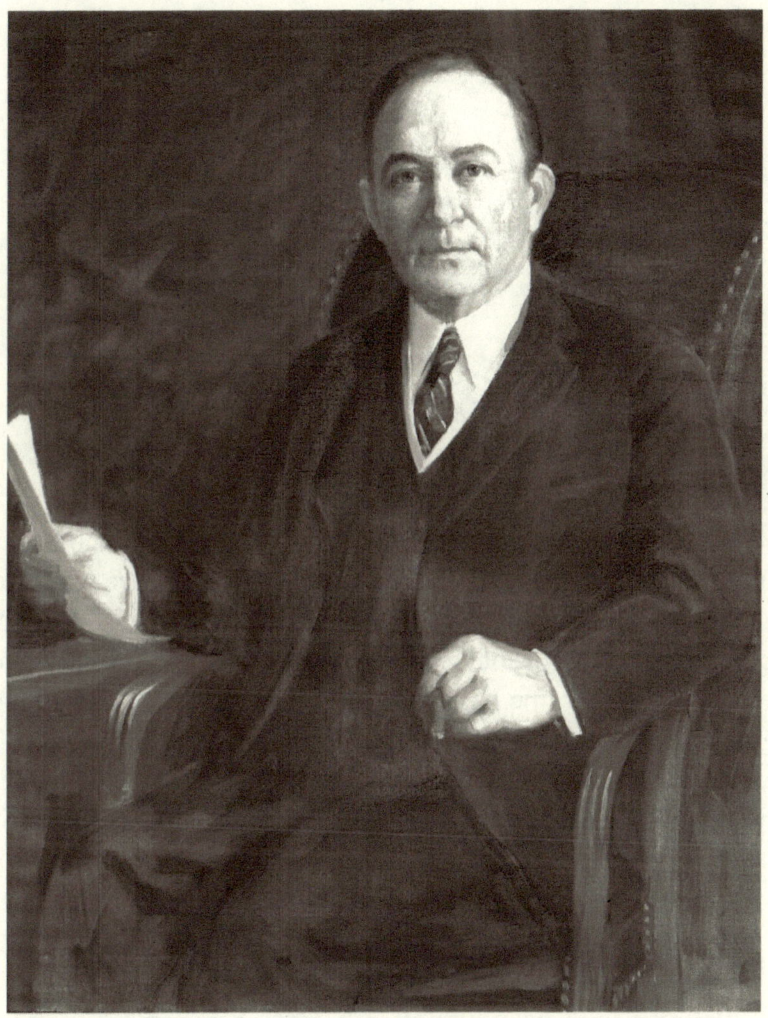

Hon. Joseph T. Robinson

Secretary Swanson of the Navy had me paint his portrait, which will eventually hang in the Navy Department. Then came Senator Norris of Nebraska, gentle and lovable, and Senator Thomas of Oklahoma, the dignified, and considered the best dressed man in the Senate; both of these men took considerable of my time in sittings.

Mrs. Robinson I painted in apple green evening wear—every inch a lady, gentle, sweet, generous. She was almost a daily visitor at my studio during the winters I spent in Washington.

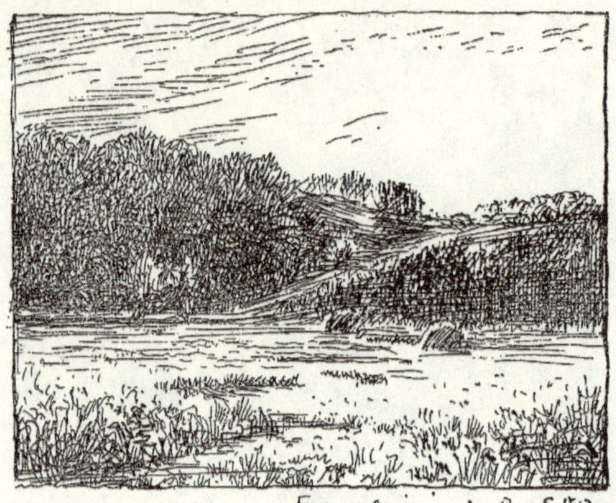

From Original By E.O.B.

During my occupancy of the studio in the Senate Office Building, I painted Vice-President John Nance Garner, whose office was directly across the hall. After the Robinson portraits were finished, Mrs. Robinson gave a luncheon for the wives of the senators and cabinet officers. Following the repast, the hostess led into the studio about fifty ladies, the elite of political society. Mrs. Garner was among them. After that, she would often step in to see what new things I had done. One day, she bought Mr. Roy Miller of Houston, Texas, an intimate friend of the Garners. Seeing the Robinson portraits, he exclaimed, "We must have John sit to Mr. Brewer for a good portrait to take the place of that horrible thing the Legislature put into the capitol at Austin."

"But," said Mrs. Garner, "he won't sit for it."

"Well, we will make him sit. I'll come here tomorrow morning and we'll pull him in and insist on it," said Mr. Miller.

The next morning about nine o'clock the door was opened, and they waltzed the Vice-President in, ostensibly to see the Robinson pictures. Presently Miller spoke his demand, "Mr. Vice-President, we have got to have a good portrait of you for the Capitol of Texas, and here is our chance."

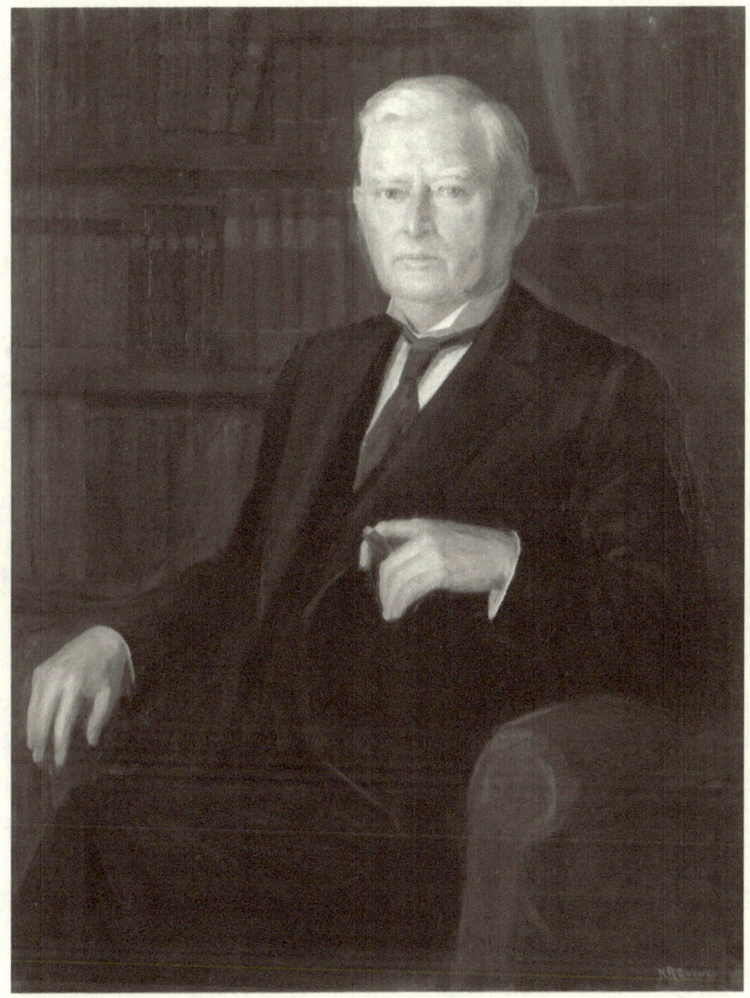

Vice-president John N. Garner

"Oh, no," replied Garner. "I won't have mine done. The one they have there is good enough."

Then Mrs. Garner urged, "Yes, John, you must, and it must be like that," pointing to the canvas of Senator Robinson. The Vice-President persisted, shook his head, "No. No." But they would not relent. Then he turned to me and meekly said, "Well, Mr. Brewer, I have lost my resistance when such people as these get after me. What else can I do?"

After they had left, Miller came back to close the arrangements, and the following day at nine, I started the first sitting. At that time, my son Adrian was with me, and he too began a sketch of the once Texas ranchman with the complexion of a red crabapple.

During the 73rd session of Congress the first year of his service as Speaker, the late Henry T. Rainey came to my studio for sittings for his portrait, which he intended eventually to hang in the Speakers' Lobby among those of previous Speakers. As he was a very busy man, some of his sittings were short, but on Sundays he was able to give me two to three hours time. Rainey was a sweet, mild-mannered man with a wonderful crown of pure white hair, a rich warm complexion, and fine skin texture. In conversation, he was smooth of voice, seemingly tolerant of other's views, however contrary they might be to his own. He was an incessant smoker when idle. While posing, his pipe was forever in his mouth. You can imagine an artist's difficulty in painting a mouth that is constantly skewed, wabbling about and puffing clouds of smoke. Occasionally, I had to suggest laying away the pipe, which he would complacently do, and fall into a brown study, but shortly out would come the pipe and go to the accustomed clamping lips, and more smoke clouds.

Rainey never expressed his views, if he had any, on art more than to say he had sat for a portrait but once, some years ago. He must have had the desire, however, that most notable men have to leave a presentment in enduring colors for succeeding generations to ponder over.

That is a feeling some attribute to a kind of vanity, but we might well be more lenient in our judgment since it is hard to fathom the reasons for so doing. Family genealogy, love of art, historic connections, may be the reason for wishing to secure "the shadow ere the substance fade." Be that as it may, a beautifully painted portrait is always a delight to intelligent art lovers.

The Rainey picture was finally finished, the session ended, and the day before the Raineys left for Illinois, the Speaker came with a friend to see it. Rainey expressed his hearty approval and said he wished the portrait hung in the Capitol when he would retire from office. He said prophetically, "It may be soon." About five weeks later he passed away.

It might be well to say why that Speakers Gallery is often referred to by artists as "a chamber of horrors." The reason is the House Library, under their chairman, who claims to, but knows nothing about art, passes upon and approves works that are a standing disgrace to art. After

Rainey's death, following the usual procedure, several artists produced portraits of him from photographs and sent them to the chairman of the committee, who, ignoring Rainey's wishes and intentions completely, opened a competitive display of six or more of these pictures. The selection will doubtless be made as heretofore, according to political "pull," and indifference to artistic merit.

I know one man who graduated from the Speaker's Chair to a more dignified position in the Administration, who swears maledictions in a good western vernacular upon that committee and their evil doings, for, he said, his portrait selected by them "is nothing but a daub."

Then, last but not least, was His White House Majesty, President Franklin D. Roosevelt, if I may add a foreign tint to his title. Of course, he will again become just plain Mr. Roosevelt. That is according to our traditions, provided they do not kill him with overwork or an assassin's bullet. We have made history along that line also, you know.

At our first meeting, when I was presented to him by Mrs. Joe T. Robinson, the President was seated at his desk running through numerous documents. He cordially grasped my hand and said, "Mr. Brewer, I have heard a great deal about you and your work, and I think that portrait you made of my uncle, Mr. Delano, is the finest portrait I have ever seen."

This, of course, shows his very gracious way of greeting and putting people at their ease. I at once perceived that the long hard hours of wrestling with trying affairs of state were leaving their marks on his otherwise handsome countenance; there were deep lines and poor color about his eyes. He has, however, a way of appearing in the best of health and spirits. He never shows weariness, or lassitude. Bravery, courage, and determination are written in every feature of his face, especially the mouth and chin. His lips are thin, but he has not what artists call a "button-hole mouth." His has a wonderful mouth, flitting instantly from determination to the sweetest smile. He talks with all his features, his head and neck. He gesticulates with his hands, but he has not Teddy Roosevelt's manner of pounding the desk with his fist to drive home a thought. When I wished him a joyous trip on his vacation to Honolulu, his eyes sparkled, and he replied with his sudden flash of delight, "Yes, I am going to have a fine time."

But how should an artist paint such a mobile face? A movie camera only could portray his facial antics. Not that his jumpy expressions are assumed, oh no. They are the natural promptings of a nature that is kindly, generous, humorous, determined, impulsive. He thinks quickly and no doubt, profoundly. Sincerity is an outstanding trait of his nature. I believe he would not be slow to rectify a mistake once he is convinced it was a mistake.

But this diversion is not painting his portrait. I chose a profile for two very good reasons: first he has a fine brow, a handsome nose, a determined contour of mouth and chin, and secondly, to avoid the mobility of his front view. One of the members of the Supreme Court, who saw the finished portrait in my studio, and who evidently was not of the President's political persuasion, referring to his profile, said, "With that forehead, nose and mouth in that dignified position one has got to concede that he is a mighty handsome man no matter how one may dislike his politics."

Of course, prejudice, political, social, religious, always make the fellow on the other side of the fence look more or less ugly, but in this case the antagonist was declared handsome.

I think I was fortunate in choosing Roosevelt's profile with the head slightly elevated. I avoided the least hint of his characteristic smile. I wanted to express his determination and an expression of responsibility, for I think those qualities should be characteristic of a President to carry down the pages of history. He was hard to catch and I had to use a substitute model for much of the figure and hands.

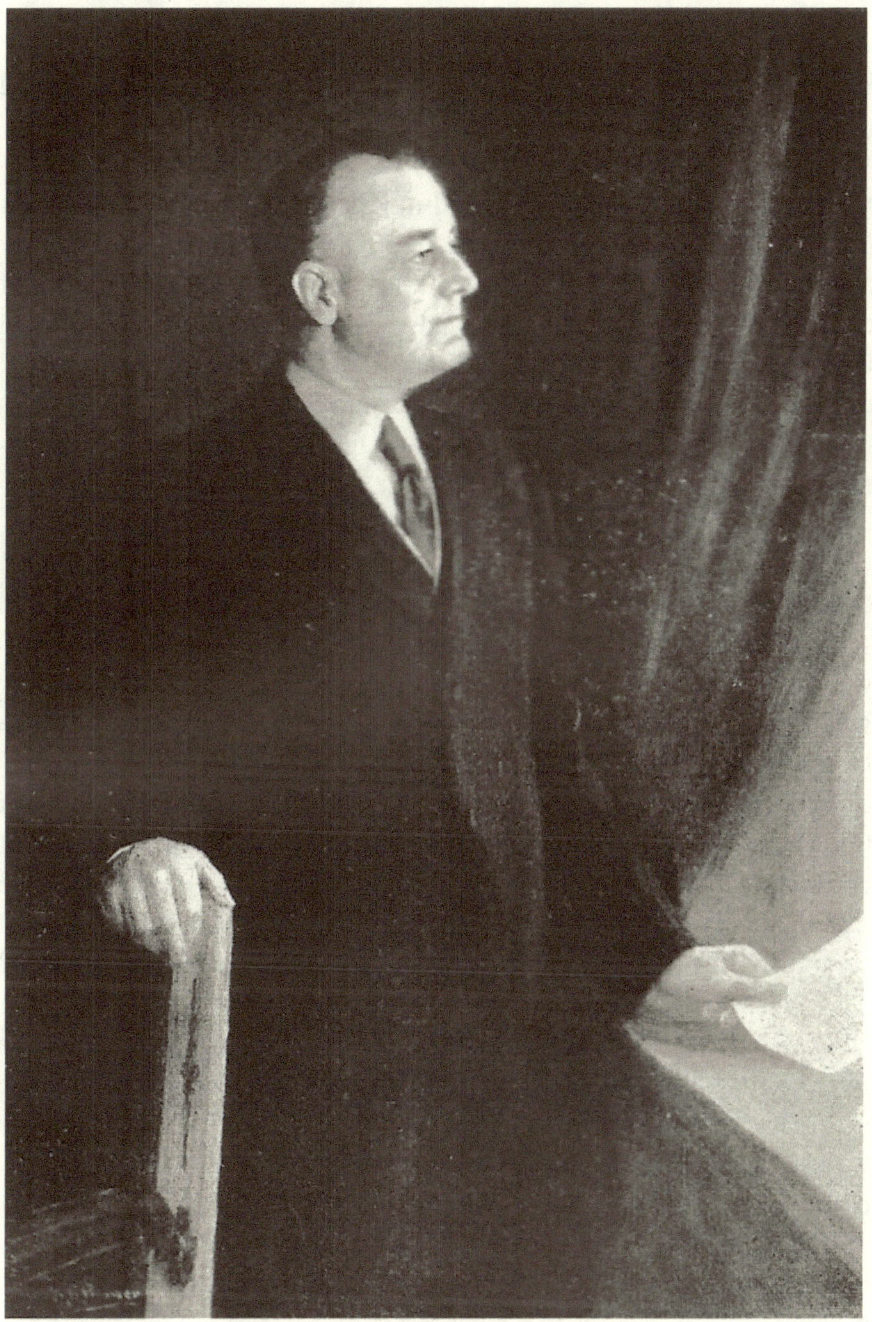

President Franklin Delano Roosevelt

* * *

Before bidding adieu to the Capitol City, I cannot refrain from paying my respects to the Corcoran Institute of Art.

The Bi-Annual Exposition, so wildly heralded through the country as broad in its scope and liberal in its aims to promote the best interests of various schools of art thought, has recently closed. The jury appointed by the management included names of conservative, half conservative, and radical artists. These men supposedly were to sit in judgment of the merits of a thousand paintings. Some four hundred canvasses out of the many were chosen and hung.

One is constrained to ask by what standard of excellence these pictures were chosen from the vast number rejected, many by notable artists; for out of the four hundred, at least three hundred of the lot could, would, and should have made an excellent bonfire. One's nerves were constantly jarred by seeing side by side along with fine academic and semi-academic works many such things as some of my six- or eight-year-old grandchildren have produced when in a spirit of mischief they would get hold of my palette and brushes and draw what they had to label, "a cow," "a man," "a pig," "a stump," "a tree," and what not—gaudy, meaningless splashings, with no message whatsoever to the lover of true art and beauty. This confession of method and treatment of the art of painting compels the conclusion in the minds of the thinking public that any or all standards of judgment were smashed to smithereens—that complete independentalism prevailed, and, if so, why a jury of selection?

An artist of the new way of thinking, recently remarked that "there is no such thing as standardized judgment of art or anything else for that matter. Truth is as every fellow sees it. That is Truth to him."

This jury must have taken turns in exercising each one's peculiar whims and trying to make all kinds of distortions and hieroglyphical, psychological neurosis agree with this artist's philosophy.

Douglas Volk once said to me, "If a painting is refused at an exhibition that does not mean that it is not a great work of art but only that it is not just what the jury wants." Evidently juries are queer, but the doings of the last Corcoran jury seems puzzling beyond question to me.

Chapter XXVII
Retrospect

Time has laid his hand Upon my heart gently, not smiting it,
But as a harper lays his open palm
Upon his harp, to deaden its vibrations.
—Henry W. Longfellow

In my youth the road of life seemed long and endless. I yearned to be of age. I fretfully said to myself, "How can I endure until I am a man and have the freedom to leave home and see life?" Life appeared to be only experience, action, and achievement. Then came responsibility, trial, and hardship; but the pangs of these quickly fell away from me one by one. I harbored no ill will over the past nor cherished resentment for misfortune and ill luck. In middle life the vigor of youth was still with me. I was never discouraged. Hope shone brightly and ever beckoned to new endeavors, adventures, and success. The dynamo of action continued to hum within me. Fatigue was short-lived and died with recurrent enthusiasm. All that my machinery needed was regular lubrication to respond to the current of my native force and run smoothly. Each flowering plant, every growing shrub, the singing birds, the sunlit landscape, the starry moonlight radiated joy.

To linger momentarily and gaze at the beauties of nature was my habit, ever with the thought of how they would look on canvas.

With the belief in the goodness and providence of God, I still felt that my life's success would depend largely upon my own hewing. At the age of fifty, I considered myself a young man with the major part of life ahead of me. The thrill given me by every sparkling bit of beauty along the wayside kept my heart young, and the ecstasy of living did not wane. Less and less sleep was needed to restore my energies as the years passed.

I painted incessantly—everything—everywhere—trying to express on canvas the beauty I saw: the landscape, portraits, figures, the laughing child, the wrinkled brow of age, flowers and fruits, rustic buildings, and ancient ruins. The subject mattered not if I thought it beautiful, nor did I try to use the methods of other painters. Fortunately, for my individuality, I lived for years away from any influence, save the inspiration of nature in the endless untraveled West with its infinite variations of scenes and beauty of subject.

Art is self-expression; the artist telling on canvas his concept of beauty, his susceptibility to the touches of nature, of life. One should turn a deaf ear to the promptings of the commercial, the popular in art, hewing ever true to one's own ideals in opposition to the false and fickle tempting's of the scribes and Pharisees. They would give the artist a purpose of their own for everything he does, forgetting that it was the artist's personal ideals and his creative genius that brought forth the greatest achievements of history.

Henry Austin Adams once said: "It is only the dreamer whose creations become immortal. It is only dreamers who see the things the average person misses, 'for many have eyes and see not.'"

Yet in my life there was ever the goading whiplash of necessity that forced regrets whenever I had to sign, for bread and butter, the canvasses I thought failures. I always drew a line between what I considered the true and the false, and that was often a hair line, for it is sometimes hard to discern just where the good ends and the bad begins.

My reward has been the joy of reveling among the things that God has made: the flower-strewn highways and byways of Texas; the purple-tinted mountains; the golden hued maples bordering the azure lakes of Minnesota; the snows of the Northland, gilded by the rays of a golden sun. Perhaps the best that can be said for my art is that I am not a one-story painter. Whatever weaknesses my work may show, a limited range of subject matter is not one of them. Perhaps my diversity in range is in itself a weakness.

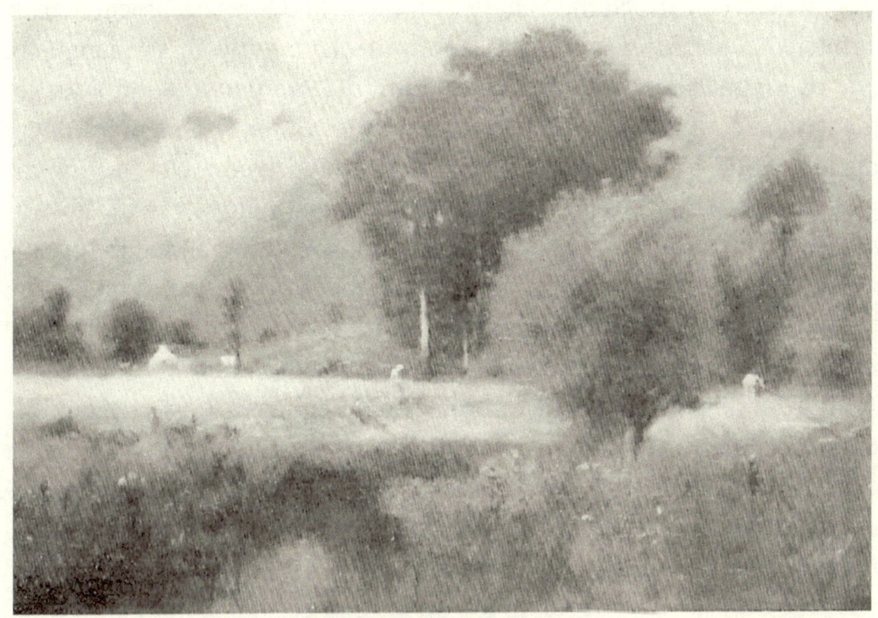

Autumn in New Jersey

Some think that to paint well one must concentrate on one line of work. In fact, the majority of artists confine themselves to a narrow range, either from personal choice or because they have neglected to study other phases of beauty.

I recall a remark to that effect of my highly esteemed friend, C. Myles Collier, who painted beautiful marines. He knew the ocean in every mood and could draw every form of sailing craft. One day he was working in my studio and I said to him, "Myles, get your kit and come with me to Bronx Park; I have found some fine subjects there that I think you will like."

When we arrived in the field, I soon selected my subject and set up for a sketch. Myles sauntered about and disappeared until I had about completed my work. When he returned, his box had not been opened. He said to me, "These things don't appeal to me. You know I have never learned to paint a tree."

I could have said, "And I have never learned to paint a ship."

Myles was a strong and lovable character, a typical Southern gentleman. He was an officer in the Confederate Navy during the Civil War, where he learned the beauty of the sea, and later became a marine painter. He asked me to paint a portrait of his wife in exchange for one of his marines, which I was glad to do. We parted soon after for the summer. He went to Gloucester and I to St. Paul. This picture was his last work, for a couple of months later I received a wire telling me that he had passed on. A venerable and much beloved man, he was respected by all who knew him, especially so in the Salmagundi Club, where a memorial exhibition of his works was given later. The picture he painted for me I still cherish, not only for its excellent qualities but as a memento of a valued friendship I shall never forget.

After I had passed my fiftieth year I noticed a change coming over me slowly. My manner of work was more deliberate with greater certainty and self-confidence. I had a keener appreciation and understanding, with a greater facility in the handling of my means—more reflective, less impulsive. The strenuous work of giving exhibitions and painting portraits had begun to tell on me and I broke under it. For three years I was permitted to work only a few hours each day. I employed my niece to travel with me as secretary and nurse. My doctor cautioned me against walks, long or rapid. Slowly, I regained my strength but not the old-time power of endurance, nor can I mount the stairs three steps at a time now. Today I only plod along, but I accomplish more in an hour than ever before, and every day I am busy. Work! Work! Without it, my life would be miserable. My diversion is with my family—the children, the grandchildren, and the great grandchild. Eighteen lovely boys and girls call us grandma and grandpa.

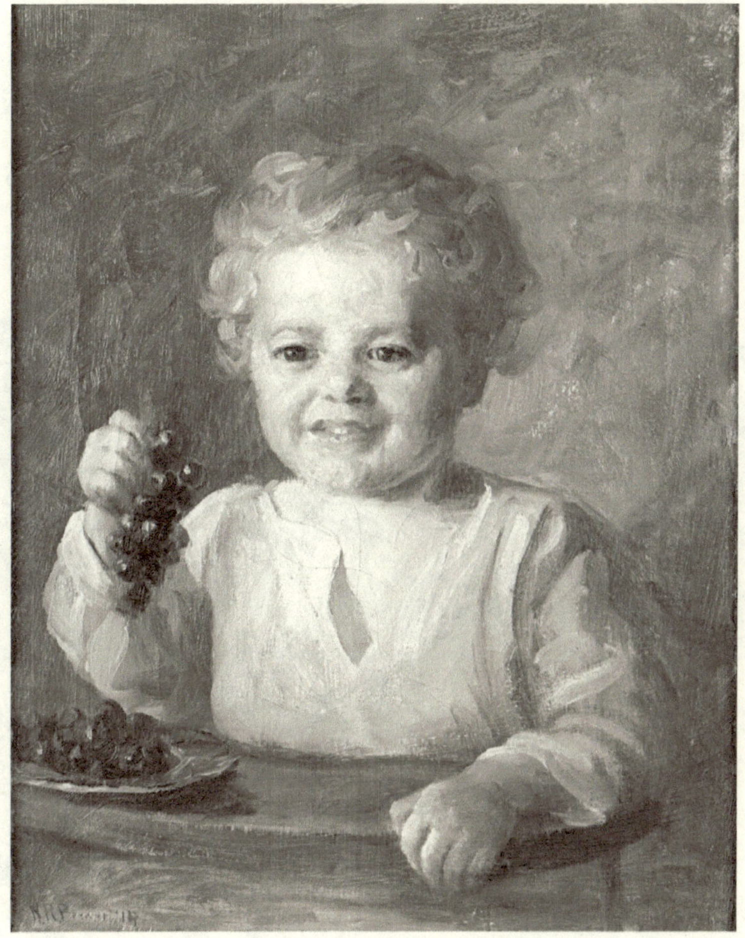

Sunny Jim—our grandson.

In my seventy-first year, thirty-four years after my last visit there, I returned to the old homestead near High Forest with Mrs. Brewer, Angelo, Edward, and their families. We motored to Rochester, Stewartville, High Forest, and two miles west to the place where I was born. It is now owned by a thrifty farmer who has extended the cultivatable acreage by clearing out some of the timber where my favorite rabbit trapping forest was.

Unfortunately, the owner and his family were not at home. The house was closed, but we wandered down through the pasture and over to the riverbank. There the log cabin once stood where my childish eyes first blinked at the fleecy clouds.

The scene today belies the memory picture I shall ever keep as the most beautiful spot in all the world. The cabin is gone and only a few of the old oaks remain. The flow of the stream is greatly lessened. The beautiful cedars that crowned the bank have been cut down and smaller and scraggier ones have grown up in their places. The stump of that great cedar, which bore the mark made by my father's axe in the hands of a powerful Indian, is still there.

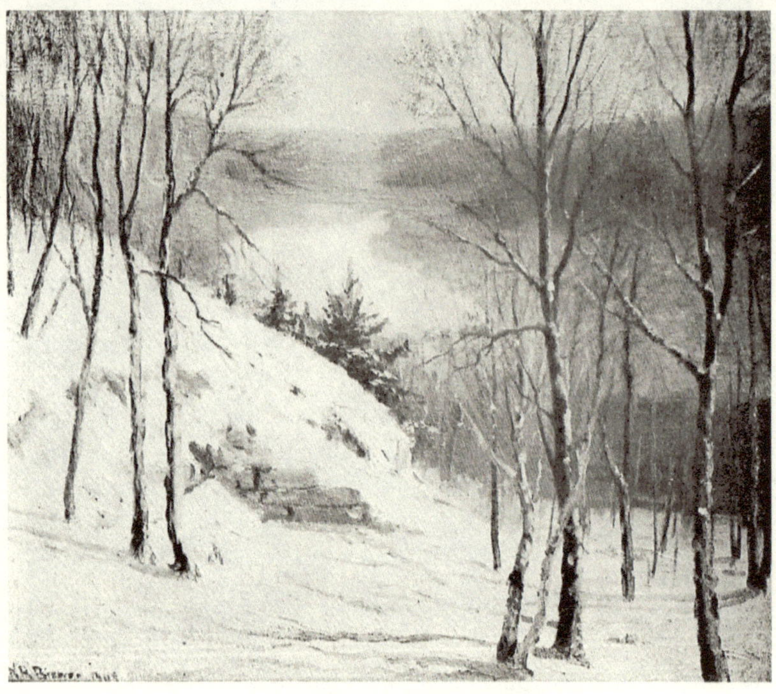

Winter on the Mississippi

We went down to the fording place. The large boulders near which we boys caught the fish with our hands are still the same. I tried to spring from one to the other across the stream as the boy Nick used to do, but what a failure I made of it! Thoughts poured through my memory of how I lifted my first sweetheart, timid Mary Goodrich, from boulder to boulder, and let her down safely on the other side.

The sun was getting low in the west, so we returned to High Forest and stopped where the old mill had formerly been. We spread our evening meal, where six feet of water once flowed, opposite the high bank now covered with trees where the gristmill stood. Further on, were traces of the sluiceway where hung the ponderous waterwheel. Edward was captivated by the charm of the spot and remarked, "What a grand place to build a romantic home."

We drove through the almost deserted village. The old Tatersall Hotel, where we danced, still remains; also, the Methodist Church where Mike Foley made me put pepper on the stove when the minister was preaching, which quickly dispersed the congregation, the blacksmith shop, and Bill Buck's store are there too, long lived and nearly as decrepit as myself. The beautiful high knoll where the flag was hoisted on the Fourth of July and where the anvil boomed has been hauled away to make roads. East of the town is the little city of the dead where Mary Goodrich sleeps. It has many more inhabitants now than the village.

We slept that night in Stewartville. In the morning some of our party returned to St. Paul, but Edward, his wife, Ida, the old folks, and the kiddies drove back to the old homestead where we met its present generous mistress. On learning who we were, she was delighted to see us and insisted on our staying for dinner.

An addition had been built to the house but the rooms in the old part were still the same as when I painted and grained the woodwork in 1876. I lingered in the room where Father died. There we closed his eyes after that indomitable spirit had fled. I asked the young folks to go with me to see the boiling spring about a mile and a half down the river. It was an unusually hot but clear summer day; however, I had no trouble in spite of the heat in persuading Ida and Ed to follow me as she is venturesome and he loves nature. For two reasons I took the lead. First, I wanted to imagine myself young; second, they did not know the trail, and I wanted to lead them over that beautiful high bank where the big oaks stood and where I used to spend so many Sundays whiling away the time watching the fish and snapping turtles in the clear water below and reading the only book in the house—the Bible.

I found that the bottomland had been used for many years for a pasture. The browsing and trampling of the cattle had destroyed all the wild plum trees, the haw bushes and the thickets of willow, hawthorn, and wild crabapple trees. Nowhere was the stream fringed with overhanging verdure. Even the soft maples and elms had been cut down for firewood. Thus, does the smiling face of nature become barren and lonely under the blighting hand of man. Those great oaks on the high knoll had yielded to the woodman's axe and around their decaying stumps a dense undergrowth made our way a greater task than I had expected. Soon we descended to the lowland close to the water and I found the cow path that led toward the spring, A little farther on, we heard the song of the boiling spring.

It was here that Fred Pierson, the fiddler, once had his fish trap, which the boys tore out because it kept the fish from ascending the stream. Now the stream is barren of fish. A little farther on the high forest of magnificent trees once stood from which the place derived its name.

Time passed and we could explore no more. Arriving at the spring, perspiring from the heat and our climb, we bathed our hands and heads in the cool water. Not having with us a glass or cup to slake our thirst, we almost stood on our heads to reach the bubbling water. Then we rested in the shade of a straggling oak tree, listening to the gurgling of the spring from a perpendicular hole in the rocks twenty feet deep. To me it seemed as if it alone remained to sing an everlasting requiem for all that had passed and gone.

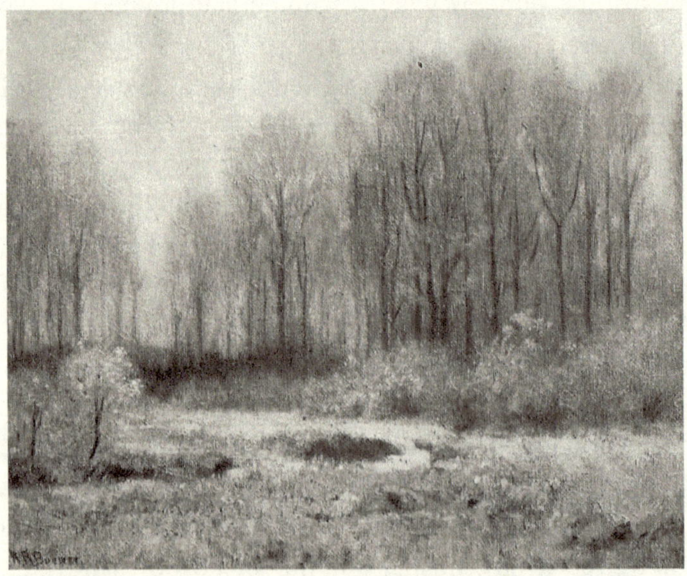

The Woodlands

A savory meal of stewed chicken and other delicious food awaited us, and our stimulated appetites did full justice to it. From our hostess I learned the history of a girl with whom I used to go to school in the old schoolhouse—Nabby Pierson, sister of John Pierson, the son of Zachariah Pierson, the brother of Fred Pierson the fiddler.

The Zack Pierson family were fine people whom everyone respected. Nabby had married. She is now Mrs. Hall, old and white-haired, but with the same sweet smile and sparkling eyes of her girlhood. She was living in Stewartville and I decided to visit her. It was fifty-eight years since I had last seen her, and I could not imagine how she looked. Her husband answered my knock at the door. I mentioned that I used to know his wife, that I was traveling and had stopped to see her. Without asking my name he led me into the dining room and called his wife from the kitchen. As soon as she saw me, she exclaimed, "Well, if that isn't Nick Brewer!" A remarkable display of memory! When she last saw me I was a timid, smooth-faced lad with a wealth of long black curly hair, without even the promise of a mustache.

When she learned that my family was in the car outside, she rushed out to meet them. Then for a while we engaged in reminiscent chatter. She asked if I remembered the red-haired teacher who spanked me for throwing dust at the girls in the road.

"Mary Powers?" I inquired.

"Well, she lives right in that next house," pointing to the comfortable looking cottage, not fifty feet away: "I'll bring her out."

Presently they returned and there was Mary. I recognized her at once and we talked pleasantly of days gone by.

* * *

Again, we headed eastward through Rochester and toward the Mississippi fifty miles beyond. We sped past broad fields that were only bleak prairies when my father used to haul his grain to Winona where river boats plied in frontier trade. Descending the great hill toward Stockton and Rolling Stone, I recalled the story Father told of the troubles he had in making the grade, how on one occasion his load was dumped into a ditch. It required five to six days for him to make the round trip, and this day we landed in Winona in less than two hours. Could my father return today and travel the same road with us, how great his surprise would be! His eyes scanned the mighty slopes, the rocky cliffs, the winding stream of the beautiful hills of Stockton just as ours do, but little did he dream that sixty years later his sons and his sons' sons and their sons would speed along their winding curves at sixty miles an hour. Such is the progress of human life.

When I was a child, one of the many questions I asked my parents was, "How long is a lifetime?" On being told it was at best about seventy years, I was grieved to know it was so short. Those seventy years and more have sped away like a dove on the wing. I now realize the brevity of human existence, nor do the sands in the dial of time flow more slowly as the sun goes down. On the contrary, the days, months, and years seem shorter than ever before. This is due to the fact that I am busy from daylight to starlight. I have so many things I want to paint, so many affairs to attend, so many cares that seem more weighty than cares ever did before. The older I grow, the greater becomes my feeling of resignation to the inevitable.

If I can only retain my faculties to my last breath that I may consciously commend my spirit into the keeping of Him Who gave me this beautiful life! When the great portals of eternity open for me, I shall gladly say the Grand Amen.

> The course of my long life hath reached at last,
> In fragile bark o'er a tempestuous sea,
> The common harbor, where must rendered be Ac-
> count of all the actions of the past.
> The impassioned phantasy, that vague and vast,
> Made art an idol and a king to me,
> Was an illusion and but vanity
> Were the desires that lured me and harassed.
> The dreams of love, that were so sweet of yore,
> What are they now, when two deaths may be mine—
> One sure and one forecasting its alarms?

Painting and sculpture satisfy no more
The soul now turning to the Love Divine,
That oped, to embrace us, on the cross its arms.
—Longfellow

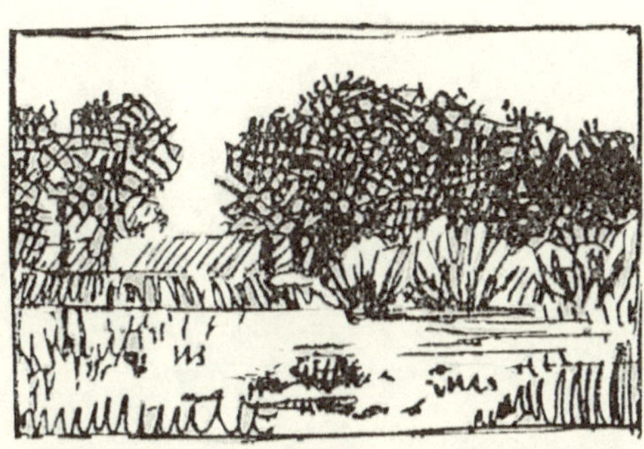

FINIS

Appendix
Thoughts from an Artist's Diary

While at work keep constantly in mind the unity of your picture.

* * *

Mystery is often resorted to as an excuse for ignorance.

* * *

Mystery does not mean a sacrifice of character or values, but a faint suggestion of details rather than a two minute and conscientious rendering of them.

* * *

Drawing is the rendering of objects in light and shade; painting is drawing in color.

* * *

To paint well, one must have no distracting cares. Art requires the whole man; care demands a part of him.

* * *

Learn to do important things first, details last.

* * *

The acquisition of a reputation is often the artist's artistic death, since feeding in the lap of luxury destroys inclination to further efforts.

* * *

A pronounced love of nature is the first indication of artistic genius.

* * *

Be careful of whom you learn your first lessons, as first impressions are never wholly effaced from the memory. First lessons have either a good or bad influence on one's after work.

***

Woman's generosity is prompted by her heart, man's by his intellect.

* * *

Genius abhors repetition and is satisfied only with new endeavors. Mediocrity glories in what it has accomplished, and cares little to climb to greater heights.

* * *

Art is a sealed book to those who will not take the trouble to study it.

* * *

One ought to see a picture ten times before passing judgment upon it.

* * *

One should rather try to paint as a thinker than think as a painter.

* * *

Art is the most catholic of all languages. It expresses the thoughts of every nation and every age. The language of Egypt perished; but her art survives to tell us of the thoughts and deeds of her people. Greek legends are closely allied with fable, but her crumbling monuments of art speak the immutable truth.

* * *

In art one must generalize and simplify but never forget truth in a broad sense.

* * *

Technical art education is the knowledge of all the good qualities which a work of art should possess. The instructor can do no more than demonstrate to the pupils those qualities. Poetry, philosophy, color, are inborn and cannot be taught.

* * *

An artist is one possessed of a superabundance of sensibility and sufficient technical knowledge to enable him to absorb and reflect in his art the conditions in which he lives. He touches with delicate fingers the chords of nature. And lo! the world beholds their harmonies.

* * *

The habit of seeing too much is the student's greatest stumbling block. In painting, one should deal with generalities. He should not try to see things individually but visualize the broad aspect of nature. Art allows license but not a distortion of truth.

* * *

If all could express what they know, the world would be ablaze with skyrockets and the earth strewn with "chestnuts."

* * *

A pool of water may be as beautiful as a mountain; a stump as picturesque as the universe.

* * *

When one has learned what beauty is, he can find it in everything from the tiniest insect to a gorgeous sunset.

* * *

Musings upon leaving the museum:

O you dumb, dead mummy! What tales might you tell of other days and conditions of civilization were you but able to speak!

Here you lie three thousand years after the date of your death, in a fireproof building, carefully enclosed in a glass case, and gazed at by the multitude who succeed you.

And there is the house you have inhabited all these long years. The tree from which it was made, perchance, stood on the banks of the Nile and nodded in the breezes from off the sunburned plains of the Sahara. It still bears the marks of the workman whose crude auger and chisel joined lid and base and sealed it over. On it the artist, with reed, brush, and waxen color, drew your likeness and recorded, perhaps, your age or the principal achievements of your life.

* * *

Great writers, like great artists, are keen observers. They give us truthful pictures of the world about us. Their success lies in their ability to select the right things from the multiplicity of material at hand.

There never was a sadder or more beautiful romance written than some of the real stories of every day, and there is nothing more ideal than some instance of the real.

* * *

Common misfortunes, like common joys, bring souls into unison.

* * *

The light of good deeds penetrating into the darkest recesses of weak hearts stimulates and vivifies them as do the sun's rays the feeble plant. Virtue, like vice, is contagious and when sweetened with kindness it is irresistible in its power to uplift sinking souls.

* * *

Some have within themselves their own greatest enemy. And the greater that enemy, the less conscious they are of his presence.

* * *

After all, life itself is man's best teacher. Consequently, the longer and more laden with experience one's life has been the more one knows.

* * *

Some women would hold the world back if Almighty God were not pulling against them. And many men damn Him for not letting these women have their way.

* * *

One should not paint from a preconceived notion of how objects look, without first having observed them. That is an exercise of neither memory nor imagination and becomes a fatal habit with many.

* * *

Be careful about your backgrounds. Everything in nature is seen against a background, which gives value to the different parts of your picture. One does not wonder that the old masters found more difficulty from this source than from many others.

* * *

Here is a head done in a day. And some ask, "How can that be a work of art since it was made so easily?" The answer is, "Because forty years have been crowded into one day."

* * *

Ignorant criticism is easier to endure than bald-faced flattery.

* * *

We estimate human greatness in proportion to our appreciation of learning. To the ignorant man greatness is but a name, a something he cannot grasp.

* * *

Work for truth of impression and get details if you can. Abandon the idea that you can finish in one direct painting. The greatest have labored much.

* * *

The painted portrait is the voice of the soul speaking through the features.

* * *

Every time we slip, we make easier succeeding slips; every time we resist, we strengthen the will and make it easier to conquer. Thus, we add our self-respect and become more assertive in the moment of temptation.

* * *

The man who does not learn from his mistakes is a dunce, and dunces are plentiful. Ingersoll said, "Colleges are places where they polish pebbles and dull diamonds." But since the great majority are pebbles, I presume colleges should be regarded as useful institutions.

* * *

There is nothing like worry to kill the creative spirit. The grocer's bill and the rent demand are frightening when one realizes he has not a dollar in the bank. One feels like rolling under the bed when he sees the collector coming.

* * *

Poverty, hardship, and struggle from youth may make a man more practical, efficient, and careful in expenditures; but may they not be too great a handicap to allow the fullest development of talent? Would the genius of Sargent have ripened into such a harvest of achievement had he been obliged to bind sheaves of grain with sore fingers and an aching back until twenty years of age and then, without guidance, go groping about a new country with no opportunities to study until he was thirty? Such have been the conditions of many a gifted soul in New America.

* * *

Never express an opinion on any subject on which you are not fully informed. Be sure of your convictions. Then, if attacked, be ready to go to the mat in defense of your principles.

* * *

Museums are sepulchers of dead men's bones. They do not foster and develop art—they embalm it. The artist must have acquired a reputation before the museums will condescend to accord him a place on their august walls. Nevertheless, every museum could well afford to make a bonfire of many canvasses by famous artists. Yet some people ask, "What is there in a name?"

* * *

What would the ancient sculptors of Greece think of some of the new sculpture being erected on the state buildings in Washington? Would it not be amusing to hear their comments?

* * *

From the beginning, man's instinct has been to rise above the sordid and material, giving expression to that divine element in his nature—love of the beautiful and the perfect. And so down through the ages his creative bent has developed certain standards of excellence, principles of execution, which can never be cast aside without loss and retrogression. The refusal to employ what has thus been formulated is, in our opinion, a false philosophy.

* * *

It is the laughter, tears, love, and heartaches that enrich the soul, the mind, and the heart of the artist, and impel him to give to the world, through the medium of form and color, his impressions of life and beauty, his message. If that message is clear and forceful, then he has produced an enduring thing which in time becomes the property of the world—something for everyone everywhere to enjoy. This is the artist's legacy to humanity.

www.ingramcontent.com/pod-product-compliance
Lightning Source LLC
LaVergne TN
LVHW041101080826
845145LV00007B/1644

9781736102121